Learn to Program

with

Visual Basic Examples

John Smiley

Active Path Ltd. ®

Learn to Program with Visual Basic Examples

© 1999 Active Path

active path

Published by Active Path Ltd, Arden House, 1102 Warwick Road, Acocks Green, Birmingham, B27 6BH, United Kingdom

Printed in USA

ISBN 1-902745-06-X.

Trademark Acknowledgements

Active Path has endeavored to provide trademark information about all the companies and products mentioned in this book by the appropriate use of capitals. However, Active Path cannot guarantee the accuracy of this information.

Credits

Author
John Smiley

Development Editor
Andy Corsham

Technical Editors
Andy Corsham
Dev Lunsford

Layout
Tony Berry

Cover
Andrew Guillaume

Technical Reviewers
Humberto Abreu
Monica Atkinson
Dr. Zoë M Backman
Eddie Correia
Antoine Giusti
Emma Morgan
Marc Simkin

Index
Seth Maislin

About the Author

John Smiley, a Microsoft Certified Professional, is the President of John Smiley and Associates, a computer consulting firm located in South Jersey, serving clients in the Philadelphia Metropolitan area. John is also an adjunct professor of computer science at Penn State University in Abington, the Philadelphia College of Textiles and Science, and Holy Family College, and has been programming and teaching for nearly 20 years. He currently teaches a number of very popular online courses at Ziff Davis University (ZDU).

On the writing front, John is the author of *Learn to Program with Visual Basic 6* from Active Path, and he has done technical editing on a number of Wrox and Que Visual Basic titles. You can find a case study he wrote in *Beginning Visual Basic 6* by Wrox Press. He is also the author of five ZDU Workbooks.

Feel free to visit John's Web Site at:

`http://www.johnsmiley.com`

Or contact him via e-mail at johnsmiley@johnsmiley.com. He religiously answers all of his e-mails, although not necessarily instantaneously!

Dedication

This book is dedicated to my wife Linda.

Acknowledgments

As with my first book, I want to thank first and foremost my wife Linda for her love and support. One of my students asked me when I ever find time to write; I told her evenings, late at night, weekends. She replied by saying that I must have a saint for a wife – and I do.

A second book is no easier on the family of the author than the first – there are still pleas for quiet, which is almost impossible with three children. My thanks also go to my wonderful children, Tom, Kevin and Melissa – each contributed to this book; Tom and Kevin (budding Visual Basic programmers) provided me with questions that beginning Visual Basic programmers need answered. Melissa, who at the time I wrote my first book spent time on my lap asking me to read Snow White to her, is now a three year old who once again kept me company while I wrote this book. Snow White is still her favorite story!

Many thanks go to the great people at Active Path. Once again, I want to thank Dave Maclean for giving me the opportunity to pursue my dream of writing innovative books on computer programming. I want to thank Andy Corsham and Devin Lunsford, my editors at Active Path, for their dedicated hard work in getting this book ready for publication. Many thanks also go to Dominic Shakeshaft, Kate Hall and Gordon Rogers at Wrox Press for their support and encouragement. The following people at Wrox Press gave me loads of help answering many emails over the last year, and provided me with fine hospitality when I met with them: Angie Doyle, Anthea Elston, Chris Ullman, Craig Berry, Dominic Lowe, Heather Gopsill, Jeremy Beacock, Sarah Bowers, Sonia Mullineux and Tim Briggs. Thank you all.

Books aren't produced in a vacuum. Behind the scenes there are reviewers, technical editors, layout specialists, indexers, and a group of marketing experts all working towards the goal of making the book a success. My thanks go to all of you.

Many thanks also go to the thousands of students I've taught over the years for your tireless dedication to learning the art and science of computer programming. Your great questions and demanding persistence in getting the most out of your learning experience truly inspired me, and contributed greatly to the book. Many of you dragged yourself to class after a long hard day of work, or rose early on your Saturday day off to learn. You have my greatest respect and admiration.

I want to thank the many readers of my first book, *Learn to Program with Visual Basic 6*, who took the time to write me about the book. I truly appreciate hearing from you, and I want you to know that I read and respond to each e-mail I receive.

Finally, I want to thank all the members of my family for their belief in and support of me over the years. Special thanks go to my mother, who said several hundred *novenas* for the success of my first book, and who has probably said just as many for this one. To my brother Bob, who calls me several times a week to encourage me and boost my spirits. To my brother Joe, who was one of the first people to read my earlier book, and who promotes it wherever he goes. To their wives, Annette and Pat, to my niece Carolyn and to my nephew Joe – thank you. Special thanks go to my nephew Jim for watching the boys in London. Thanks to my mother-in-law Leona for bragging about me. To my brother-in-law Bill for his many words of encouragement. To Tom and Sandy for being good family and good friends these many years. To their children, my nephew David, who right now is reading my first book, and to my niece Laura, whom I hope will read it soon.

And even though he is not physically here to see this book, thanks to my father for giving me a great example of what a husband and father should be. Whenever I wake up early to work on my book, I think of you. I believe that somehow, someplace, you are already flipping through the pages of *this* book. And I know that, someday, God will permit us all to be together again.

Examples

Table of Contents

Learn to Program with Visual Basic Examples

Week 2

Week 3

Week 4

Week 5

Week 6

Week 7

Week 8

Week 9

Table of Contents

Examples

Introduction

Picture this.

You've read my first book, *Learn to Program with Visual Basic 6*. And now you're working on your first real program. You try to change the `BackColor` of the command button on your form, but nothing happens. Now you're in a panic because you've promised this feature to a prospective client, or to your new boss! What do you do now?

You thumb through your manuals, but can't find anything. You call a friend. Good question, they say, but *they've* never been able to get it to work either. You check out some Visual Basic websites – but the questions asked out there are pretty advanced – and *this* one's not out there. Now what?

This question, and 99 others, are asked and answered in this book, in the form of a simulated call-in television show. These 100 questions are the questions that I anticipate a beginner programmer, working on their first real Visual Basic program, might ask. In fact, having taught Visual Basic for the last five years, I can assure you that these *are* the questions you will ask sometime during the course of writing your first real programs.

I hope you enjoy the book. Good luck, and happy programming!

John Smiley

Who is this book for?

You've already taken your first steps into Visual Basic programming. You understand the basics of how a program is put together, from design to interface to code. This book will make the most sense if:

❑ You've read an introductory text on Visual Basic programming (John Smiley's *Learn to Program with Visual Basic 6* is our ideal choice), or

❑ You've been playing around with VB long enough to be familiar with controls, variables, menus, arrays, events, methods and properties.

If you're not sure about any of these, consider running through *Learn to Program with Visual Basic 6*, where all these topics are explained from the ground up.

What will you need?

You could learn a lot from this book even without a PC in front of you – the examples are all explained and described in detail. But we think that the material is more likely to sink in if you try it out yourself. So you'll need to be running some version of Visual Basic. The examples in this book should all work fine on Visual Basic versions 3 and newer. Again, if you don't already have Visual Basic, consider purchasing *Learn to Program with Visual Basic 6*, which actually includes the Visual Basic **Working Model Edition**.

There are a few examples here that require a fully working version of VB, such as the *Learning Edition,* to run. These are mostly the ones that require a program to be *compiled*. The rest of the book will work just fine with the *Working Model Edition* and, by the end of the book, you'll have probably got an idea of what you can do with Visual Basic, and you'll know it's worth purchasing the full version.

What's covered?

Wow, that's a tough one. There's a little bit of everything in here. From simple 'why isn't this working the way I expect?' questions, through to handy tips to get your program to behave the way you want it to, covering a vast area of beginning VB. There are even a few tasters of more complex matters, like API calls, to give you a sneak peek at the world of intermediate VB programming. You'll be challenged to look at areas you've never thought about, but always in terms you're already familiar with.

How's the book structured?

Wouldn't it be great if there were a beginners' VB hotline? Where you could just call up someone you know will be always able to give you the answer you need? Well, if you find one, call me, because I could use one. Here's the next best thing. The 100 most commonly asked beginner questions, as compiled by John Smiley from his wealth of teaching experience. There's a good chance that if you have a question, it's in this book.

The book follows John Smiley as he presents a cable TV program devoted to answering VB questions for aspiring programmers. Each of the callers has a question to ask John their question, and he answers it in an easy-to-understand way, taking the opportunity to teach them (and you) other important concepts along the way.

You'll find that there are a number of ways you can read this book. If you really just want to broaden your knowledge of Visual Basic, you can read the book straight through. We actually think that this is the best way to get full value from it.

If you have a specific question, you can look it up in the table of contents – all the questions are listed there. Or, if you decide you want to find out everything there is to know about, for example, list boxes, you can check our thematic index inside the back cover, which will give a list of all questions on that theme. There's a full index too, for more detailed searching. Some questions also have related questions, and you'll see those referred to under the question title. Whatever you do, there's so much in here you might miss out if you don't read it all – but you might find the direct access methods give you other helpful ways to use the book.

What is *Learn to Program?*

Learn to Program with Visual Basic 6 Examples is the second in a series of foundation-level Visual Basic books designed to take someone from having no programming experience up to the level where they can really understand how programming is done. By the end of a 'Learn to Program' book, you might not be a professional programmer yet, but you will have established the beginnings of your programming knowledge. Remember that learning takes time, though, and don't get discouraged. We at Active Path will keep nurturing that skill, all the way up to the professional level.

Do I get any support?

OK, so if this was a real TV show you could just call up John Smiley and ask him a question. What do you do if you get stuck in a book?

You're not alone, OK? Just remember that. The Active Path website on `www.activepath.com` is there as a resource for you to use. There'll be the opportunity to ask the book's editors questions and give us feedback (positive or negative – we can take it). Just email us at `feedback@activepath.com` if you have a question or suggestion about the book. Please don't ask us about general VB questions, though, unless they're really related to the books – we'd love to be able to help you out individually but there just isn't enough time in the day to do that *and* bring out the great books you want to see from Active Path.

What is Active Path?

Active Path is a reasonably new publishing house with a fresh attitude to learning about computer programming. As a publisher, we understand your need to have the most up-to-date, cutting edge information about the computing world around you. We also understand that the computing world is full of jargon, and awash with unhelpful books that either treat you like an idiot or talk over your head, making no attempt to help you *learn* and build your skills.

So what makes Active Path different? Books from Active Path start at your level. There will always be an entry-level book, for which there's no previous experience required – guaranteed. We're not going to blindly show you everything about a subject in one massive brain-dump; we'll present the concepts when they become relevant to the problem. We don't believe anything is too complicated to learn; but we do believe that if you can imagine the problem, we should be able to illustrate the solution in terms you can understand.

We like detailed examples, and giving you the chance to work out your own solutions to problems designed to get you thinking and applying your knowledge. Most books try to cover everything, but end up leaving you baffled. We think that if you can pick it up and use it yourself, you're well on the way to thinking it's not so hard after all.

Basically, we believe that you should be able to learn what you want, how you want, when you want, and at a pace you feel comfortable with. All we do is write books to let you do that.

What about text styles?

To help you pick out important pieces of information and distinguish a piece of code in a paragraph of text, we've used certain fonts and styles throughout the book. We've kept it simple, so we don't distract you from the content, which we believe is the key here. Here are examples of each kind of style we use:

Question 1: Question titles will appear like this

(see also question 1) ←   you'll see this after any questions that have related information in other questions. It shows the **question number**, not the page number.

Since this book is about programming, there are quite a few times when we need to point out pieces of code. There are three ways of doing it, but they all look similar, so you can easily pick them out of a crowd. Sometimes we'll use `this style` to refer to a `procedure` or `code-related thing` in the middle of the text.

```
When we describe a new chunk of code, it'll be displayed on gray like this.

If you see this twisted arrow symbol,
↳ it means that you should type all the code on one line,
↳ leaving out the twisted arrow.
↳ Don't try to find this symbol on your keyboard -
↳ it's not there!
```

[By the way, if the line's *really* big, you might want to use the VB line continuation character, the underscore (_). If you're not sure how to use that, there's a good explanation in question 41 of this book.]

```
Code that has already been explained won't have the gray background.
↳ Quite often it will be a chunk of code you've seen before, but we've
↳ changed one line of it, or added something. So the new part looks like
this.
```

New **terms** or **new phrases** will be bolded.

Text from a Menu or on buttons appears like it does on the screen.

> **If we want to point out something important that you need to know, it will stand out like this.**

And if John's scribbling merrily away on his whiteboard in the studio, it'll show up like this.

OK - let's Learn to Program.

John Smiley's Prolog

I'm an educator at heart.

I have this idea that if I can teach everyone to program with Visual Basic, ultimately the world will be a better place. Judging by the numbers of my first book sold, I'm already reaching a sizable number of people. But there are more I need to reach, and here's why...

I think that people who are unemployed, but who learn Visual Basic, can be employed in good paying jobs.

I think that by teaching Visual Basic to children who may not care very much for reading, writing and mathematics, we can improve key reading, writing, and math skills.

I think that programming in Visual Basic can increase the self-esteem of people who are caught in failure chains.

But I can only do these things if I can reach these people. And the problem is, the folks in the second and third groups aren't all that likely to be buying books. Sad to say, group number two may not have the reading skills to get through my *Learn to Program with Visual Basic 6* book.

That's where a TV show comes in.

In the United States, we have loads of cooking and home repair shows. People tune in, check out the techniques, and try those techniques for themselves. And the great thing about these shows is that you don't need to be a reading genius to absorb the material. You just sit and watch. Why couldn't that be done with a show about computer programming – specifically Visual Basic?

Well, it hasn't happened yet. That's a shame. This book is, so far, as close as I've got to making that TV show. For now, we'll just have to pick up where we left off...

Those of you who have read my *Learn to Program with Visual Basic 6* book will probably remember Dave, one of my brightest (and most vocal) students. Well, it turns out that Dave was a sales representative for a local Cable TV station. Of course, I'd casually mentioned that I'd always wanted to present a TV show about VB programming. The next thing I knew, Dave had set up a meeting with the managing director of his station, and I was stepping across the deep blue carpet of their corporate headquarters, feeling very small and nervous.

The first problem was that Matt, the managing director, had noticed that another TV station already *had* a programming show – and it didn't appear to be doing too well. "I'm not surprised," I said. "All they're doing there is lecturing. It's on at 3 am, the students are expected to videotape the show, and it's boring," I asserted.

My idea was quite different, I told him. I had grown up watching a television show called Mr. Wizard. Each Sunday afternoon, Mr. Wizard would demonstrate a new scientific concept and, through the use of an experiment, make it come alive. Mr. Wizard also had several school-age assistants, drawn from his audience each week, who would help with the experiments.

"That's the kind of thing I mean," I said. "It'll be sort of interactive, and we'll make it interesting. You can't teach people unless the people want to learn. Mr. Wizard made science fun, and that's the way I want to teach programming."

He didn't seem quite convinced. He suggested a show which he thought would do well, one where I'd discuss more widely interesting computer topics, like the Net, operating systems, hardware, and so on. That's not my dream, though – there's plenty of that out there already. I pushed my idea out again, but Matt said that to him, it seemed like just another cooking show.

It looked like a lost cause, until the Vice President of Sales, Tim, came into Matt's office, and asked us how the meeting was going. Matt gave him a quick summary, explaining our barrier.

"What about," said Tim, "a show where the host would field questions from a live television audience, and use those questions to teach Visual Basic?" I liked the sound of that, as I knew that questions are a great gateway to teaching. If someone's asking a question, they're usually receptive to an answer. And Matt was receptive to the idea because it didn't fit the 'cooking' show formula.

The major difference was that my audience wouldn't be people with absolutely no experience, but people with *some* experience who needed help. No one in the room really knew if the idea would fly, but one thing we knew for sure was that we would find out very quickly.

I signed a standard contract for ten 90-minute television shows to be aired on Saturday afternoons at 1 pm. We all agreed to re-evaluate the idea at the end of the ten-week run.

I was feeling pretty happy about the fact that I'd got the show, but I also knew that from my point of view, the 'call in' format wasn't ideal. The lack of structure meant I'd never be able to prepare any material. And I'd have to type pretty fast…Tim sensed my reluctance, and reassured me that he thought a show of this nature could actually benefit more people than my original idea would.

Tim said that I could suggest to the viewers that they read my book, *Learn to Program with Visual Basic 6*, if they needed the type of step-by-step instruction I had wanted to televise. I could then use the show to allow the readers of my book – and anyone else with a Visual Basic problem – to ask questions about the types of pesky problems that seem to baffle beginners. Matt suggested calling the show "Professor Smiley's Visual Basic Programming Workshop," and that's what we settled on.

Examples

Week 1

"Five minutes," shouted my producer Linda.

I have to admit I was a bit nervous prior to the start of the show. Although I had taught hundreds of Visual Basic classes before, I had never done so on live television with a potential audience of thousands.

Everything was in place.

I sat down in front of the long desk, and surveyed my PC, keyboard and mouse. Linda asked me to double check that all of the equipment was working properly. I anxiously tested their correct operation and started up Visual Basic, while Linda confirmed that the video feed from the PC was working normally.

"Two minutes," Linda intoned. Looking towards the back of the studio, I could see the Visual Basic IDE (**Integrated Development Environment** – the main Visual Basic screen) displayed on a huge monitor behind her. From my end, the technical side looked fine. One less thing to worry about.

"Suppose no one calls in?" I thought to myself. "What an embarrassment that would be."

I sipped nervously from a can of soda, and looked at the clock on the wall as its hands moved unstoppably toward 1pm. The studio floor staff scurried around and spoke matter-of-factly to each other, and I wondered if I was the only one trying to suppress a bubble of panic rising in my chest.

Linda's voice buzzed in my earpiece, informing me that we already had two callers with Visual Basic questions waiting on the telephone line.

"That's fast," I thought to myself, "there's only been bare bones advertising for the show. Perhaps this might work after all?"

"Thirty seconds," Linda called out. I took one last sip of soda and prayed that my mouth wouldn't dry up. Well, here I was, and my dream was about to come true. Let's hope there wouldn't be a rude awakening.

Linda counted down the seconds.

"You're on the air," she said.

Learn to Program with Visual Basic Examples

"Welcome to the first segment of Professor Smiley's Visual Basic Programming Workshop," I began, right on cue. "I'll be answering your Visual Basic questions at this time for the next ten weeks. Of course, I'll need your help, since without your calls there will be no show! Please write down the toll free number that my producer is flashing across your television screen right now, and use it to call in with your beginning to intermediate Visual Basic questions. Furthermore, if you have some code that you would like me to check out, you can send that in to the studio by e-mailing me at `johnsmiley@johnsmiley.com`."

Linda signaled that we were ready for our first caller.

Question 1: How do I change the colors of a command button?

"Hi, my name is Mario from South Philadelphia," the caller began. "I've been programming for a few months, and I've been trying to change the colors of a command button, but I've had absolutely no success. Can you help me?"

"Mario, this has to be one of *the* most frequently asked VB questions. The answer to your question depends in part on which version of Visual Basic you're running."

"It's – uh – I'm running VB 5," said Mario.

"That's good – you're in luck," I replied. "Until the release of Visual Basic 5, you simply *couldn't* change the colors of a command button."

"Even though there's a `BackColor` property?" Mario interjected.

"That's right," I said, as I created a new Visual Basic project on my studio PC. "In every version of Visual Basic, the command button has had a `BackColor` property. Instinct tells you that this should change the color of the command button's face, but prior to Visual Basic 5, changing the `BackColor` property of a command button had *no effect* on its color. However, in Visual Basic 5 and 6, you *can* change the command button's `BackColor` property and affect the color of the button face – but first you must change the `Style` property of the command button to `Graphical`..."

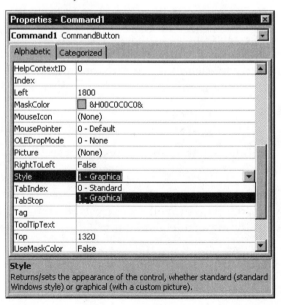

"Then, when you change the `BackColor` property of the command button..."

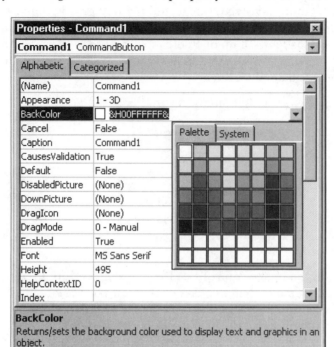

"...the button's face color will change:"

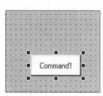

"Wow," Mario said, "that did it. Thanks a lot. One other question, though. Is there any way to change the color of the caption – the words, that is – on the command button's face?"

"Changing the color of the text in the caption is a problem," I replied. "The technique I just showed you allows you to change the `BackColor` property of the command button. But changing the caption's color is not easily accomplished. However, there are some alternatives if you want to pursue them."

"Such as?" Mario asked eagerly.

"Well, if you think about it," I said, "an **image control** will work just as well as a command button. Although it's a little more involved, this technique will give you more flexibility on how your command buttons look. What you can do is this: customize a graphic using your favorite Paint program, such as Paint Shop or Photoshop, and then place an image control on your form, size it just the way you want it, and set the `Picture` property of the Image control to the graphic you've customized."

I took this opportunity to do exactly that on my studio PC:

"You can then place code in the image control's `Click` event procedure to initiate whatever action would have been performed when the user clicked on your command button. If you're clever, you can even simulate the default action of a command button (for example, making it appear 'pressed down' when the user clicks on it)."

"I see what you mean," Mario said. "I never would have thought of that. Thanks a lot."

"Thanks for calling," I said as Linda signaled that another caller was ready with our next question.

Question 2: How do I Center a Command Button within a Form?

"Hi, my name's Katherine. Thanks for that tip on the `Style` property, by the way," she said, "I've been wondering about that for ages. While we're on the topic of command buttons, I was wondering if you could tell me how to center a command button on a form. I've created a program at work where the form is resizable, and I think it would look tons better if I could re-adjust the command button to be centered automatically whenever the user resizes the form."

"Hello, Katherine," I said, "and thanks for calling. I think you gave yourself a clue to the answer when you used the word 'resizable'. We can place code in the `Resize` event of the form so that the command button is *always* centered. Let me ask you this: are you interested in centering it vertically, horizontally, or both?"

"I need to center the command button slap in the middle of the form," she said.

"Take a look at this code on your television screen," I said, as I created a new Visual Basic project with a single command button. I placed the following code in the form's `Resize` event procedure and displayed it for the television audience at home:

```
Private Sub Form_Resize()

Command1.Left = (Form1.ScaleWidth - Command1.Width) \ 2
Command1.Top = (Form1.ScaleHeight - Command1.Height) \ 2

End Sub
```

"What I'm doing here," I continued, "is setting the `Left` and `Top` properties of the command button, dependent on the changing size and dimensions of the form. This is a little formula I learned a long time ago, in which we calculate the `Left` position of the command button to be equal to the width of the form, minus the width of the command button, divided by 2:"

```
Command1.Left = (Form1.ScaleWidth - Command1.Width) \ 2
```

"The same formula can be applied to calculate the top position of the command button, this time using the height of the form and the height of the command button:"

```
Command1.Top = (Form1.ScaleHeight - Command1.Height) \ 2
```

I then ran a quick demo of the project in which I resized the form repeatedly, and the command button remained perfectly centered within the form, both horizontally and vertically, each time I resized it.

"That's great," Katherine said. "Now may I ask another question?"

"Sure, Katherine."

"OK. I noticed that you used two properties of the form in your formula that I'm not familiar with – `ScaleHeight` and `ScaleWidth`. Are these properties the same as the `Height` and `Width` properties?"

"Not quite," I said. "The `Height` and `Width` properties of the form measure the height and width of the form, *including* the borders and title bar. `ScaleHeight` and `ScaleWidth` are the 'internal' height and width dimensions of the form, *not* including the borders and title bar. `ScaleHeight` is measured from directly *underneath* the title bar of the form to just *above* the bottom border of the form. `ScaleWidth` is measured as the internal width of the form, not including the left and right borders."

"Can using one set of properties versus another have an impact on centering the command button?" Katherine asked.

"It sure can," I said. "If we use `Height` and `Width` in our formula instead of `ScaleHeight` and `ScaleWidth`, as the form becomes smaller and smaller, the command button will no longer appear to be centered. This is because the title bar and the borders take up an increasing proportion of the entire height and width of the form. Let's compare these in an example."

To demonstrate this phenomenon, I added a second command button on the form, called `Command2`. I modified the code in the form's `Resize` event procedure as follows (changed code is highlighted, as it will be throughout this book):

```
Private Sub Form_Resize()

Command1.Left = (Form1.ScaleWidth - Command1.Width) \ 2
Command1.Top = (Form1.ScaleHeight - Command1.Height) \ 2

Command2.Left = (Form1.Width - Command1.Width) \ 2
Command2.Top = (Form1.Height - Command1.Height) \ 2

End Sub
```

"Instead of the `ScaleHeight` and `ScaleWidth` properties we used to 'center' the first command button, let's use the `Height` and `Width` properties of the form to 'center' the second command button," I said, as I ran the program, and progressively re-sized the form.

"Take a look at what happens. As the form gets smaller, the second command button begins to stick out like a sore thumb. It no longer appears to be centered within the form – at least not vertically – and that's because it's really being centered within the *entirety* of the form, including the title bar and borders."

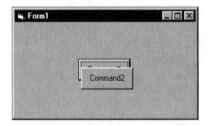

"That's great," Katherine said, "that illustrates it beautifully for me. And this formula will help me out quite a bit. I have just one more little question if I may. I thought the operator for division was the forward slash (/). What is the purpose of the backslash (\) in the formula?"

"The forward slash (/) operator," I said, "represents the type of division most people are familiar with – and that's **floating point division**, where there can be a fractional part in the result (such as 10 / 3 = 3.33 recurring). The backslash operator (\) represents **integer division**. Integer division discards the fractional part of the result, and therefore the answer is *always* a whole number or integer. In the case of this formula, we're not concerned with the fractional part of the result, since the answer is in **twips** (there are 1440 twips to an inch) – and a fractional part of a twip isn't going to make much difference in the placement of the command button. Besides, integer division is much faster than floating point division. It's good programming practice to use integer division wherever possible."

"Thanks, Professor Smiley," Katherine said. "I appreciate your help."

"Thanks for calling, Katherine," I said.

I looked to my producer Linda, and she was holding up ten fingers, then nine, then eight, and progressively counting down. I wasn't exactly sure what that meant. I knew we had been on the air for about ten minutes, but that wasn't it. Oh yes! Suddenly I remembered. A commercial break – we did have advertisers, after all!

"We'll be right back," I said, "after a word from one of our sponsors."

I sat for a while, cleaning up the little projects that I've created, then got up from behind the studio desk and asked Linda how things were going.

"Just fine," she said, "we've got five people on hold waiting to ask you questions. We've already received a number of phone calls to the station switchboard telling us what a great idea the show is. You'd better get back to your desk; you only have a few seconds left."

Question 3: Can you explain the Visual Basic Mod Operator?

"Hi, I'm William from London – well, originally, anyway," the caller said. "Katherine's question about that backslash division operator is a bit like something that's always confused me. Can you explain the Visual Basic `Mod` operator? Better yet, can you do something that no one has ever been able to do for me, and that's explain why I would ever use it in the first place?"

"Sure thing, William," I said, starting to feel more comfortable in the role of television host. "We saw how integer division discards the fractional part of a division operator in the code I just displayed for Katherine. Well, the `Mod` operator returns *only* the remainder of a division operation as a result. `Mod` is short for *modulus*, which in this context means the remainder of one number divided by another."

"Can you give me an illustration of how it works?" William asked.

Learn to Program with Visual Basic Examples

I created a new Visual Basic project with a single command button and placed the following code in the command button's Click event procedure:

```
Private Sub Command1_Click()

Form1.Print 10 Mod 3

End Sub
```

"In this code, we 'mod' the number 10 by the number 3, which is another way of telling Visual Basic to display the *remainder* of the number 10 divided by the number 3. We all know that 10 divided by 3 is 3, with a remainder of..."

"1", William said over the telephone.

"Exactly," I replied, "and that's what will be displayed on the form when we click the command button:"

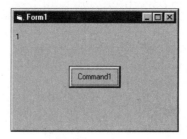

"OK," William said, "I see how the Mod operator works. It returns the remainder of a division operation as a result. Now how about a practical use for it?"

"In order to discuss a practical use for it," I replied, "let's change the code in the Click event procedure of the command button to look like this:"

```
Private Sub Command1_Click()

Form1.Print 10 Mod 5

End Sub
```

"In this example," I said, "we're using the Mod operator to display the remainder of 10 divided by 5. What will be displayed on the form?"

"10 is evenly divisible by 5," William said, "so there is no remainder."

"Of course, and that's an important point to remember – when a number is evenly divisible by another number, the Mod operator returns a result of 0," I said as I ran the program, and clicked on the command button:

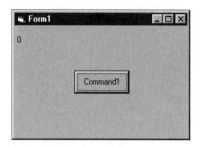

"I understand that now," William confirmed. "When you 'mod' two numbers, if the first number is evenly divisible by the second number, the result will be 0. Now how can we put *that* to practical use?

"Well," I said, "coincidentally, an example came up earlier this week in my Penn State University Visual Basic class. One of the students in the class was executing a long-running loop, and she wanted to give the user a visual clue as to what was happening behind the scenes. But she didn't want to give this visual cue to the user every time the loop was executed, but maybe every 100 or 1,000 times."

"So you were able to use the Mod operator for that?" William asked, apparently a bit stumped.

"Yes, we were," I answered, "and it worked out quite well. Look at this code, in which I'll code a For...Next loop that 'counts' from 1 to 100,000. Notice that after the loop is finished, we display a message box saying we're 'All Done'."

I typed the following code into the Click event procedure of a new command button:

```
Private Sub Command1_Click()

Dim lngCounter As Long

For lngCounter = 1 To 100000
Next lngCounter

MsgBox "All Done!"

End Sub
```

When I ran the program and clicked on the command button, the message box appeared in a second or two telling us that the program was finished.

Learn to Program with Visual Basic Examples

"Suppose," I continued, "we wanted to let the user know what number our loop was up to in its counting? It's pretty easy to do this by using the `Print` method of the form – like so."

I modified the code to look like this:

```
Private Sub Command1_Click()

Dim lngCounter As Long

For lngCounter = 1 To 100000
Form1.Print lngCounter
Next lngCounter

MsgBox "All Done!"

End Sub
```

"The problem with this code," I said, "is that every time the loop executes, the number we're counting is printed on the form, and we wind up with an ugly bunch of numbers (and eventually gibberish) on the form, because Visual Basic forms don't scroll. Not only that, but our program, which ran in a second or two before we decided to print numbers on the form, now takes much longer to finish – all because we decided to get fancy and display numbers on the form!"

I then ran the modified program, and sure enough, execution time went from one second or so to twelve seconds.

"It would be better all around," I said meanwhile, "if we could think of a way to display only *some* of the numbers – like every 10,000th one – on the form. That's where the `Mod` operator comes into play. Look at this code:"

```
Private Sub Command1_Click()

Dim lngCounter As Long

For lngCounter = 1 To 100000
If lngCounter Mod 10000 = 0 Then
    Form1.Print lngCounter
End If
Next lngCounter

MsgBox "All Done!"

End Sub
```

"By 'modding' the value of the variable `lngCounter` with 10,000," I said, "and then checking to see if the result is 0, we are able to determine if the current value of the variable `lngCounter` is evenly divisible by 10,000. If it *is*, then we know that we have an increment of 10,000, and we print the current value of `lngCounter` on the form. In this way, we print every 10,000th number on the form. Let's run the program and see what happens."

I did exactly that, and the following screen shot was displayed (in about a second, by the way):

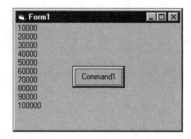

"So," William said, "if we wanted to print every 50,000th number, we would just change the code to read '`lngCounter Mod 50000`'?"

"That's right, " I said, "pretty easy, isn't it?"

"I'm impressed," William said. "And I think I can see a bunch of other practical applications for the `Mod` operator. I'm really interested in animation and game programming, and I might be able to use it there. Thanks for the demo."

"Glad I could help," I said, and Linda put our next caller on.

Question 4: The correct properties don't show up in the code window – only Count, Item, LBound and UBound. Why?
(see also questions 32 & 50)

"Hi, I'm Betsy from Center City Philadelphia," the voice said. "I've been working on a Visual Basic project at work for the last two weeks, and I'm really frustrated with it. I've been trying to change the `Caption` property of a label control at run time. However, when I begin to write code in the code window, where I would ordinarily see a list of the label control's properties and methods in those pop-ups, all I see are four entries: `Count`, `Item`, `LBound` and `UBound`. When I go to the `Properties` window for the label control, I can see all of the properties for the label there. But I can't change them using code when I run the program – it's as if they've disappeared. And when I run my code, I get an error message saying '`Method or data member not found`'. Can you explain this?"

Learn to Program with Visual Basic Examples

"Hi, Betsy. Don't worry, this is an easy one," I said, "and the fix is also very easy. Let me illustrate what's happening here."

I added a label control and a command button to a form in a new project, and wrote some code in the `Click` event procedure of the command button. This code would change the label control's `Caption` when the program ran and the command button was clicked.

In Visual Basic 5 and Visual Basic 6, with Auto List Members specified in the Options tab, a list of properties and methods 'belonging' to a form or control will show up automatically as soon as you reference the object. As soon as I typed `Label1`, followed by a dot (`.`), Visual Basic displayed the label control's **members** (its properties and methods):

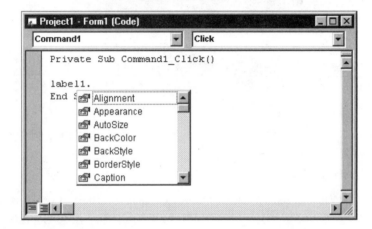

"This is what we would expect to see," I said, "a full listing of the members – properties and methods – for the label control. But you're not seeing this, are you Betsy?"

"No I'm not," Betsy said, "it's as though I've lost all of my properties. Do you think I need to download the Service Pack for Visual Basic?"

> **Visual Basic Service Packs update Visual Basic with the latest upgrades and fixes for the software. When you apply a service pack you need to consider what stage of your development cycle you are at – for example, if you are in the final testing phase the impact of updating your software and thus changing your development environment could have unpredictable results on your half-developed programs. Things that worked before the service pack was applied might stop working after the application of the service pack. So while it's good to have all the latest fixes in your software, it's important that you consider the timing of the service pack installation.**

"That's not the problem here, Betsy," I said. "What you've done – and it's very common – is accidentally put something in the label control's `Index` property. When you did that, you turned the label control into a **control array** – and when you reference a control array in your code without typing in a `Index` value, the four methods you described are displayed as members, rather than the *full* range of members that you'd expect to see for an individual label control."

To illustrate my point, I then changed the `Index` property of the label control to `0`, thus turning the single label control into a control array:

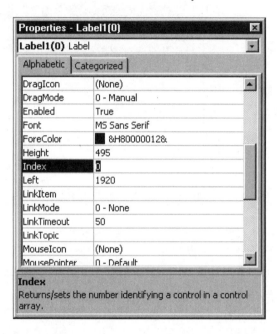

"Notice," I said, "that as soon as I change the `Index` property of a control to anything other than its default value of 'nothing', the control becomes a control array. You can tell that this has happened because some parentheses appear after the name of the label control:"

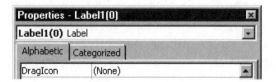

Learn to Program with Visual Basic Examples

"Those of you who may have read my beginner's book on Visual Basic (*Learn to Program with Visual Basic*) should know control arrays pretty well. For everyone else, a control array (in this case a control array of labels) is like a *family* of label controls. All of the 'family' members of a control array have the same *name* (in this case, **Label1**), but each has a *unique* **Index** property that identifies each individual label control that make up the array. **As soon as a control becomes a member of a control array, all references to it *must* include its Index value**. If you don't include the reference to the **Index** value in your code, you get exactly what Betsy is seeing."

I then went back into the code window, and started entering code referencing the label control. This time, instead of seeing a full listing of the properties and methods of the label control, only four methods appeared:

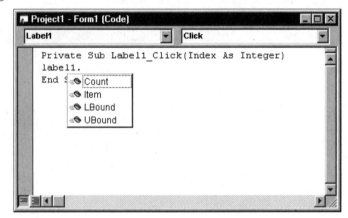

"These four members," I said, "are the properties of the control array itself – *not* a particular member (i.e. not an individual control in the family of controls)."

There was silence on the other end of the phone – Betsy must have been trying it herself.

"You know," she said after a moment or two, "you're right. Somehow I had placed the number **4** in the **Index** property of the label control. Hmm...I bet I know what I did! When I was setting the **Tab Order** of the controls on my form, I probably confused the **TabIndex** property of the label control with its **Index** property."

"That's likely," I said, "and it happens all the time. Just remember, whenever you see just these four properties show up in your **Code** window, then you know that your control is actually a control array, and has a value of some kind in its **Index** property."

"But how can I fix it?" Betsy asked, eager to get her problem sorted out. "Do I need to re-do my entire project? I have an important deadline to meet."

"No, you don't have to do anything that drastic," I said. "Just bring up the Properties window for the label control, find its **Index** property, select the value using your mouse, and press the *Backspace* key. That will clear it, and set it back to its default."

Again there was a moment of silence.

"That worked," she said excitedly, "now all of my properties and methods are showing up – and now the code's working! Thanks. I'm well on my way now."

"You're quite welcome," I said, "and thank you for calling. Let's move on to our next caller before taking a commercial break."

Question 5: I have Require Variable Declaration specified in my options, but I don't see Option Explicit in my code window – why?

"Hi, this is John," he said. "This isn't a big deal, but it's been bugging me. I'm taking a Visual Basic class at the Community College down here, and our instructor this morning said that it's a good idea to turn Require Variable Declaration 'on' in the VB Options window. She said that if we did that, we should see the words 'Option Explicit' in the code window, but I don't see it. How come?"

"Hi, John. There are a number of possible reasons for this. First, for the rest of the viewers at home, let me just reinforce what you said. By checking Require Variable Declaration in the Editor tab of the Visual Basic Options menu, we tell Visual Basic to ensure that if we refer to a variable in code, we must have explicitly declared it already. Visual Basic reminds us that we've turned Require Variable Declaration 'on' by inserting the words 'Option Explicit' in the General Declaration section of a form, code module, or class module. Let's see how this works," I said, and selected Tools | Options | Editor from the main Visual Basic menu:

Learn to Program with Visual Basic Examples

"It's important to note," I said, "that checking this option only applies to any *new* forms or modules that you subsequently create. In other words, if you already have forms or other types of modules in your project, Visual Basic won't add 'Option Explicit' to those existing modules – only to forms or modules that you create thereafter."

"This option isn't project-specific, is it?" John asked. "What I mean is this: if I exit VB and restart it, Require Variable Declaration will still be selected. Is that right?"

"That's right," I said, "all of the options that you see here are global Visual Basic options – not project-level ones. So if Require Variable Declaration was not checked, and you then checked it on, this means that when you start a new Visual Basic project, or even add a new module to an existing project, you should see Option Explicit in the General Declarations section of the module."

In the pause I could hear John tapping away at his keyboard. I looked the camera straight in the eye and waited.

"I did that," reported John. "I checked Require Variable Declaration on, then started a new VB project, but I still don't see those words."

"There's another possibility, then," I said. "If you take a look at the Editor options tab, you'll see that there's another checkbox there labeled Default to Full Module View. Do you see it?"

"Yes, I do," John answered. "It's not checked on. I'm not really sure what that means."

"**Full Module View**," I said, "means that when you view your code window, you can see the code in all of your event procedures at once. This also includes any code in the General Declarations section of your module – including the words 'Option Explicit'. The alternative view is something called **Procedure View**, where Visual Basic only shows you the code from one event procedure at a time. That's what I have got selected here in the studio. If you have procedure view selected, as I do, you won't see the words 'Option Explicit' unless you either turn Full Module View 'on' or actually go to the General Declarations section of the form."

"Can you show me what you mean by that?" John asked. "I'm a bit confused."

"Sure thing," I said, and quickly created a new Visual Basic project. I put two command buttons on the form, with code in each to display message boxes, reading "I love Visual Basic" and "I can teach everyone to program" respectively. Then I double-clicked on the command button in design view to bring up the Visual Basic code window:

26

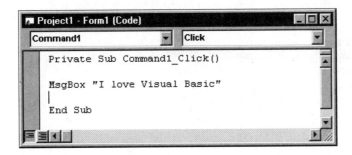

"See, John," I said, "We don't see 'Option Explicit' anywhere, even though I know that 'Require Variable Declaration' is turned on. For that matter, notice that the code I have in the Click event procedure of the second command button is not visible either. And I know it exists, because I just typed it in."

"So where is 'Option Explicit?" John asked.

"Option Explicit is there, switched 'on' in the project," I assured him, "we just can't see it in this view."

"So how can we see it?" he replied, starting to sound a little irritated.

"As I mentioned earlier, we have two choices," I said. "If you look at the top of the Visual Basic code window, you'll see that there are two list boxes. The list box on the left is called the Object list box, and the one on the right is called the Procedure list box. If we click on the Object list box, and then select General..."

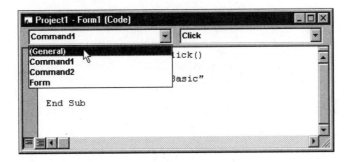

"...we'll then be in the `General Declarations` section of the form, and you'll then be able to see the words `'Option Explicit'`:"

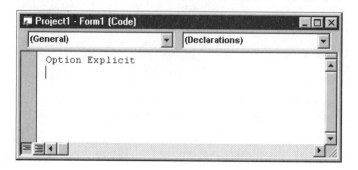

"Oh...*there* it is," John said, sounding surprised. "But in class this morning, I could swear that `Option Explicit` appeared at the top of the code window, and there was a line underneath it. I believe our instructor called it a separator bar."

"That's right, John," I said. "That's how the `General Declarations` section will appear if you have Full Module View selected. Full Module View can either be specified in the Editor options window from the Tools menu of Visual Basic, or you can switch from Procedure View to Full Module View while you have the code window up."

"How can we do that?" he asked.

"Take a look at the bottom of the code window," I said. "Do you see the two buttons on the left of the window?"

"Yes, I do," John answered.

"The button on the left," I continued, "is the one selected on my PC here in the studio – and it indicates that Procedure View is in effect. That means we can only see *one* event procedure at a time. If we were to click on the second button from the left, we'd turn 'on' Full Module View."

I did exactly that:

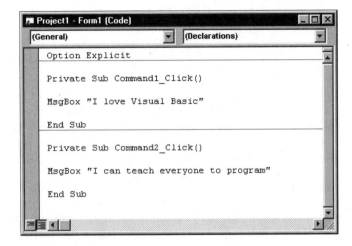

```
Option Explicit

Private Sub Command1_Click()

MsgBox "I love Visual Basic"

End Sub

Private Sub Command2_Click()

MsgBox "I can teach everyone to program"

End Sub
```

"That's it," John said excitedly. "That's what we saw in class. Thanks. It really did puzzle me before. Just let me get this straight in my mind: if I want to set Full Module View permanently, all I need to do is select Full Module View from the Editor tab of the Options window?"

"That's all," I answered.

"And then, provided I have Require Variable Declaration turned 'on', I'll always see Option Explicit?" he asked.

"That's right," I said.

"Thanks a lot, Professor," John said, "maybe I'll have another question for you next week!"

"Thanks for calling," I said, and with a cue from my producer Linda, I announced a commercial break.

During the break, Linda told me that since the beginning of the show 40 minutes ago, the phones had been pretty busy. In fact, she told me, she had been forced to turn away callers, as with the number of callers now on hold, it was obvious that we wouldn't be able to accommodate any more today. We had about 45 minutes left to go.

Question 6: Is there a way to make a form scrollable? (How to write multiple lines to a text box)

"Hi, this is Eleanor from Philadelphia," she said. "I've been trying to create a scrollable form in Visual Basic. Is there a way to do that?"

"Well, Eleanor," I said, "the short answer is no. Forms in Visual Basic are not scrollable. In Visual Basic, the form is basically just a container for other controls, so we have to rely on some of those other controls to give us a scrollable feature if that's what we want. For instance, text boxes, list boxes and combo boxes implement scrollbars where necessary. What reason did you have for wanting the form to scroll?"

"I've written a program," she said, "where I'm writing output to the form using the form's **Print** method. With each successive **Print** to the form, my output automatically moves down one line on the form. Finally, when the program gets to the bottom of the form, it just goes right off the lower edge. I was hoping I could get it to scroll."

"That's probably the most common reason that people look for some kind of scrollable feature on the form," I answered. "Unfortunately, this kind of facility doesn't exist – at least not in Visual Basic."

"I tried placing **Vertical** scrollbars alongside the right edge of the form," she said, "hoping that might do the trick – but it didn't."

"Scrollbars by themselves won't do anything," I said. "If you want to implement a feature like that, you would have to write some pretty sophisticated code, and even then you would only be making the form 'appear' to scroll. But there *are* alternatives. For instance, you could place a list box control on the form, and, rather than using the form's **Print** method, you could use the **AddItem** method of the list box. You could also write your output to a text box where, if you set the text box's **MultiLine** property to **True**, and specify a **Scrollbars** property of **Vertical**, you have in essence made yourself a scrollable form."

"Can you show me the code for that?" Eleanor asked. "I've had some confusion writing to a text box in the past."

"Sure thing," I said, swiftly creating a Visual Basic project containing a command button and a text box. I then changed the **MultiLine** property of the text box to **True**, and specified '**Vertical**' for the **ScrollBars** property.

"The trick here," I said, "is how to write the output to the text box. Just specifying **True** for the **MultiLine** property won't do the trick – you need to concatenate a Visual Basic **Carriage Return** and **Linefeed** to the current value of the **Text** property in the text box, *then* concatenate the value you want to write to the text box. Here's the full code to do this:"

```
Private Sub Command1_Click()

Dim intCounter As Integer

For intCounter = 1 To 100
    Text1.Text = Text1.Text & intCounter & vbCrLf
    DoEvents
Next intCounter

MsgBox "All done"

End Sub
```

"What I've done here is set up a `For...Next` loop to count from 1 to 100:"

```
For intCounter = 1 To 100
    Text1.Text = Text1.Text & intCounter & vbCrLf
    DoEvents
Next intCounter
```

"Within the body of the loop, I've concatenated a Carriage Return and Linefeed character (**vbCrLf**), plus the value of the variable '**intCounter**', to the **Text** property of the text box (**Text1.Text**). Remember that the ampersand (**&**) acts as the concatenation character that joins all the separate elements into a single string. Let's see what happens when we run this code."

When I then ran the program, the following screen was displayed on the studio monitor and in the homes of the viewers:

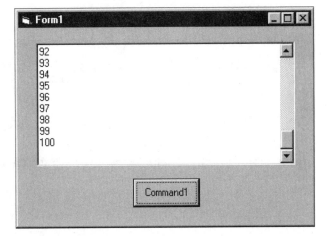

"Not quite a scrollable form," I said, "but pretty close. In fact, if you really wanted to, you could make the text box appear to be a scrollable form like this: set its `BorderStyle` property to `None`, the `BackColor` property of the text box the same value as the `BackColor` of the form, and its `Height` and `Width` properties equal to the `ScaleHeight` and `ScaleWidth` properties of the form."

Eleanor seemed to be satisfied with that.

"Wow you're right," she said. "That does look like a scrollable form – just like it in fact. Can I ask you another question? What is `vbCrLf` again?"

"Good question," I said, "sorry if I glossed over that. `vbCrLf` is a Visual Basic **Intrinsic Constant** – which means it's defined as a fixed part of Visual Basic itself. It represents the ASCII value for a Carriage Return and Linefeed, which is what we use to 'force' the next value we want to enter in our text box to appear on the next line of the text box:

```
Text1.Text = Text1.Text & intCounter & vbCrLf
```

"Without it, we would just get a single stream of numbers, like this:"

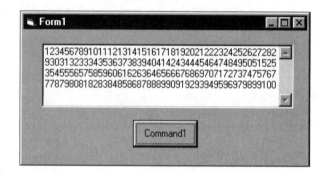

"OK. One more question: what's the purpose of `DoEvents` in the code?" Eleanor asked.

"Well," I explained, "*Without* `DoEvents`, the contents of the text box would appear all at once when the `Click` event procedure ended. *With* `DoEvents`, the text box contents appeared as the `Click` event procedure was running."

"Um, I'm afraid I still have another question – what about the message box `'All Done'`?" Eleanor asked.

"Just a habit of mine," I said. "Whenever I'm doing a demonstration of loop processing, I like to know when the loop has ended."

"Thanks, Professor Smiley," she finally said. "This has been a big help – plus I've learned something about text boxes as well."

"Thanks for calling, Eleanor," I said. "Who's next on the line?"

Question 7: I specified a graphics file in the Picture property of a form or picture box, but now I want to clear it. How can I do this?

(see also question 8)

"Hi, I'm Albert from Rome, New York," he said. "I'm afraid that Eleanor stole my thunder. I had a problem with the `MultiLine` property of the text box, or so I thought. I couldn't get the text box to display more than one line, no matter what I tried – everything came out on a single line. I just realized, after seeing your example, that I wasn't concatenating the Carriage Return and Linefeed."

"Well, Albert," I said, "I'm glad we could help. You're certainly welcome to ask another question if you want – after all, you've been on hold for quite some time."

"OK," he said, "how about this one? I feel a little dumb asking this, though."

"No problem," I reassured him, "just ask away."

"OK. I don't do a lot of work with graphics, but on occasion I specify a `Picture` property in either a form or a picture box control. I'm OK with selecting a graphics file for the `Picture` property. I just use the dialog box that pops up in the Properties window to find a graphics file. Then, once I find it, I double click on it and it's automatically entered into the `Picture` property of the form or picture box control for me. My problem occurs after I've successfully selected a `Picture` property – I just haven't been able to figure out how to *get rid* of it."

"First of all, Albert," I said, "remember, there isn't any such thing as a dumb question. I hear this question all the time, and not just from beginners. You'll be happy to hear that the answer is really quite easy. First though, let me show everybody exactly what we're talking about."

I brought up the Properties window for the form in a new Visual Basic project and specified a graphics file for the `Picture` property:

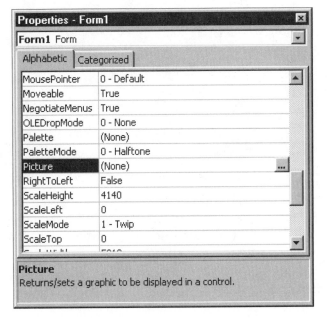

By clicking on the ellipsis in the `Picture` property of the form, I used this dialog box...

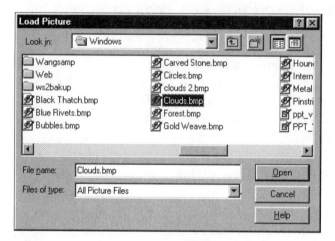

...to specify a `Picture` property equal to the path of the graphics file '`Clouds.bmp`'. As soon as I had done that, the form's background changed to incorporate the graphic:

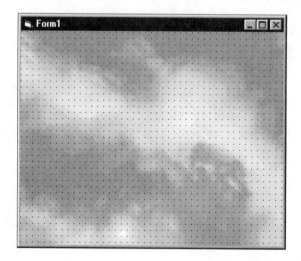

"So far, so good," Albert said. "I should mention that I know how to change this to a *different* graphics file...you just go through the process of re-selecting another graphic. But how do you get rid of the graphic entirely, so you have no background graphic on the form or picture box?"

I smiled because I knew Albert would believe he had somehow missed the obvious – but as I always tell my students, nothing is obvious with programming or Visual Basic.

"Albert," I said, "To remove the reference to the graphics file, bring up the Properties window again. You'll see that the value in the `Picture` property reads '(`Bitmap`)'. Now select the value in the `Picture` property with your mouse..."

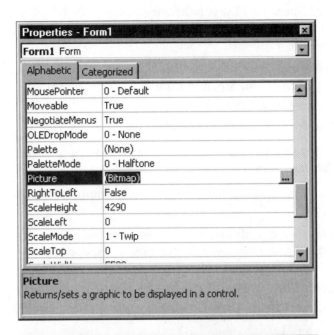

"and then press the *Delete* key. The `Picture` property value will now go back to its default of '(`None`)':"

"You're kidding," I heard him say, half-embarrassed. "Is that all there is to it? I bet I tried a hundred different ways. I could swear I even tried your method, but I bet I pressed the *Backspace* key instead. Thanks."

Albert was gone. I had thought about discussing the `LoadPicture` function a little bit more with Albert, but he had hung up, and Linda was gesturing wildly to me that I had a commercial break coming up.

"Time for a word from one of our sponsors," I said, as we cut away for a commercial.

I explained to Linda that I had wanted to discuss loading pictures into forms a little more, but Albert had hung up too quickly.

"This is your lucky day," she said, "the next caller wants to discuss the `LoadPicture` function with you."

Linda told me that we had about 25 minutes left in the program, so we could probably take another three calls or so. Our goal had been ten calls, and we were right on track for that.

Question 8: I specified a graphics file in the Picture property of a form using the LoadPicture function. Can I clear it using the LoadPicture function also?

(see also question 7)

"Hi, this is Henry from Doylestown," the voice on the other end of the line said. "My question is very similar to Albert's. I've been trying to clear a graphics file from the `Picture` property of the form. The difference is that I want to clear it at run time, not via the Properties window in design mode."

"Hi, Henry; thanks for calling." I said. "May I presume that you are using the `LoadPicture` function to set the value of the `Picture` property of a form or picture box?"

"That's right," he replied. "Again, just like Albert, I'm having no problem assigning a graphics file to the `Picture` property using the `LoadPicture` function. I just haven't been able to figure out how to clear it once I've set it. Is there another function I need to use?"

"No, you don't need to use another function, " I said. "The `LoadPicture` function is the beast that you're after here. However, like some other areas of programming, there's a little trick you need to know. Before I show you that trick, I'd like to show how to use the `LoadPicture` function to set the `Picture` property of a form. Let's keep this example consistent with the previous one I showed Albert by using the same graphics file."

I typed the following code into the `Click` event procedure of a new command button:

```
Private Sub Command1_Click()

Form1.Picture = LoadPicture("c:\windows\clouds.bmp")

End Sub
```

When I ran the program and clicked on the command button, the 'Clouds' graphic was loaded as the background image for the form:

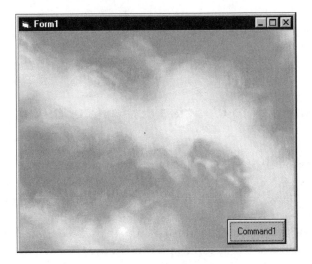

"OK," Henry said." How do we clear it? I'm anxious to see this."

I typed the following code into the `Click` event procedure of a second command button:

```
Private Sub Command2_Click()

Form1.Picture = LoadPicture()

End Sub
```

I then ran the program again and clicked on the first command button. As before, the 'Clouds' image appeared on the form. I clicked the second command button and the image 'disappeared'.

"What we're doing here, Albert," I explained, "is using the first command button to pass the `LoadPicture` function the 'clouds.bmp' graphic as an argument in the function's brackets:"

```
Form1.Picture = LoadPicture("c:\windows\clouds.bmp")
```

"Next, with the second command button, we pass the LoadPicture function a value of 'nothing'. This is called a **null argument**, and it essentially tells the function to load 'no picture':"

```
Form1.Picture = LoadPicture()
```

"So that's it," Henry chuckled to himself. "I never would have thought of it. Pass the LoadPicture a null argument."

"Tricks of the trade," I said. "Thanks for your call, Albert."

We were starting to get a little tight with time, so Linda passed the next caller right through.

Question 9: Is there any way to clear the contents of the Immediate window?

"Hi, this is Deborah from Philadelphia," she said. "I've been reading your book – loved it by the way – and in Chapter 6, the chapter where you discuss debugging, you talk about the Immediate window, and how useful it can be in debugging your programs. There's something that's been bugging me – pardon the pun – and that's this: is there any way to clear the Immediate window? If I write output to it using a Debug.Print statement, the output just stays there, and keeps building up in the Immediate window. It would be real useful if you could clear it out."

"Hi Deborah," I answered, "I know exactly what you mean. The Immediate window can get cluttered pretty quickly. Wouldn't it be great if there were a 'CLS' method of the Debug object, just like there is of the form or picture box? Unfortunately there isn't, and there's no way of doing this using Visual Basic itself, although you might be able to use the Windows API to do it."

"The Windows API?" Deborah asked, obviously confused.

"That's an advanced topic for another show, or rather another *series*," I said. "Working with the API is something only the advanced Visual Basic programmer should attempt."

"So there's really no way to clear it then?" Deborah asked.

"Not using code," I confirmed. "There *is* a manual method, though."

"Oh," said Deborah, "How does that work?"

"Watch this," I replied, creating a few `Debug.Print` statements to generate some content for the Immediate window:

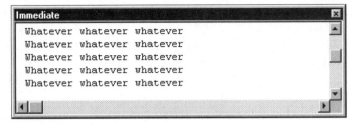

"OK," I continued, "Now stop the program running, make sure you've got the Immediate window visible (use View | Immediate Window if you can't see it), highlight the contents of the Immediate window with the mouse..."

"...and press the *Delete* key."

"And voilà! – the Immediate window is clear."

"Doh!" said Deborah.

"Never underestimate the power of the mouse," I said, laughing. "It's just a shame that we can't do this programmatically."

Linda held up one finger to indicate that the next one would be our last caller for the day. We had a little over five minutes left in our inaugural show.

Question 10: How do I add a second form to a project?

"Hi, this is Edgar," he said. "I know you're short on time, but hopefully this question is a quick one. I've just finished your book, completed the project you build in it, and everything has worked out great. The only thing I wanted to do to enhance the project was to add a second form to it. I figured out that if I selected Project | Add Form from the Visual Basic main menu, I could add another form to the project that way. Then I figured I needed to load `Form2` using code from somewhere on `Form1`, so I placed a command button on `Form1` to load `Form2`. So far, so good. The only problem is that when I run the code to load the second form, I never actually *see* the form. It's as though `Form2` is invisible."

Learn to Program with Visual Basic Examples

"OK, Edgar," I said, "we still have a few minutes left, so we can take this slowly. Many Visual Basic applications require more than one form in the project. And you're right – in my book, we used just a single form – something that made learning Visual Basic much easier for the beginner. But eventually, there comes a point where you need to add another form to your project. You hit the nail on the head when you say that to add another form to a project, you need to select Project | Add Form from the Visual Basic main menu. Let's show the home viewers what we mean by that."

I started a new project and added a second form to it by selecting Project | Add Form from the main menu:

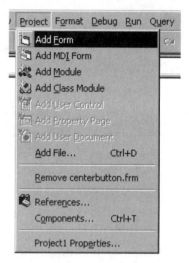

"Edgar is right," I continued, "Once a second form is added to the project, then you need to write some code to make it visible. I should mention at this point that every Visual Basic project has something called a `Startup Object` – which is, by default, `Form1`."

"`Form1` is automatically loaded and displayed by Visual Basic when your program starts to run. The programmer doesn't need to do anything special to make the form visible."

"Which is why," Edgar interrupted, "I figured that all I needed to do was use the `Load` statement to load `Form2`."

"You were on the right track, Edgar," I said. "Let's follow your suggestion by placing a command button on `Form1`, and put some code in the command button's `Click` event procedure that will bring `Form2` into view. Let's code that up now, and see what happens:"

```
Private Sub Command1_Click()

Load Form2

End Sub
```

I ran the program, and when I clicked on the command button nothing appeared to happen, just as Edgar had described.

"The problem with using the `Load` statement," I explained, "is that when a form, other than the `Startup` form is 'loaded', it isn't automatically made visible. Occasionally, you might *want* to preload a form and leave it invisible until you need it – for example, a form that would take a long time to load because it uses a large number of controls. To make the second form visible, you must explicitly 'show' it by using `Form2`'s `Show` method. In fact, it's not even necessary to load `Form2` explicitly – just using the `Show` method of `Form2` both loads *and* shows it."

I then changed the code in the command button's `Click` event to look like this:

```
Private Sub Command1_Click()

Form2.Show

End Sub
```

When I ran the program and clicked on the command button, the second form became visible.

"That seems kind of stupid, doesn't it?" Edgar said. "What about the `Startup` form? I know that a `Load` event takes place on the `Startup` form, and I know that the `Startup` form *automatically* gets shown – you don't need to explicitly show that one, do you?"

"You're right to see a bit of a conundrum here," I replied, "but there's something unique about the `Startup` form. At the end of the `Load` event for the `Startup` form, Visual Basic issues an implicit `'Show'` method of the form. This means that the programmer doesn't have to code anything to show the `Startup` form. Strange, but true."

Linda began to gesture that we had just one minute left in the show.

"Well," I said, "that's about all the time we have for today. I want to thank everyone for watching. Special thanks go to the people who called in with questions today. If you tried to call, but couldn't get through, remember, we'll be here next week, same time, same channel."

Linda signaled that we were 'off the air', and I breathed a sigh of relief. "How do you think it went?" I asked her nervously.

"Well, I've seen a lot of new shows," Linda began, "and I think you're doing just fine. Nothing went wrong, which is always nice. Listen, some of the crew are going for a quick coffee – would you like to join us?"

"I'd like that," I replied. I wasn't much company, as it turned out. I was filled with a mixture of emotions, from elation at the apparent success of the first show, through to a slight fear that the success wouldn't be repeated in next week's show. I still felt I had something to prove, and I wouldn't be able to relax until I could be confident that the show wouldn't flop.

As I drove home, my mind replayed the show. Had I been helpful to the callers? Instructive? I felt that I had. Still, it's hard to tell when you can't see them directly. And with such a limited timeframe, it's a challenge to get your message across effectively. But I had definitely enjoyed it. I returned home, and was greeted by my family, who had been watching the show. Whether it had been as much of a success as I'd hoped or not, their supportive comments and smiles were a real comfort to come back to.

Week 2

Around mid-week I received a phone call from Tim and Matt at the Cable Television Channel. They told me that our first week's ratings had been extremely promising, and that our advertisers were very pleased. The trick now, they said, was to maintain the momentum of Week 1 in our second show this Saturday.

As 1pm approached that Saturday, I found that I wasn't nearly as nervous as I had been the previous week. I'd still prepared some Visual Basic teaching material just in case not enough people called in, though.

Once again, a quick review of my equipment revealed that everything was in place. You never would have guessed that just a few hours earlier, this studio set had been host to a French cooking show – that is, apart from the subtle fragrance of sautéed mushrooms and tarragon.

As the five-minute mark approached, I sat down at my studio desk. I could see the Visual Basic IDE displayed on the big monitor at the back of the studio. Everything looked fine.

Linda, my producer, informed me that we already had ten callers ready to begin asking Visual Basic questions. Provided that no one tired of waiting, all of the callers for the day were probably already queued. Standing room only already – no wonder the advertisers were happy.

"One thing before you go on," said Linda. "Try not to refer to me too much when you're on air. As far as the viewing audience is concerned, everything just happens by itself – commercials, phone calls, and so on. They don't want to know the details."

"Sure thing," I replied. "I'll try, anyway – I haven't been doing this for very long, so..."

"No problem," she said. "It's just that little bit more professional, you see. Anyway, you're on shortly. Good luck!"

"Thanks, Linda," I said, and took a few deep breaths.

"Ten seconds," Linda called out, and cued me in for my standard introduction.

Learn to Program with Visual Basic Examples

"Welcome to Professor Smiley's Visual Basic Programming Workshop," I began. Each week at this time, for the next nine weeks, I'll be answering your Visual Basic questions. Of course, I'll need your help, since without your calls, there will be no show! Please write down the toll-free number that's flashing across your television screen right now, and use it to call in with questions about beginning to intermediate Visual Basic issues. And if you have some code that you would like me to examine, you can send that to me here in the studio by e-mailing me at `johnsmiley@johnsmiley.com`. I'd like to thank those of you who tuned in last week. I've received some great e-mail about the show, and I appreciate your comments. Special thanks go to those of you who called in last week with questions."

Linda signaled to me that we were ready for our first caller.

"Before we take our first call," I said, "I want to address an email that I received during the week from a viewer who has obviously taken to heart the advice I gave in my book about using Hungarian notation in Visual Basic when naming controls and variables. Let me read his email...."

Professor Smiley,

I'd like to tell you how much I enjoyed your television show last week, and I hope you continue with this endeavor for a long time.

I would like to express my concern, however, that in the code examples you used last week, you weren't always using Hungarian notation. For example, you left command buttons with their default names, like Command1, and I know you went to great extremes in your book to point out that you shouldn't name controls like this.

Sincerely

Bob Lautenbach

"I want to thank Bob for raising this issue," I said, "and I must confess, I'm guilty. Naming a command button `Command1` is a cardinal offense – but I do have a good reason. With only ninety minutes to cover as many questions as possible, it's a lot quicker for me to leave the controls with their default names – that's the *only* reason I did it. If I named every control in my coding examples according to Hungarian notation, our show would probably run over two hours instead of its scheduled ninety minutes. I must confess, you'll probably see the same thing today, and in the coming weeks. So please forgive me for it – I have a good reason – but please don't do it yourself. Remember, always name your own controls and variables meaningfully, and according to Hungarian notation."

"And now, we're ready for our first call of the day," I said.

Question 11: How can I pre-select an item in a list box?

(see also questions 12,13,16 & 26)

"Hi, my name is Gil from Bridesburg," the voice on the other end of the line began. "I'm working with a `ListBox` control, and after I add items to the list box, I'm wondering how I can 'pre-select' a particular item."

"Thanks for calling, Gil," I said. "Your name and voice sound very familiar – have you been in one of my classes?"

"Yes – I took your *Introduction to Programming* online class last year, and I called you afterwards to say how much I enjoyed it."

"I remember. I'd love to talk more, but we're on air...you say you want to pre-select an item in the list box?" I said. "May I ask why?"

"I want to establish one of the items in the list box as a default," he replied. "For instance, if I load all fifty of the United States into a list box, I'd like to pre-select and highlight Pennsylvania as the default item in the list box, since most of my users are from Pennsylvania."

"I understand," I said. " We can do that. Let me show you how."

I started a new Visual Basic project, placing a list box control and a single command button on the form.

"There are actually several ways of doing this, Gil," I said. "Let's start with what I consider the most straightforward approach. First, I'm going to put some code in the `Click` event procedure of the command button to load some items into the list box – in this case the first ten letters of the alphabet – it's faster than loading up the fifty United States! We'll use the `AddItem` method of the list box control to do this. Then, with a single line of code, we'll pre-select the letter 'E' in the list box, just by setting the `Text` property of the list box control to the value we want to have selected in the list box."

I then displayed this code to Gil, and to the rest of the television audience:

```
Private Sub Command1_Click()

List1.AddItem "A"
List1.AddItem "B"
List1.AddItem "C"
List1.AddItem "D"
List1.AddItem "E"
List1.AddItem "F"
List1.AddItem "G"
List1.AddItem "H"
```

```
List1.AddItem "I"
List1.AddItem "J"

List1.Text = "E"

End Sub
```

Then I ran the program and clicked on the command button:

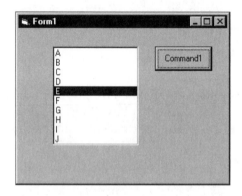

"Ah," I heard him say on the other end of the phone, "*that's* the trick. Set the **Text** value of the list box to the name of the item that you want selected. I hadn't thought of that. I didn't even know there *was* a **Text** property of the list box."

"The **Text** property," I said, "contains the name of the item that the user selects in the list box. Ordinarily, it's the action of the user selecting an item in the list box that sets this value – but as you can see, the programmer can also achieve the same thing by using code at run time. That first method will serve you just fine. As I mentioned though, there are several approaches to accomplishing this. They're a little more obscure, though, so I'll only give you an overview of them. The first of these alternatives is to set the **ListIndex** property of the list box."

```
List1.ListIndex = 4
```

"**ListIndex** property of the list box," Gil said, puzzled. "I'm afraid that's a new one on me."

"The list box control," I said, "is actually a 'behind the scenes' array, and each item added to the list box, becomes a member (or **element**) of this 'behind the scenes' array. The first item added to the list box is, by default, added as element number 0, the second item added to the list box is element number 1, and so forth."

"So the fifth item," Gil interjected, "in this case the letter 'E', is actually element number 4?"

"You've got the idea, Gil," I said.

"So where does the `ListIndex` come into play?" Gil asked.

"The `ListIndex` property of the list box control," I said, "indicates the element number of the item that's selected in the list box. Ordinarily, this is set when the user clicks on an item in the list box – but the programmer can set it in code the way we did here and select an item in the list box at run time."

"I think I see what's happening here," Gil said.

"Good. I think you'd agree, Gil," I said, "that the first approach is by far the most straightforward. This example with ten letters of the alphabet is pretty vanilla, because we know that the letter 'E' is the fifth letter of the alphabet. But for the example you cited earlier, where you wanted to pre-select the State of Pennsylvania in a list box, the first approach is easiest: you would just set the `Text` property of the list box control to 'Pennsylvania'. Using the second approach – where you set the `ListIndex` property to the number of the item within the 'behind the scenes array – is more difficult; you would need to know where Pennsylvania ranked alphabetically within the 50 United States, and then subtract 1. That's too much trouble for my liking."

"Did you imply that there was a third method?" Gil said.

"Yes, I did," I said, "and this method is perhaps just as obtuse as the second one. Take a look at this line of code:"

```
List1.Selected(4) = True
```

"I see what you mean," he said. "That's not very transparent, is it? How does this line work compared to the other methods?"

"The number '4' within the parentheses is referring to element number 4 in the array we discussed – which in this case represents the fifth item added to the list box, the letter 'E'."

There was a moment of dead air.

"I just took a look at the Properties window for a list box control," Gil said, "and I don't see a `Selected` property. In fact, I don't see the `ListIndex` or `Text` properties either."

"That's because those properties are **run time-only** properties of the list box control," I said. "They don't appear in the properties window at *design* time. The `Selected` property is a `Boolean` – `True` or `False` – property. `False` means that the item is not selected in the list box; `True` means that the item *is* selected. Therefore, one way to pre-select the letter 'E' in the list box control is to set its `Selected` property to `True` – but, as you can see, we also need to refer to its element number when we do so."

"Do I have time to ask another question related to this?" Gil asked.

"Sure thing," I said. "Take your time."

"There's a property of the list box control that I use all the time and which I find invaluable, and that's the **Sorted** property," he said. "But how does setting the **Sorted** property of the list box affect what you've just shown us? I presume it has no effect on the first approach you showed me – using the **Text** property of the list box control to pre-select an item. But what about the other two methods? In other words, if we loaded the items into a list box in no particular sequence, and set the **Sorted** property of the list box control to **True**, how should we refer to the letter 'E' in the 'behind the scenes' array – by its original, unsorted position, or by its sorted position?"

"That certainly is a great question, Gil," I said. "Before we examine that, let me make sure that people in our audience who are unfamiliar with the **Sorted** property understand what you're getting at. Setting the **Sorted** property of a list box control to **True** automatically sorts the items in a list box alphabetically. For instance, if we change the code behind the command button to read like this..."

```
Private Sub Command1_Click()

List1.AddItem "B"
List1.AddItem "J"
List1.AddItem "D"
List1.AddItem "E"
List1.AddItem "A"
List1.AddItem "C"
List1.AddItem "I"
List1.AddItem "G"
List1.AddItem "H"
List1.AddItem "F"

End Sub
```

"...our list box will look like this when we run the program and click on the command button:"

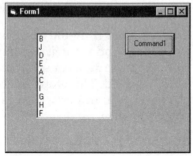

"However," I continued, "if we set the `Sorted` property of the list box control to `True`..."

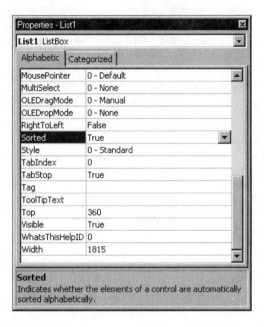

"...then once again the contents of the list box control are sorted alphabetically:"

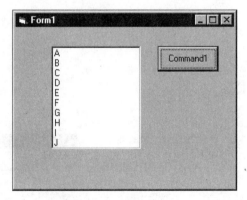

"We're now presented with another question," I continued. "With the `Sorted` property of the list box set to `True`, is the letter 'E' array element number 3 in the list box, or is it element number 4?"

"Uh...I don't know," Gil said.

"Well," I explained, "when we originally loaded the unsorted items in the list box, the letter 'E' was the fourth item in the list box - i.e. what *should* be array element number 3. However, in the sorted version of the list box, the letter 'E' appears as the fifth item, which would be array element number 4. So, is the letter 'E' array element number 3, or array element number 4?" I asked rhetorically.

"I'm betting it's array element number 4," said Gil.

"Seeing is believing," I said. "Let's see – we've modified the code in the command button to add the items in no particular order to the list box – and we've set the **Sorted** property of the list box to **True**. Now, let's change the code in the **Click** event procedure of the command button to set the **Selected** property of element number 4 to **True** – will it be the letter 'E', or the letter 'A' that is selected?"

I modified the code in the command button's **Click** event procedure to look like this:

```
Private Sub Command1_Click()

List1.AddItem "B"
List1.AddItem "J"
List1.AddItem "D"
List1.AddItem "E"
List1.AddItem "A"
List1.AddItem "C"
List1.AddItem "I"
List1.AddItem "G"
List1.AddItem "H"
List1.AddItem "F"

List1.Selected(4) = True

End Sub
```

When I ran the program and clicked on the command button, the letter 'E' was selected, as before:

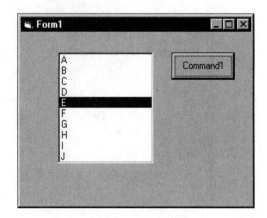

"So," Gil observed, "we *do* need to reference the element number of the *sorted* list box items, not the unsorted ones. Wow, is *that* confusing. All the more reason to use the first, straightforward method."

"All the more reason indeed," I agreed. "Let's move on to our second call."

Question 12: Is it possible to select more than one item in a list box?

(see also questions 11, 13,16 & 26)

"Hi, this is Bernice from Andalusia," she said. "This must be a day for questions about the list box control. I was wondering if it's possible for the user to select more than one item in a list box control, and if so, what code I need to write to deal with the user's multiple selections."

"That's a good question," I replied, "and the answer is yes – the user can make multiple selections in a ListBox control, provided that you set the `MultiSelect` property of the list box to something other than its default value of '`None`'. Now that's the easy part. Once the user has made their multiple selections, you need to write some code to detect which items in that 'behind the scenes' array have been selected."

This was going to be complicated. I thought for a moment about the best way to approach this and continued.

"I have an example that I sometimes use in my university classes," I said, "which illustrates how to work with multiple selections in a list box. Follow along with me."

I created a new project, and placed two list boxes and three command buttons on the form, placing the list boxes side by side on the form, with the three command buttons arranged vertically between them:

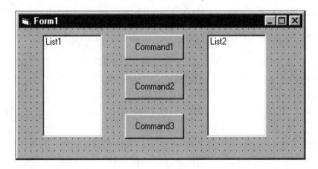

I then changed the captions of all three command buttons, changed the **Sorted** property of both list boxes to **True**, and finally changed the **MultiSelect** property of both list boxes to 'Extended':

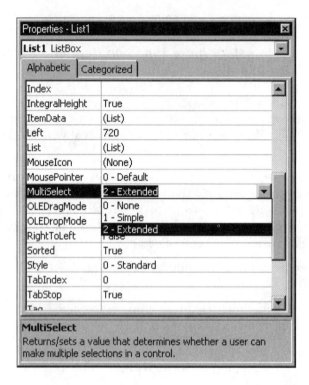

"Changing the **MultiSelect** property to **Extended**," I said, "allows the user to select more than one item from the list box."

"What's the difference between **Simple** and **Extended**?" Bernice asked.

"**Extended** provides more of a true Windows feel," I said. "With **Extended**, if the user selects an item in the list box, presses and holds the *Shift* key, and then selects another item, everything in between is selected as well. On the other hand, if the user selects an item, presses and holds the *Control* key, and then selects another item, only those two items are selected, and the user can continue to select discrete items like this by holding the *Control* key down. With the **Simple** setting, a mouse click or press on the *Spacebar* selects or deselects an item in the list. As I said, the **Extended** setting provides a more typical Windows feel. Why not try both methods out, so you can see the difference?"

In no time at all, I had created and displayed the screenshot below:

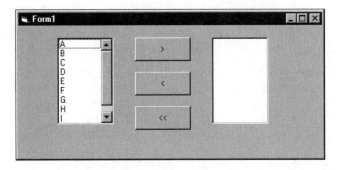

I explained to Bernice that I had placed code in the form's **Load** event to add the letters A through J to the list box on the left, much as we had done for our last caller, Gil.

"What about those buttons in the middle of the form?" Bernice asked. "What do they represent?"

"The top button," I explained, "will be used to move all items selected in the left list box to the list box on the right. The middle button will be used to move all items selected in the right list box to the list box on the left. And the bottom button will be used to move *every* item in the right list box to the list box on the left, regardless of whether or not the user has selected individual items."

"OK," Bernice answered. "I've seen programs like this. In fact, that's why I called, really. I wanted to do something along those lines."

"I'm glad you did call, Bernice," I said, "I'm sure there are other people who were wondering how to do the same thing. Now, let's place some code in the **Click** event of that first command button so that we can move selected items in the left list box to the list box on the right."

"This is where I got lost when I was trying this on my own," Bernice interjected. "I discovered the **Text** property a while back, and I thought I could just check the **Text** property of the list box like you did with Gil earlier. But if the user makes a *multiple* selection, what's in the **Text** property?"

"If the user makes a multiple selection," I said, "the **Text** property of the list box contains the *last* item the user selects – so we can't use this property to let us know each of the items that the user has selected. To do that, we'll need to use the **Selected** property of the 'behind the scenes' list box array I spoke of in our first question today."

"I think I followed that discussion," Bernice answered, "I mean I understand that each element or item in the list box has this 'hidden' **Selected** property. But how can we check all of the items?"

"To do that," I said, "we need to perform some loop processing."

"Loops? Oh no," Bernice sighed. "I'm afraid loop processing isn't a big favorite with me."

"Not to worry," I said, "it's not that bad. Let's take a look at the code in the click event of the first command button, and I think you'll agree."

With that, I displayed this code:

```
Private Sub Command1_Click()

Dim intCounter As Integer

For intCounter = List1.ListCount - 1 To 0 Step -1
  If List1.Selected(intCounter)= True Then
   List2.AddItem List1.List(intCounter)
   List1.RemoveItem intCounter
  End If
Next intCounter

End Sub
```

I ran the program, selected the letters 'A' and 'D' in the left-hand list box, and clicked on the top command button. As if by magic, the selected items in the left-hand list box were then 'moved' to the list box on the right:

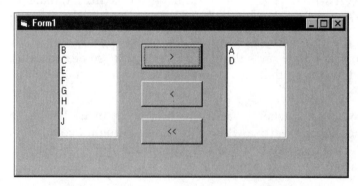

"OK," I heard Bernice say. "I can see that you're using a For...Next loop to 'move' through the elements in that 'behind the scenes' list box array. Let's see now...if the Selected property is equal to True, that means that the item is selected, so you add that item to List2 using the AddItem method. And to make it look like it's been moved, you have to remove it from List1, and you do that using the RemoveItem method."

"That's great," I said. "You should be teaching Visual Basic. And you're right – by adding the items to the list box on the right, and then removing the same items from the left list box, it appears as if the selected items are being 'moved' from one list box to the next."

"Can I ask what the reference to `ListCount` is for?" Bernice asked.

"`ListCount` is a property of the list box control," I said, "that tells us how many items are in the list box. In the case of our list box, there are ten items, so the `ListCount` property is equal to 10."

"Why is the `Start` parameter of the `For...Next` loop '`ListCount -1`' then?" Bernice asked.

"It's all to do with that 'behind the scenes' array we were looking at a moment ago. We know that the last element's index is equal to the total number of items minus one, so we start there. If we used `ListCount` instead of `ListCount - 1`, we'd be trying to reference an item that doesn't exist, and we'd run into problems there," I explained.

"Also," I added, "we mustn't forget to count down to zero instead of 1."

I waited a few seconds to ensure that Bernice and the rest of the viewing audience were getting this.

"I presume," Bernice said, "that the code for the `Click` event of that middle button is basically the same, but works in the opposite direction?"

"That's right," I said, "here we remove selected items from `List2`, and add them to `List1`:"

```
Private Sub Command2_Click()

Dim intCounter As Integer

For intCounter = List2.ListCount - 1 To 0 Step -1
  If List2.Selected(intCounter) = True Then
    List1.AddItem List2.List(intCounter)
    List2.RemoveItem intCounter
  End If
Next intCounter

End Sub
```

I did exactly that, selecting an item in the right-hand list box, and 'moving' it to the left side.

"That makes sense," she said, "no problems there...now what about that third command button?"

Before showing Bernice the code in that last command button, I added some more items to the right-hand list box, and then clicked on the bottom command button. This time, every item in the right-hand list box was 'moved' to the left-hand list box, regardless of whether the items were selected.

"This button effectively clears that right-hand list box and returns all the selections back to the left-hand one," I explained. "Let's look at that code now." I said. "Here, we use the same type of loop processing as in the `Click` event procedures of the first two command buttons, except that this time we don't bother checking the `Selected` property of the array elements, since we're going to 'move' the item regardless:"

```
Private Sub Command3_Click()

Dim intCounter As Integer

For intCounter = List2.ListCount - 1 To 0 Step -1
    List1.AddItem List2.List(intCounter)
Next intCounter

List2.Clear

End Sub
```

"I'm OK with everything I see here," Bernice said, "except for the `Clear` method. That's a new one on me."

I explained that the `Clear` method of the list box control is used to remove *every* item in a list box control in one fell swoop.

"Thanks, Professor Smiley," Bernice said. "I'm anxious to try this out now."

I thanked Bernice for calling and saw that Linda was signaling for a commercial break. Our first two callers had consumed about twenty minutes of air time.

Linda's voice came through my earpiece, saying "John, I have a caller on hold, Bill from Levittown, who's at position 5 in the call list, but his question is also related to list boxes, and I think it will be a quick one. If you don't mind, I think I'll move him up."

"That's fine," I said. "Should I let the next caller know we're coming back to them?"

"No, leave that to me," she replied. "Just make it flow together naturally. I really think you're getting the hang of this."

"You think so? I feel pretty relaxed out there, actually. How long do I have before the end of the commercial break?"

"One minute. Better get into position," said Linda, "and I'll count you in."

Question 13: How can I deselect all the items in a list box?

(see also questions 11, 12, 16 & 26))

"Welcome back. Our next question is also about list boxes, and it's Bill from Levittown, I believe. Bill?"

"Hi, Professor Smiley," came the bright voice from the other end of the phone, "this is Bill. Thanks to you and Gil, I now know how to pre-select an item in a list box, and thanks to Bernice, I know how to process multiple selected items in a list box. Now can you tell me how I can 'un-select' every item in a list box? Not clear them, like you just did, but 'un-select' each one? Based on what you just showed Bernice, I suppose I could use loop processing to make my way through each item in the list box, and set the `Selected` property to `False`. But is there a quicker way?"

"That's an interesting question, Bill," I replied, "and there are two answers, depending on whether you permit the user to select more than one item in the list box - which I think is what you're asking. Let's begin with the simple scenario where you are permitting the user to select only a single item in the list box – you can then use this single line of code to 'un-select' the selected item:

```
List1.ListIndex = -1
```

"I think I mentioned earlier today," I said, "that the `ListIndex` property refers to the element number of the 'behind the scenes' array that has been selected by the user. Setting this property to minus 1 un-selects that item. If you wanted, you could also use *this* code:"

```
List1.Text = ""
```

I waited to see if Bill had any problem with this.

"If you permit the user to make multiple selections in a list box," I continued, "the process becomes more complex, as you might imagine. In a multi-selection list box, the `ListIndex` property is set to the element number of the last item in the list box that the user selects, so that isn't going to do us much good. For a multiselect list box, about all you can do is use the type of loop processing we saw earlier in today's show, and set the `Selected` property of each item in the list box to `False` – as you suspected. It's not complicated, though – the code would look something like this:"

```
Dim intCounter As Integer

For intCounter = List1.ListCount - 1 To 0 Step -1
  If List1.Selected(intCounter) = True Then
   List1.Selected(intCounter) = False
  End If
Next intCounter
```

"So I was on the right track," Bill said. "I was certain there must be a faster, more efficient way of doing this."

I cautioned Bill and the rest of the viewing audience not to be overly concerned with the notion of efficiency.

"I've seen so many beginners toss and turn over the efficiency of their code," I said. "But a 300 megaHertz PC is processing somewhere in the neighborhood of several million instructions per second. It doesn't make much of a difference to that PC if the program uses a loop with a dozen or so instructions to set the `Selected` property of each element in the list box to `False`, or if somehow there's a magical way to set a single property value. In the end, both scenarios are executed in a millionth of a second anyway."

Bill thanked me for the answer to his question and told us that he was anxious to get back to his programming.

"What, you're not going to watch the rest of the show?" I joked.

"Oh, I'm taping it. I know I'll learn a lot, but right now I really want to make progress with my program."

"I understand you, Bill. I still feel that way when I have a program to write. Good luck. Now, who's next?"

Question 14: Is there a way to 'clear' option buttons so that none of them are selected?

"Hi, this is Joe from Frankford," said the next caller. "I don't have a question about list boxes – is that OK? It seems like the theme of today's show is list boxes."

"That's OK, Joe," I said, "*any* question on Visual Basic is fine."

"In that case," he continued, "here's my question. I have a form that I've put three option buttons on. When I run my program, and after the user has made a selection of one of the three option buttons, I'd like to be able to 'reset' them for the next user, so that none of them are selected. I haven't been able to figure out how to do that."

"That's not a problem," I said. "Let me give you a little demonstration."

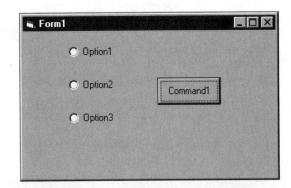

I quickly placed three option buttons on a form in a new project, along with a single command button. When I ran the program, the following screen shot was displayed:

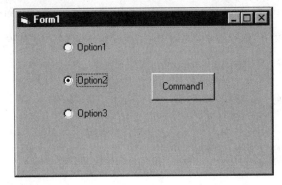

"As you can see, Joe," I said, "when the program is first run, none of the option buttons are selected. Now let's select the second option button – Option2." I clicked on the second option button:

"Now Option2 is selected," I said. "The question is, how can we un-select it? Nothing the user can do at this point will un-select all three."

"That's right," he said in frustration. "I've tried using the SetFocus method of each one of the option buttons in code, but that didn't work. One of the programmers I work with suggested that I create an 'invisible' option button, and set its Value property to True in code."

"Moving focus to the other controls in code using the SetFocus method definitely won't work," I said. "That's like playing the old shell game. Now, as for creating an invisible option button, and setting its Value property to True – in effect selecting it, so that the others in the option button group are therefore un-selected – that *will* work. In fact, I seem to recall doing that way back in Visual Basic 1. But it's not really necessary. All you need to do is set the Value property of each of the option buttons to False. That will 'un-select' all of them. Here's the code to do this:"

```
Private Sub Command1_Click()

Option1.Value = False
Option2.Value = False
Option3.Value = False

End Sub
```

Placing this code in the command button's **Click** event procedure, I ran the program, selected one of the option buttons, and then clicked on the command button. As I promised Joe, all of the option buttons were then 'un-selected'.

"Somehow," Joe said, "I thought that it would be harder than that. Thanks a lot!"

"Glad I could help," I said. "I think we can fit one more question in before our next break."

Linda confirmed that we could, and put the next caller through.

Question 15: How can I change my form icon?

"My question's probably got a really simple answer," the voice on the other end of the phone said, "but it's been bothering the heck out of me. Oh, my name's Rita, from Frankford."

"Do you happen to know Joe, who just called?" I asked her.

"Why, yes I do," she replied. "He works just down the hall from me. What a small world. Anyway, my question's kind of a silly one, but..."

"Rita," I interrupted, "you know the teacher in me can't resist saying this – remember, there is no such thing as a silly question. You never know, I might put your question in a book some day. Go ahead."

"Well," she continued, "you know the icon on the title bar of the form? I've noticed that same icon appears on the Windows Taskbar when you minimize the form. It also appears if you generate an executable version of your program, and then create a Windows desktop shortcut for the executable – that same icon appears on the desktop. My question is this: Is there a way to change the icon? I'm sure there must be a way to change it, but I haven't found it yet."

"You're right, Rita," I said, "there is a way to change that icon, but there are two pieces to the puzzle we have to work with. First, you're really talking about two separate icons here. The icon you mentioned that appears when you create a Windows desktop shortcut for your executable program is actually the *application's* or *project's* icon."

"Where is that specified?" Rita asked.

"Nice question," I said. "You don't actually specify an application icon; what you do instead is designate the form in your project whose icon will be the application's icon. It's kind of a round-about way of doing it. Here, take a look at this."

I created a new Visual Basic project and selected Project | Project1 from the Visual Basic menu. This brought the Properties window for the project into view, and I selected the Make tab:

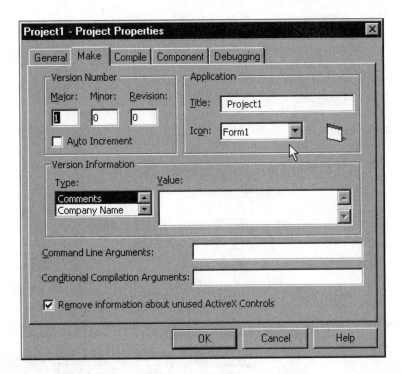

"Do you see the Icon property of the application in the top-right pane?" I asked. "The icon displayed there is the icon specified in Form1's Icon property."

"Does that mean," Rita asked, "that if we have multiple forms in our Visual Basic project, we can specify any of their icons to act as the application's icon, just by selecting the form?"

"Excellent," I said, "that's exactly what I mean."

Rita seemed to be thinking for a moment.

"Does this mean," she said, "that this is the icon I see when I create a Windows Desktop shortcut to the executable?"

"That's right," I said, "the application's icon is the one that appears as a Desktop shortcut."

"And you mentioned, I believe," Rita continued, "that the icon that appears in the title bar of the form, and on the Windows Taskbar when the form is minimized, is specified elsewhere. In the `Icon` property of the form?"

"That's right," I said. "The icon that appears in the title bar for the form is specified via the `Icon` property for the form – and you can easily change it in the Properties window. In fact, let's do that in a moment so I can show you how easy it is to do. But before we do that, let's add another form to this project."

I added a second form to the project by selecting Project I Add Form from the Visual Basic main menu. After doing that, I selected `Form1` in the Project Explorer window and brought up its Properties window:

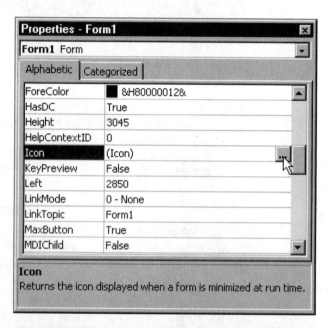

"Each form has a default icon," I continued, "and changing the form's icon is just a matter of selecting the `Icon` property in the Properties window, and finding an appropriate icon file to use. Let's select 'Ctrusa.ico':"

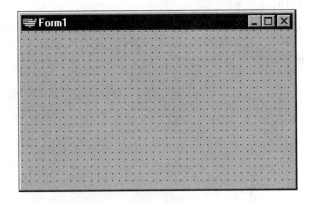

I selected the `Ctrusa.ico` file for the icon property of the form. Immediately, the default icon on the title bar of the form changed:

"You made that look so easy," Rita said. "Are only files ending in `.ico` valid for the icon property?"

"Yep. You can usually find a selection in an icons subdirectory somewhere within the Visual Basic directory."

I then minimized the form, and the form's new icon appeared on the desktop.

"So far so good," I heard Rita say. "Now we've changed the form's icon - what about the application's icon?"

"OK," I continued, "let's see what impact changing the form's icon has on our choices for the application's icon."

I brought up the Make tab on the project's Properties window again.

"Notice," I said, "that the application's icon still reads 'Form1', but now the icon's graphic has changed – reflecting the fact that the icon for `Form1` has changed:"

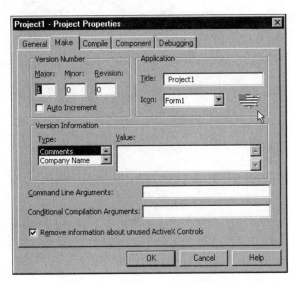

"Why did you add a second form to the project?" Rita asked.

I explained that I wanted to show that Visual Basic gives us the flexibility of choosing another form's icon to act as the application's icon. I selected Form2 in the Icon's drop-down list box:

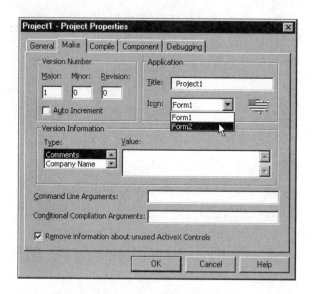

"If I select Form2 in the drop-down list box," I said, "I tell Visual Basic to use Form2's icon as the application's icon:"

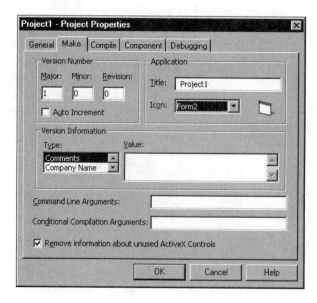

"Back to that ugly default icon," Rita said. "I see now. Thanks for the illustration. Bye!"

During the break Linda told me that once again, our phone line had been really busy. Not only that, but she had been monitoring our e-mail traffic, and we had over 100 e-mails from viewers writing in with questions and comments.

After our commercial break, we started in with another question about list boxes.

Question 16: I'm entering items in the List property of a list box in the Properties window. When I hit the ENTER key, the Properties window closes. What am I doing wrong?

"Hi," the voice said, "this is Dottie from Holmesburg. I have another question about list boxes."

"Seems like this is national list box day," I said jokingly. "Go ahead."

"I already know," she said, "that one way to add items to a list box control is to use the `AddItem` method of the list box. But I'm more comfortable adding these items at design time through the `Item` property in the Properties window. There's nothing wrong with that, is there, provided you know ahead of time what the list box will hold?"

"No, Dottie," I said, "there's nothing wrong with that. My personal preference is to use the `AddItem` method at run time, but adding the items to the `Item` property of the list box control is perfectly fine. Now, what's the problem?"

"The problem," she said, "is that when I bring up the `List` property of the list box control in the Properties window and start entering the items that I want to appear in the list box, as soon as I hit the *Enter* key, the `List` property 'window' closes. If I want to add another item to the list, I then need to re-select the `List` property, then add the second item. Once again, as soon as I hit the *Enter* key, the 'window' closes and I have to repeat this process all over again until I have added all the items for my list box. It's getting on my nerves, frankly. I must be doing something wrong – but I don't know what it is."

"I know what the problem is," I said, "but before I show you the correct technique for adding items to the list box through the Properties window, let me show the viewers at home exactly what is happening."

I created a new project containing a single list box control, and then brought up the Properties window for the list box control:

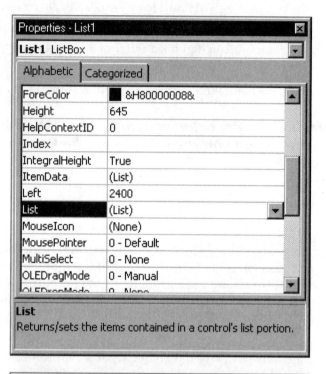

"Clicking on the List property," I said, "opens up the List Window. We should then be able to type in the Items for our list box."

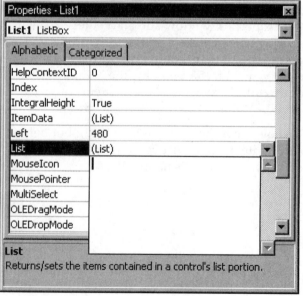

"Now the problem," I said, "is that if we type 'Tom' into the **List** window, as soon as we hit the *Enter* key, the **List** window closes."

I did just that, and sure enough, the **List** property window closed.

"That's right," Dottie said. I could hear the frustration in her voice as she continued. "That's exactly what happens to me. I've tried everything – using the *Enter* key, the *Tab* key…"

"I bet you didn't try *Ctrl+Enter*," I said.

"No, I don't think I did," she answered. "I never would have thought to do that. Will that help?"

"Let's see," I said.

I then re-selected the **List** property in the Properties window, and brought up the List Window. 'Tom' was already in there. I typed 'Kevin' into the **List** Window, after 'Tom'. This time, instead of pressing the *Enter* key, instead I pressed the *Ctrl+Enter* combination. Sure enough, the **List** window stayed open, and I was able to type in another name – in this case, 'Melissa' for good measure.

"So that's the trick," Dottie said, with obvious relief. "I never would have figured that out on my own."

"Don't feel bad about this one, Dottie," I said. "it's certainly not an intuitive key combination. For the life of me, I know this is documented somewhere – but I really couldn't tell you where."

"Thanks again, John," Dottie said, and then she was gone.

Question 17: I want to start the Microsoft Calculator in my program, but don't know how

(see also question 74)

"OK, who's next?" I wondered aloud.

"Hi, I'm Marion from Lansdale," the caller introduced herself, "and I'd like to be able to display the Windows Calculator from within my Visual Basic program. Can that be done?"

"That's not a problem," I said, "I just need to introduce you to the Visual Basic **Shell** function."

"The **Shell** function?" echoed Marion.

"That's right. The **Shell** function is used to run an executable program from within Visual Basic. For instance, if I place the following code in the **Click** event procedure of a command button, I can fire up the Windows Calculator from within my Visual Basic program."

Learn to Program with Visual Basic Examples

I created a Visual Basic project with a single command button on its form, and placed the code below in the **Click** event procedure:

```
Private Sub Command1_Click()

Shell "calc.exe"

End Sub
```

I then ran the program.

"Hold on," Marion interrupted, "I don't see the Calculator anywhere."

"Good point," I agreed. "The Windows Calculator is running, but the default mode of the **Shell** function is to run the program, and minimize it to an icon on the Windows Taskbar. If you take a look at the Taskbar, you'll see an icon for the Calculator there."

I directed Marion's attention to the Windows Taskbar, where the Calculator's icon could be seen.

"Can you explain the format of the **Shell** function?" Marion asked.

"The **Shell** functionhas two parameters or arguments," I said. " The first, and most important, is the name of the program that you want to run. The second parameter is optional, and it's called the **WindowStyle**. It's this parameter that specifies how the program you start will appear. As I mentioned, by default the program is minimized on the Taskbar. Here are the possible values for the **WindowValue** parameter:"

I displayed this list from the Visual Basic Help files:

Constant	Value	Meaning
vbHide	0	Window is hidden and focus is passed to the hidden window.
vbNormalFocus	1	Window has focus and is restored to its original size and position.
vbMinimizedFocus	2	Window is displayed as an icon with focus.
vbMaximizedFocus	3	Window is maximized with focus.
vbNormalNoFocus	4	Window is restored to its most recent size and position. The currently active window remains active.
vbMinimizedNoFocus	6	Window is displayed as an icon. The currently active window remains active.

"There is no argument with the value 5, by the way. That's not a mistake," I assured everyone.

"If we change the WindowStyle parameter to 1," I continued, "we can start up the Calculator right in the middle of our Visual Basic desktop."

I changed the code in the Click event procedure of the command button to look like this:

```
Private Sub Command1_Click()

Shell "calc.exe," vbNormalFocus

End Sub
```

I then ran the program – and up popped the Windows calculator, right in the middle of the desktop.

"I notice," Marion commented, "that we seem to have two copies of the Calculator running – one is on the desktop, and the other is minimized on the taskbar. Is that possible?"

"Indeed it is," I replied. "When we clicked on the command button earlier, we started one copy (sometimes called an **instance**) of the Calculator program. When we clicked on the command button a second time, we started up a second instance of the Calculator."

"Windows allows that?" Marion asked.

"It's up to the *program* to allow or disallow a second instance of itself from running," I answered. "In the case of the Calculator, you can have as many instances of it running as you have available memory on your PC. This isn't the case with *all* Windows programs, but it is with the Calculator."

There was silence for a moment or two. I was just about to ask if there was anything else I could do for Marion when she asked:

"You said that Shell is a function, does that mean that it returns a value?"

"An interesting question," I said, "Shell is a function, and in Visual Basic, a function will return a value to the calling procedure. In this case, the return value is equal to the Task ID of the running program."

"What's a Task ID?" Marion asked, "and is that useful in any way?"

"Each program that runs in Windows is assigned a unique Task ID," I said. "This value is not very useful for a beginner programmer. More advanced programmers might find the Task ID useful for something called Windows API programming, but that isn't something I would recommend to the newcomer to Visual Basic."

Again there was a moment of silence. I could tell that Marion was thinking about something.

"How come we don't need to specify a full path name for the Calculator program?" Marion asked. "Aren't we required to do that?"

"Well," I said, "that depends on whether Windows knows the location of the program you wish to execute. If it does – and that means that the location of the program can be found in one of the directories included in your PC's path property – then you only need to specify the name of the executable as the argument to the **Shell** function. If, however, Windows *can't* find the program in any of the directories included in the PC's path, then you need to specify the full path of the program for Windows to be able to find it. Since the Windows Calculator is a program supplied with the operating system, Windows has no trouble finding it, and that's why I only referenced its name as the argument to the **Shell** function."

"One more question if I may," Marion said. "Suppose I start a long running program using the **Shell** function – will my Visual Basic program wait until the program finishes?"

"No, it won't," I said, "the **Shell** function runs a program **asynchronously** – that means that the 'other' program is running independently of your Visual Basic program. Your Visual Basic program continues executing with the line of code immediately after the line containing the **Shell** function."

"Thanks, Professor Smiley," she said, "I can't wait to try this out."

"Thanks for calling, Marion," I said. "Now, let's take a commercial break."

During the break, Linda told me that our next caller wanted to ask a question that she thought would be a perfect follow-up to this one.

Question 18: How can I prevent more than one 'instance' of my program from running at once?

The next caller introduced himself; "Hi, this is Frank from Lawndale," he said, "thanks very much for taking my call. My question is somewhat related to the previous questions. I've written a Visual Basic program, and I've given a copy to some of my friends and members of my family, as an executable. My program does some disk file manipulation, so I only ever want one instance of my program to run at one time – but I haven't been able to figure out how to do this in Visual Basic. I gather from your discussion with Marion, where you said that certain Windows programs can prevent a second instance from running, that there might be a way to do it?"

"That's right, Frank," I said, "there is. Let me elaborate on this just a bit for the rest of the viewing audience. There are valid reasons to prevent the user of your program from being able to run more than one instance of it at a time. For instance, if your program is reading a database table or records in a disk file, you probably won't want to have multiple instances of it running at the same time. Also, there are times when it just doesn't make sense to have more than one copy of your program running at once – it might simply confuse the user. On the other hand, there are some Windows programs that permit it – the Calculator and even Visual Basic, for instance – and you could probably think of other examples as well. At any rate, Frank, let me show you how you can stop a second instance of your program from running."

I created a new Visual Basic program with my now familiar single command button, and placed the following code in the form's Load event procedure:

```
Private Sub Form_Load()

If App.PrevInstance = True Then
  MsgBox "Only one instance of this program may run at one time"
  End
End If

End Sub
```

I explained to Frank, and to the viewers, that the programs we write in Visual Basic have a 'built in' System object called the Application object. Like any object in Visual Basic, the Application object has properties, and one of the properties is called the PrevInstance property.

"The PrevInstance property," I said, "is a Boolean (True/False) property that lets us know if another instance of our program is currently running. By checking to see if the PrevInstance property of the Application object is True, we can display an appropriate message to the user, and then unload our form."

"I assume the End statement just ends the program, is that right?" Frank asked.

"That's right," I said. As a demonstration, I ran the program. Since at the time there was only one instance of the program running, the program fired up as normal, displaying the one and only form in the middle of the desktop.

"How can we test our code's reaction to a second instance of the program?" Frank asked. "Do we need to generate an executable file?"

"Well, it's either that or start up another instance of Visual Basic," I said. "Since the user of your program will be running your program as an executable anyway, let's generate an executable to test the program. There may be some viewers at home who are unfamiliar with generating one who will find the process educational. Once we have the executable, we'll be able to launch two instances of it using Windows Explorer. Let's generate that executable now."

I selected File I Make from the Visual Basic main menu, and saved the executable as `frank.exe` in a directory I had created earlier called `\Practice`. Using Windows Explorer, I then located the executable and double clicked on it. As was the case when we ran the program from within Visual Basic, the program started right up, and the one and only form displayed, right in the middle of our desktop.

"Now," I said, "that's the first instance of our program running. Let's try to fire up a second instance of the program, once again using the Windows Explorer, and see what happens."

Once again, I located the executable on the PC's hard drive, and double clicked on it. This time the results were different – as this screen shot shows:

"That's beautiful," Frank said, "that's exactly what I want to happen. Thanks, Professor Smiley."

"My pleasure, Frank," I said. "Now on to our next caller."

Question 19: I gave a program I wrote to my brother-in-law to run. The program loads a graphics file into my form at run time. When he ran the program, a 'File Not Found' error was generated. What happened?

(see also question 69)

"Hi, I'm Donna from Clementon," the voice on the other end of the line said. "Recently I wrote a Visual Basic program, and I was so proud of it that I gave it to my brother-in-law to run on his computer at home. Someone at work told me that I couldn't just give him an executable – that I needed to provide him with a setup program to install my executable and the Visual Basic run time DLLs on his PC. I did that, and he installed the program successfully, but the program won't run properly. Here's what I think might have happened; I got fancy, and when the program starts up, it loads a graphics file that I custom designed in PhotoShop as the background for my start up form. At least it tries to, I should say. The program runs fine on my PC, but when my brother-in-law runs it, a 'File Not Found' error is displayed. I don't understand this, because as I said, I did run the Setup/Distribution Wizard in Visual Basic to produce a setup program. Can you tell me what I'm doing wrong?"

"I think I know what the problem is, Donna," I said. "And thanks for telling our audience about the Setup/Distribution Wizard. To emphasize, you can't merely provide a user with an executable file you generate out of Visual Basic, and expect it to run on their PC. Your executable requires some support programs to run on a PC that does not have Visual Basic installed – and those are the run time DLLs that Donna is talking about here. Using the Setup/Distribution Wizard in Visual Basic 4 and 5, or the Package/Deployment Wizard in Visual Basic 6, will generate a set of diskettes that contain all of the files your end-user will require to run your program."

"So what did I do wrong?" Donna asked.

"How are you loading the graphics file into the form?" I asked. "Did you specify a graphics file in the form's `Picture` property?"

"No," she said, "I used the `LoadPicture` function – someone at work told me that was more efficient than specifying the graphics file in the Properties window– and specified the full path and name of the graphics file to be loaded. I don't understand – it works fine on my PC at home. Was I wrong to use the `LoadPicture` function?"

"Using the `LoadPicture` function is fine," I said, "and can provide you with a great deal of flexibility in terms of loading graphics files at run time. For instance, by using the `LoadPicture` function, you can load different graphics files at different times in the program. Unfortunately, with this flexibility, there comes a slight drawback, and that drawback is the danger that the graphics files won't load at run time."

"What can make that happen?" Donna asked.

"Usually," I replied, "exactly what you're seeing here. The program doesn't find the files where it's expecting them. Are you sure the graphics file is on your brother-in-law's PC?"

"Yes," she answered, "he double checked that the file is there."

"Then there's one more possibility," I said. "Is there any chance that perhaps he didn't install your program in the same directory that you had the program running in on your PC?"

"I hadn't thought of that," Donna said. "But how could that happen? I thought if I used the Setup/Distribution Wizard, and specified a location for both my executable program and any graphics files, that the Setup program would install the files exactly where I specified."

"Not quite, Donna," I said. "Unfortunately, the Setup program gives the user the option of changing the directory into which the program and other files will be stored. This isn't at all unusual for Setup programs – you have probably done the same thing yourself when installing software. For instance, you may have two or more hard drives. The Setup program might suggest installing the software on Drive 'C', but you decide Drive 'D' is a better choice because it has more space available."

"Come to think of it," Donna said, "my brother-in-law does have two hard drives – and he told me last week that he was short of space on Drive 'C'. I wonder if he did change the location for the program? And if he did that, that would explain why the program is bombing – since the `LoadPicture` function is looking for the graphic file in one location, and it's actually stored in another. I would think this would be a problem in almost every program I write."

"I think you're right," I said, "that's probably why your program is bombing. But don't worry, it doesn't have to be a problem. I can show you a technique that will basically eliminate the potential for trouble in every program you write in the future. And it doesn't involve the obvious fix of having your brother-in-law move the executable and graphic files to where your program is expecting them. After all, the programs we write should be more flexible than that."

"How do I fix the program then?" she asked.

"I don't know if you were listening to the previous caller's question while you were on hold," I said, "but we were talking about a Visual Basic System Object called the `App` object."

"Yes," Donna answered, "I caught that conversation."

"As it turns out," I continued, "there's another property of the `App` object which can come in very handy – and that's the `Path` property. The `Path` property tells us the drive letter and directory from which our program is being run."

"I bet I know what that means," Donna said excitedly. "If we know the drive and directory from which the program is running, that's most likely where any graphics files are also located. We can then specify the drive and directory, along with the file name in the **LoadPicture** function. Can you show me how to do that?"

"I'd be glad to," I said, as I created a new Visual Basic program containing a single command button. I hunted for a graphics file on my studio PC to use in my demonstration, and finally settled on a file called '**Bubbles.bmp**' which I found in my Windows directory. To aid in my demonstration, I copied it into the 'Practice' directory on my hard drive that I had created earlier.

"I'm going to code a very simple **LoadPicture** function here, and place it in the command button's click event procedure," I said, and displayed this code for the viewing audience:

```
Private Sub Command1_Click()

Form1.Picture = LoadPicture("c:\Practice\bubbles.bmp")

End Sub
```

Next, I ran the program and clicked on the command button. When I did this, the graphics file '**Bubbles.bmp**' was loaded into the **Picture** property of my form, and the following screen shot was displayed:

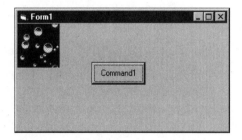

"This," I said, "is exactly what we want to happen. That is, the **LoadPicture** function finds the graphics file where we have specified, loads it into the **Picture** property of the form, and the background changes. But let me show you what happens if the program doesn't find the file where it's looking for it – perhaps because the user doesn't install the program and its associated graphics files into the directory our program is expecting. Suppose, for instance, the user installs it into a directory called 'Bob' instead."

Learn to Program with Visual Basic Examples

Using Windows Explorer, I renamed my 'Practice' directory to 'Bob'. I ran the program again, and the following error was displayed:

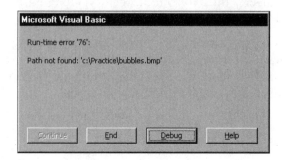

"That's the error my brother-in-law is getting," Donna called out. "Since the Practice directory doesn't exist anymore, the graphics file couldn't be found, and an error is generated."

"Right," I said. "Now let me show you how we can anticipate this kind of problem and react to it, with just a couple of lines of code. Before we do that, let's first save both our project and form in the Bob directory. Doing that will give the App object a chance to get an accurate reading on its Path property."

I saved the project and form in the 'Bob' directory, ran the program again, and immediately paused it.

"What are you doing?" Donna asked.

"I wanted to give you a chance to see the Path property in the Immediate window," I said. "By pausing the program, this will give us a chance to see visually the Path that our program believes it is being run from."

I brought up the Immediate window by selecting View | Immediate Window from the Visual Basic main menu, and typed ?App.Path into the Immediate window. The result was displayed:

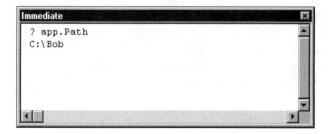

"What's the question mark mean?" Donna asked. "Is that a shortcut for Print?"

78

"That's exactly right," I said. "All I've done here is ask Visual Basic to report the directory from which our program is running – and in this case, it's telling us that it's the 'C' drive, and the Bob directory."

"Does the `Path` property of the `App` object work the same for an executable?" Donna asked.

"Exactly the same," I replied. "The `Path` property of the `App` object always reports the drive and directory from which our program is being run, regardless of whether it's a compiled program or one being run in the Visual Basic IDE."

"I notice that you took great pains to save the project and form before running this demo," Donna continued. "Suppose we had created a new project in Visual Basic, and had not saved it. What would the `Path` property be?"

"In that case, the `Path` property would be the Visual Basic directory itself," I answered.

I waited a moment to see if Donna had any more questions. She didn't.

"OK, now let's see how we can use the `App.Path` property to good effect in our code," I said.

I placed the following code in the command button's `Click` event procedure:

```
Private Sub Command1_Click()

If Right(App.Path,1) = "\" Then
  Form1.Picture = LoadPicture(App.Path & "Bubbles.bmp")
Else
  Form1.Picture = LoadPicture(App.Path & "\Bubbles.bmp")
End If

End Sub
```

When I ran the program we saw that, even though I no longer had the full path of the graphics file explicitly coded, the program successfully found the graphics file in the 'Bob' directory, loaded it into the `Picture` property of the form, and displayed it in the form's background.

I explained to Donna and to the viewers that what we had done was to take the value of the `Path` property, in this case `'C:\Bob'`, and concatenated a backslash plus the name of the graphics file to it – giving us a full path name.

"I'm finding that code to be a bit confusing," Donna said.

"Maybe it'll help if I draw it out," I said as I wrote up this illustration on the electronic whiteboard in the studio, and displayed it to the audience:

"C:\BOB" + " \BUBBLES.BMP" = C:\BOB\BUBBLES.BMP

"All right," she said, "I think I'm OK with that, but why the `If` statement? Why are we concatenating two different file names to the `Path`? And what's the purpose of the `'Right'` function in the code?"

"Actually," I replied, "we're not concatenating two different file names – the file name never changes. What we're doing here is checking for a special case – the program being run from the root directory of the hard drive – that could give us a problem. Did you notice earlier, when we displayed the `Path` of our program in the Immediate window, wheteher the `Path` property ended with a backslash?"

"I don't believe it did," Donna said. "I don't think the `Path` ever ends in a backslash."

"Actually, there's only one instance where the `Path` will end in a backslash," I said, "and that's when the program is being run directly from the root directory of a hard drive. That's the point of the `'If'` statement in our code – to detect this special case. And we use the `'Right'` function to examine the rightmost character of the `Path` property – which is where the backslash will be located."

"By root directory," she said, "do you mean where system files such as the `AUTOEXEC.BAT` are stored?"

"Yes," I said, "that's the root directory, at least on Drive 'C'. Every hard drive has a root directory. Because of this possibility, we need to check the rightmost position of the `Path` property, and if it's a backslash, we concatenate a slightly different string to the value of the `Path` property, like so..."

I then drew this illustration on my electronic whiteboard:

"C:\" + "BUBBLES.BMP" = C:\BUBBLES.BMP

"I understand what you've done here," Donna said. "and I'm ready to go back and modify my program now. But I must confess – I just don't understand how the `App.Path` does what it does?"

"Understanding everything is great," I said, "but there are some things going on behind the scenes with Windows that you may never fully understand. That's the magic of the Operating System at work here – Windows needs to know the directory from where the program is being run, because that's where the program instructions are kept. When the program is started, Windows records that directory in the `Path` property of the `App` object."

"Thanks again," Donna said.

"Thanks for calling, Donna."

I took a look at my producer Linda to see if we had time for one more question. She held up two fingers, which meant that we only had two minutes.

"I have time for one more question," I said. "Let's go to the next caller, but we need to make this a quick one."

Question 20: I'm using the Print method of the Printer object, but nothing is printing – why not?

"I think this is quick," he said. "My name is Matt from Springfield. I was browsing through your book in the bookstore – and in the second half of the book, you mentioned the Print method of the Printer object as a way to send something to the printer. Anyway, I've spent all week coding the Print method, but nothing's being printed. What am I doing wrong?"

"In addition to the Print method of the Printer object," I said, "Did you use the EndDoc method?"

"The EndDoc method?" Matt said in a puzzled tone. "Never heard of it. I must have missed that in the book."

"Next time, Matt," I said jokingly, "*buy* the book. I cover that in the same chapter of the book where I discuss the Print method. Here's what you need to do. Use the Print method of the Printer object to format your output. Then, to actually release the output to your printer, you need to use the EndDoc method – that will do the trick. Without EndDoc, you're just sending output to a Visual Basic object – and nothing will ever print. Take a look at this code."

I typed the following code into the click event procedure of a command button that I created in a new project:

```
Private Sub Command1_Click()

Printer.Print "Repeat after me, I love Visual Basic"
Printer.Print "Repeat after me, I love Visual Basic"
Printer.EndDoc

End Sub
```

"See the EndDoc method, Matt?" I asked. "As soon as that line of code is executed, you should hear your printer fire up."

"Thanks, Professor Smiley," Matt said, and he paused, presumably trying this out. A second or so later, he said "That did the trick. Thanks a lot."

Linda gave me a signal that we had come to the end of today's show.

"That's all the time we have for today's show," I said. "Once again, I want to thank everyone for watching. As always, special thanks go to the people who called in with questions today. You make the show what it is. If you called but couldn't get through, remember, we'll be here next week, same time, same channel."

Linda pulled off her headphones and shouted – "Let's get some donuts and talk about the show!"

Examples

Week 3

It had been a hectic week leading up to our third show.

In what was now becoming a familiar scenario, the cable network executives had placed a call to me mid-week, and asked me to meet them in their offices in Philadelphia. Nervous that the show was being canceled, I hurried to their offices. I found to my delight that they had exciting news for me (and also for themselves). The show was going national: news of its local success had spread westward, and a national cable television network had decided to 'pick up' the remaining eight shows.

"A national audience – you're not joking, are you?" I asked.

Tim, the Vice President of Sales, looked at me and said, "It's no joke. Maybe as early as your next show. Of course, we still have some logistics to work out but, conceivably, this Saturday you could be receiving calls from people all over the country."

I was on cloud nine for the remainder of the week. My early fears about appearing on TV, and about the viability of the show had dissipated a little, and when I arrived at the studio on Saturday for our third show, Linda was there waiting for me.

"I heard the great news," she said enthusiastically. "The show has been syndicated nationally. I guess soon we'll be talking with people from all over the country about Visual Basic."

We began our pre-show preparations. As usual, all of our equipment was ready to go. The residual aroma of olive oil and garlic lingered around the studio from the previous show – but aside from that, everything was in position.

"Imagine that," I thought to myself, "soon I might be taking calls about Visual Basic from viewers in Los Angeles."

"3 minutes," Linda shouted.

Linda already had ten callers ready to ask Visual Basic questions, just like the previous week. However, the network executives had instructed her to 'work in' any out-of-town callers who might get through. She had already informed the callers on hold that they might be 'bumped' by out-of-town callers if necessary. This seemed a little harsh to me, but I bowed to the wisdom of the professionals.

"Ten seconds," Linda called out. "Have a good show, John."

I smiled back and nodded, crossing my fingers for luck.

"You're on air," mouthed Linda.

After giving my standard 'start of show' speech, I said, "I'm also delighted to tell you that our show is now reaching a national audience, and we have viewers tuning in from outside the Philadelphia area. To any of them watching the show right now, welcome, and I do hope you call."

We were ready for our first call of the day.

Question 21: Can you assign a hotkey to a textbox, like you can in Microsoft Access?

(see also questions 22, 39,87,95 & 98)

"Hi, I'm Lil from Mount Laurel," the voice on the other end of the phone said. "I've only been working with Visual Basic for a few weeks. I'm primarily a Microsoft Access user. Anyway, in Access, text boxes have attached captions. That is, the caption is actually part of the text box control. From what I've seen, that's not the case in Visual Basic. Furthermore, I don't see a `Caption` property for the text box in Visual Basic – am I missing something?"

"No, you're not missing anything," I assured her. "Visual Basic doesn't have an associated caption for the text box the way that Access does. The alternative in Visual Basic is to place a label control next to the text box, and use *that* to describe the text box."

"I thought so," she said, "and that's actually what I've been doing – placing a label control next to the text box, that is! But can you answer another question? In Access, where the text box *does* have an attached caption, you can assign an **access key** to a text box, so that the user can set focus to a text box quickly. As there's no `Caption` property, I presume that there's no way to set focus to the text box the same way in Visual Basic?"

"You're right, Lil," I said. "There *is* a way to do it. But before I explain how, let me clarify your question for the home audience. Let's say that you have three text boxes on a form, into which you want the user to type their Name, ID Number, and Phone Number. Furthermore, you want to give the user the ability to 'hot key' to these text boxes quickly by pressing *Alt+N*, *Alt+I*, and *Alt+P* respectively. These key combinations are the **access keys** (or 'hot keys') used to take us straight to the control that they're associated with."

"Exactly what I want," Lil said emphatically. "Also, exactly what I haven't been able to do!"

"You need to use a bit of a Visual Basic trick here," I said, "and that's to place three label controls next to the text boxes, as I suggested earlier. Since there is no `Caption` property for the text box, you can't set an access key *directly* on the text box. However, you can set the access key on the label control."

"So," Lil said, "if you want the text box to be accessed via an *Alt+N* combination, you set the `Caption` of the corresponding label control to `&Name`?"

"That's right," I said, "you guessed it. Take a look at this…"

I started a fresh
Visual Basic project,
and arranged some
controls on its form in
the following order: a
label control,
followed by a text box
control; then a second
label control, and a
second text box; and,
finally, a third label
control and a third
text box:

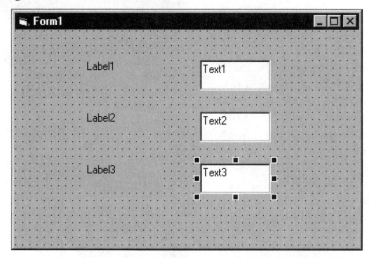

"Is the order that you placed these controls on the form significant?" I heard Lil say.

"Yes, the order *is* significant," I said. "This 'trick' of using a label control's `Caption` to set the focus to the adjacent text box works on the basis of the `TabIndex` properties of the label and text box controls – they *must* be consecutive. In other words, if `Label1`'s `TabIndex` property is `0`, this means that when its access key is pressed, Visual Basic looks to set the focus to a control with a `TabIndex` property of `1`."

"I see," said Lil, "that's why you didn't just place the three label controls on the form, followed by the three text box controls."

"That's right," I said, "the order is critical. If you are going to use this technique, you've got to give some thought to the placement of the controls on the form ahead of time – either that, or (after the fact) change the `TabIndex` properties of all the controls."

"Can you tell me why the label controls themselves don't receive the focus when the user presses the access key combination?" Lil asked.

"That's easy," I said. "A label control *can't* receive focus – it's only used for displaying information, and therefore it can't receive focus. "

"Of course," Lil said. "I should have thought of that."

Lil seemed satisfied with the explanation so far, so I set about defining the `Caption` properties of the three label controls using the Properties window.

"For those of you at home who don't know how to do designate an access key for a control," I explained, "the nub of the matter is the use of the ampersand (`&`) character. The ampersand, when placed in front of a letter in the `Caption`, marks that letter as the designated 'hot key'. For instance, we want the access key combination for the first text box to be '*Alt+N*', and so the `Caption` property will read `&Name`:"

I quickly changed the `Caption` properties of the remaining two label controls, and while I was at it, 'cleared' the `Text` properties of the three text boxes by selecting their `Text` properties and pressing the *BackSpace* key. This left us with the form looking like this:

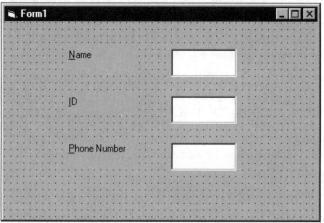

"Notice," I said, "that the ampersand doesn't appear in the displayed caption. Instead, the relevant letter is underlined, indicating the hot key's identifying letter."

When I had finished with the Properties window, I ran and tested the program for the viewing audience. Sure enough, when I pressed *Alt+N*, focus was moved to the text box to the right of the 'Name' label. When I pressed *Alt+I*, focus was moved to the text box to the right of the 'ID' label. When I pressed *Alt+P*, focus was moved to the text box to the right of the 'Phone Number' label.

"Well," Lil said, "you have certainly answered my question. Thanks for your help, Professor Smiley."

"Glad I could help, Lil," I said, "feel free to call again. And now, let's move on to our next caller."

Question 22: My MultiLine text box has funny characters in it when I concatenate text

(see also questions 21, 39, 87, 95 & 98)

"Hi, this is Florence from Lansdale. I believe it was last week that you talked about the MultiLine property of the text box control. My problem is in a similar vein – I'm using code to write text to a text box control. Not only is it not wrapping to multiple lines, but I'm getting this strange character in the text box – it looks like a double set of vertical lines. I've mailed you my code, by the way, if that helps. When I found it going wrong, I set up a mini-project just to test this part of the code, which I find usually lets me see what's going wrong. No luck on this one, though. Do you have any idea what I'm doing wrong?"

"Yes, Florence, I do," I answered quickly. "I know *exactly* what is going on. Let's paste your code into a new project so we can test it out – it's a pretty common problem."

With that, I created a command button and a text box in a shiny new Visual Basic project. I set the MultiLine property of the text box to True, and the ScrollBars property to Vertical. I named the command button and text box in keeping with the code Florence had e-mailed me, and pasted the code into my project:

```
Private Sub cmdCount_Click()

Dim intCounter As Integer

For intCounter = 1 To 100
    txtCount.Text = txtCount.Text & intCounter & Chr(10) & Chr(13)
    DoEvents
Next intCounter

MsgBox "All done"

End Sub
```

I then ran the program, clicked on the command button, and the following screenshot was displayed for the viewers at home:

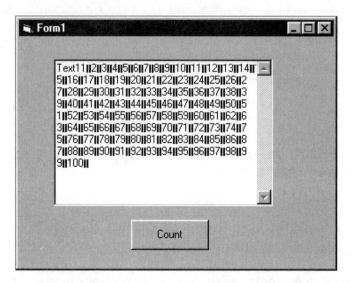

"All I've done here," Florence said, "is write a simple **For...Next** loop to display the numbers from 1 to 100 on multiple lines in the text box."

"Oops – hold on, Florence, I forgot one thing. I forgot to clear the **Text** property of the text box – sorry about that. Let me just do that now."
I did this by going to the Properties window for the text box control, clicking on the drop-down box for the **Text** property...

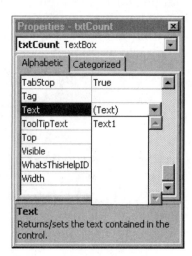

...and highlighting its contents (Text1) before pressing the *Delete* key. When I ran the program again, the unwanted text was no longer there:

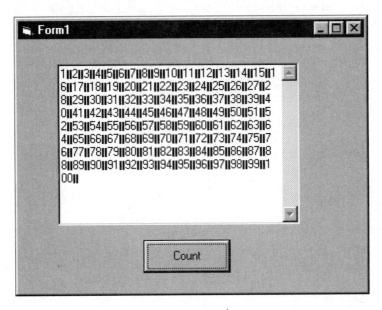

"That's solved the first problem," I said. "The next issue is that the output from the loop wraps around – the numbers aren't displayed on individual lines. The final problem is that there are funny characters between the numbers. Is this the character you were telling us about, Florence?"

"That's the one." Florence replied. "What is that? And what's causing it?"

"The problem," I said to Florence, "is how you are trying to write multiple lines to the text box control in code. You cleverly concatenated a Carriage Return and Line Feed to the text box, knowing that in effect you needed to simulate the press of the *Enter* key in your code. Unfortunately, you made a tiny mistake with this. By the way, where did you find this code?"

"It may have been out of a book," she said, "or I might have done this on my own – I don't really remember. My memory hasn't been all that great since I turned 80 last year.Still, I don't see what the problem is – after all, I'm concatenating the ASCII code for the Carriage Return – 10, followed by the ASCII code for the Line Feed – 13."

"Florence," I said, "you'll find that you have those reversed. ASCII code 10 is the Line Feed character, and ASCII code 13 is the Carriage Return."

"I seem to always get those two confused," she said, pausing momentarily. "Is that significant? Is there all that much difference in concatenating a Line Feed plus a Carriage Return in a text box, instead of a Carriage Return and a Line Feed? I know I've done this in my 'C' programs with no problem."

"Unfortunately," I said, "the difference in Visual Basic is significant. Visual Basic is just *pickier* when it comes to the order of the Carriage Return and Line Feed – if you reverse them, you see those funny characters instead of having the text move to the next line of the text box. Let me show you what happens when we reverse the order."

I changed the code in the command button's click event procedure to look like this:

```
Private Sub cmdCount_Click()

Dim intCounter As Integer

For intCounter = 1 To 100
    txtCount.Text = txtCount.Text & intCounter & Chr(13) & Chr(10)
    DoEvents
Next intCounter

MsgBox "All done"

End Sub
```

I ran the program again and clicked on the command button. This time, the numbers were properly formatted within the text box:

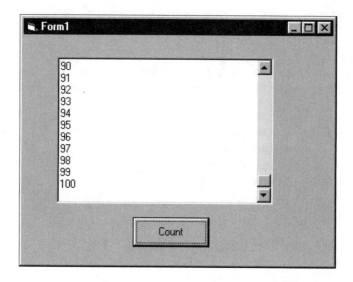

"That's better," Florence said. "I wish Visual Basic wasn't so picky about this. I'm probably going to confuse the two again somewhere down the road. I always do."

"Actually, Florence," I said, "during our first show, instead of using the ASCII characters for a Carriage Return and Line Feed, I used the Visual Basic Intrinsic Constant representing the correct combination of those two – vbCrLf. This constant has been available ever since the introduction of Visual Basic 5."

"Visual Basic intrinsic constant," Florence said dubiously. "What exactly is that? I don't think I've ever heard of that."

I explained that an intrinsic constant is a Visual Basic constant, not defined by the programmer, but actually contained inherently within Visual Basic itself.

"Visual Basic intrinsic constants," I said, "are used in place of hard to remember values – such as the Carriage Return or Line Feed, or in the case of vbCrLf, both of those!"

"So if I use vbCrLf in my code," she said, "that's the same as explicitly referencing the ASCII code for both the Carriage Return and Line Feed?"

"That's right, Florence," I replied. "Plus, you don't need to remember what order they need to be used in. Visual Basic does that for you."

"Can you show me some code," she asked, "that uses this intrinsic constant?"

"I'd be glad to," I answered, as I made the following change to the command button's click event procedure:

```
Private Sub cmdCount_Click()

Dim intCounter As Integer

For intCounter = 1 To 100
    txtCount.Text = txtCount.Text & intCounter & vbCrLf
    DoEvents
Next intCounter

MsgBox "All done"

End Sub
```

I then ran the program, and clicked on the command button. Once again, the program properly formatted the output in the text box – this time using the intrinsic constant instead of the ASCII characters themselves.

"I guess I should have paid more attention to that first show," Florence said. "Thanks for your help."

"My pleasure, Florence," I said, "you wouldn't believe how often I've been asked that question. Let's take one more caller before our first break."

Question 23: Is there a way to permanently add a control to the Toolbox?

(see also question 64)

"Hi, my name is Buddy, and I'm from Lubbock, Texas," began the caller. "Your producer told me that I'm your first out-of-state caller. Let me tell you, this show is a welcome addition to my cable channel's lineup down here."

"Buddy, thanks, and welcome to the show," I said. "How can we help you today?"

"I'm not exactly sure that this is a question appropriate for beginners, but it's been driving me crazy," he said. "I'm sure you know that when you start up Visual Basic, there are only so many controls in the Toolbox. Well, it seems that just about every project I work on these days requires using the common dialog control. What I have to do every time is select Project I Components from the main menu, and add the common dialog control to the project. I was wondering, is there any way that I can add the common dialog control to the Toolbox permanently?"

"Yes, there is," I said. "How you do it is another thing, however. That depends on the version of Visual Basic that you are now using. Versions 3 and 4 of Visual Basic installed with a Visual Basic project already loaded into the default Visual Basic directory called AUTOLOAD. In VB3 and VB4, you could open this project in Visual Basic like any other project, add a control to your Toolbox by selecting Project I Components from the Visual Basic menu bar, and then save the project. The next time you created a new Visual Basic project, the controls you added to the Toolbox would be there, all ready and waiting for you."

"That sounds like what I want," Buddy says, "but I'm not using VB3 or VB4. I'm running Visual Basic 5. Do VB5 or 6 have an AUTOLOAD project?"

"No, they don't," I said, "although I have had some enterprising students of mine create a new project in Visual Basic 5 and 6, and then save the project as AUTOLOAD.VBP in the default Visual Basic directory. That seems to do the trick, but I wouldn't recommend it..."

"Why not?" Buddy said. "If it works..."

"VB5 and VB6 have provided a more elegant solution," I said, "and that's the use of project and form templates. Through the use of project templates, you can have *any number* of different Toolbox set-ups available for your use – not just one. Let me show you."

I opened up a new Visual Basic project.

"When you tell Visual Basic that you want to start a new project," I began, "ordinarily you see this New Project window – depending, of course, on what edition of VB you have:"

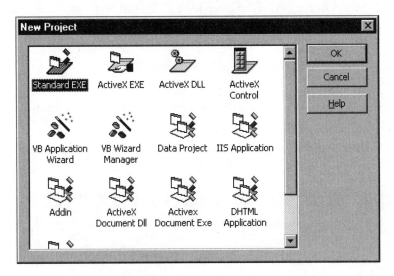

"That's right," Buddy said. "For the type of work I do, I just select the Standard EXE project – that's all I ever use. Is that OK?"

"That's fine, Buddy," I said, "most beginners only use the Standard EXE project type. I'll select that now."

"Now in case anyone missed your question," I continued, after selecting the Standard EXE project type, "you want to know how to add the common dialog control permanently to the Toolbox. As you pointed out earlier, if you add the common dialog control to the Toolbox now, when you start a new Visual Basic project, you will need to add it all over again."

"Exactly," Buddy affirmed, "even though if we save this project and open it up again, the common dialog control is still there. It's only *new* projects that don't contain it in the Toolbox."

"You're right," I said. "Thanks for clarifying that. It's only new projects that we're talking about here. Back to your question: I think you'll find that this situation is pretty easy to remedy through the use of a Visual Basic project template. What that means is this: after we add the common dialog control to the Toolbox, we'll immediately save this project in a Visual Basic Template directory."

"Where is that located?" Buddy asked, "and how does it get created?"

"The Templates directory is a special directory that is created for you when you first install Visual Basic," I replied. "It's intended to be used to hold any project templates that a programmer might create. Thereafter, whenever we tell Visual Basic that we want to start a new project, any project templates that we have created (including this one, whose Toolbox contains the common dialog control) will appear in the Project window."

"Sounds pretty neat," Buddy said. "What do we need to do?"

"The first thing we need to do," I replied, "is to add the common dialog control to the Toolbox of this project. We can do that now by selecting Project | Components from the Visual Basic menu bar."

I selected Project | Components and scrolled through the list box to the Microsoft Common Dialog control and selected it:

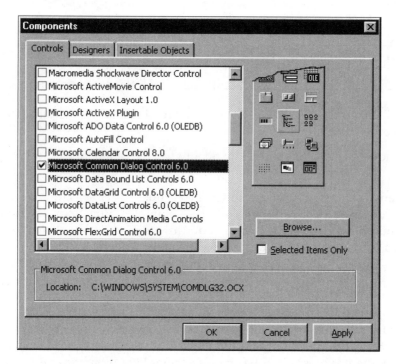

After I clicked on the OK button, the common dialog control was included in the Toolbox:

"So far, so good," I heard Buddy say. "Now what?"

"At this point," I said, "we need to check a couple of things. First, we need to confirm the location of the Templates directory in Visual Basic, so that we know where to save the project template. We do that by selecting Tools | Options | Environment from the Visual Basic menu bar:"

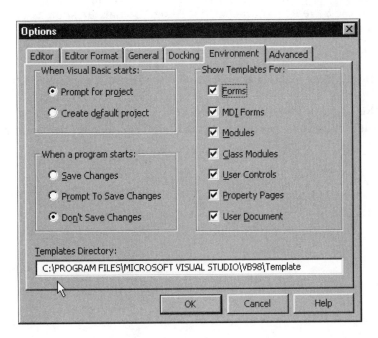

I pointed out the location of the Templates directory to Buddy and the rest of the viewing audience.

"Also notice the frame that reads Show Templates For:," I said. "By default, project templates are shown when you go through the process of creating a new project in Visual Basic. There are also other types of templates that can be shown while you're working in Visual Basic – such as form and module templates. If the check boxes for those are not selected here, you won't see them."

"I understand where and when I'll see the project templates," Buddy said. "But what about some of the others?"

"Yes, let's look at that," I said. "Form templates appear when you select Project | New Form from the Visual Basic menu bar; and modules, when you select Project | New Modules."

I waited a moment to see if all of this was sinking in before moving on.

"Now we need to save this project, complete with its customized Toolbox, in the project templates directory," I said, "and give it a unique name so that we can identify it in the Project window. In honor of you, Buddy, why don't you name this template?"

Buddy pondered a name for a couple of seconds. The phone line clicked and echoed.

"Do you mind if we name the project template after my girlfriend, Peggy Sue?" he asked. "I know she's watching the show!"

"Sure thing, Buddy. We can do that, but we'll need to remove the space between Peggy and Sue," I said, clicking on the Save icon on the Visual Basic Toolbar. As soon as I clicked on this icon, a dialog box to save the form appeared.

"Do we need to save the form, too?" Buddy asked.

"I should have mentioned that earlier," I answered. "When we save a project template, we also need to save the form along with it – there's just no other way. This isn't necessarily a bad thing, as doing this also allows us to customize the project's form or forms. But be careful. If you want the look and feel of VB default behavior associated with your project template, don't change the form!"

In the Save File As dialog
box, I navigated to the
template directory, as
specified in the Tools |
Options | Environment tab we
had checked earlier:

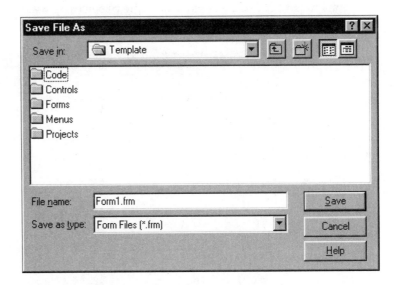

I pointed out that many people make the mistake of saving their templates in this directory
– which makes a lot of sense, since it is named the 'Template' directory.

"The Template directory," I warned, "contains subdirectories for all of the different types of
Visual Basic templates you can create – projects, forms, etc. We need to save the project
template in the 'Projects' subdirectory of the Templates directory."

I then selected the Projects
subdirectory, and saved the
form there as
'PeggySue.frm':

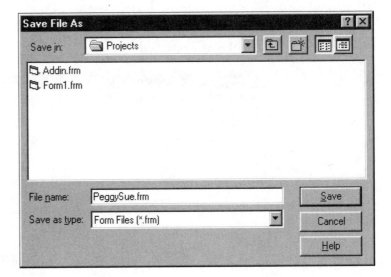

"The final step," I continued, "is to save the project file itself: in this case, we'll save it as 'PeggySue.vbp':"

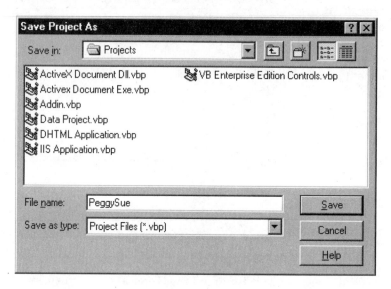

"So now," Buddy said, "when we tell Visual Basic that we want to create a new project, we should see the name 'PeggySue' in the Project window."

"That's right," I affirmed, "and if we then select it, the Toolbox will contain the common dialog control."

Seeing is believing, so I then selected File | New Project from the Visual Basic menu bar, and the following screen shot was displayed:

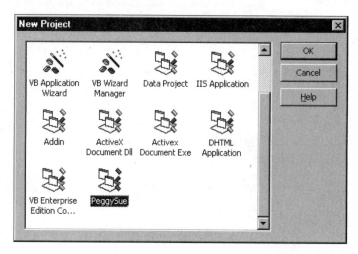

"I see PeggySue," Buddy said excitedly. "Can we select it, and see if the common dialog control is in the Toolbox?"

"Sure thing," I said, and selected 'PeggySue' in the Project window. When I did so, the project loaded, although there was no form visible in the IDE. The Visual Basic Toolbox was visible, however, and it contained the common dialog control.

"Hey, that's great," Buddy said, "I see the common dialog control – but where's the form we saved along with the project? Why don't I see it anywhere?"

I explained that the form is not opened automatically for you after you have created a project template and select the project template in the New Project window.

"That's not a big deal," I said, "as we can view the Project Explorer window, double click on the form there, and make the form visible."

"You've answered all of my questions. Thanks a million!"

"My pleasure, Buddy," I said.

During the ensuing commercial break, Linda congratulated me on taking our first national call before putting through our fourth caller of the day.

Question 24: Can you place a quotation mark in a label's caption at run time?

(see also question 33)

"Hi, my name is Sonny. I'm from Pasadena," he said. "I have to tell you I've been looking forward to this show all week. I hope you can help me with a nagging question I have. I guess it's a pretty frivolous one, but I just hate not to be able to figure something out."

"Go ahead, Sonny," I said, "I know that feeling. Let's hear your question. There's probably someone in the viewing audience that's also dying to know the answer."

"OK," he said, "I want to include a quotation mark in the `Caption` of a label control on my form. I know I can do this easily by typing the quotation mark into the `Caption` property in the Properties window. But I'm being stubborn... I want to do this at *run time*, using code. That's where I'm having trouble."

"I was about to say," I said, "why not just set the `Caption` in the Properties window – but you beat me to it. You're right, though – setting the `Caption` for the label control at run time does pose a problem. Because the quotation marks delineate a **string** (i.e. a string variable, like a name or address) in code, Visual Basic tends to get confused as to how to treat strings that contain a quotation mark themselves. But don't worry, there's a way around this. As you'll see in a minute or two, it's just another trick of the programming trade."

I placed a single command button and a label control on a form in a new project.

"I want to illustrate the basic problem," I said. "Using the Properties window to assign quotation marks to the label's caption is easy – you just type the quotation mark directly into the `Caption` property. But at run time we have a problem, in that the `Caption` property of the label control is a string – and to assign a string to a property at run time, we have to 'sandwich' the string within a pair of quotation marks. For instance, if we want to assign my name, John Smiley, to the `Caption` of a label control, we would use this code."
I then typed this code into the `Click` event procedure of the command button, and ran the program.

```
Private Sub Command1_Click()

Label1.Caption = "John Smiley"

End Sub
```

My name appeared as the label's `Caption`:

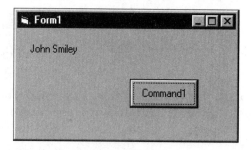

"No problem here," I said, "since the string we are assigning to the `Caption` does not contain a quotation mark. But we would have a problem if we wanted the `Caption` to display my name with quotation marks around it. Again, this is easy to do in the Properties window."

I 'cheated' by typing this string directly into the Properties window...

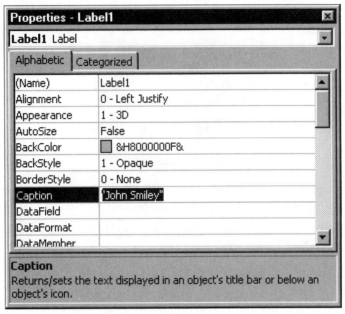

...and then ran the program:

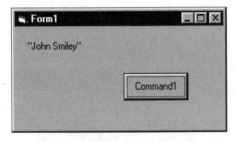

"That's it, that's exactly what I want to be able to do," Sonny said. "I thought that anything that could be done at design time in the Properties window can be done at run time through code. Is it possible?"

"Definitely," I said. "Most beginners are inclined to believe that this code will do the trick:"

```
Private Sub Command1_Click()

Label1.Caption = ""John Smiley""

End Sub
```

"But all you get from this is a Visual Basic error, because this syntax just confuses Visual Basic..." I said, as the following error was displayed on my studio PC and for the viewers at home:

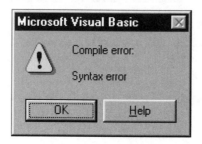

"I tried that also," Sonny said. "I was certain that was the trick. And you're right, all I received was an error for my troubles. So what's the solution?"

"The solution," I answered, "is to use a *triple* set of quotation marks instead of a double pair wherever you want a quotation mark to appear as part of a string. Like so..."

```
Private Sub Command1_Click()

Label1.Caption = """John Smiley"""

End Sub
```

"Count the quotation marks. There are six in total; one on either side of the string to delineate it, and two more each side, sandwiching my name, telling Visual Basic to display a single quotation mark on either side of my name. I know this is confusing, but it does work," I said, as I ran the program and clicked on the command button. Sure enough, my name appeared in the label's caption, surrounded by quotation marks:

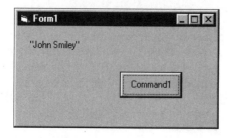

"So the technique here," Sonny asked, "is that wherever I want to display a *single* quotation mark in a `Caption` – or assign it to a string – I need to use *two* in the code to specify the single one shown? Is that right?"

"That's the trick," I said.

"I never would have figured that out on my own. Thanks."

"Thank you for calling, Sonny," I said, "and now time for our next caller."

Question 25: How do you change the default font size in the code window?

"I'm Frank from Chestnut Hill," he said. "I'm probably one of your older callers – I'll be 70 on my next birthday – and I find that the default font size of the code in the Visual Basic code window is way too small for me. Is there anything I can do to make it larger?"

"You're about 20 years younger than my oldest student, Frank," I said. "Remember, age is no barrier to learning Visual Basic, although I understand your feelings about the print in that code window. I sometimes have trouble making that out myself. But that problem is easy to solve; all you need to do is make your way to the Editor Format tab by selecting Tools | Options from the Visual Basic menu bar."

I did that myself in the studio, and the following screen shot was displayed:

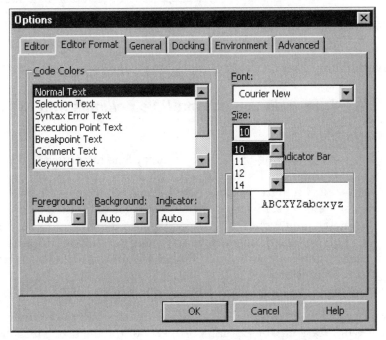

"Once you're here, Frank," I continued, "just select the **Size** list box, and change the **FontSize** to whatever you feel comfortable with. You can also change the **FontStyle** from this tab also. Let's try 18 point."

I then clicked on the OK button.

"Are the changes you make here permanent?" Frank asked. "Or will I have to do this every time I start Visual Basic?"

"These changes are permanent, Frank," I said. "You won't have to make these changes more than once. Let's see what the code window looks like now," I said, as I switched to the code window. The size of the **Font** was obviously larger – and much easier to view:

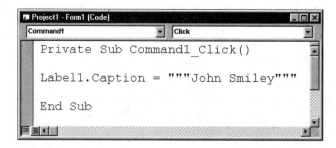

"That's great – I should be able to see that fine now, " I heard Frank say. "Thanks for the tip."

"My pleasure." I said. "Now on to our next caller."

Question 26: How do you get multiple columns in a list box?

(see also questions 11, 12, 13 & 16)

"Hi, I'm Pelle from Lindenwold, New Jersey," he introduced himself. "I'm enjoying your show quite a lot. I tried to call in last week, when it seemed like there were a lot of list box questions, but I couldn't get through. I don't believe anyone asked this question last week, though, so here goes; I want to display multiple columns in a list box control. I'm a bit of an ice hockey fan, and what I'd like to do is use a list box to display my favorite hockey players. The problem is that I have two pieces of distinct information I want to display – their names, and their uniform numbers. I want to display each type of information in separate columns of a list box. Is there a way to do this? I see that the list box does have a **Columns** property, but I'm not sure if that's exactly what I need."

"You're right, Pelle," I said. There *is* a **Columns** property of the list box control, but that won't work for you. The **Columns** property of the list box affects 'wrapping' of the items in the list box. What you want to do is have two distinct columns in a list box, and that feature isn't really supported. But there is a way to *simulate* that behavior, if you want to see it."

Pelle agreed that he would.

I created a fresh Visual Basic project containing a list box control and a command button. After changing the font type and size back to the defaults (remember, I had changed the settings for my previous caller), I typed the following code into the command button's `Click` event procedure:

```
Private Sub Command1_Click()

Dim intCounter As Integer

For intCounter = 1 To 99
List1.AddItem intCounter
Next intCounter

End Sub
```

Then I ran the program and clicked on the command button:

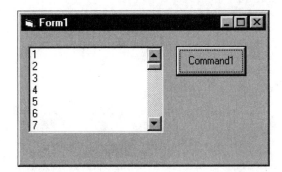

"This is almost identical to the code I used last week," I said, "which loaded the numbers from 1 to 100 into a list box. I've modified it to load the numbers from 1 to 99 so that – eventually – we can have three columns of numbers with the same number of entries in each column. With this many numbers, there's no way that all of them will fit into the list box without the list box having to scroll vertically. Notice that I didn't need to do anything 'special' to make the vertical scrollbar appear. The list box does that on its own – it just *knows* that if it's not 'tall enough' to display all of the items in the list, that it should provide a vertical scrollbar – a nice example of default Visual Basic behavior."

"I see," Pelle said.

"OK," I continued, "let me ask you this question; have you ever seen a horizontal scrollbar in a list box?"

"No," Pelle said, "I don't think I have."

"That's right," I said, "by default, you don't see horizontal scrollbars in a list box. If the list box needs to provide scrollbars, it automatically supplies *vertical* scrollbars. Now *this* is where the Columns property comes into play. If the Columns property of the list box is set to anything *except* 0, and the list box is not large enough to accommodate the data items, then instead of seeing vertical scrollbars, we get *horizontal* ones instead. Watch this."

I changed the Columns property of the list box control to 3...

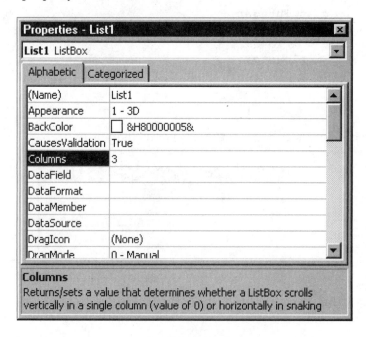

...ran the program again, and clicked on the command button. This is the screen shot that Pelle and the viewing audience saw:

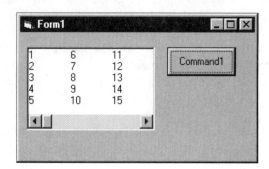

"I think I see," Pelle said. "By specifying the value 3 for the `Columns` property, the items in the list box are now arranged in three columns, and we no longer have a vertical scrollbar – instead, we have a horizontal one."

"That's right," I agreed. "But in fact we actually have *more* than three columns in total here – what the `Columns` property specifies is how many columns we *see* at one time. The rest of the columns are off to the right. The items in the columns are 'snaking' – in order to see the rest of the items in the list box, we must scroll to the right:"

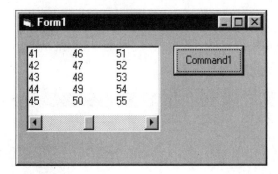

"I entirely misinterpreted the meaning of the `Columns` property," Pelle said. "I thought using the `Columns` property could tell Visual Basic that I wanted a list box with three columns *in total*, and still retain the vertical scrollbars. But in this example, we actually have many more columns than the three that I want to display."

"That's right," I agreed, "So the `Columns` property won't give you the effect that you're looking for."

"You mentioned earlier that there was something you *could* show me that was close to what I want?" Pelle asked. "Can you show me that now?"

"OK," I said, "let's start by loading into a list box the names of five of my favorite ice hockey players. Before I do that, let me widen and lengthen the list box just a bit. Also, I don't want to forget to change the `Columns` property of the list box back to its default value of 0."

I made those changes, and then keyed this code into the `Click` event procedure of the command button:

```
Private Sub Command1_Click()

List1.AddItem "ERIC LINDROS"
List1.AddItem "RON HEXTALL"
List1.AddItem "ROD BRIND'AMOUR"
List1.AddItem "JOHN VANBIESBROUCK"
List1.AddItem "JOHN LECLAIR"

End Sub
```

I then ran the program, clicked on the command button, and the following screen shot was displayed to Pelle and the viewers at home:

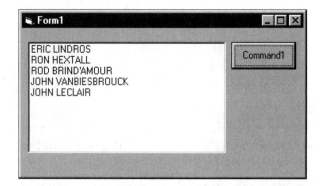

"Now let me double-check," I said to Pelle, "you want to be able to display the uniform number of the player in a second column of the list box – is that right?"
"Yes," he answered.

"The way I would do this," I said, "is to concatenate a tab character to the player's name, and then concatenate their uniform number to that. Like this..."

I changed the Click event procedure of the command button to look like this:

```
Private Sub Command1_Click()

List1.AddItem "ERIC LINDROS" & vbTab & "88"
List1.AddItem "RON HEXTALL" & vbTab & "27"
List1.AddItem "ROD BRIND'AMOUR" & vbTab & "17"
List1.AddItem "JOHN VANBIESBROUCK" & vbTab & "34"
List1.AddItem "JOHN LECLAIR" & vbTab & "27"

End Sub
```

...ran the program, and clicked on the command button. This gave us the following:

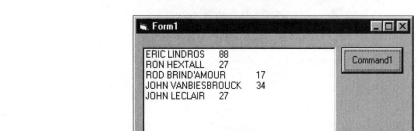

"Well, in live television," I said, "not everything works perfectly the first time! We'll need to fine-tune this just a bit."

I explained that the code I had placed in the command button's `Click` event procedure was designed to concatenate the Visual Basic intrinsic constant `vbTab` to the name of the player, and then concatenate the player's uniform number to that.

"For those of you familiar with the concept of Visual Basic **print zones**," I said, "the list box 'window' also has print zones, which subdivide the list box 'window' into discrete areas, each of which is eight characters in width. By concatenating a tab character to the player's name, we tell Visual Basic to 'skip' to the next print zone – in this case, the 9th character position across the list box."

"So that's why the output looks like it does," Pelle interjected. "But because of the variable length of the player names, you get that skewed appearance of the items in the list box?"

"Right," I agreed, "but all is not lost. We can estimate the number of tab characters we'll need to make our output look better. Let's concatenate *three* tab characters to the names that are 'short', and *two* tab characters to the names that are 'long'. It isn't perfect, but it will work."

I entered this next lot of code into the command button's `Click` event procedure:

```
Private Sub Command1_Click()

List1.AddItem "ERIC LINDROS" & vbTab & vbTab & vbTab & "88"
List1.AddItem "RON HEXTALL" & vbTab & vbTab & vbTab & "27"
List1.AddItem "ROD BRIND'AMOUR" & vbTab & vbTab & "17"
List1.AddItem "JOHN VANBIESBROUCK" & vbTab & vbTab & "34"
List1.AddItem "JOHN LECLAIR" & vbTab & vbTab & vbTab & "27"

End Sub
```

After typing up the code I ran the program and clicked on the command button:

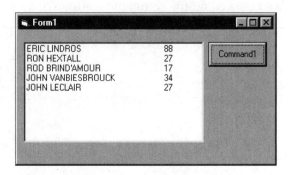

"That's the effect I was looking for," Pelle said. "I hadn't thought of using the tab character. That's pretty clever."

"Thanks," I said. "So much in programming is just knowing the right technique or trick. Thanks for calling – and good luck with your program."

After the next commercial break, we picked up with caller number seven.

Question 27: Why do I get an error message saying I have no fonts installed when I use the ShowFont method of the common dialog control?

(see also question 37)

"Hi, this is Frank from Hoboken," he said." I recently discovered that you can use the ShowFont method of the common dialog control to let the user change the default font in your application. I thought this would be the greatest thing since sliced bread, but whenever I display the Font dialog box to the user at run time, they get an error message telling them that there are no fonts installed, and that they should install some via the Windows Control Panel. What am I doing wrong?"

"Hi, Frank," I said. "You're not doing anything wrong by using the ShowFont method of the common dialog control; that's exactly what you *should* be doing. However, there's a property of the common dialog control that needs to be set before you use the ShowFont method – otherwise, you'll receive this nasty error message. Let me first show the viewing audience exactly what you're seeing – then I'll show you how to fix it."

Creating a new project, I added a single command button and a common dialog control, before typing the code below into the command button's Click event procedure:

```
Private Sub Command1_Click()

CommonDialog1.ShowFont

End Sub
```

When I ran the program and clicked on the command button, we saw the following result:

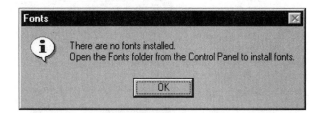

"Yep, that's the error message I'm receiving," Frank said from the other end of the line. "But I'm certain I have Windows fonts installed – don't I? I just can't figure out what I was doing wrong."

"If you check Visual Basic's on-line help for the **ShowFont** method of the common dialog control," I said, "buried deep in the Remark section, there's a warning that says: if you use the **ShowFont** method, you must first set the **Flag** property of the common dialog control to either **&H1**, **&H2**, or **&H3**."

"What exactly do those values mean?" Frank asked.

"The **'H'** indicates that these are hexadecimal values," I said, "and they are used to tell Visual Basic whether you want the user to be presented with a list of available Screen fonts (**&H1**), Printer fonts (**&H2**), or both (**&H3**)."

"So to use the **ShowFont** method, I need to enter either **&H1**, **&H2**, or **&H3** as a value in the **Flag** property in the Properties window at design time – and I'll be OK?" he asked.

"That's right," I said. "Don't forget though, that in addition to setting the **Flag** property at design time via the Properties window, you can also set the **Flag** property at run time. And to make things easier for you, you might want to consider substituting the Visual Basic intrinsic constant name of **cdlCFScreenFonts** for '**&H1**', **cdlCFPrinterFonts** for '**&H2**', or **cdlCFBoth** for '**&H3**' in your code. Let's see how that works now."

I modified the **click** event procedure of the command button to look like this:

```
Private Sub Command1_Click()

CommonDialog1.Flags = cdlCFBoth
CommonDialog1.ShowFont

End Sub
```

Then I ran the program, and clicked on the command button. This time, we got this result:

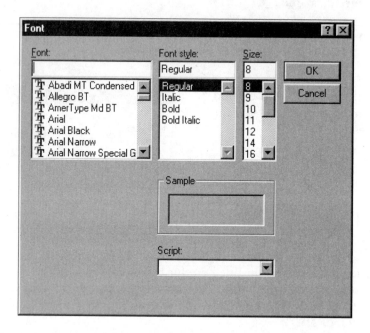

"That's better," I explained, "now we're actually seeing the Font dialog box. And since we used `cdlCFBoth`, that means what we're seeing here is a list of all of the PC's fonts – both Screen and Printer fonts – installed on the PC."

"Uh-huh," said Frank, "I see that."

"Now don't forget," I added, "that once the user has made a selection in this Font window, you still have some work to do. You'll need to check the common dialog control's `Font` properties, and use them to change the font characteristics of your form, labels, text boxes, and whatever else you desire."

"Yes, I understand that," Frank said. "This was my biggest hurdle. I think I'll be OK now. Thanks so much – this is a lifesaver."

"You're quite welcome, Frank," I said, "and now on to our next caller."

Question 28: What does the error message 'Variable not defined' mean?

(see also question 40)

"Hi, I'm Marilyn from Los Angeles," she said. "I'm pretty new to Visual Basic, and I've been coding some of the examples in your *Learn to Program With Visual Basic* book. I was doing pretty well, but now I'm getting an error message, 'Variable not defined'. I'm a bit mystified by this, because I've read far enough into your book to know that I should have Option Explicit specified in the General Declarations section of my form – and it *is*. And I'm not using any variables in the code procedure that are being flagged as errors."

"Hi, Marilyn," I said, "thanks for calling. This is a very common problem – particularly with beginners. Nine times out of ten, the reason for the error message is that in your code you're referencing a control whose name is not what you *think* it is. Unfortunately, the error message that Visual Basic displays in this case isn't a very clear one, mainly because Visual Basic is pretty confused by this state of affairs. When Visual Basic sees a control name in code, it immediately looks at all of the controls in your project. If it can't see a matching name, Visual Basic figures that you are actually referring to a *variable*. If you have Option Explicit entered into the General Declarations section of your form, it then looks to see if you have declared a variable with that name, and when it *doesn't* see a variable declared anywhere with that name, it displays this error message. Let me show you what I mean."

I created a new Visual Basic project with a single command button and a label control. I entered this code in the command button's Click event procedure:

```
Private Sub Command1_Click()

Lab11.Caption = "I love Visual Basic"

End Sub
```

"I want you to notice," I said, "that I've intentionally mistyped the name of the label control on the form. It should be 'Label1', but I did something that anyone can easily do – I made a typo, and referenced the label control as 'Lab11' instead. Since I have Option Explicit specified in the General Declarations section of my form, when I run the program, and click on the command button, see what happens:"

"I see what you mean now," Marilyn said. "Visual Basic doesn't exactly come straight out and tell you that there isn't a control with that name, does it? And while you were doing that demonstration, I checked my code here at home, and I can see that the name of the control in my code window doesn't match the name of the control in the Properties window. You were right."

"I figured that," I said. "It would be great if Visual Basic came right out and said that the control name was wrong – unfortunately, it doesn't. But I do have a few tips that may help you avoid this kind of mistake in the future."

"What are they?" Marilyn asked.

"First," I continued, "name your controls in a meaningful way. If you just accept the default name that Visual Basic assigns to a control when you place it on your form, you're more likely to make a mistake when you refer to that control in your code. Secondly, use the Hungarian Notation that I've mentioned in an earlier show and in my book. The use of a standard naming convention such as Hungarian Notation also reduces the likelihood that you'll wrongly reference a control's name in your code. For example, if you place a command button on your form, and it's an 'OK' button, name it `cmdOK`, where `cmd` is the Hungarian Notation prefix for a command button."

"Those two make a lot of sense," Marilyn agreed. "Anything else?"

"Yes," I continued. "In my experience, probably the most important tip I can give you is to name your controls using what I call 'mixed case' syntax. That is, when you name a control, name it so that it contains a mix of upper and lower case letters. Then, any time you type the name of the control in your code window, type it using all lower case letters. When you move to the next line in the code window, Visual Basic should then change the control's name to mixed case. If, instead, the name remains in all lower case, which means that Visual Basic doesn't recognize the name. This way, you know something is wrong somewhere – either with your code, or with the control's `Name` property."

I re-displayed the `Click` event procedure of the command button again:

```
Private Sub Command1_Click()

labl1.Caption = "I love Visual Basic"

End Sub
```

"Notice," I said, "that I typed the name of the label control in lower case in code, and that it remained in lower case. Now, the default name of the first label control that Visual Basic places on the form is *capital* 'L', *lowercase* 'abel1'. If I had typed the name of the control *properly* in the code window, Visual Basic would have automatically changed it to mixed case when I moved to the next line in the code window. The fact that Visual Basic *didn't* do that should have given me a visual clue that something was wrong with the name of the control I was typing."

"That's a great tip," Marilyn said.

"My pleasure, Marilyn," I said.

I looked over at Linda to see if we should take a commercial break, but she signaled me to take our next caller.

Question 29: Can I write to, and read from, the Windows Registry?

(see also question 30)

"Hi, I'm Janis from Port Arthur, Texas," the caller began. "I was wondering if there's a way for Visual Basic to save values in the Registry?"

"Hi, Janis," I said. "Welcome to the show. And yes, there is. In Visual Basic, you can easily write to and read from the Windows Registry. For those of you who don't know, the Registry is where Windows stores the information that it needs to run Windows programs – this information remains stored there even after you turn off your machine. This means that Windows can use it the next time it starts up. Let me code up a little example for you."

I thought for a moment, and then created a new Visual Basic project with a single command button.

"It makes sense to demonstrate *writing* to the Registry first," I said, "that way, we'll have values to read later. Let's put some code in the command button's Click event of the which will accept the user's name from a Visual Basic input box, and then save that name to the Registry. After that, we'll write some code in the form's Load event procedure that *reads* the name we've just written name from the Registry, and display the name in the form's Caption. But first things first – here's the code to write to the Registry:"

```
Private Sub Command1_Click()

Dim varRetVal

varRetVal = InputBox("What's your first name?")
```

```
If varRetVal <> "" Then
    SaveSetting "Janis", "STARTUP", "UserName", varRetVal
End If

End Sub
```

Then I ran the program, and clicked on the command button. When I did, a Visual Basic input box was displayed on the form. I entered my first name...

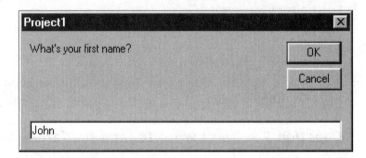

...and clicked on the OK button.

"Nothing visible has happened," I said, "but we just wrote my name to the Windows Registry. Now for the magic – the code to read my name from the Registry and put it in the form's Caption when the program runs."

I placed the following code into the Load event procedure of the form:

```
Private Sub Form_Load()

Dim strUserName As String

strUserName = GetSetting("Janis", "Startup", "UserName", "User")
Form1.Caption = "Good day, " & strUserName

End Sub
```

...and ran the program. When I did, the Caption of the form changed to 'Good day, John':

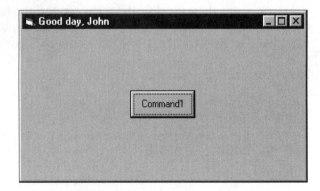

"I'm impressed!" Janis said. "You just did what I've been trying to do for two weeks. Now can you explain to me exactly what you did?"

"Sure thing," I replied. "Let's look at the code to save a value to the Registry first. To do this, we used the Visual Basic statement `SaveSetting`:

```
SaveSetting "Janis", "STARTUP", "UserName", varRetVal
```

"`SaveSetting` requires four parameters; `Application Name`, `Section Name`, `Key Name`, and `Value` – with `Value` being the information (in this case the first name) that you want to save to the Registry."

"It looks to me," Janis said, "that you took the return value of the `InputBox` function, and used it as the value parameter in the `SaveSetting` function. Is that right? And can the values for `Application Name`, `Section Name`, and `Key Name` be anything you want?"

"Yes," I said. "`SaveSetting` writes values to a special 'area' of the Windows Registry used just for application programs like ours – and you can use just about anything for the `Application`, `Section`, and `Key` names. But don't forget, as is the case when naming variables and controls, choose those names logically."

"As far as the code in the `Load` event procedure of the form," Janis said. "I think I see what is happening here. You already know the `Application Name`, `Section Name`, and `Key Name` that you used to save the value with the `SaveSetting` statement. What you're doing is using the `GetSetting` function to return that same value – in this case, the return value is being assigned directly to a variable called `strUserName`, whose value you are then assigning to the `Caption` of the form."

"That's right," I said. "`GetSetting` retrieves and returns the value we saved in the Registry using `SaveSetting`."

"My only question," Janis said, "is this; what's that fourth parameter – `User` – used for in the `GetSetting` function?"

"`GetSetting`," I replied, "*requires* only three parameters; `Application Name`, `Section Name`, and `Key Name`. But there is an optional fourth parameter, called `Default`, which can be used to specify a default value to be returned should the combination of `Application`, `Section`, and `Key` name not be found in the Windows Registry."

"And if you don't specify a `Default` parameter?" Janis asked.

"In that case," I said, "the return value of the `GetSetting` function will be something called a zero length string – nothing really. A zero-length string could wreak havoc with your program, especially if you blindly take the return value and do something with it, like assigning it to a variable, or using it in a calculation."

"So in other words," Janis said, "by specifying a **Default** parameter – **User** – here in the **Load** event procedure of the form, we guard against the we are looking for not existing in the Registry. If that combination *isn't* found, the default value is used, and the form's caption would read, Good day, User."

"That's right," I said, "And while it's not ideal, specifying a **Default** parameter can be very useful – especially if you are executing code looking for a value in the Windows Registry that for some reason hasn't been established there yet."

"I see," she said. "That makes a lot of sense. Can you give me any pointers about *when* to save settings to the Registry?"

"Well, " I said, "I think I did a pretty good job of covering that in my introductory book, *Learn To Program With Visual Basic*. You may want to pick up a copy."

"Thanks, Professor Smiley," Janis answered. "My husband Bobby and I may do just that. Thanks again."

After we came back from our break, we were ready to tackle the final call of the day.

Question 30: How do I back up the Windows Registry?

(see also question 29)

"Hi, this is Jack from Boston," he said. "I'm afraid I may be one caller too late. A friend of mine recently told me about a Visual Basic statement called **SaveSetting** which allows you to save values in the Windows Registry so that your program can always find them? This means that you can set values there permanently, rather than having to create them in code every time the program runs. I was calling to ask you how to use this statement to save values in the Registry, and then how to get to the saved values again. But Janis beat me to it. You've done a fine job of illustrating how that's done; still, I must confess, I'm a bit nervous about updating the Windows Registry. Is there any way to back up the Registry before we start working with it?"

"Hi Jack," I said, "First of all, let me say I understand your nervousness about working with the Windows Registry – it sounds so forbidding, doesn't it? But believe me, there's really nothing to be concerned about. While your PC is running Windows, the Registry may be updated thousands of times while you run your various software applications over the course of an hour, say. Your Visual Basic programs are using the same routines to update and read the Registry as any other Windows application – so you really have little to fear. Still, backing up the Windows Registry is probably something you should do periodically anyway – regardless of whether you are updating the Registry using Visual Basic. Let me show you one technique for doing that now. I should also mention that you should consult your Windows operating manual for more information about the Registry."

"To back up the Windows Registry, " I said, "we need to run a Windows program called 'RegEdit'. You normally won't find this in a program group anywhere – to start it, you'll need to click on the Start button, click on Run, then type 'RegEdit' into the text box:"

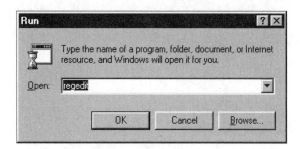

"As soon as you click the OK button," I said, "the Windows Registry Editor will appear:"

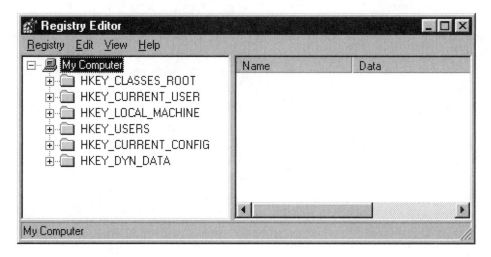

"At this point, select Registry | Export Registry File from the Registry Editor's menu bar," I said:

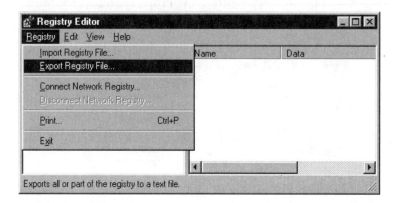

"A dialog box," I continued, "will appear asking you to specify the name and location of your Registry Backup file. For safety's sake, I would recommend saving the Registry file on a floppy. It's usually small enough to easily fit on a floppy. I also usually name my Registry Backup files according to the date on which I back it up. For instance, since today is March 6, 1999, let's name the Registry Backup 030699. The extension .reg will automatically be added to the file. Make sure that you specify All as the Export Range:"

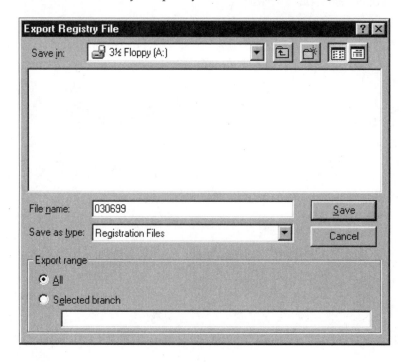

"Finally," I concluded, "just click on the Save button, and a backup of the Registry will be saved for you on your floppy disk."

"That's great," Jack said, "but suppose I need to restore the Registry from my backup. How can I do that?"

"Good thinking," I said. "If you need to restore the Registry from your backup, just open up the Registry Editor, and from the menu bar select Import Registry:"

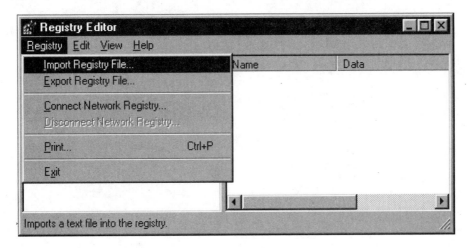

"Specify the location and name of your Registry backup file, and the Registry will be restored."

"That's cool," said Jack.

"Well, Jack, looks like that's all the time we have for today's show. Once again, I want to thank everyone for tuning in. As always, special thanks go to the people who called in with questions today. Remember, you make the show what it is. And if you called, but couldn't get through, remember, we'll be here next week, same time, same channel."

I removed my earpiece and prepared for a debrief over coffee and donuts.

Week 4

It had been a fabulous three-week run – and from all indications, things promised to get better. Unlike the previous weeks, there had been no mid-week phone call from anyone at the cable television network. My fears of an early termination had pretty much vanished, and I was able to spend the week teaching classes, writing, and enjoying the prospect of show number 4.

When I arrived at the studio for Saturday's show, the now familiar perfume of French cooking from the previous show filled my nostrils (good thing I ate lunch that day – it smelled delicious!). Still, I couldn't help but feel a little hungry as I tested my equipment setup.

"Thirty seconds," called out Linda, before continuing, "Oh, John? We don't need to give priority to out of town callers today - every call in the queue is from out of town!"

I readied myself as she silently counted me down with her hand signals.

"Welcome to Professor Smiley's Visual Basic Programming Workshop," I began. "Each week at this same time, for the next seven weeks, I'll be answering your questions about Visual Basic programming. Of course, I'll need your help, since without your phone calls, there will be no show! Our toll free number is being flashed on your television screen at this very moment. And if you would like me to examine your code on the air, you can e-mail that to me now at `johnsmiley@johnsmiley.com`. I've received some great e-mail about the show this week, and I appreciate your comments."

Linda signaled me that we were ready for our first caller.

"And now," I said, "for our first phone call of the day. Go ahead."

Question 31: What's the difference between a list box and a drop-down list box?

"Hi, my name is Karen, and I'm from New Haven, Connecticut," she said. "I've been developing a Visual Basic program that displays a list of musical artists in a list box. A friend of mine suggested that I use a drop-down list box control instead. She told me that it would provide a much more polished look to my program – but I don't see the drop-down list box control in my toolbox. Can you tell me where it is?"

"Hi Karen," I said, "thanks for calling. Actually, there is no specific drop-down list box control. The control you really want to use is the **combo box** control – I'm sure that's what your friend was talking about. The combo box control contains a `Style` property that has three possible values – one of which is the drop-down list box. Let me show you the difference between the list box control and the combo box control."

I started a new Visual Basic project and created a command button and a list box control on the form, before keying the following code into the command button's `Click` event procedure. This could would load up the list box items:

```
Private Sub Command1_Click()

List1.AddItem "Artie Shaw"
List1.Additem "Benny Goodman"
List1.AddItem "Billie Holiday"
List1.AddItem "Charlie Parker"
List1.AddItem "Dizzy Gillespie"
List1.Additem "Duke Ellington"
List1.AddItem "Ella Fitzgerald"
List1.AddItem "Fats Waller"
List1.AddItem "Louis Armstrong"
List1.AddItem "Louis Jordan"

End Sub
```

I then ran the program and clicked on the command button, and the following screenshot was displayed to the viewing audience:

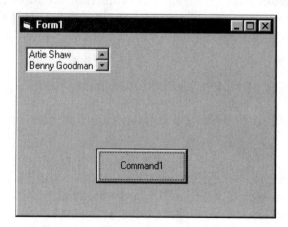

"This is what I call the plain old vanilla list box look," I said. "Perhaps this was the reason that your friend suggested using a drop-down list box instead. One of the problems with the list box control is what I call the 'real estate issue'. That is, how large should you size the list box control? If it's too 'short', the user has to scroll too often to see the entire list. If it's too tall, then the list box consumes too much of your form, and can make your form look cramped and crowded. If you are going to use a list box control, my rule of thumb is to size the list box control large enough to accommodate about five entries. Like this:"

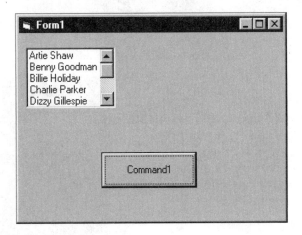

"Now," I said, "I think that's better, and gives the user a nice interface to work with. But sometimes your form *will* be cramped and crowded – you just can't help it if you have a lot of information to display. In that case, allocating this much space for your list box may be a problem. This is where the combo box and its drop-down list box style can come in handy. Let me show you."

I then stopped the program, removed the list box control, and placed a combo box control on the form instead:

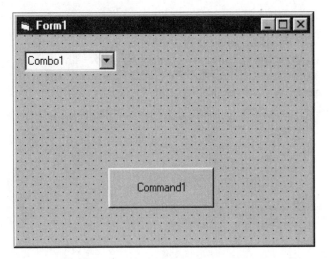

"Notice, Karen," I said, "that when I first put the combo box on the form in design mode, I can size the *width* of the control, but I can't change its height. That's because the default `Style` property of the combo box is something called 'drop-down combo', which looks like this when I run the program:"

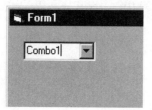

"Don't forget, we also need to change the code to refer to `Combo1` instead of `List1`," I reminded her, and did so myself. I also blanked out the `Text` property of the combo box. I ran the program, and clicked on the command button to load the items into the combo box:

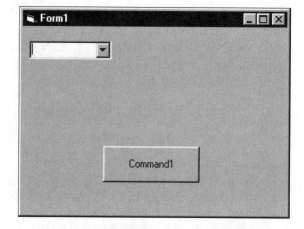

"Where are the items in the list box...I mean, the combo box?" Karen asked.

"That's what you get with the drop-down combo style of the combo box control," I said. "The user won't see the items in the combo box until they actually *click* on the drop-down arrow. Like this:"

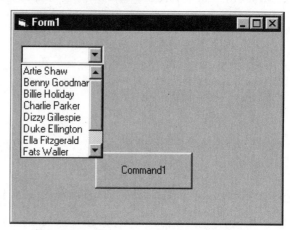

128

"OK," Karen said, "I see what you mean by real estate now. The combo box is good because it takes up less space on the form, and the user can click on the drop-down arrow to open up what amounts to a large list box. That's useful. But what's that empty text box at the top of the combo box control?"

"Good observation," I said. "The combo box does have what's essentially just a text box at the top. The theory with a combo box control is that if the user doesn't see an item in the list that they want to select, they can type an entry of their own into the 'text box' portion of the combo box."

"So the user can actually type something into that text box?" she asked. "And it doesn't have to appear already in the list?"

"That's right," I answered. "With *this* style of combo box. But there are two other styles – and you'll see that their behavior is different. Watch this."

I typed 'Lester Young' into the text box portion of the combo box:

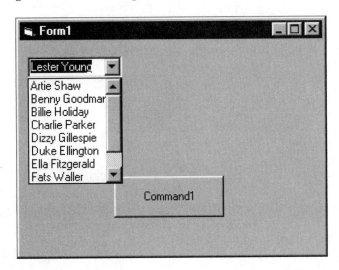

"Even though 'Lester Young' is not in the list portion of the combo box," I said, "I'm still able to type it into the text box portion. This can come in quite handy when the programmer wants to present a list of possibilities to the user – but recognizes that they may have a valid entry of their own that they need to communicate to the program. Rather than having a finite list, this is a little bit more open ended."

"Wow," Karen said, "I can see that this is very powerful. But it must be a pain to program – I mean, programming just for possibilities you *are* expecting can be hard enough!"

"You're right," I said. "Using the combo box, and programming for the possibilities of the user's entries, does pose a much greater programming challenge than a simple list box.

Obviously, if you place a combo box on a form, and then allow the user to make an entry of their own into it, you need to write code to deal with that."

"I would imagine that can be complicated," Karen said. "You said that there are three styles of combo boxes – will one of them allow me to display a drop-down list box, without having to worry about the user being able to type an entry of their own?"

"Yes there is," I replied, "but I must warn you, you're not going to be 100 percent happy with it. Let me show you..."

I brought up the Properties window for the combo box, and changed the `Style` property from 0-Dropdown Combo to 2-Dropdown List:

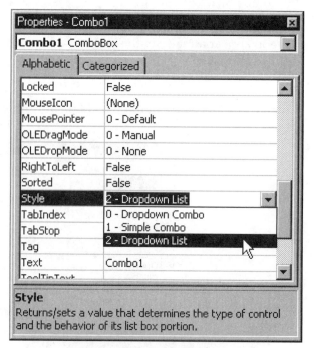

I ran the program, and clicked on the command button to load the items into the combo box:

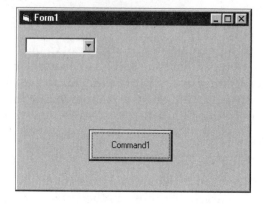

"The empty text box is still there," Karen said.

"Yes, it's there," I said, "which is why I warned you that you wouldn't be 100 percent pleased; however, the user *can't* make an entry in the text box portion of the combo box that doesn't appear in the list. As before, the user is presented with an empty 'text box' – until they click on the drop-down arrow."

"If the user can't make an entry in the text box portion unless that choice exists in the list, then why is the text box there?" Karen asked.

"Because of an interesting phenomenon," I said. "I think you'll like it. If I type the letter 'D' into the text box, the list box automatically scrolls 'down' to the first entry that begins with 'D', and it's selected in the item portion of the combo box:"

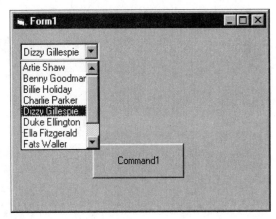

"If I type 'D' *again*, the selection will move to the next item starting with that letter," I continued.

"I do like that," Karen said. "Kind of like a search box. Yes, I like that behavior. On a related topic, I recall that a few weeks ago you discussed 'pre-selecting' an item in a list box control. Can you also pre-select an item in a combo box?"

"Yes, you can," I answered. "Take a look at this code."

```
Private Sub Command1_Click()

Combo1.AddItem "Artie Shaw"
Combo1.Additem "Benny Goodman"
Combo1.AddItem "Billie Holiday"
Combo1.AddItem "Charlie Parker"
Combo1.AddItem "Dizzy Gillespie"
Combo1.Additem "Duke Ellington"
Combo1.AddItem "Ella Fitzgerald"
Combo1.AddItem "Fats Waller"
Combo1.AddItem "Louis Armstrong"
Combo1.AddItem "Louis Jordan"
```

```
Combo1.Text = "Dizzy Gillespie"

End Sub
```

"So setting the `Text` property of the combo box will pre-select the item in the combo box?" she asked.

"That's right," I said, "just like the list box. Of course, since we're dealing with a combo box, you might expect a little different behavior. Let's run this code and see what happens:"

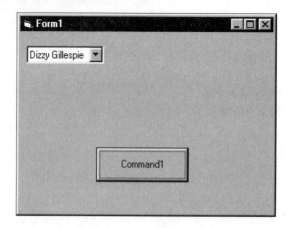

"Not only will the item be selected in the item portion of the combo box when the user clicks on the drop-down arrow," I said, "but the text box portion of the combo box will also initially contain the pre-selected item."

"I can certainly live with that," Karen said. "I think my friend was right – the combo box control will come in quite handy. I want to thank you for your explanation. I feel much more confident about the combo box. Oh, I almost forgot – you said there was a third style. What is it?"

"The third style," I replied, "is called the Simple Combo. Unlike the other two styles of combo boxes, there is no saving on real estate whatsoever with this style. You size this type of combo box at design time the way you do with a list box control – and its size at run time is identical. Because of that, there's no drop-down component with it – in fact, the only real difference between the Simple Combo and a list box control is that you can make an entry in its text box portion that doesn't exist in the list."

"I see," Karen said. "Doesn't sound like I'll be using that style of combo box much, if at all. Thanks very much. I'm going to put the combo box control to good use right away. I'll send you an email, and let you know how it works."

"Thanks for calling, Karen," I said, "and please do let me know how you're doing. And now onto our second caller."

Question 32: Can you put controls inside a frame control at run time?

(see also questions 4 & 50)

"Hi, my name is Sammy, and I'm calling from Beverly Hills," he said. "This question may be a little bit beyond the beginner's scope of your show, but I'm hoping you'll take it anyway – this is driving me crazy, and I don't think it will take much time."

"Go ahead, Sammy," I said, "let's take a shot at it."

"Well," he said. "I was experimenting with some of the code in your *Learn to Program with Visual Basic* book – specifically the section you have on control arrays. You didn't mention it in the book, but I did a little research and experimentation on my own, and I found out that you can dynamically make copies of a control at run time, provided that control already exists on your form as a control array."

"That's right, Sammy," I agreed, "it is possible to create controls dynamically at run time from a control already present on the form – provided that control has an `Index` value other than 'blank'. Are you having a problem creating controls at run time?"

"No," he replied quickly, "I've been able to dynamically create the controls fine. My problem is that on my form I have a frame, and I want to dynamically create the control within the frame. Do you see what I mean? I don't want the dynamically created control to rest on the form – but inside the *frame* on the form. Does that make sense?"

"That's really a great question, Sammy," I said. "Yes, that makes perfect sense – to me, anyway. To make sure everyone else understands this, let me just show our viewing audience how we can go about creating a control dynamically at run time."

I created a new project and placed a frame, a command button, and a check box on the form:

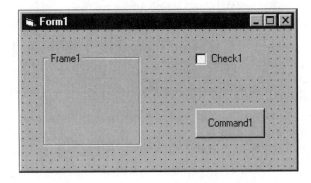

"As Sammy said," I explained, "it's possible to dynamically create a new control at run time. The ability to create new controls - or even new forms - at run time can give your program an incredibly powerful dimension. You could set up controls to alter the characteristics of a variably-sized number of entities, for example the sex, age, hair and eye colors of children in a family. You'd make the correct number of controls appear as the number of children was entered."

"The requirements are these," I continued. "First, you must already have at least one control of the type you wish to dynamically create on the form – in this case, the check box control. And secondly, that control must be a member of a control array. Those of you who have read my book will know that a control array is like a family of controls. Each member control of a control array shares the same name and the same event procedures. We designate a control as being a member of a control array by changing the `Index` property to something other than its default value of 'blank' – usually changing the `Index` property of the first member of the control array to 0, the second to 1, and so forth. When we create a new control dynamically at run time, all we need to do is use the `Load` statement, and specify an unused `Index` value or subscript for the new control – ideally, the next one in succession. Let me show you how we can turn the check box we have on the form into a control array – in this case, with just a single member."

I brought up the Properties window for the check box, and changed its `Index` property to 0:

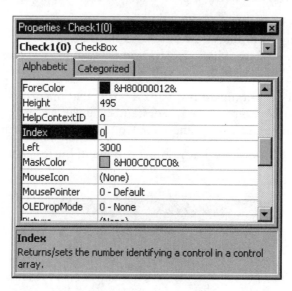

"Changing the `Index` property of the check box," I said, "tells Visual Basic that this control is a member of the control array `Check1`. Take note how the name of this check box designated at the top of the Properties window now includes a subscript of 0 within parentheses – matching the value of its `Index` property. That's one tip-off that a control is a member of a control array."

I waited a moment for this to sink in. I knew that Sammy already knew this, but I wanted all of the viewing audience to have a chance to absorb it also.

"Now," I said, "the requirements are fulfilled. We have one control on the form of the type we want to create at run time, *and* it's a member of a control array. Let's take a look at the code we need to dynamically create another check box control at run time."

I placed the following code in the command button's `Click` event procedure:

```
Private Sub Command1_Click()

Load Check1(1)

Check1(1).Visible = True
Check1(1).Top = 800
Check1(1).Left = 3000

End Sub
```

When I ran the program and clicked on the command button the following screen shot was displayed:

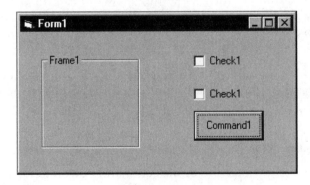

"As I indicated a minute or so ago," I said, "all we need to do to create a control at run time is to use the `Load` statement, and to specify an `Index` property for the new control that is not already in use. `Load Check1(1)` tells Visual Basic to dynamically create a new control that is a member of the `Check1` control array, and to create it with an `Index` property of 1. Pretty impressive, isn't it?"

"Professor Smiley," Sammy interjected, "can you explain why you had to set the **Visible**, **Top** and **Left** properties?"

"Great point, Sammy," I agreed. "When a new control is created dynamically at run time, it inherits all of its properties from the control on the form – in effect, it's been *cloned*. As a result, it contains the same **Height**, **Width**, **Left** and **Top** properties, along with all of the other properties except for two: the **Index** property, which we specified with the **Load** statement, and the **Visible** property – which is automatically created as **False**."

"As a result," Sammy broke in, "if you don't change the **Visible** property to **True**, you'll never see the newly created control. And if you don't change the **Left** and **Top** properties, you'll only see one check box, since the new one will be sitting on top of the old one!"

"Well said, Sammy," I agreed enthusiastically. "Great job! You can always check the **Left** and **Top** properties of the existing control to see where you should place the new one. Now let's get back to your problem – creating a control at run time, and placing it within the frame at the same time. Let me just mention why we'd want to put controls into a container control."

I explained that the frame control is one of two Visual Basic container controls, the other one being the **PictureBox** control.

"Many beginner programmers," I said, "believe that the frame control is just a border to be placed around other controls. But a frame control is much more than this. Controls placed within a container control (such as a frame or a picture box) take on some of the characteristics of their container. For instance, if we make a frame control invisible by setting its **Visible** property to **False**, every control contained within the frame becomes invisible. If we *disable* a frame control by setting its **Enabled** property to **False**, every control contained by the frame becomes disabled. In short, the frame control can be very useful if you need to do something to an entire group of controls – such as disabling all of them, or making them all invisible."

"That's exactly why I wanted to dynamically place the control within the frame," Sammy said. "I wanted to create a group of controls at run time, and have the ability to make them all invisible by setting the frame's **Visible** property to **False**. I can't wait to see how it's done."

"A piece of cake," I said. "Watch this."

I modified the **Click** event procedure of the command button to look like this:

```
Private Sub Command1_Click()

Load Check1(1)
```

```
Set Check1(1).Container = Frame1

Check1(1).Visible = True
Check1(1).Top = 200
Check1(1).Left = 200

End Sub
```

I ran the program and clicked on the command button, with the following result:

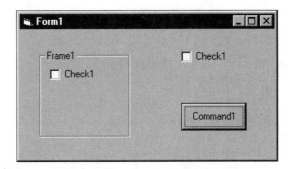

"You're kidding?" Sammy said. "Just that single line of code? That's great. I never would have thought of it."

I explained that each control on the form has a run time-only property called `Container`, which can be used to change the container of the control, just the way we did here.

"In this case," I said, "just by specifying `Frame1` as the name of the container control, in effect we 'drew' the check box within the frame control at run time. The `Left` and `Top` properties apply to the *container* the control is in, so in this case it's relative to the top left of the *frame*, not the *form*."

"Not that I'm doubting you, Professor Smiley," Sammy said, "but I remember the problems I had early on with placing controls within frames. At design time, if you double-click in the Toolbox instead of explicitly 'drawing' the control within the frame, it appears as though the control is contained within the frame, when it really isn't. I suppose that we could verify that the dynamically created control is really contained with the frame, by writing some code to make the frame invisible. If the check box is really contained within the frame, the check box should disappear also."

"Good idea, Sammy," I said. I created a second command button on the form, and entered the following code in its `Click` event procedure:

```
Private Sub Command2_Click()

Frame1.Visible = False

End Sub
```

I ran the program, and when I clicked on the first command button, the check box was dynamically created within the frame. Then I clicked on the second command button – and both the frame and the newly created check box control disappeared!

"I'm convinced," Sammy said. "Thanks so much for this – it'll come in very handy!"

"Glad I could be of help, Sammy," I said. "And thank you for calling."

Question 33: How do you put an '&' in a caption?

(see also question 24)

"Hi," the voice on the other end of the line said, "I'm Leonard from Cincinnati, Ohio. I have a question that is similar to one you had last week about specifying the Caption of a Label control with quotation marks in it. In my case, I want to display an *ampersand* (&) as the Caption for a command button. Of course, since the ampersand is used to designate the hot key or access key for a command button, trying to do this is causing me a lot of grief."

"This isn't a big problem technically, Leonard," I said. "You just need to know the right technique. Before I show you how to do this, let's illustrate the problem - as is my custom - to the viewers at home."

I started up a new project, with one form that contained two command buttons. In the Properties window, I assigned the value '&A' to the Caption of the first command button:

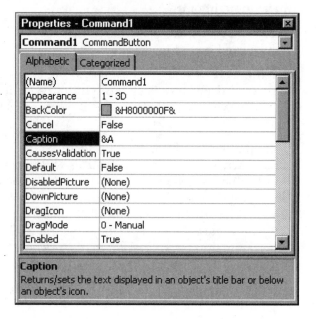

and the value '&B' to the `Caption` of the second command button.

"Nothing fancy yet," I said. "Let's observe the effect that the ampersand has on the behavior of the program."

When I ran the program, instead of clicking on any of the command buttons, I pressed and held the *Alt* key, and at the same time pressed the letter 'B'.

"There are two things to notice here," I said. "First, the first letter of the captions of each of the command button is underlined – this is to alert the user that these letters are serving as **access** or **hot keys** for those buttons. In other words, pressing the *Alt* key plus the underlined letter is the same as clicking on the command button with the mouse. Secondly, notice that as soon as I press the access key for the second command button, *Alt+B* in this case, that button immediately receives the focus... "

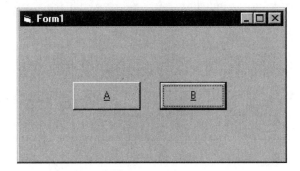

"Focus is indicated by the presence of the dotted line around the face of the button. Now," I continued, "back to your problem, Leonard: how to specify a caption for a command button that contains the ampersand character. As soon as we type the ampersand character in Visual Basic, the character immediately following it becomes the access key. The access key can be the first letter in the caption, it can be the last letter in the caption, or it can be any letter in between. The thing that tips Visual Basic to the access key is the ampersand. Now suppose we wanted to specify a `Caption` for a command button that reads 'Bits & Pieces'?"

"This is where I got completely lost," Leonard said. "I tried all kinds of combinations, but never got it to work."

"I bet the first thing you tried, Leonard, was the obvious thing," I said. "Like this."

I then changed the `Caption` property of the first command button to 'Bits & Pieces', and ran the program.

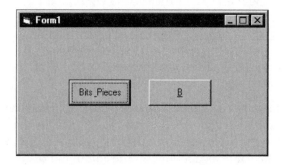

"See the problem?" I said to Leonard and the viewing audience. "Instead of the ampersand appearing in the caption, Visual Basic assigned an access key to the first command button that consists of the *Alt* key plus the space bar. Not exactly what we wanted to do."

"So what's the trick?" Leonard asked.

"This is similar to the technique we used to specify a quotation mark in a `Caption` property several weeks ago," I said. "We just use *two* ampersands."

"Two ampersands?" Leonard said. "All I needed to do was repeat the ampersand to get one to appear in the caption?"

"That's all," I said, as I changed the `Caption` property of the first command button to 'Bits && Pieces':

I ran the program, and the following screen shot appeared:

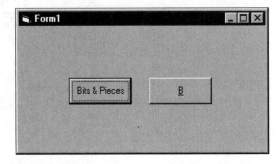

"That does the trick," I heard Leonard say. "Thanks very much! I really appreciate it."

"Thanks for your call, Leonard," I said, "glad I could help. And now, time for a commercial announcement."

After a short break, we picked up with caller number four.

Question 34: Is there a way to place an icon on a menu bar?

"Hi, my name is Richard, and I'm from Yorba Linda, California," he said. " I've been working with Visual Basic for a while now, and this question has been nagging at me for some time. I've asked a number of people about it, received conflicting advice, and I would be very appreciative if you could give me a definite yes or no."

"I'll try, Richard, what's your question?" I said.

"Is there any way to place an icon on a menu item?" he said. "The same way, for instance, that you see an icon next to the Open Project or Save Project menu items on the Visual Basic File menu?"

"That's an interesting question, Richard," I said. "I am usually asked that question in my intermediate to advanced Visual Basic classes after my students have had an opportunity to work with Visual Basic menus for a while. I don't mean to intentionally keep you in suspense, but before I give you the answer to your question, let me just demonstrate for the viewers at home exactly what you want to do in Visual Basic. Let's take a look at the Visual Basic File menu:"

"Look at the icons that you see next to Open Project, Save Project, Print and Print Setup options," I said. "Those are the types of icons you would like to be able to specify using the Visual Basic editor – is that right, Richard?" I asked, as I pointed to the Open Project menu item using my mouse pointer.

"That's right," he answered, "for the life of me, I can't figure out how to associate an icon with a menu item in the Visual Basic menu editor. The first thing I looked for was an `Icon` property, then a `Picture` property, but it seems like there's simply no way to do it. Can it be done?"

"Unfortunately, the answer is 'no'," I said. "There is no way to assign an icon to a menu item using the Visual Basic menu editor."

"How do other Windows programs provide this functionality, then?" Richard asked. "You would think if any Windows program had menu icons, surely the same functionality would exist in Visual Basic?"

"Those programs are written in other languages – most likely C++," I answered. "But all is not lost. I only said that the Visual Basic *menu editor* does not provide this functionality."

"Well," Richard said, "if you can't do this using the Visual Basic Menu Editor, how can it be done?"

"If you're willing to use the Windows API," I said, "then there's a good chance you can do this."

"API," Richard said cautiously. "What's that?"

"API," I replied, "stands for **Application Programming Interface**. The Windows API is really just a collection of the Procedures and Functions available in Dynamic Link Libraries, or DLLs, that comprise the Windows Operating System. It's possible to get at and execute those procedures and functions using Visual Basic."

"And that's the Windows API," Richard said. "These functions and procedures?"

"That's right," I said. "By gaining access to the Windows API through Visual Basic, you can tap into functionality that is not an innate part of Visual Basic itself."

"Such as placing an icon on a menu?" Richard asked.

"Exactly," I said. "Whenever there's something that can't be done through Visual Basic itself, almost certainly the functionality exists by executing a function or procedure through the Windows API."

"Sounds great," Richard said. "Can you tell me how to do this?"

"Unfortunately, Richard," I continued, "it's not quite as easy as that. It's relatively easy to call the procedures and functions in the Windows API – almost as easily as you invoke Visual Basic methods and functions. However, it can be pretty complex trying to find out which function and procedure to call, the parameters to pass to them, and what may or may not be passed back as a return value can be pretty complex. Worse yet, there's no documentation, unless you pick up something called a Software Developer's Kit from Microsoft, or invest in a good book describing the Windows API. In short, the use of the Windows API is definitely an advanced topic, and not one that I can go into in any depth in this forum. I teach the Visual Basic API interface as part of my university Advanced Visual Basic courses – perhaps one of your local colleges offers something similar? And as I mentioned, you can always pick up a book on the Windows API. I highly recommend Daniel Appleman's *Visual Basic Programmers Guide to the Win32 API*. That book contains a list of just about every API procedure and function call – in fact, I bet if I had it here with me today, we would find one that allows us to specify an icon for a menu item."

"Well, you gave me my answer; I appreciate that," Richard said.

"Sorry I couldn't do more for you, Richard." I said, "Just remember, although Visual Basic is a great Windows Development tool, it's been estimated that Visual Basic probably incorporates only about 60% of the functionality found in the Windows API. Just about everything you would ever want to do in the Windows world can be done through Visual Basic itself – but as you advance in your programming career, you may find that you need to turn to the API. A good book to introduce you to how to use the API is Jason Bock's *Win32 API Tutorial*, but since the API is such an advanced topic, I must warn you that book does assume a good knowledge of VB."

"Thanks, Professor Smiley," Richard said.

"Thanks for calling, Richard," I said, as I prepared to take call number five.

Question 35: How can I get the Minimize and Maximize buttons to disappear?

"Hi, my name is Bo, and I'm from Falls Church, Virginia," he said. "I just started working with Visual Basic about a week ago, and I'm a little confused. I want to prevent the user of my program from Minimizing or Maximizing the program's form. A friend of mine told me that if I set the `MinButton` or `MaxButton` properties to `False`, that the buttons would disappear – but I did that, and the buttons are still there."

"Hi, Bo, thanks for calling," I said. "That's peculiar; those buttons should disappear if you set the `MinButton` or `MaxButton` properties of a form to `False`. Let me show you."

I created a new project and changed the `MinButton` and `MaxButton` properties of the form to `False`:

I then ran the program, and both the Minimize and Maximize buttons were absent:

"Do you see what I mean, Bo?" I asked, as I displayed the form for the viewers at home.

There were a few seconds of silence.

"I'm half embarrassed to say this," Bo said, "but I realize now what the problem is. I expected the buttons to disappear while I was working in Design mode. I see now that they don't disappear until you run the program. I was so hung up on the fact that when I changed the properties the buttons were still there, I never ran the program, and got the chance to see that they weren't there!"

"Don't feel embarrassed about that, Bo," I said. "That's quite understandable, and you've raised an excellent point. There are so many of the properties of the form and controls that take effect immediately in design mode that we almost take for granted that *every* property we change in the Properties window will have an immediate effect in the design time environment. For instance, `Caption`, `Top`, `Left`, `Height`, and `Width` all have an immediate effect in design mode. But `MinButton` and `MaxButton`, along with some other properties such as `Visible`, `ControlBox` and `BorderStyle` *don't* have immediate effects in design mode – rather, you have to wait until run time to see their impact. Let me stop the program now, so that I can show our viewing audience that the Minimize and Maximize buttons are still visible in design mode – while *invisible* at run time."

I stopped the program, and the following screen shot was displayed:

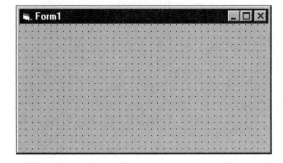

"As you can see," I said, "both the Minimize and Maximize buttons are there in design mode – despite the fact that both the `Minbutton` and `MaxButton` properties are set to `False`. Bo, you've done everyone a great service by asking this question. I'm sure you're not the only one who was confused by this. Thanks for your call."

"Thanks, Professor Smiley," Bo said. "Give me a few weeks, I'm sure I'll have another!"

"Fine. Let's take our next caller," I said.

Question 36: Why isn't there an Undo function when you delete a control?

"Hi," he said, "this is James from Marion, Indiana. I accidentally deleted a control from my form. I thought I remembered reading somewhere that Visual Basic had an 'Undo' command. I checked on-line help, and it said that I should find it under the Edit menu – but after deleting the control, and looking under the Edit menu, I found no 'Undo' menu item to enable me to restore the control. Do you have any idea what I may be doing wrong?"

"Hi, James," I said, "thanks for calling. Yes, I have a pretty good idea, only because I think I've done the same thing myself. First, let me demonstrate to our home viewers exactly what we're talking about here."

Creating a new Visual Basic project containing a single command button, I selected the command button in design view and pressed the *Delete* key.

"The command button has been deleted," I said. "Now let's take a look at the Edit menu:"

"Darn," James said, "Undo Delete is there. I wonder why it doesn't show up for me."

I then selected Undo Delete from the Edit menu, and the command button was restored.

"The important thing to note here," I said, "is that if you *do* delete a control by accident, Visual Basic will restore the control – all you need to do is select Edit | Undo Delete from the Visual Basic menu bar, or press the *Ctrl+Z* combination."

"But what happened in my case?" James said. "Why do you think the Undo Delete option was not available?"

"I have a suspicion," I said. " Were you, by any chance, writing code in the Code window when you realized that you had deleted the control?"

"Yes I was," James said, "how ever did you know that?"

"When I first started using Visual Basic," I said, "I did the same thing. I accidentally deleted a control, but I didn't realize it until I was in the middle of writing code that referenced the deleted control. At that point, I immediately did what you did – selected the Edit menu, because I was certain there was an Undo Delete option, but the option wasn't available. I finally realized the reason I didn't see it was because I was 'in' the Code window. You see, when the Code window is open, Visual Basic keeps track of any text deletions that you make in the Code window – at that point, it's no longer concerned with providing you a means to undelete a control."

"I see what you mean," James said. "That's exactly what happened. I started writing some code, and then I realized that I had lost the control – and tried to find the Undo Delete on the Edit menu."

"For the heck of it," I said. "Let's see if we can duplicate that here."

Once again I deleted the command button. This time, however, instead of immediately selecting Edit | Undo Delete from the Visual Basic Menu bar, I double clicked on the form to open up the Code window, then selected the Edit menu from the Menu bar:

"Just as we thought," James said. "There is no Undo Delete option here. I bet if I had just closed the Code window, the Undo Delete option would have been on the Edit menu."

"I reckon you're right," I replied, and did exactly that – closed the Code window. Sure enough, when I closed the Code window, the Undo Delete option appeared. I selected it, and the command button was restored.

"Thanks," James said. "I must say, you really have a feel for the types of mistakes and questions that beginners make and have. Maybe you should consider writing another book!"

"Thanks, James," I replied, "that comes from teaching many, many Visual Basic courses."

I saw Linda signaling for a commercial break.

"How's it going at your end?" I asked Linda during the commercial break.

"Well, we have enough callers, if that's what you mean," she said.

"That's great, but I really meant how are you doing in general? Do you enjoy being a producer?"

"Yes, I do, as a matter of fact. It's a great feeling when you know that something you're working on is appreciated by so many people."

"I know what you mean," I said. "Just getting so many nice comments from readers of my book really brightens my day. But do you never feel like you want to do something from the front of the camera?" I asked her.

"Well, when I was a little girl I swore I'd become a movie star, but we all do that, right? I'd get too nervous. I'm much happier behind the scenes, making sure it all happens smoothly. Like telling you when you have one minute left."

"Yes, I see what you mean. You're an organized person, all right..." I began, but broke off, somewhat confused, because Linda was waving her hands at me. "I'm sorry?" I said, puzzled.

"John, that was a *hint*. You really *do* have one minute left. Or should I say forty seconds? Get up there. We can talk when you're not on air, OK?"

"Oops. OK, thanks, Linda," I said, and took my place in front of the camera. Linda counted me in, and we resumed with the show's seventh caller.

Question 37: Clicking the Cancel button makes my form turn black. Why?

(see also question 27)

"Hi," the voice on the other end said, "this is Franklin, and I'm from Hyde Park, New York. I'm enjoying your show greatly, and I hope you can help me out here. I've written some code – I'm quite proud of it – that enables the user of my program to change the color of the form by using the Common Dialog control. Most of the time it works fine – however, on occasion, when the user clicks on the Cancel button of the Common Dialog control, the form turns black. Do you have any idea why?"

"Thanks for calling, Franklin. Yes, I think I do know what the problem is," I said, as I set up a project with a command button and a Common Dialog control.

> If you've never used the Common Dialog control, I should point out that it's not part of the standard Toolbox – you'll have to add it yourself. To do this, select **Project | Components...** and scroll down in the resulting dialog box until you see **Microsoft Common Dialog Control 6.0.** Make sure the checkbox is selected and click on **OK.**

"I would bet that you have code much like this in your project. I'll place some code in the `Click` event procedure of the command button:"

```
Private Sub Command1_Click()

CommonDialog1.ShowColor
Form1.BackColor = CommonDialog1.Color

End Sub
```

Next, I ran the program and clicked on the command button. The Color box of the Common Dialog control appeared. I made a selection of Cyan and pressed the OK key. The form's color immediately changed to Cyan.

"Yes, that code is just like mine," Franklin said. "I use the `ShowColor` method of the Common Dialog control to display the Color Dialog box. When the user makes their selection, I then take the value in the `Color` property of the Common Dialog control, and set the form's `BackColor` property to that value. This works fine, except..."

"Except when the user presses the Cancel button of the Common Dialog control," I said, finishing the sentence for him.

"That's right," he said. "That's when the form turns black – but it doesn't happen *every* time the user presses the Cancel button."

"Let me guess," I said. "I bet it only happens the first time the Common Dialog control is shown – and only then if the user presses the Cancel button."

"I think you're right," Franklin said. "The first time the Common Dialog control is shown, and only if the user then presses the Cancel button. I have a feeling I called the right person about this question – I think you've seen this before."

"There isn't much about Visual Basic that I haven't seen," I replied. "Actually, this is a pretty common beginner error – and like all beginner errors, we all make them when we're starting out. Let me show you what's happening here, Franklin. The problem is this; if the user presses the Cancel button on the Common Dialog control..."

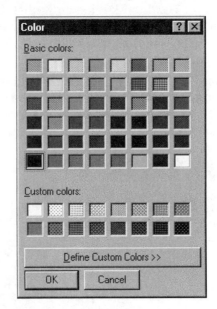

"...the `Color` property value of the Common Dialog control is never changed – it remains whatever it was. If it so happens that the first time the Common Dialog control is displayed in your program, the user presses the Cancel key, your next line of code assigns the value of the `Color` property of the Common Dialog control to the Form's `BackColor` property. Now the problem is that the default value for the `Color` property of the Common Dialog control is 0 – which equates to black."

"Let me get this straight, then," Franklin said. "When the Cancel button is pressed, the `Color` property of the Common Dialog control remains as is...there's no change."

"That's right," I said.

"So the first time I present the Color dialog box to the user," he continued, "the `Color` property is by default 0."

"Again, that's right," I agreed.

I stopped the program, then re-ran it in order to re-initialize all of my controls. Then I clicked on the command button to display the Common Dialog control. When it was presented, I pressed the Cancel button, and the following screenshot was displayed:

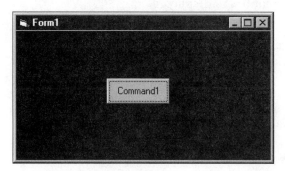

"There's that black form," Franklin said. "I think I see now. I thought that when the user pressed the Cancel button, that Visual Basic would somehow magically skip by the rest of my code. I see now that in actual fact, the next line of code *was* executed – which assigns the value 0 to the `BackColor` property of the form – making the form black."

"Correct," I said. "Remember, there's very little 'built in' to a computer program. Just about everything that happens in code is based on your explicit instructions."

"I'll remember that," Franklin said. "That explains why the form turns black, but why does this behavior only occur the first time the Color dialog box is displayed? If the user presses the Cancel button on the second or third display, the color of the form remains as it was – it doesn't turn black."

"Actually," I said, "the color only *appears* to stay the same. You're still setting the `BackColor` property of the form equal to the value already present in the `Color` property of the Common Dialog control. However, if the user presses the Cancel button after the Common Dialog control has already been displayed once, the `Color` property contains a valid color value – which just so happens to be the same as the form's `BackColor`."

"How can I get around this problem, then?" Franklin pressed. "It doesn't happen very often, but it is affecting the reputation that I'm trying to build. Should I use an 'If' statement to check the `Color` property of the Common Dialog control to see if it is equal to 0 prior to changing the `BackColor` property of the form?"

I thought for a moment.

"That would work," I said, "but suppose the user really wanted to change the `BackColor` of the form to black? Unlikely, but possible. No…there's a better way to fix this problem, and that's to have Visual Basic alert your program that the user has pressed the Cancel button."

"You're kidding!" Franklin said. "Is that all?"

"Well, that's only part of it," I said. "If you check the Properties window for the Common Dialog control, you'll see that there's a `CancelError` property. Let's set that property to `True` now, and see what happens when we run the program, and click on the Cancel button when the Common Dialog control is displayed."

I did exactly that – changed the `CancelError` property of the Common Dialog control to `True`...

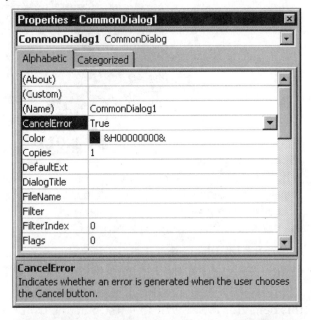

...ran the program, clicked on the command button, and then clicked on the Cancel button. The following message box came up on my screen:

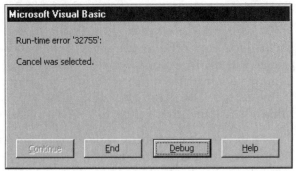

"A run time error?" Franklin asked. "Is this Visual Basic's way of telling us that the user has pressed the Cancel key? I have a sneaky suspicion that you're going to tell me that we need to incorporate error handling in the procedure."

152

"Yes, Franklin," I said, "I am going to tell you that – but don't fret over it, error handling is not all that bad. In fact, we can incorporate error handling in this procedure with just a few lines of code. Look at this…"

```
Private Sub Command1_Click()

On Error GoTo ICanHandleThis

CommonDialog1.ShowColor
Form1.BackColor = CommonDialog1.Color

Exit Sub

ICanHandleThis:

If Err.Number = 32755 Then
    Exit Sub
Else
    MsgBox "Unexpected Error " & Err.Number & "has occurred."
    Exit Sub
End If

End Sub
```

After entering this amended code into the command button's Click event, I ran the program again. Then I clicked on the command button to display the Common Dialog control, and then pressed the Cancel button. Nothing appeared to happen – the color of the form remained the same.

"Well," Franklin said, "the error handler seems to have taken care of the black screen problem. Should we make sure that we can still change the color of the form?"

"Sure thing," I said. I then clicked on the command button to display the Color dialog box, chose my favorite color of Cyan, and the form's color immediately changed to Cyan.

"All right," Franklin said, "I'm convinced. Now can you explain to me what you did in the event procedure to make this work?"

I explained to Franklin and the viewing audience that when I pressed the Cancel button on the Common Dialog control Visual Basic generated something called a 'trappable' error, because the CancelError property of the Common Dialog control was set to True.

"A trappable error," I said, "is just an error that your program has the ability to detect – *if* you have an enabled error handler. That's what the line of code that reads 'On Error Go To ICanHandleThis' means."

"I thought," Franklin said, "that the use of the `GoTo` was frowned upon."

"In all cases but one," I answered, "and this *is* that case. In Visual Basic, the only way to enable an error handler is to use the `GoTo` syntax."

"What is the significance," Franklin asked, "of the word `'ICanHandleThis'` that appears after the `GoTo` statement?"

"That's the name of a Visual Basic line label," I replied, "which needs to appear somewhere within in the procedure. You can identify Visual Basic line labels (not to be confused with a label control) because they appear on a line by themselves somewhere within the procedure, and they end with a colon."

"I see the label in this procedure," Franklin said. "It's about halfway through the procedure, right after the `Exit Sub` statement."

"That's right," I said. "The line label here designates the beginning of the error handler code. What you see after that label comprises the code we want Visual Basic to execute in the event a trappable error occurs in the procedure:"

```
ICanHandleThis:

If Err.Number = 32755 Then
    Exit Sub
Else
    MsgBox "Unexpected Error " & Err.Number & "has occurred."
    Exit Sub
End If
```

"So," Franklin answered, "the name following the `GoTo` is the name of a Visual Basic label, which appears somewhere in the procedure on a line of its own, ending with a colon. And the code following that label is the error handler code."

"That's excellent," I said. "By the way, please don't read too much into the name of the `ICanHandleThis` label – it could be anything. In fact, I could just as well have named it `Franklin`."

"OK, so far, so good," Franklin said. "You enable the error handler with the `GoTo` statement, and if some kind of trappable error is generated by the code in the procedure, Visual Basic jumps to the label designated after the `GoTo`, and starts to execute that code. Is that right?"

"That's better than right," I said, "that's perfect."

"Now in the case of the user pressing the Cancel button," Franklin continued, "it appears that we are checking for an `Error` code of '32755':

```
If Err.Number = 32755 Then
   Exit Sub
```

Franklin continued his exposition: "This is the error that was generated when we clicked on the Cancel button a while back. So `Err.Number`? Is that the number of the error generated?"

"That's right," I said, "`Err` is a special Visual Basic system object. Each time an error is generated in a Visual Basic program, an instance of the `Err` object is created. The `Err` object contains both `Number` and `Description` properties, and the `Number` property contains the number equating to the generated error. We can use a simple `If` statement to check for the error number. In this case, if the `Number` property contains a number telling us that the user has pressed the Cancel key – there's really nothing else for us to do in this procedure. At that point, we really want to bypass the rest of the code in the procedure – we certainly don't want to be setting the `BackColor` property of the form, that's for sure."

"OK," Franklin said, "if we find the number we are looking for in the `Number` property of the `Err` object, we 'bail out' by executing an `Exit Sub` – which just exits the event procedure."

"And if the `Number` property contains something unanticipated," I said, "then we display a message to the user, telling them that something unexpected has occurred – and also bail out of the procedure."

```
Else
   MsgBox "Unexpected Error " & Err.Number & "has occurred."
   Exit Sub
```

"I think I'm OK with everything going on here," Franklin said, "except for the `Exit Sub` that appears right before the error handler label. Is that there to prevent the code in the error handler from executing when no error is generated in the procedure?"

"Right you are," I said. "I think you've done this before! What would happen if we didn't have the `Exit Sub` statement right before the error handler? We would 'fall' right into the error handler code if the user made a valid color selection in the Common Dialog control and pressed the OK button immediately after we set the `BackColor` property of the form equal to the `Color` property of the Common Dialog control. I mean that the next line of code executed would be the *first* line of the error handler. Just because we didn't explicitly state it with a `GoTo` statement doesn't mean we won't enter that section of code. We don't want to execute it *unless* there's a generated error – so we bypass it through the use of the `Exit Sub`."

"I thought," Franklin said, "that error handling would be more complicated – thanks for the explanation."

"It can be," I replied. "If you want to learn a little bit more about error handling, you might want to consider picking up my *Learn to Program with Visual Basic* book. I have an entire chapter in the book devoted solely to error handling."

"I think I might just do that," Franklin said. "Thanks again."

"Thanks for calling," I said. "Let's go to our next caller."

Question 38: I'm printing to the form in the Load event but nothing is showing up. Why not?

"Hi, this is Lucille from Jamestown, New York," she said. "My question is about a problem I'm having with the **Form Load** event. I wrote some code there to display some text on the form when my program starts up – but it isn't being displayed on the form. Am I doing something wrong?"

"Hi, Lucille," I said, "You may not be doing anything wrong, as such. There are some subtleties at work in displaying text or graphics on the form at startup time that you may not be aware of. Let me give you a quick demo."

I opened up a new project and keyed the following code into the **Load** event procedure of the form:

```
Private Sub Form_Load()

Form1.Print "I love Visual Basic"

End Sub
```

"If I asked ten beginner programmers," I said, "to tell me what would happen when this program starts, and the form loads, I would wager that all ten would say that the phrase 'I love Visual Basic' would be printed on the form."

"That's what I would expect," Lucille replied.

"Let's see what happens, though," I said, running the program. Nothing was printed on the form.

"This is the time," I said, "when a beginner starts to second guess themselves. They check their code, then double check their code, perhaps even run the program in Step mode to see that the code is being executed – but still nothing."

"You're not kidding," she said, "I've spent the last two days doing exactly that. So, what's the answer? What's going wrong?"

"The problem here," I said, "is that the `Print` method of the form is being executed prior to the form actually being drawn."

"In other words, " Lucille said, "I'm basically losing the output of the `Print` method."

"That's right," I said. "In Visual Basic terms, the `Print` method is known as a `Graphics` method. And in Visual Basic, by default, Visual Basic does not 'remember' the output of `Graphics` methods when it either draws or re-draws a form."

"I understand that a form is 'drawn' when it's opened for the first time," Lucille said. "I would think that happens when the form is first loaded. But when does a form get re-drawn?"

"Good question," I said. "Believe it or not, the form is re-drawn pretty frequently in Windows. For instance, when the form is minimized, and then restored, it's re-drawn. When a form is re-sized, it's re-drawn. And when a form is covered by another window, it's also re-drawn."

"I had no idea," Lucille said. "And you say that when a form is re-drawn, any output placed on the form as a result of a `Graphics` method is lost?"

"Exactly," I answered. "That, in effect, is why 'I love Visual Basic' never showed up on the form at run time – the `Graphics` method took place before the form was initially drawn, and once the form was drawn, Visual Basic just never bothered to write the text on the form."

"This all sounds vaguely familiar," said Lucille. "Didn't you mention something about an `AutoRedraw` property in your book? Can that help this problem?"

"You have an excellent memory," I replied. "In fact, there are two ways to solve this problem. The easy way is to set the `AutoRedraw` property of the form to `True`. Setting this property to `True` tells Visual Basic to 'remember' the results of any `Graphics` method on the form, and to re-display the results of this output whenever the form is re-drawn. Let me try to illustrate that now."

I brought up the Properties window for the form, set the `AutoRedraw` property of the form to `True`...

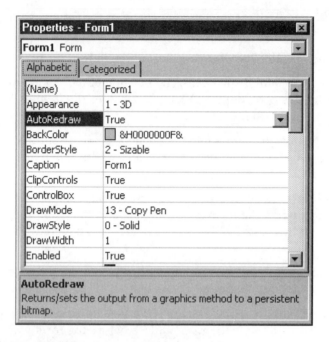

...and re-ran the program. This time, the text output to the form was displayed:

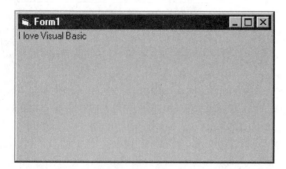

"That did the trick," Lucille observed. "And I guess that will solve my problem. Just set the `AutoRedraw` property to `True`. You said there was a second method – what would that be?"

"The other method," I said, "is to 'force' Visual Basic to display the form before you use the `Print` method in the `Load` event of the form. You can do this by explicitly coding the form's `Show` method, like this..."

```
Private Sub Form_Load()

Form1.Show
Form1.Print "I love Visual Basic"

End Sub
```

To test this method, I changed the AutoRedraw property back to its default value of False, and re-ran the program. Once again, the words 'I love Visual Basic' were printed on the form.

I explained that, implicitly, the last thing that takes place in the form's Load event is a Show method of the form.

"By explicitly coding the Show method here," I said, "we've also affected the order in which the form is drawn. Since it takes place prior to the Graphics method of the form being executed, the output of the Graphics method is not lost."

"That's interesting," Lucille said. "So both methods work – either setting the AutoRedraw property to True, or coding the Show method of the form prior to writing output in the form's Load event procedure."

"From a program performance point of view," I said, "setting the AutoRedraw property to True can slow down the speed of your program just a bit. But on the other hand, if you have a program that uses quite a bit of the Graphics methods, such as Print or Line, then you probably want to set the AutoRedraw property to True."

"I heard you mention earlier," she continued, "that the output of these Graphics methods can also be 'lost' if the user minimizes the form, or if the form is covered by another application's window."

"Yes," I said. "If you've written output to the form using any of the Graphics methods (with AutoRedraw is set to False), and if the user then either minimizes the form, or if the form is covered by another application's window (the Calculator for instance), any output on the form produced by a Graphics method will disappear. Basically, that means anything written to the form at run time will be lost. Let me illustrate what I mean."

I fired up the Windows Calculator, and used it to cover some of the phrase 'I love Visual Basic':

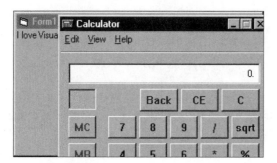

"Notice how I've covered the letters I-B-a-s-i-c," I said. "Now watch what happens when I move the Calculator off of the form - we lose some of our text:"

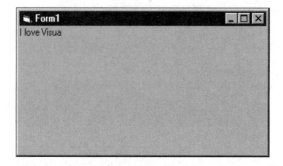

"Wow," Lucille said, "I didn't realize there was so much going on behind the scenes. And we can also prevent this by setting the `AutoRedraw` property to `True`?"

"Exactly right," I said. To demonstrate, I changed the `AutoRedraw` property to `True`, and repeated the Calculator experiment. This time around, the text on the form was intact after uncovering the letters with the Calculator.

"Thanks, Professor Smiley," Lucille said, "I think I understand more about `Graphics` methods and form's `Load` event procedure than I did before."

"You're welcome, Lucille," I said, "And now time for our next caller."

Question 39: How can I create a multi-line text box?

(see also questions 21, 22, 87, 95 & 98)

"Hi, my name is Shari, and I'm calling from Los Angeles," she said. "I have a question about the text box – specifically about permitting the user of my program to enter more than one line into a text box. Your producer said you might have covered this topic while answering another question in earlier weeks – but you'll have to forgive me, your show wasn't picked up in my area until this week."

"That's OK," I said, "Go right ahead. What's your question?"

"Well," she went on, "I'm trying to write a program for children that gathers their responses to some questions. I have a series of text boxes set up to accept their answers. My problem is this: since the children using the program are quite young, I've selected a pretty large font for the text box, and there simply isn't enough room in the text box for them to type their responses into without needing to go to another line. I know somehow I should be able to allow them to enter more than one line in the text box, but I've been unable to get it to work. Whenever I hit the *Enter* key, nothing happens. Can you help me?"

"I think so," I answered. "What you really want to do is to allow the user to 'wrap' text in a text box. Doing this is really a three-step process. First, you need to size the text box to accommodate more than a single line of text. This may seem obvious, but you would be surprised how many programmers neglect to do this. You don't want a text box sized for a single line while it's wrapping – the user of the program really needs to see several lines at one time so that they are not confused."

"I thought of that," she said. "My text boxes are sized for about three lines of text."

"That's great, Shari," I said. "I think now would be a good time to perform a demo of what we're talking about for the home viewers."

At that point, I created a new Visual Basic project with a text box. I increased the font size in the text box by clicking on the **Font** property of the text box and changing the value in the dialog box that appeared. I ran the program, and typed 'I love Visual Basic.' into the text box:

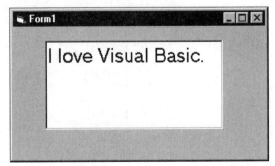

"How's this look, Shari?" I asked.

"That looks fine," she said. "Your font size is just about the same as mine. Now show us what happens when you continue typing."

"Good point," I said. "By default, a text box can hold 2,048 characters – and since by default, this text box doesn't wrap (not even if I hit the *Enter* key), if I continue typing, the existing text will scroll to the left to accommodate my typing – like this:"

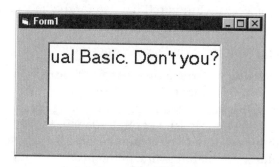

"Exactly my problem," she said. "This is confusing the children using my program. I want the children to be able to hit the *Enter* key at this point, and start typing on another line."

"No problem there," I said, "to enable that, all we need to do is set the `MultiLine` property of the text box to `True`. Like this:"

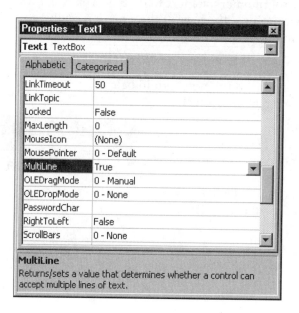

I ran the program again and typed 'I love Visual Basic.' into the text box. At this point, I hit the *Enter* key. The cursor moved to the second line in the text box, allowing me to type 'Don't you?' on the second line:

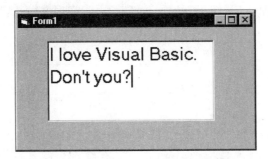

"That's it," Shari said, "that's what I want the children to be able to do!"

"That's an improvement," I said, "but we still have a little problem. As soon as I type more than 3 lines, the lines in the text box start to scroll 'up':"

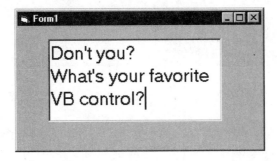

"This scrolling can give the user the impression that they've lost some text," I continued, "especially if you're working with children, or people not very familiar with the Windows environment. Even though the user can use the arrow keys to move 'up' in the text box, ordinarily in a Windows program, you would expect to see scrollbars that help you to do this."

"Earlier," Shari said, "you said that creating a 'wrappable' text box was a three step process. I have a feeling that the final step is the creation of scrollbars."

"Right you are!" I said. "First, you size the text box so that the user will be comfortable with the number of lines they can see at one time. Secondly, you set the MultiLine property of the text box to True. And thirdly, provide for scrollbars."

"And how do we do that?" Shari asked.

"We adjust the `Scrollbars` property of the text box," I answered.

I displayed the Properties window of the text box for the viewers at home:

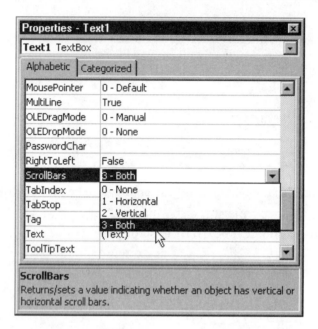

"The `Scrollbars` property of the text box," I said, "has 4 possible values. None, Horizontal, Vertical, or Both."

"I think those are pretty much self-explanatory," Shari replied. "What do you suggest in this case?"

"My personal preference is for both," I said.

I then changed the `Scrollbars` property of the text box to '3-Both', re-ran the program, and once again typed into the text box:

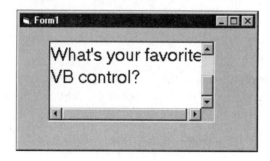

"See the difference," I said. "With scrollbars, the user can easily navigate through the text box."

"Thanks, Professor Smiley," Shari said. "You've answered my question. Let me go try this out now."

"My pleasure, Shari," I said. "Glad I could help. And now on to our final question of the day. It will have to be a quick one – we only have a few minutes left in the show."

Question 40: Can I declare more than one variable on a line?

(see also question 28)

"Hi, my name is Roy, and I'm from Winneta, Illinois," he said. "I've done some C programming, and in C, you can declare more than one variable at a time. Can that be done in Visual Basic? Or do I need to use separate Dim statements?"

"Hi Roy, welcome to the show," I said. "The short answer is 'yes', you *can* declare more than one variable at a time, and 'no', you don't need separate Dim statements to do it. However, you need to be very careful of the syntax. For instance, quite often I see code like this…"

```
Dim intA, intB, intC As Integer
```

"Judging from the prefix 'int'," I continued, "you would believe that the programmer intended to declare three Integer type variables named intA, intB, and intC, and so decided to just string their declaration like this. For those of you familiar with 'C', this is something you can do in that language. Unfortunately, it doesn't quite work out that way in Visual Basic. In Visual Basic, after this line of code is executed, what you'll wind up with is two Variant variables, named intA and intB, and one Integer type variable named intC."

"So, the first two variables, intA and intB, are assumed to be Variants by Visual Basic because they don't have an explicit data type specified?" observed Roy.

"Exactly, Roy," I replied. "Visual Basic will not apply that final 'As Integer' to all three variable names the way the C programming language does. Visual Basic evaluates each variable name separately. As a result, Visual Basic treats the statement as if you had coded it like this…"

```
Dim intA as Variant, intB as Variant, intC As Integer
```

"I would bet," Roy said, "that when you see this syntax, most times it's coming from an experienced C programmer."

"That's usually the case," I replied. "No-one else would really think of declaring the variables this way."

"So then," Roy continued, "if you want to declare three `Integer` type variables on the same line of code, there's no way to do it but the long way – by using three distinct `'As'` statements?"

"That's right, Roy," I said. "Just like this…"

```
Dim intA as Integer, intB as Integer, intC As Integer
```

"That's clear to me now, Professor Smiley," Roy said. "Thanks very much for taking my call."

"Thanks for calling, Roy," I replied, "and good luck with your programming."

Linda gave me a signal that we were out of time.

"Wow," I said, "where did the time go? I hope you all enjoyed the show today as much as I did. Thank you for tuning in, and for calling. Remember, without you, there would be no show. And if you called, but couldn't get through, remember, we'll be here next week, at the same time. I hope to see you then!"

The red light on the camera blinked off, and the show was over. I could almost feel the adrenaline draining out of my system. The show was like a big roller coaster ride - scary while I was on it, but as soon as it finished I wanted to get straight back on.

Examples

Week 5

Week five of my ten-week television trial run found me more comfortable than ever before. There had been a Monday morning courtesy call to let me know that for the fourth week in a row, ratings were good, and our commercial advertisers were very pleased; and Tim asked me once again if I had made up my mind about a longer-term contract. I promised I would let him know my decision soon.

When I arrived at the studio on Saturday for our fifth show, Linda was already there.

"Good morning," she said. "Did you hear anything about the possibility of the show going international?"

This was news to me, and I snorted with laughter, "Which countries?"

"I don't know – maybe it's just a rumor," she said. "That happens a lot in this business. Apparently, there was some talk about changing the air time from 1pm to 11am to accommodate a wider audience. Probably nothing to it."

An international audience, I thought – wouldn't that be great?

"By the way," Linda continued, "during the week, we received some phone calls from viewers complaining that by the time the show starts, the phone lines are already busy. So I won't be opening the phone lines until you make your introductory remarks."

"That's fine with me," I said, and took up my position at the now-familiar desk.

While I waited for the show to start, I found myself pondering, over and over, the possibilities of an international audience.

It was during one of these daydreams that I heard Linda's familiar voice call out:

"Ten seconds," she said, and cued me in.

"Hi, everybody," I said, "welcome to Professor Smiley's Visual Basic Programming Workshop..."

After my usual introductory remarks, I said, "Let's go right to the phone lines. Caller number one, you're on the air."

Question 41: I get syntax errors using the line continuation character. Why?

"Hi, this is Ben from Philadelphia," he said. "I've been using the Visual Basic line continuation character to split my code onto more than one line – or rather I should say I've been *trying* to use it. Most of the time I just receive a syntax error. Can you help me?"

"Hello, Ben. This is a good question – and another very common one," I answered. "Using the Visual Basic line continuation character can be confusing when you first start out. My viewers at home may be wondering what a line continuation character *is*, and why do we use it at all? Allow me to explain. In Visual Basic, the line continuation character is the underscore (_). Here's how it looks in the code window," I said, and quickly typed up a piece of 'nonsense code' that showed the line continuation character:

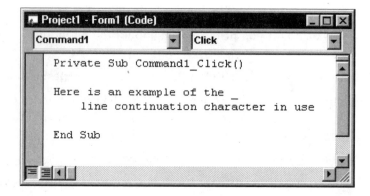

"So," I explained, "We use the underscore to take a line of code that would usually be typed on just a single line, and break it into two or more lines of code. There are two reasons to do this: first, if the line of code you are entering into the Visual Basic code window exceeds the 1,023 character Visual Basic limitation, you need to split the code onto more than one line. Secondly, splitting your code onto more than one line can make your code more readable – and I think those of you who have either read my book or watched this show for the last four weeks know how important that is to me."

"Wow," Ben said, "1,023 characters – I didn't know a line of code could be that long. I just can't conceive of writing a single line of code like that."

"I'm with you, Ben," I said. "I don't think the typical programmer is likely to write code that hits that limit. Most likely, the reason you will use the line continuation character is for readability purposes. Long lines of code are more difficult to read and debug."

"I can identify with that from my own experience," Ben said.

"Yes," I continued, "This is a very common phenomenon. Frequently, students ask me, 'What is good code?' I believe the essence of good code is that it's crisp, clean and concise, and produces a program that meets the user's expectations and requirements. Secondly, good code is readable, both by the person who originally wrote it, and the person who will come along next and need to modify it. So if I'm typing code into the Visual Basic code window and the code starts to scroll past the right margin, I consider using a line continuation character to break the code onto more than one line."

"I guess I'm just a bit confused by the rules governing the use of the line continuation character," Ben said. "Can you tell me what they are?"

"There are three rules," I said, as I displayed this list on my studio electronic whiteboard:

First, you must insert a space between the last character of the line you are continuing, and the line continuation character – which is the underscore character (_).

Second, once you type the line continuation character nothing – not even a comment character (') – may follow it.

Third, you may not place a line continuation character in the middle of a String Literal.

"Let me demonstrate these rules," I continued, "by entering a line of code into the Visual Basic code window. This line of code isn't long enough to *require* a line continuation character – but we can use it to demonstrate these three rules."

I started up a new project containing a single command button and placed the following code in its `Click` event procedure:

```
Private Sub Command1_Click()

MsgBox "I love Visual Basic"

End Sub
```

Learn to Program with Visual Basic Examples

When I ran the program and clicked on the command button, the message box was displayed:

"Look familiar?" I asked, referring to the code in the Click event procedure. "I've used this statement a number of times during the last few weeks. There's no real necessity to break this single line into two using a line continuation character, but for the purpose if illustration I will. Look at this code..."

I then modified the Click event procedure to look like this:

```
Private Sub Command1_Click()

MsgBox _
    "I love Visual Basic"

End Sub
```

I re-ran the program and clicked on the command button, and the same message box was displayed once again.

"No problem there," I said. "This code still works fine, even though we've used the Visual Basic line continuation character here to split into two. Be sure to use the underscore. Some beginners accidentally use the hyphen (-), which is the subtraction operator. Notice also the space between the last character on the line – the 'x' in MsgBox – and the underscore character. If you *don't* insert that space, as in this piece of code..."

```
Private Sub Command1_Click()

MsgBox_
    "I love Visual Basic"

End Sub
```

"...you'll receive an error when you run the program and click the command button:"

"See what I mean?" I said. "Without the space between the last character of code and the line continuation character, we really confuse Visual Basic."

"Does it matter where you start the next line of code?" Ben asked. "I noticed that you indented it – do you need to do that?"

"No, it's not essential," I replied. "Personally, I indent code to make it more readable. Let's get back to those three rules for the line continuation character. We just saw number 1 in action – the space between the last character on the line and the line continuation character. What about the second rule? Once you type the line continuation character on the line nothing – not even a Visual Basic comment – can follow it on that line. Let's see this in action by modifying our code to include a comment after the line continuation character:"

I changed the code in the command button's `Click` event procedure to look like this:

```
Private Sub Command1_Click()

MsgBox _                'Line Continuation Character
"I love Visual Basic"

End Sub
```

This time when I ran the program and clicked on the command button:

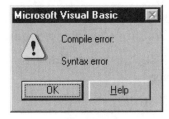

"Again," I said, "we managed to confuse Visual Basic by not following the rules. Remember, once you type the line continuation character, nothing else can follow it."

"I guess," Ben said, "that the problem I'm having must be with rule number three – but that's the one that I just don't understand. String literal? Can you illustrate that for me?"

"Sure," I said. "Let's change the code in the `Click` event procedure one more time."

This time, I modified the code to look like this:

```
Private Sub Command1_Click()

MsgBox "I love _
    Visual Basic"

End Sub
```

"This is a violation of rule number three," I said, "because we used a line continuation character to 'break up' the string literal 'I love Visual Basic'."

"Oh," Ben said, "*that's* what a string literal is – I think I've also heard it called a 'quoted string'."

"That's right, Ben," I said. "Regardless of what we call it, string literal or quoted string, we can't place a line continuation character in between two quotation marks. Again, we just wind up confusing Visual Basic."

I ran the program, clicked the command button, and the following screen shot was displayed:

"That's the error message I received," Ben said, "because that's the mistake I made. I guess I just didn't realize that Visual Basic wouldn't be able to handle something like this."

"Don't worry, Ben," I assured him, "I see this particular error all the time when beginners discover the line continuation character."

"Thanks for your help," Ben said. "That clears that up."

We moved on to our second call.

Question 42: What's the difference between the two concatenation operators (+ and &)?

"Hi, my name is Joe, and I live in Hollywood, Florida," our second caller said. "I'm a little confused over the difference between the two Visual Basic concatenation operators – the plus (+) operator, and the ampersand (&) operator. What are the differences, and is it better to use one rather than the other?"

"Hi, Joe, welcome to the show," I said. "This is an interesting question. For those viewers not familiar with string concatenation operators, just let me say that they allow you to join two or more **strings** (a series of text characters, such as your name) together. For instance, take a look at this code..."

Starting a new project, I added a single command button and keyed the following code into its Click event procedure:

```
Private Sub Command1_Click()

Dim strCombined As String

strCombined = "Visual Basic has " + "2" + " Concatenation Operators"

MsgBox strCombined

End Sub
```

I ran the program and clicked on the command button:

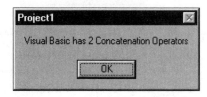

"In this code," I said, "we joined three string literals together using the string concatenation operator (+), and assigned the result to a variable called strCombined."

"String concatenation reminds me a lot of arithmetic," Joe said. "Because of the plus sign operator."

"That's a fair analogy," I said. "It's OK to imagine that you are 'adding' two strings together. I should point out to the viewers at home that my book has a chapter devoted just to String Manipulation. It's a very useful tool, and being comfortable with string concatenation certainly makes you a more well-rounded programmer. But let's get back to your original question – let's change our code to use the ampersand instead of the plus sign and see if there's an impact."

I changed the code in the `Click` event procedure to look like this:

```
Private Sub Command1_Click()

Dim strCombined As String

strCombined = "Visual Basic has " & "2" & " Concatenation Operators"

MsgBox strCombined

End Sub
```

When I re-ran the program and clicked on the command button we were presented with the same message box:

"So the plus sign and ampersand operators are the same?" Joe asked.

"Almost," I said. "If you check the Visual Basic documentation you'll see that Microsoft recommends using the ampersand instead of the plus sign for string concatenation. Let me show you why. Let's change our code slightly; instead of concatenating the *string* '2', let's concatenate the *number* 2:"

```
Private Sub Command1_Click()

Dim strCombined As String

strCombined = "Visual Basic has " + 2 + " Concatenation Operators"

MsgBox strCombined

End Sub
```

176

"Is this code all that much different than what we had before?" Joe asked. "Before, the number 2 was inside of quotation marks – now it's not. Is that significant?"

"The difference," I said, "*is* significant. When the number 2 was inside quotation marks, it was a string literal. Now that the number 2 is *not* inside quotation marks, it's a numeric value. Since we're doing *string* concatenation, you might imagine that Visual Basic could be confused if you ask it to perform string concatenation on something that is not really a string. In reality, Visual Basic becomes *extremely* confused if you use the plus sign operator to concatenate a number to a string. Let's see what happens when we run this code."

When I ran the modified program and clicked on the command button, the program 'bombed' with this error:

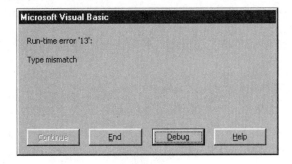

"Ouch," Joe said. "I didn't realize that would be a problem. So when you concatenate, you can only concatenate real string data?"

"That's true if you use the plus sign operator," I said, "and this is where the ampersand character comes in to its own."

I modified the `Click` event procedure to look like this...

```
Private Sub Command1_Click()

Dim strCombined As String

strCombined = "Visual Basic has " & 2 & " Concatenation Operators"

MsgBox strCombined

End Sub
```

...and re-ran the program:

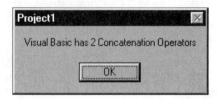

"No error message this time," Joe said. "The program didn't bomb the way it did before when we used the plus sign operator. Why not?"

"The ampersand character," I answered, "is a lot more forgiving. It actually converted the numeric value 2 to a string literal "2" behind the scenes prior to performing the concatenation. Using the ampersand operator for string concatenation allows us to join not only true string data together, but other data types as well. We can even concatenate dates – look at the following code."

I modified the code in the **Click** event once more:

```
Private Sub Command1_Click()

Dim strCombined As String

strCombined = "Today's date is " & Now

MsgBox strCombined

End Sub
```

...re-ran the program, and clicked on the command button – the following screen shot was displayed to Joe and the viewing audience:

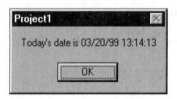

"That's impressive," Joe said. "I didn't know you could do that. You actually *joined* the System Date from your PC to a string?"

"That's right, Joe," I said. "We can use the ampersand operator to concatenate today's date and time – in the form of the Visual Basic function `Now` – to the string `"Today's date is"`. The `Now` function is an integral Visual Basic function that returns the system date as its result. By the way, if we had tried to do this using the plus sign operator, our program would have bombed."

"Are you recommending that we always use the ampersand operator for concatenation?" Joe asked.

"Not only am I recommending it," I replied, "so are Microsoft. Don't forget, that recommendation is even in Visual Basic Help."

"Thanks for your help, Professor Smiley," Joe said.

"You're quite welcome," I said. "I think we have time for one more caller before we go to our first commercial break. Go ahead, caller."

Question 43: How can I include 'Yes' and 'No' buttons in a message box?

"Hi, my name is James, and I'm from Indiana, Pennsylvania." the caller said. "I've been working on a program where I ask the user a question that has two possible answers, 'Yes' or 'No'. I saw a program in a Visual Basic magazine that displayed a message box with two buttons captioned 'Yes' and 'No'. Quite honestly, the only time I have ever used the `MsgBox` statement in a Visual Basic program is when I display a message to the user – and in those cases, I just display a message box with just a single button labeled 'OK'. I guess my question is how to display a message box that has something other than the single 'OK' button in it – and if I do that, how will my program know which button the user selected?"

"I can help you, James," I said. "The Visual Basic message box has a lot of capability. At times, `MsgBox` is used as a *statement*, and at other times its used as a *function*. When it's used as a statement we're telling VB to display a default message box with a single 'OK' button; when we use it as a function, we want VB to do something more sophisticated – we're using it to discern which of the buttons the user has clicked."

"If `MsgBox` is a function," James said, "why is it that we don't need to account for its return value when we execute it? Shouldn't we do something with its return value?"

"That's a very perceptive question, James," I replied. "`MsgBox` is a special case in Visual Basic, in that we can use it as a statement or as a function. When it's used as a *function*, then you're right – you *do* need to account for its return value."

"How do I know the difference?" James asked. "When do I use the `MsgBox` as a statement, and when do I use it as a function?"

"If you've been using it to display a message box with the single 'OK' button, then you've been using it as a statement all along," I said. "When used as a statement, the MsgBox requires just a single argument – the Prompt argument, which defines the message that will be displayed for the user in the message box. But there are four optional arguments that can be passed – Buttons, Title, Helpfile, and Context. You can read more about these optional arguments in Visual Basic Help, or you can check my *Learn to Program with Visual Basic* book for more information. The important point to note is this: if you specify any argument in addition to the required Prompt argument, then you are using the MsgBox as a function – and that means you *must* account for its return value in your code."

"Hmm. I'm still not quite clear about this," said James dubiously.

"OK," I said, "Let's take a look at some code to illustrate this. First, let's code MsgBox as a statement."

In my usual fashion, I created a clean Visual Basic project containing a single command button and typed the following code into its Click event procedure:

```
Private Sub Command1_Click()

MsgBox "I love Visual Basic"

End Sub
```

"Note that after the MsgBox statement we supply the required Prompt argument that tells Visual Basic what to show to prompt the user – I love Visual Basic," I said.

I ran the program and clicked on the command button:

"Nothing new here," I said. "Just a message box with a single button labeled 'OK'. Do you notice the default title 'Project1' on the message box's title bar? Suppose that we decided that we don't like this default title, and wanted to customize it? That's when we'd use the Title argument to specify the title we wanted to display. Take a look at this code."

This time, I changed the `Click` event's code to look like this:

```
Private Sub Command1_Click()

MsgBox "I love Visual Basic",,"James"

End Sub
```

"Why did you place those two commas side-by-side?" asked James.

"The two commas are related to the optional arguments that we can use. In this instance, we want to pass argument number three, which is the optional `Title` argument, but I didn't want to pass argument number two – the optional `Buttons` argument – just yet. That's because the default value for the `Buttons` argument is the single 'OK' button," I said. "That's fine for our purposes at this stage."

"And the two commas?" James persisted.

"Whenever you want to skip an optional argument in a *series* of arguments, you need to specify a comma in the argument string to act as a placeholder – in other words, it marks the place of the optional argument you aren't supplying. You have to supply this placeholder to satisfy Visual Basic's expectations about the number (and order) of arguments that you can pass for a particular statement or function."

"I see," James said. "The gap between the two commas is where the `Buttons` argument would go if we were to pass it."

"Exactly right," I said. "Visual Basic really helps you out here," I said. "When you key in the commas, Visual Basic highlights which argument you are currently typing:"

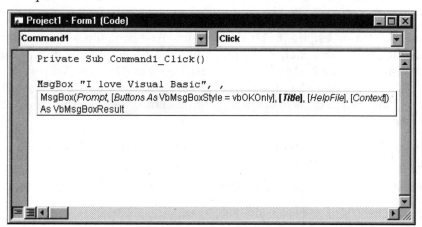

"See?" I asked, "As soon as I type the placeholder comma for the `Buttons` argument, the `Title` argument is highlighted in the tip box."

I then re-ran the program and clicked on the command button:

"Notice the difference," I said. "We now have a customized title bar – James – on our message box."

"I must confess that I half expected this code to bomb," James said.

"Why is that?" I asked.

"Well," James replied, "I thought you said that if we specified anything in addition to the required **Prompt** argument, this means that the **MsgBox** statement is being used as a function, and we have to account for the return value. But you didn't do anything with the return value in this code."

"Yes I did," I said, smiling, "but in this case, we discarded it. In other words, we ignored the return value."

"Now I'm really confused," James said. "You discarded it? I didn't know you could discard the return value. How did we tell Visual Basic that we wanted to do that?"

"I know that it seems strange to call a function (which by definition returns a value) and then to discard it," I said, " but it can be done. And sometimes there are perfectly valid reasons to do so. For instance, the return value here would just be a number corresponding to the button that was selected. Since there's only one button that *can* be selected, there really isn't any need to handle the return value. So, how do we discard the return value? Well, all we need to do is to call the function and *not* enclose the argument list within parentheses."

"So if you had placed parentheses around the argument list," James said, "then we would have had a return value to deal with."

"Absolutely right," I said. "Watch this..."

I changed the **Click** event's code once again:

```
Private Sub Command1_Click()

MsgBox ("I love Visual Basic",,"James")

End Sub
```

As soon as I finished modifying the code, even before I ran it, Visual Basic displayed this error:

"The change I made to the code – enclosing the argument list within parentheses – tells Visual Basic that I'm no longer discarding the return value. With this error message, Visual Basic is reminding us that we need to deal with the return value from this function in our code."

"And how do we deal with it?" James asked.

"Let me show you," I answered.

I modified the code again:

```
Private Sub Command1_Click()

Form1.Print MsgBox ("I love Visual Basic",,"James")

End Sub
```

"Return values must either be used in an expression (passed on to another control, method, or property)," I said, "or assigned to a variable. Here, we've used the return value in an expression by passing it as an argument to the **Print** method of the form:"

"Visual Basic 'knows' that the **MsgBox** function will return a value, and this syntax passes that value – in this case, the value of the button that's pressed in the message box – to the **Print** method of the form."

"There won't be much excitement when we run this code," I continued. "Since we're displaying a message box with just a single button (the OK button) the return value will be '1'."

I re-ran the program, and clicked on the command button. As before, a message box was displayed with a prompt reading 'I love Visual Basic'. When I clicked on the OK button of the message box, the following screenshot popped into view:

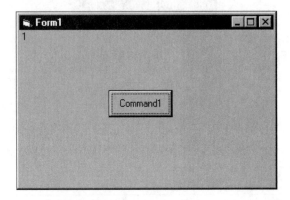

"The number 1 in the upper left-hand corner of the form," I said, "is the return value of the **MsgBox** function. There are actually seven possible return values for the **MsgBox** function, depending which button the user selects. A return value of '1' means that the user pressed the OK button."

"What are the other return values, then?" James asked.

I displayed a list on the studio's electronic whiteboard.

MsgBox Return Values:

Value	Description	VB Constant
1	OK	vbOK
2	Cancel	vbCancel
3	Abort	vbAbort
4	Retry	vbRetry
5	Ignore	vbIgnore
6	Yes	vbYes
7	No	vbNo

"Now," I said, "Armed with this knowledge, let's get back to your original question, James. How to display a message box with two buttons, 'Yes' and 'No', and how to detect which of the two buttons the user has clicked. Take a look at the following code."

I modified the code in the `Click` event procedure again:

```
Private Sub Command1_Click()

Dim intRetVal As Integer

intRetVal = MsgBox("Do you love Visual Basic?", vbYesNo, "James")

    If intRetVal = vbYes Then
       Form1.Print "You love VB - Great!!!"

    ElseIf intRetVal = vbNo Then
       Form1.Print "Oh dear - I'm sorry to hear that..."

    End If

End Sub
```

I then ran the program, and clicked on the command button. The new message box appeared:

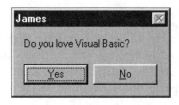

"There's the message box with two buttons that you're aiming for," I said. "Now watch what happens when I click on the 'Yes' button:"

Next, I clicked on the command button again, and this time clicked on the 'No' button:

"I think I see what's going on here," James said. "In this example, you passed the **MsgBox** function the optional **Buttons** argument. I presume that **vbYesNo** is another of Visual Basic's intrinsic constants?"

"That's right, James," I replied. "In our line of code..."

```
intRetVal = MsgBox("Do you love Visual Basic?", vbYesNo, "James")
```

"...the **vbYesNo** argument tells Visual Basic to display both 'Yes' and 'No' buttons in the message box. Using this argument implies that the **MsgBox** function will return one of two values; either **VbYes** – i.e. a numerical return value of '6' (when the 'Yes' button is clicked); or **VbNo** (a numerical return value of '7', when the user clicks the 'No' button)."

"What happens when we run the code, then?" interjected James.

"Well," I continued, "we take the return value from the **MsgBox** function and assign it to an integer type variable, **intRetVal**. Using an **If** statement, we then evaluate the value of that variable to determine what to print on the form. If the return value was equal to the value of the intrinsic constant **vbYes** we print one statement:"

```
If intRetVal = vbYes Then

    Form1.Print "You love VB - Great!!!"
```

"If the return value is equal to the value of the intrinsic constant **vbNo**, we print the alternative response:"

```
ElseIf intRetVal = vbNo Then

    Form1.Print "Oh dear - I'm sorry to hear that..."
```

"Well," said James, "that's a lot clearer to me now. I want to thank you for your help."

"My pleasure, James," I said, "thanks for calling. And now, it's time for a commercial break. We'll be back in a few minutes."

After the commercial break, we picked up with caller number four.

Question 44: How do I display a context-sensitive or pop-up menu?

(see also question 54)

"Hi, my name is Jacqueline," the caller said, "I'm from New York City. Could you take a few minutes to show me how to generate a context-sensitive menu? I think Visual Basic calls them pop-up menus."

"Sure, Jacqueline," I said, "I'd be glad to do that for you. And you're right – Visual Basic does call context-sensitive menus pop-up menus – they're also known as shortcut menus, and are typically displayed in Windows when the user clicks on the right mouse button. Context-sensitive menus display different menu items depending upon *where* the right mouse button is clicked on the form – so the user gets a menu that relates to the control or area of the form that the mouse pointer is pointed at when they right-click. In Visual Basic, the important thing to remember is that the pop-up menu structure must have been created using the Visual Basic Menu Editor – are you familiar with that, Jacqueline?"

"Yes, I am," she confirmed. "I should say that I've had no problem creating standard Visual Basic menus. It's only the context-sensitive or pop-up menu that I have no experience with."

"OK," I continued. "First, let me provide some more background. In Visual Basic, a pop-up menu is a menu that 'pops up' (naturally!) or floats somewhere over the form – this in contrast to the more conventional menu displayed on a menu bar. To display a pop-up menu in Visual Basic, the programmer needs to use the `PopUpMenu` method and, by default, the pop-up menu will be displayed exactly where the user clicked the right mouse button."

"So is Visual Basic pop-up menu the same as a context-sensitive menu?" Jacqueline asked.

"Well," I said, "a context-sensitive menu is one whose menu items vary according to the location on the form where the right mouse is clicked. For instance, if the mouse is right-clicked over an open area of the form, a specific menu is displayed. Right-click over a text box control, and another, different menu is displayed. To make a pop-up menu context-sensitive, we have to do a little more work."

"So how do we begin?" Jacqueline queried.

"Let's start out by creating a simple pop-up menu. The first step is to create the menu using the Visual Basic Menu Editor. Remember that all we do when displaying a pop-up menu in Visual Basic is display a menu that we've already created using the menu editor. So let's create the menu that we want to pop up. I'll have to assume that you know how to use the menu editor," I said, "as I don't have time to describe this process in full detail. There's a section on creating menus in my book."

I created a new Visual Basic project and added a text box control to the form. Then, using the Visual Basic menu editor, I built a standard Visual Basic menu consisting of two 'top-level' menu items, each with two submenu items:

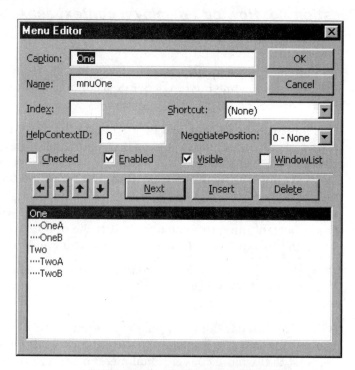

Concluding the menu design, I ran the program and the following form was displayed:

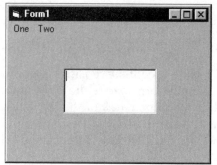

"At this point," I said, "the program doesn't do anything, but we do have a menu bar in place with two top-level menu items, each with two submenu items. Now, it's possible that you don't want all of the items that you create in the pop-up menu to appear on the standard menu bar on your form; for example, this will help to reduce clutter. To show how to do this, let's set the `Visible` property of one of the top-level menu items – `mnuTwo` – to `False`."

I did just that, using the menu editor to click the check mark out of the `Visible` box:

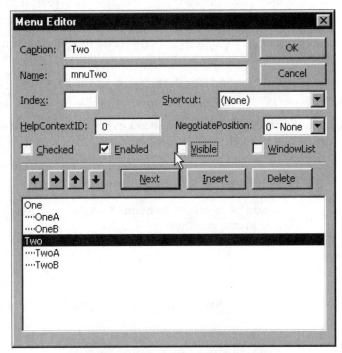

Then I ran the program again to see what the form looked like now:

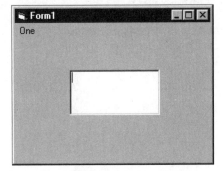

"The second top-level menu item is invisible," I said, "But the first one is still visible. For the sake of neatness, I'll make the first top-level menu item invisible as well; this will fit in better with the concept of pop-up menu items only appearing in their desired context."

Using the menu editor again, I did just that.

"Now," I continued, "let me show you how to create a pop-up menu. In Visual Basic, we typically put code in the **MouseDown** event procedure to display the pop-up menu (we'll see how Visual Basic knows if it's the right or left mouse button later). Since I also want to show you how to create a context sensitive pop-up menu, we'll display menu item 'One' when the user right-clicks the mouse somewhere *over the form*, and we'll display the menu items in menu item 'Two' when the user right-clicks the mouse *over the text box*."

"Does that mean we'll need to write code in two different event procedures?" Jacqueline asked.

"Yes, it will," I replied. "Both the form and the text box control have their own **MouseDown** events."

I started with the form's **MouseDown** event procedure, inserting the following code there:

```
Private Sub Form_MouseDown(Button As Integer, Shift As Integer, X As Single,
Y As Single)

    If Button = vbRightButton Then
        PopupMenu mnuOne
    End If

End Sub
```

Next, I typed the following code into the *text box's* **MouseDown** event procedure:

```
Private Sub Text1_MouseDown(Button As Integer, Shift As Integer, X As
Single, Y As Single)

    If Button = vbRightButton Then
        PopupMenu mnuTwo
    End If

End Sub
```

"Both `MouseDown` event procedures," I said, "are passed arguments which give Visual Basic information: about which mouse button that the user clicked (the `Button` argument); about whether the *Shift*, *Control*, or *Alt* keys were pressed simultaneously with the mouse button (the `Shift` argument); and about the X and Y coordinates of the mouse pointer within the form or the text box. Using the information supplied by the `Button` argument, Visual Basic can determine if the right mouse button was clicked by checking if the `Button` argument is equal to the intrinsic constant `vbRightButton`. If it *is*, VB uses the `PopupMenu` method to display the appropriate menu items. For the form, the relevant part of the code is:"

```
If Button = vbRightButton Then
    PopupMenu mnuOne
```

"And for the text box, the important code is:"

```
If Button = vbRightButton Then
    PopupMenu mnuTwo
```

I then ran the program, and right clicked the mouse over the *form*. A pop-up menu consisting of the submenu items of `mnuOne` was displayed:

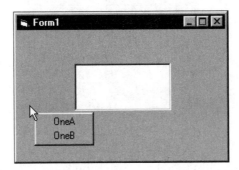

"That's impressive," I heard Jacqueline say.

I then right-clicked the mouse over the *text box* control – *not* over an open area of the form. Instead of seeing a pop-up menu consisting of the submenu items of `mnuTwo`, the following menu was displayed:

"What happened there?"Jacqueline interjected. "That's not the menu you designed in the menu editor."

"You're right, it's not," I said. "Text box controls behave a little differently when the user right-clicks the mouse over them. That's one of the reasons I chose a text box control for this little demonstration. When the user right-clicks the mouse over a text box control, they trigger some built-in Visual Basic behavior. Since the text box control is intended to be used for data entry, when the right mouse button is clicked over it, some built-in editing commands – among them Cut, Copy and Paste – are automatically invoked."

"That's logical, I guess," Jacqueline said, "and I can see that being useful. But does that mean we can't have a pop-up menu of our own associated with a text box control?"

"No, not at all," I replied. "If the user right-clicks the mouse one more time, our pop-up menu will be displayed. As you can imagine, this behavior can be confusing to your users, and it's something that you should definitely alert them to. Unfortunately, there's no simple way of coding your way around it."

To show what I meant, I right-clicked the mouse one more time over the text box. The built-in editing menu went away, and the following screen shot was displayed:

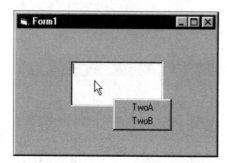

"That's better," Jacqueline said, "but I do have a couple of questions. What determines the location of the pop-up menu, and why did we need to place code in two separate MouseDown event procedures? Couldn't we have used the x and y coordinates passed to the form's MouseDown event procedure to determine whether the user was right-clicking over the textbox, or an open area of the form?"

"In answer to your first question – what determines the location of the pop-up menu – by default, the pop-up menu will appear at the same location as the mouse pointer when the user clicks it. I should point out that the `PopupMenu` method has several optional arguments – one of which allows you to specify the *exact* location of the menu when it is displayed. And your second question – why can't we just use the `MouseDown` event procedure of the form to display all of the pop-up menus? That's because when the user clicks the mouse over the text box control, *only* the `MouseDown` event of the text box is triggered – not the `MouseDown` event of the form. So it's impossible to use the `MouseDown` event procedure of the form to determine if the mouse was clicked over other controls on the form."

"That means," I continued, "that if we have a form containing many controls and we want to display different pop-up menus depending upon which control the user right-clicks the mouse over, then we need to put code into the `MouseDown` event procedure of each control on the form."

"OK," said Jacqueline, "How about this; are the `x` and `y` coordinates passed to the `MouseDown` event procedure relative to the *form*, or relative to the *control* associated with the event procedure?"

"That's a tricky one," I answered. "The `x` and `y` coordinates can be relative to the form *or* the control. For instance, if you are passed a value of 0 for both the `x` and `y` coordinates in the *form's* `MouseDown` event, this tells you that the user clicked the mouse in the upper left hand corner of the form. That same X and Y value passed in the *text box's* `MouseDown` event procedure means that the user clicked the mouse in the upper left hand corner of the text box. See the difference?"

"Yes, thank you," Jacqueline said. "The coordinates relate to the form or control that the mouse pointer happens to be over – they're not absolute coordinates on the screen."

"That's right," I replied.

"Thanks so much," Jacqueline said. "This will come in very handy in my program."

"Glad I could help," I said, "and thanks for calling. Let's take our next caller now."

Question 45: I'd like to generate a random number in a program – how do I do it?

"Hi, my name is Jessica," the caller said. "I'm from New York City. I'm intrigued by the idea of generating random numbers in a Visual Basic program, and I was wondering if you could show me how?"

"Hello, Jessica," I said. "Generating random numbers is a pretty useful function in any programming language – for example, in gaming or in simulations. To generate random numbers in Visual Basic, you use the `Rnd` function. It's really quite simple – take a look at this."

In a project, I added a command button on the form and keyed the following code into its Click event procedure:

```
Private Sub Command1_Click()

Form1.Print Rnd
Form1.Print Rnd
Form1.Print Rnd

End Sub
```

I then ran the program and clicked on the command button:

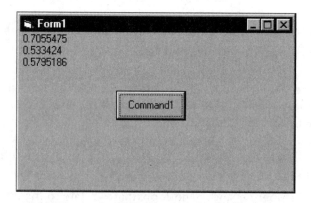

"Those numbers are all less than 1," Jessica said. "Is that a coincidence?"

"No, it's not a coincidence," I answered. "By default, the Rnd function returns a value greater than 0 and less than 1. If you want to change that range, say to generate numbers between 1 and 6, you need to do a little manipulation. Like this."

I amended the code in the Click event procedure...

```
Private Sub Command1_Click()

Form1.Print Int((6 * Rnd) + 1)
Form1.Print Int((6 * Rnd) + 1)
Form1.Print Int((6 * Rnd) + 1)

End Sub
```

...and ran the program again:

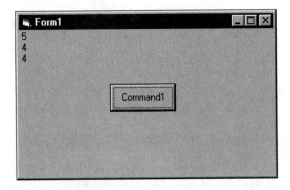

"That's better," I said. "Now we have whole numbers between 1 and 6."

"Can you explain what's going on in that code?" Jessica asked.

"Sure thing, Jessica. We're still using the **Rnd** function to generate a random number between 0 and just less than 1. We then take that number and multiply it by 6, which gives us a number between 0 and just less than 6. Then we add 1 to it (giving us a number between 1 and just less than 7), and use the **Int** function to return just the integer portion of that calculation – the *whole number* part. Ultimately, that produces a random number between 1 and 6."

"I see," Jessica said. "And if I wanted to generate a random number between 1 and 10, I would change the number 6 in the code to a 10?"

"Absolutely correct," I said. "Just like this:"

```
Private Sub Command1_Click()

Form1.Print Int((10 * Rnd) + 1)
Form1.Print Int((10 * Rnd) + 1)
Form1.Print Int((10 * Rnd) + 1)

End Sub
```

"This gives us the following:"

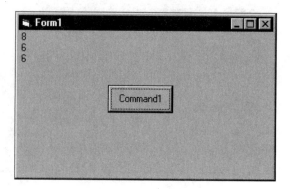

"I just noticed something peculiar," Jessica said. "I just executed this program at home on my PC, and the exact same numbers were displayed on my form as the ones you generated in the studio. Not only that, but I've now stopped the program and started it several times – and every time I click on the command button the first time, I get the same sequence of numbers. In fact, when I click on the command button the second time, I get the same second set of numbers. Isn't this supposed to be random number generator?"

"Jessica, you have just found the fallacy in the notion of a random number generator," I said. "Visual Basic – most languages really – provide to the programmer what is known as a *pseudo random-number generator* for their use. The Rnd function can optionally be passed something called a 'seed' number, which the Rnd function uses to generate the random number. If you omit this argument, Visual Basic always uses the same 'seed' value the first time you call the Rnd function. Visual Basic then uses the last random number generated as the seed for subsequent calls to the Rnd function."

"That would mean that the numbers the Rnd function generates aren't really random," Jessica said. "If the seed for the first random number is always the same, and if the subsequent number's seed is based on the result of the preceding number, the pattern is all very predictable."

"You're absolutely right," I said. "If we run this program again, we will get the identical three numbers displayed on the form."

"As you pointed out, Jessica," I went on, "these numbers are not *truly* random. But as I mentioned, you could pass a seed value as an argument to get a more random generation of numbers."

"What a pain that would be," Jessica said.

"I agree," I said. "Fortunately, Visual Basic has a `Randomize` statement that will take care of this problem. The `Randomize` statement 'reinitializes' the random number generator every time it is executed, which means that the initial 'seed' value passed to the first execution of the `Rnd` function will always be different."

"That should be an improvement," Jessica said.

"It is," I agreed. "Like the `Rnd` function, you can pass an optional seed value to the `Randomize` statement, but if you don't supply one, Visual Basic a seed value based on your PC's system timer – and that's as close to random as you can get."

"How often should you execute this `Randomize` statement?" Jessica asked.

"Some programmers," I said, "'reinitialize' the random number generator before each execution of the `Rnd` function. Other programmers execute the `Randomize` statement just *once* in their program. If you execute the `Randomize` statement once, then the first time you use the `Rnd` function, you produce a truly random number, but subsequent random numbers generated by `Rnd` function use the prior generated random number as a seed. If you execute the `Randomize` statement prior to executing each `Rnd` function, each number produced should – theoretically – be random. Let's see what effect the `Randomize` statement can have on our program, and if it solves that problem you noted earlier."

I made the following changes to the code in the command button's `Click` event...

```
Private Sub Command1_Click()

Randomize

Form1.Print Int((10 * Rnd) + 1)
Form1.Print Int((10 * Rnd) + 1)
Form1.Print Int((10 * Rnd) + 1)

End Sub
```

...and ran the program:

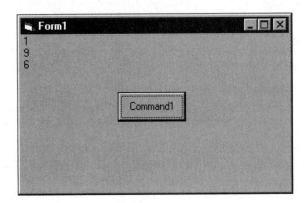

"Different numbers – at last!" Jessica exclaimed.

When I stopped and re-ran the program, we saw the following result:

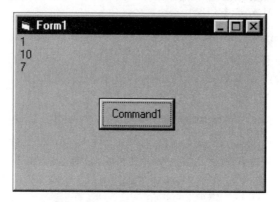

"Another set of numbers," Jessica said. "OK, I'm convinced, it looks like the `Randomize` statement will do the trick. Now you said that some programmers might code the `Randomize` statement before each call of the `Rnd` function?"

"That's right," I said. "That would ensure a perfectly random number – or at least as far as possible – each time."

"I'd like to thank you for your help, Professor Smiley," Jessica said. "I know I never would have figured this out without you!"

"My pleasure," I answered. "Thanks for calling. And now time for our sixth call of the day."

Question 46: Can I implement Cut, Copy and Paste in a program?

"Hi, my name is John, but most people call me Jimi (that's J-i-m-i). I'm from Seattle," the caller announced. "I'm interested in using cut, copy and paste functionality in my program. I've written a program that has several textboxes on a form, and I want my users to be able to perform the standard copy, paste, and cut operations between the various textboxes, and between other applications such as Notepad and Word. Can you help me?"

"I'm sure we can, Jimi," I answered. "First, are you aware that Visual Basic text boxes automatically support standard Windows cut, copy and paste operations through the use of *Ctrl+U*, *Ctrl+C* and *Ctrl+V* shortcuts, and also via the right-click shortcut of the mouse?"

"Yes, I am," Jimi said. "But I want to provide that functionality through my program's *menu bar*, just like other Windows programs, and I just haven't been able to figure out how to do it."

"This won't be difficult at all," I said. "The first thing we need to do is create the menu structure for Edit | Cut, Edit | Copy and Edit | Paste."

I started a clean project and placed two text box controls on it. Then I set about building a menu using the menu editor; this menu consisted of an Edit menu, and three submenu items captioned 'Cut', 'Copy' and 'Paste':

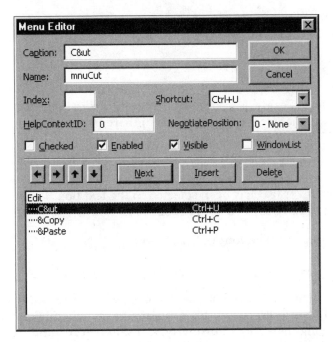

"Notice, Jimi," I said, "that I have taken care to follow the Windows design standards in terms of naming the `Captions`, and assigning access keys and shortcut keys for each item. Now for the code."

I explained to Jimi and the viewing audience that menu editor items only react to one event – the `Click` event.

"To provide cut, copy and paste functionality," I went on, "we need to place code in the `Click` event procedure of *each* of the three menu items. I should warn you in advance that each one of the three menu items will be using a Windows object called the Clipboard – which you are probably familiar with if you use Windows for copying, pasting, and cutting data. Let's look at the code for the cut menu item first."

I opened up the `Click` event of the `mnuCut` object in the code window and keyed in the following code:

```
Private Sub mnuCut_Click()

Clipboard.Clear
Clipboard.SetText Screen.ActiveControl.SelText
Screen.ActiveControl.SelText = ""

End Sub
```

"Cutting text from the text box," I said, "is a three-step operation. First, we need to clear the Windows Clipboard object of whatever may already be in there using this syntax:"

```
Clipboard.Clear
```

"*Second*, we need to grab whatever text has been selected in the text box. To do this we use the `Seltext` property of the `Screen` object's `ActiveControl`:"

```
Clipboard.SetText Screen.ActiveControl.SelText
```

"What's the `ActiveControl` property of the `Screen` object?" Jimi asked.

"The `ActiveControl` property of the `Screen` object," I answered, "lets us know which control on the form currently has *focus*. Using this property, we can then take whatever text is selected in that control (using the `SelText` property, as I said before), and put the text into the Windows Clipboard using the Clipboard's `SetText` method:"

```
Clipboard.SetText Screen.ActiveControl.SelText
```

"Finally," I continued, "having safely stored the cut text in the Windows Clipboard, we can then clear the selected text from the `ActiveControl` by assigning an empty string to it:"

```
Screen.ActiveControl.SelText = ""
```

"Makes sense to me," Jimi said. "I guess that the code for the copy operation will be very similar, with the exception that we don't want to *clear* the selected text?"

"Right on the mark," I said. "Here's the code:"

```
Private Sub mnuCopy_Click()

Clipboard.Clear
Clipboard.SetText Screen.ActiveControl.SelText

End Sub
```

"As you predicted, Jimi," I said. "These two lines of code are identical to the code in the mnuCut Click event, except that here – since we are performing a *copy* operation – we don't clear the selected text from the ActiveControl, so we just leave it there. Finally, here's the code for the Paste Click event procedure:"

```
Private Sub mnuPaste_Click()

Screen.ActiveControl.SelText = Clipboard.GetText()

End Sub
```

"For the paste operation," I said, "we use the GetText method of the Clipboard, which copies the contents of the Windows Clipboard and assigns it to the SelText property of the ActiveControl."

"Again, that seems pretty straight forward to me," Jim said.

I ran the program, and entered "I love Visual Basic" into the first textbox. Next, I selected the text in the first text box, and when I chose Edit | Cut from the menu bar, the text disappeared. I then set focus to the second text box by clicking in it with the mouse, and selected Edit | Paste from the menu bar. The 'cut' text then appeared in the second textbox:

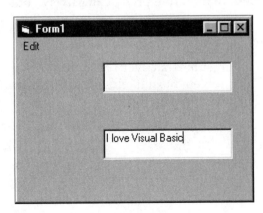

"That works like a charm," I heard Jimi say. "Exactly what I needed to be able to do."

In the same fashion, I tested the Edit | Copy menu item.

This time, the text that I selected in the first text box remained there after I selected Edit | Copy. I then set focus to the second text box, and selected Edit | Paste from the menu bar. The 'copied' text appeared in the second textbox.

"That works beautifully," Jimi said. "Thanks for your help. I'll put this to good use right away."

"Thanks for calling, Jimi," I said. "Now it's time for our final commercial break of the day. We'll see you in a few minutes."

After our break, it was time for call number seven.

Question 47: I put a check box in a frame. Why doesn't it act like it's contained in the frame?

(see also question 63)

"Hi, my name is Gracie, and I'm from San Francisco," caller number seven said. "I'm having a little problem with a check box control I placed on a frame. Perhaps I got just a bit too fancy. I've only been programming in Visual Basic for a few weeks, but I read that the frame control is a container control, and that if I placed another control in a frame and then made the frame invisible, all of the controls on the frame would become invisible also. So what I did was place a check box control on a frame and, at run time, ran code to change the `visible` property of the frame to false. However, I could still see the check box control, even though the frame disappeared. What's up?"

"First, Gracie, welcome to the show," I said. "Don't feel bad about this – this is a common ailment with the frame; so much so that I wrote pretty extensively about this problem in my book."

"Oh, I'm sorry, Professor Smiley," Gracie said. "Should I hang up?"

"Oh no," I quickly replied. "I don't presume that every caller has read my book. I'll be glad to answer your question here. The problem most likely is *how* you placed that check box control on the form. Do you remember how you did it?"

"I double-clicked on the check box control in the Toolbox," she said. "That placed the check box control right in the middle of my frame."

"Or so you thought," I said. "That's a very common mistake that beginners make when placing controls on a frame. Container controls like the frame control or picture box, must have other controls *explicitly* 'drawn' on them. Double-clicking a control from the Toolbox onto the frame places the control *on top of* the frame, but not *within* it – in other words, the control is *not* contained by the frame, but is sitting *over* it. Here, let me show everyone what I mean..."

I started a new project and added a frame control roughly in the middle of the form, with a command button just underneath the frame. I then double-clicked the check box control in the Toolbox. Visual Basic placed the check box right in the middle of the form, on top of the frame:

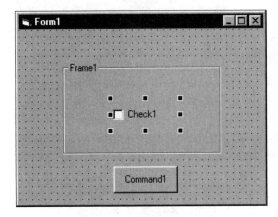

"The check box appears to be contained within the frame," I said. "But really it isn't. We'll see that in a minute."

I then typed the following code in the `Click` event procedure of the command button:

```
Private Sub Command1_Click()

Frame1.Visible = False

End Sub
```

"Nothing fancy here," I said, "just some code to make the frame invisible when we click on the command button. Now, if the check box is really contained by the frame, the check box should become invisible when we set frame's `Visible` property to `False`."

I then ran the program and clicked on the command button, with the following effect:

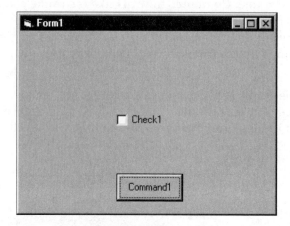

"The check box is still there," Gracie said. "That's exactly what is happening to me. Now, you say that means that the check box is not really contained within the frame? I wish there was a way to check at design time."

"Actually," I said, "there is. If you move the frame in design mode, and any controls you put within the frame don't move with it, you know that the controls are not really contained within the frame."

I moved the frame and, sure enough, the check box control stayed put – a sure sign that it was not really contained within the frame:

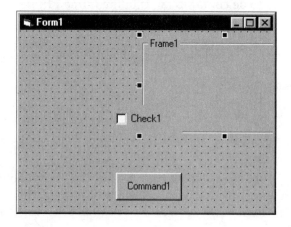

"OK, that will help me identify the condition," Gracie said. "But how can I do this right? You said earlier that I need to explicitly draw the check box within the frame if I want it to be properly contained within the frame. How do I do that?"

"Well," I said, "we've seen that we can't *double-click* the check box into the frame. What we have to do is this: first, select the check box in the Toolbox by clicking and releasing the left mouse button. Next, click on the form and explicitly drag and draw the check box onto the frame."

I stopped the program, selected the check box in design view, and pressed the *Delete* key to clear it off the form. I then single-clicked on the check box in the Visual Basic toolbox, then moved the mouse pointer across to the form and explicitly drew the check box within the frame:

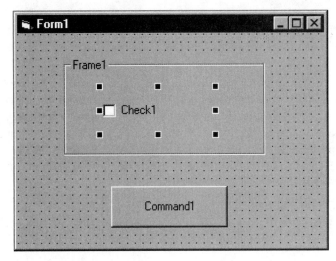

"It doesn't look any different, does it?" I asked Gracie.

"Not really," she answered. "Should we verify that the check box is actually contained within the frame by moving the frame just as we did before? If we did this right, the check box should then move with it, correct?"

"That's right," I replied, and I did exactly as Gracie suggested. This time, the check box moved with the frame.

"Now if we re-run this program," I said, "when we click on the command button, both the frame *and* the check box should disappear. Let's see:"

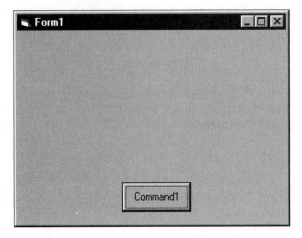

"I must echo the comments of the other callers when I say thank you very much," Gracie said.

"My pleasure, Gracie," I said, "and thanks for calling. And now for caller number eight."

Question 48: Can I automatically capitalize the 1ˢᵗ character of a string and leave the rest in lower case?

"Hi, my name is Lou, and I'm from New York City," the caller said. "I've written a Visual Basic program where the user inputs address information. My problem revolves around the input of their city into a text box. I take the user's input and write it to a database. What I'd like to do is write their city to the database with the first letter capitalized and the remaining letters in lower case. I bought a copy of your book and I've tried to use some of the techniques you illustrate in your chapter on string manipulation. But I'm a little unsure of what I'm doing. Can you help me?"

"Hi Lou," I said, "welcome to the show. There's an amazing little Visual Basic function that will do exactly what you need – this is a good alternative to using the string manipulation functions I mentioned in my book. May I show you?"

"Please do," Lou said.

I created a sparkling new project and placed two text boxes and a command button on the form. I cleared the **Text** properties of the text boxes and placed the following code in the command button's **Click** event procedure:

```
Private Sub Command1_Click()

Text2.Text = StrConv(Text1.Text, vbProperCase)

End Sub
```

I ran the program and entered 'new york' into the first textbox before clicking on the command button:

"See?" I said, "That little bit of code – and the `StrConv` function in particular – has turned the lower case entry into the format that you want."

"That's exactly what I need," Lou said. "I haven't heard of the `StrConv` function."

"It's not all that widely known," I replied. "Essentially, it's designed for manipulating strings and converting them based on the arguments that you pass it. Here, we pass the `StrConv` function the intrinsic constant `vbProperCase` as an argument. Using this, the function takes the entry in the first text box and returns a string with the first letter of each word capitalized. In this program, we took the return value and placed it in a second textbox – but you could easily write this value to a database record instead."

"Can you explain the argument to this function?" Lou said, "`vbProperCase` – that's another one of those Visual Basic intrinsic constants I've heard you speak about during the course of your shows. Are there any other possible arguments?"

"Yes, there are," I said. "For instance, there's an argument which will make the function return a string all in upper case, and an argument to return a string all in lower case. There are also some obscure argument values that you may want to check out further on your own in Visual Basic Help."

"Thanks, Professor Smiley," he said. "You sure answered my question."

"Thanks for calling, Lou," I replied, "Who's our next caller?"

Question 49: Is there an easy way to load the elements of an array?

(see also questions 59 & 60)

"Hi, my name is Walter, and I'm from West Allis, Wisconsin," the caller said. "I've written a Visual Basic program that performs some array processing. I understand array processing pretty well, having worked with them in 'C' for a number of years. Here's my problem; I need to initialize a 30-element one-dimensional array with some startup values when my program begins, and I was wondering if there was an easier way to do that besides the method I've been using. The way I do it at the moment is to write 30 separate assignment statements. That can get old pretty quickly. I know the 'C' programming language has the capability to assign all the values to an array with a single line of code – how about VB?"

"Hi, Walter," I said, "Thanks for your call. I'm familiar with the 'C' notation for initializing variables, and I must tell you up front that there isn't really an equivalent in Visual Basic. However, there *is* an easier way of assigning initial values to a one-dimensional array, and that's to use the Visual Basic `Array` function. Unfortunately, though, it doesn't work for *multi-dimensional* arrays. If you need to initialize a multi-dimensional array in Visual Basic, you have to use separate assignment statements for each element of the array. As you said, that can get tiresome pretty quickly. Let me show you how to use the `Array` function to initialize a one-dimensional array. We'll do this in two stages; first, I'll show you the long way round, *then* I'll show you how to do it with a single line of code."

I started a new project and, as so often, placed a single command button on the form. "Rather than work with a 30-element array," I said, "let's make things a little easier for demonstration purposes, and work with a 4-element array instead. This will still enable me to illustrate my point."

I coded up the command button's `Click` event with the following code:

```
Private Sub Command1_Click()

Dim strArray(3) As String
Dim intCounter As Integer

strArray(0) = "I"
strArray(1) = "love"
strArray(2) = "Visual"
strArray(3) = "Basic"

For intCounter = LBound(strArray) To UBound(strArray)
    Form1.Print strArray(intCounter)
Next

End Sub
```

I ran the program and clicked on the command button:

"Nothing too clever going on here," I said. "I just declared a 4-element array..."

```
Dim strArray(3) As String
```

"...individually assigned values to the elements in the array..."

```
strArray(0) = "I"
strArray(1) = "love"
strArray(2) = "Visual"
strArray(3) = "Basic"
```

"...and then used a `For...Next` loop to display the values on the form:"

```
For intCounter = LBound(strArray) To UBound(strArray)
    Form1.Print strArray(intCounter)
Next
```

I was just starting to move on to my next point when I realized I should probably point something out to the viewing audience at home.

"Just a word to my viewers at home," I said. "Remember that the number in parentheses in the array declaration is *not* the number of elements in the array – it's something called the **Upper Bound** of the array:"

```
Dim strArray(3) As String
```

"In my *Learn to Program with Visual Basic* book, I analogized the upper bound of an array to the top floor in a skyscraper or hotel. There's a corresponding lower bound value in an array that represents the 'bottom floor' number. In Visual Basic, by default, numbering of arrays begins with the number 0, and memory allocation for the array proceeds up to (and includes) the upper bound. Since I didn't specify a lower bound for this array, an array declared with an upper bound of 3 has a total of 4 elements – 0, 1, 2 and 3."

"Could you specify a lower bound if you wanted to?" Walter asked.

"Yes, you could," I said, "the declaration would look like this:"

```
Dim strArray(0 To 3) As String
```

"Back to our code," I said. "Notice the start and end arguments of the `For...Next` loop:"

```
For intCounter = LBound(strArray) To UBound(strArray)
```

"Instead of using the numeric literals 0 and 3, I used the LBound and UBound functions. Both of these functions take, as their single argument, an array name. The LBound function returns the lower bound of the array. The UBound function returns the upper bound of the array."

"Why use those instead of 0 and 3?" Walter asked.

"Just habit, I guess," I explained. "Experienced programmers tend to avoid numeric literals whenever possible."

"So the LBound and UBound functions just return the bottom and top 'floors' of the array," Walter said. "I can see why using these functions would be preferable to using numeric literals. That way, if for some reason, you changed the array declaration, you wouldn't have to change this section of code."

"Exactly," I said. "We've done it the hard way, using individual assignment lines for each variable in the array. Now let's get back to your question – assigning values to the array with a single line of code."

I then modified the Click event procedure of the command button to look like this:

```
Private Sub Command1_Click()

Dim strArray As Variant
Dim intCounter As Integer

strArray = Array("I", "love", "Visual", "Basic")

For intCounter = LBound(strArray) To UBound(strArray)
    Form1.Print strArray(intCounter)
Next

End Sub
```

I ran the program, clicked on the command button, and the same results were displayed on the form:

"Looks good," Walter said. "The array has been properly loaded, and its elements printed on the form."

"That's right," I said. "Let's take a look at the code. I modified the code in two different spots. First, the declaration for the array itself has been changed."

"I noticed that," Walter said. "Correct me if I'm wrong, but this isn't even an array declaration anymore. This looks more like a straight variable declaration, and the `string` type has been replaced with a `Variant` data type."

```
Dim strArray As Variant
```

"You hit the nail right on the head, Walter," I said. "The Visual Basic `Array` function doesn't load values into an existing array – more to the point, it *dynamically* creates an array at run time. When you execute the `Array` function, you supply as arguments the values for the array. The return value of the function is then assigned to a plain old `Variant` variable type:"

```
strArray = Array("I", "love", "Visual", "Basic")
```

"In fact," I continued, "if you were to try to assign the return value of the `Array` function either to an existing array or to a variable declared as anything other than a `Variant`, a run-time error would be generated."

"Let me make sure I understand this," Walter said. "The variable you assign the return value of the `Array` function to *can't* be declared as an array, and its data type *must* be a `Variant`?"

"That's correct," I said.

"And furthermore," Walter continued, "the `Array` function can only initialize a one-dimensional array – is that correct?"

"Right again, Walter," I said. "The `Array` function falls a bit short – but for one-dimensional arrays, it can be a great time saver."

"I agree," Walter said, "the `Array` function will help me immediately. Thanks for your help!"

"Thanks for calling, Walter," I replied. "And now, on to our final caller of the day."

Question 50: When typing code in a command button's Click event, an Index argument is passed to the event procedure. Why?

(See also questions 4 & 32)

"Hi, my name is Jerry, and I'm from San Francisco," the voice said. "I know you don't have much time left, so I'll make this quick. I was writing some code in the `Click` event of a command button, when I noticed that an `Index` argument was being passed to the `Click` event procedure. Can you tell me why that is?"

"That's easy," I answered, "your command button is a member of a control array. Check the `Index` property of your command button – I bet it has a number in it."

There was a momentary pause.

"You're right," Jerry said. "My `Index` property has a number in it. I certainly didn't intend to create a control array; I wonder how that happened."

"It's actually pretty easy," I answered,"Beginners frequently do this by accidentally placing a value in the `Index` property of the control – most likely intending to update the `TabIndex` property instead. Let me demonstrate."

In a new project, I added a single command button on the form and double-clicked on the command button to bring up the Visual Basic code window:

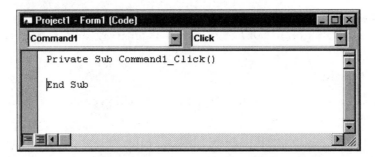

"Notice," I said, "that there is no `Index` argument being passed to this event procedure. In fact, there's no argument *at all*. Now let me close the code window and modify the `Index` property of the command button by changing it from its default empty value to `0`. Remember, any numeric value in the `Index` property of a control tells Visual Basic that the control is a member of a control array."

I then brought up the Properties window for the command button, and changed its `Index` property to `0`:

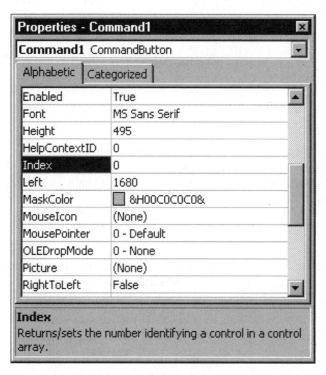

"Now let's take a look at the `Click` event procedure of the command button again," I suggested:

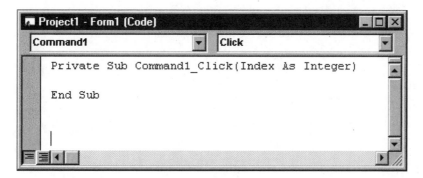

"Do you see the difference, Jerry?" I asked. "There's now an `Index` argument being passed to the event procedure."

"I see it," was his response. "Now what – how can I fix it?"

"The first thing to do is to clear the `Index` property in the Properties window," I said. "Then, you should erase this event procedure from the code window by highlighting it from the '`Private Sub`' header line to the '`End Sub`' line and pressing the *Backspace* key. Then close the code window, double-click on the command button, and you should see the `Click` event procedure properly formatted – *without* the `Index` argument."

"That worked!" Jerry said emphatically. "Thanks a lot for your help. By the way, is there any chance there will be re-runs of the show, or even a videotape based on the show for people like me who are out of town frequently?"

"Who knows, Jerry? I'll check into that. Well, it looks like we are just about out of time. I hope everyone enjoyed today's show, and I hope you tune in again next week. Special thanks to all of our callers. And if you called, but couldn't get through, remember, we'll be here next week, same time, same channel."

"Whew!" said Linda. "Were those questions as hard as they sounded from my side of the room?"

"Well, yes, I think they were," I said. "Keeps me on my toes, though. It's making the explanations concise and instructive that's the real challenge. It's a real change from classroom teaching, where I'd be able to devote a whole lesson to a difficult topic, and really go into detail."

"Looks like you're doing fine to me," she said. "I've got a few things to do, so I'll have to say 'bye' now, and see you next week."

"Right. Bye, Linda, and thanks," I said as I made my way towards the door.

Week 6

It was Saturday the 27th of March. As I drove in to the studio on for the sixth show, I gave some thought to the pressure I was under to sign the contract to present the show on an extended basis. I was moderately relaxed about the show itself, but I still had to weigh up the implications of continuing the contract.

As usual, Linda was already in the studio, and she was talking to one of the show's camera operators, Sue.

"Good morning," said Linda. "Sue's just asked me if I'd heard anything about the show going international?"

I told them that *I* still hadn't heard anything concrete about it.

"It's just that my cousin Kate saw the show when she visited me last week," said Sue, "and she was wondering if she'd get to call in from home. She lives in London, England."

"I'm sure we'd have heard for sure by now if it was going to happen today," I said.

Our pre-show setup was now routine. I ran all of my equipment and software through a quick test, but I must admit I soon found myself daydreaming about an international audience again, and I rose with a start as I heard Linda call out:

"All quiet on the set. Ten seconds."

As she counted me in, I took a quick gulp of water and cleared my throat. I was midway through my introductory speech when I suddenly found that I had a loud case of the hiccups. "Our phone lines are now open," I continued, "and if you'll just excuse the slight technical hitch I seem to be having, we'll take our first caller."

I tried holding my breath as the first caller introduced himself.

Question 51: What's the point of a creating a Grayed check box?

"Hi, my name is George, and I'm from Westmoreland County, Virginia."

"Hi, George," I said between hiccups. "Do you know of any good hiccup cures?"

"I thought I was supposed to ask *you* questions," he replied, laughing. "First, try not to laugh – although I'm finding that to be a problem myself right now," he said apologetically. "There's always the old favorite – juggle three fresh sea bass while humming the 'Star Spangled Banner' – or why not try drinking some water from the wrong side of the glass?" he suggested.

"It's never worked before, but I guess national TV is as good a time as any," I said. "Why don't you ask me your question meanwhile?"

"Can we have a drum roll, please?" he quipped. "OK, here goes. My friend and I are a bit confused about the `Grayed` property of the check box control, and we're hoping that you can enlighten us."

"I knew this was bound to come up sometime," I said. "The `Grayed` option of the check box's `Value` property has got to be one of the most confusing things programmers come upon in Visual Basic."

"It's good to know we're not alone," said George. "I discovered the `Grayed` setting of the `Value` property of the check box control a few weeks ago. I just assumed that once the `Value` property of the check box was set to `Grayed`, the user would no longer be able to click the mouse in it. After all, once the check box is set to `Grayed`, it looks like a disabled check box, except that it has a checkmark in it."

"That's a common misconception," I said. "It's easy to think that setting the `Value` property to `Grayed` has the same effect as disabling it."

"That's right," George answered. "Then my friend was experimenting with the program I wrote, and he discovered that if you click the mouse on a `Grayed` check box, not only can the check box be clicked on, but the check mark disappears, and the check box loses its `'Grayed'` quality. After that, the user can click the check mark off or on at will."

"You're right about that," I said. "It sounds to me as though you understand the behavior of the `Grayed` check box fine now – what's your dilemma?"

"To be honest with you," George said, "my friend and I simply can't see a *use* for it. Can you enlighten us?"

"I'll try," I said. "And I'll have to be honest with you; it's a 'stretch' to find a good use for it, but I'll be able to give you an example of where it's used in the Windows world. After that, you're pretty much on your own in deciding if you would ever want to use it. First, though, let me demonstrate the `Grayed` value of the check box for our home viewers who may not be familiar with its characteristics."

I started a new Visual Basic project and placed three check boxes on the form. I left
`Check1`'s `Value` property set at the default; `0-Unchecked`. I also left `Check2`'s `Value`
property set at `0-Unchecked`, but I changed its `Enabled` property to `False`. Finally, I set
`Check3`'s `Value` property to `2-Grayed`:

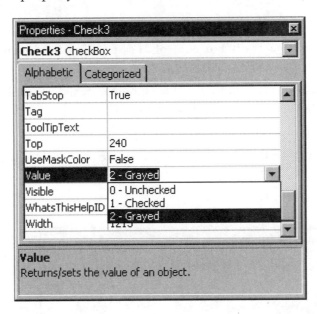

"`Check1` and `Check3` are now enabled," I said, "and `Check2` is *disabled*."

When I ran the program, the following screen shot was displayed to the viewing audience:

"What we have here," I said, "is three check boxes with distinctly different looks. The first
check box, `Check1`, is the basic default look of the check box – `Enabled`, and with a `Value`
property of `0-Unchecked`. In the middle, `Check2`, we have a disabled check box, whose
`Value` property is set to `0-Unchecked` also. Finally, on the right, `Check3`, we have an
enabled check box, whose `Value` property is set to `'2-Grayed'`."

"`Check2` and `Check3` do look similar, don't they?" George said. "You can't help but believe that `Check3` is disabled."

"Well," I said, "they do look a little similar, with the exception that `Check3` has a checkmark in it, and its caption isn't grayed out."

I clicked on the first check box, clicking it 'off' and 'on' repeatedly.

"That's the normal behavior for the check box control," I said. "Click it once and a check mark appears. Click it again, and it disappears, and so on."

Next, I clicked on the check box in the middle, but nothing happened, since it was disabled. "The middle check box is disabled," I said, "so we can't affect it at all."

I then turned my attention to the rightmost check box.

"This check box," I said, "is the most intriguing. It *looks* like we shouldn't be able to interact with it – it does appear dimmed – but if we click on it right now..."

I did that, with the following result:

"As you can see," I continued, "not only was I able to click on the check box, but when I did, the check mark disappeared, and now `Check3` looks just like `Check1` – it's no longer `Grayed`. In fact, its `Value` property is now set to `0-Unchecked`, and there's no way, once the `Grayed` property has been changed by the user, to toggle that `Grayed` property back on. As you can see, clicking on it now just places a check mark in the check box..."

"...the same as with the ordinary check box on the left, `Check1`."

"That's exactly right," George chimed in. "So what's the point of the `Grayed` property of the check box to begin with?"

"Believe it or not," I said, "you'll find a `Grayed` check box in almost every application that Microsoft ships. For instance, just the other day, I was installing Visual Basic in one of my classrooms, and I had the occasion to choose a custom installation. Would you believe when I chose that option, a window was displayed with a number of check boxes, and nearly almost all of them were grayed out? As was the case here, I could still click on the check box. I believe what Microsoft was trying to tell me was that the check boxes were already selected for a good reason, or maybe that some elements of the item it described were selected. Still, I could change them if I wanted...."

"I hadn't thought of that," George said. "Now that you mention it, I do remember seeing check boxes like that here and there. I have to be honest with you – I can't see myself using a `Grayed` check box in a program of my own – I don't think most users would have any idea what it means."

"I have to agree with you," I said. "Microsoft doesn't attempt to explain or give an example of the use of the `Grayed` check box in their documentation. The `Grayed` check box must certainly be one of the biggest Visual Basic mysteries there is. Thanks for bringing this up."

"Thank you for explaining it," George said. "And, Professor?"

"Uh – yes, George?" I said.

"Your hiccups are gone," he pointed out.

"Thanks, George," I chuckled. "And now it's time for our second caller."

Question 52: Default properties – what are they?

"Hi, this is Abe, calling from Springfield, Illinois," the caller said. "A friend of mine recently showed me some code he'd written, and I pointed out what I was sure was a syntax error in the code. It looked like he had forgotten to specify the property name of a control in an assignment statement. Not only that, but he was also invoking methods of the form without specifying the form name. When I pointed this code out to him, he told me that his code was perfectly fine. He said that each control in Visual Basic has something called a **default property**, and that if you refer to a control *without* a property name in your code, Visual Basic presumes the operation is being carried out against that default property. And as for not referencing the form name in his code, he told me that if you reference a property or method in code without specifying a form or a control name, Visual Basic presumes that you are referring to the active form. I'm really puzzled by this."

"Thanks for calling, Abe," I said, "and let me say, I don't blame you for feeling uncertain. Everything your friend told you is true – but in my opinion, coding like that is really a bad habit to fall into. As a beginner, you read and hear over and over again about the importance of good coding practices, and then you come upon an example of this type of real-world code that violates all the rules! Code like this is much more difficult to maintain and modify than properly written code. Mark my words, if this code needs to be modified in a month or so by someone else, or even by the person who wrote it, it's going to take some time for the programmer to figure out what's going on. Let me show the home viewers exactly what we're talking about."

I started a fresh project and placed a command button and a label control on the form. I used the Properties window to change the `Caption` of the label control to "John Smiley"...

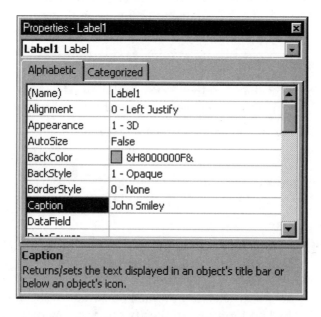

...and then typed the code below into the `Click` event procedure of the command button:

```
Private Sub Command1_Click()

MsgBox Label1

End Sub
```

Next, I ran the program and clicked on the command button. The following message box was displayed to Abe and the viewers at home:

"It looks like you've displayed the `Caption` of the label control in the message box," Abe said, "but all you did was pass the `MsgBox` function the name of the label control. Does that mean that the `Caption` property is the default property of the label control?"

"You hit the nail on the head," I said. "This code..."

```
MsgBox Label1
```

"...is functionally equivalent to this code:"

```
MsgBox Label1.Caption
```

"Every control in Visual Basic," I explained, "has a default property, which means that if you choose, you can refer to that property implicitly in your code by typing the control name alone."

"That seems really weird to me," Abe said. "Why would a programmer want to do that anyway?"

"There are three reasons that I can come up with," I said. "First, some programmers are poor typists, and this shortcut means less to type. Secondly, in older versions of Visual Basic, you could actually make your program run faster by reducing the amount of what is known as '**dot notation**' in your programs."

"Dot notation?" Abe asked.

"Yes," I answered. "Dot notation refers to that period or dot between the name of a form or a control and its corresponding property and method. If you only reference the form or control, and not the property, you eliminate the dot."

"I see," he said. "So eliminating the dot can make your programs run faster."

"That was true with earlier versions of Visual Basic," I said. "In fact, eliminating dot notation as a way to 'speed up' your program appeared as a recommendation in Visual Basic documentation. But with newer versions of Visual Basic, and with the introduction of today's faster computers, eliminating dot notation really isn't necessary any more."

"What's the third reason?" asked Abe.

"Habit," I said. "Programmers who've used these shortcuts for years continue to do so because it's become their – er – default behavior."

"How do these programmers even know what the default properties are for each control?" Abe asked.

"That's a good question," I said. "In the documentation for earlier versions of Visual Basic, the one that comes to mind is the Visual Basic Version 4 Programmer's Guide; there was a table listing the default properties of all of VB's intrinsic controls – but later versions of the documentation don't mention default properties *anywhere*."

"OK," Abe said, "I think I understand the idea of a default property – although based on what you've just told me I would never use it myself. What about referring to properties and methods of the form without specifying the form name? Is that an attempt to save processor time too?"

"I think the same reasons apply," I said. "Typing, Speed, and Habit. Let me show the home viewers an example of this. Let's place some code in the `click` event procedure of the command button..."

```
Private Sub Command1_Click()

Print "I love Visual Basic"

End Sub
```

I ran the program and clicked on the command button:

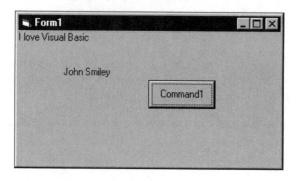

"As you can see," I said, "even though I didn't specify the name of the form, Visual Basic presumed that the `Print` method 'belonged' to the form object. Again, this is just another programming 'shortcut' – one I don't endorse or recommend. Are you OK with all of this, Abe?"

"I think so, Professor Smiley," Abe replied. "I'll follow your words of advice, and avoid both of these shortcuts."

"You'll be much better off if you code objects and properties *explicitly*," I said. "You'll never confuse others, or yourself! And your code will be much easier to modify in the future. Thanks for your call," I continued, "and now on to our third caller of the day."

Question 53: I wrote code in the Click event procedure of a command button, and then re-named the command button. I lost my code!

"Hi, I'm hoping you can help me," the slightly agitated voice on the other end of the line said. "My name is John, and I'm calling from New York, although I'm originally from Toronto. Yesterday I wrote a lot of code in the `Click` event of a command button. Today I renamed the command button, and all of my code disappeared. Tell me it's not gone forever!"

"Don't panic, John," I said. "It's not lost, and we can get it back for you. Before we do that, let me show everyone at home what happened to your code. Whatever you do, don't touch a thing in the meantime."

"I won't," he said, obviously relieved. "I'll hang on..."

I continued using the project I'd used for the last caller, but deleted the label. As a reminder, here's the code that was already in the button's `Click` event procedure:

```
Private Sub Command1_Click()

Form1.Print "I love Visual Basic"

End Sub
```

When I ran the program and clicked on the command button, we saw this:

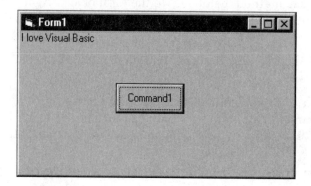

"Nothing too original here," I said. "The code in the command button's `Click` event just prints 'I love Visual Basic' on the form. Now let's change the name of the command button from `Command1` to `cmdOK`..."

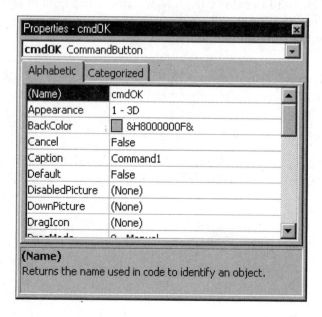

"...and run the program again."

I ran the program, clicked on the command button, and the following screen shot was displayed:

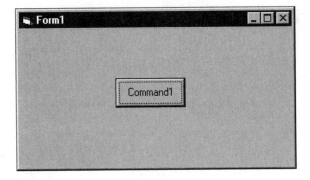

"Nothing's been printed," John said. "That's kind of like what happened to me. The code just didn't run. I bet now that if you open up the code window, the code that was in the Click event procedure of that command button will be gone!"

"I'll wager you're right," I told John. "But don't worry, I know exactly where it is. Let's stop the program and open up the code window."

I stopped the program and double clicked on the command button to open up the code window. This is what we all saw:

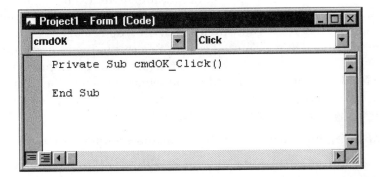

"Just like you said, John," I confirmed, "the Click event procedure of the command button is now empty. There's no code here – and that's why when we ran the program and clicked on the command button, nothing happened. Now let's see if we can find that code. To help us find it, let's click on the Full Module View button at the bottom of the code window – it's the second from the left – so that we can see *all* of the code in our form module at one time."

I did that – clicked on the second button from the left at the bottom of code window. The 'missing' code appeared:

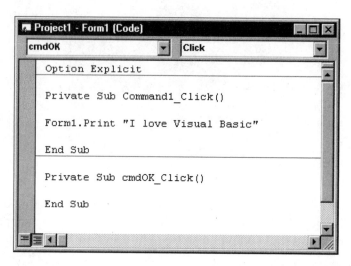

"What happened?" I heard John say. "I see the missing code. Where was it?"

"The missing code wasn't really 'missing' at all," I said. "It was actually in its own little section of code. Have you noticed that when you write code in the Click event procedure of a command button the name of the event procedure 'header' contains the name of the command button? For instance, if your control is named 'Command1', its Click event procedure is named 'Command1_Click'. Unfortunately, when you re-name a control, Visual Basic *doesn't* rename the event procedure header. As a result, if you double-click on the control that has been renamed, it seems that there's no code in its event procedure. Not only that, but since the header of the event procedure no longer 'matches' the name of the control, and because no code is associated with the Click event, nothing appears to happen when the program runs and you click on the command button."

"So where does the code go," John asked, "when the command button is renamed?"

"When a control is renamed," I said, "the code associated with the old control name isn't lost – you just have to hunt for it a little, as it retains the name of a nonexistent control in its header."

"Great," John said, "so now that we know where to find it, how can we get it back?"

"The easiest thing to do," I said, "is to Cut the code from the old command button event procedure and to Paste that code into the new one. Like this..."

I selected the code in the old event procedure `Command1_Click` and chose Cut from the Visual Basic menu bar. Then I pasted the code into the new `cmdOK` event procedure.

"There," I said, "that will restore the code. Now, John, as a tip for the future, avoid renaming controls after you've written code for their associated event procedures. If you rename controls *first*, that will save you from this kind of headache later on."

"What about the old event procedure?" John asked. "It's empty now – but should we delete it anyway?"

"Yes, that's a good idea," I said, as I selected the old event procedure 'stub' and pressed the *Backspace* key to erase it.

"Thanks a lot, Professor Smiley," John said. "Thanks to you, I found my event procedure code, and put it where it belongs. Everything is running fine now."

"Thanks for calling, John," I said. "And now it's time to take our first commercial break of the day. We'll be back in a few minutes."

After a short commercial break, we continued with our fourth caller.

Question 54: The right click of my mouse doesn't make Pop-up menus go away - why?

(see also question 44)

"Hi, my name is Nathan, and I'm calling from New York City," he said. "My wife was lucky enough to get through last week to ask you a question about the frame control. Now I have a question about Visual Basic pop-up menus, a topic you also discussed last week. As soon as last week's show ended, I started coding a VB program with a pop-up menu. I've been extremely pleased with the results, but I noticed some behavior that I can't explain, and which I don't particularly care for…"

"Hello, Nathan," I said. "What behavior is it that you're referring to?"

"Well," Nathan continued, "in my experience of Windows applications, when you right-click the mouse, a pop-up menu appears; and if you right-click the mouse again anywhere else on the form, the original pop-up menu goes away and a new one is displayed at the new cursor position. After I had coded my pop-up menu in Visual Basic, I noticed this isn't happening. When I right-click the mouse, the pop-up menu doesn't go away. It isn't until I *left*-click the mouse somewhere else on the form that the original pop-up menu disappears. Is there anything I can do to change this behavior?"

"I know exactly what's happening, Nathan," I said, "and yes, you can change this behavior. Let me take a minute to simulate your problem for everyone else."

I created a new project and quickly built a menu using the Menu Editor. The menu I made consisted of two top-level menu items, each with two submenu items:

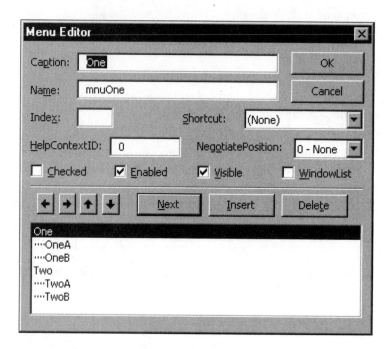

"This is identical to the menu structure I created last week, I believe. As we did last week," I said, "let's make the top level menu items invisible by setting their **Visible** properties to **False**."

I did just that.

"Again, as we did last week," I said, "let's type some code into the **MouseDown** event of the form:"

```
Private Sub Form_MouseDown(Button As Integer, Shift As Integer, X As Single,
Y As Single)

If Button = vbRightButton Then
    PopupMenu mnuOne
End If

End Sub
```

"Now let's observe the behavior that Nathan is talking about," I continued, "by right-clicking the mouse over the form."

I did that, with the following result:

icking the mouse causes the pop-up menu to appear. Now click the right mouse button over the form *again*."

the left of the pop-up menu that was already displayed.

d. "Don't you agree that in most Windows programs, right-have resulted in one menu disappearing, and another one

od news is that there is an easy way to achieve this ss the `PopupMenu` method an optional argument. Take a

```
n(Button As Integer, Shift As Integer, X As Single,


  Then
upMenuRightButton
```

```
End Sub
```

"I believe I mentioned last week," I continued, "that there are optional flag arguments that you can pass to the `PopupMenu` method to fine-tune its behavior. One of these flags, `vbPopupMenuRightButton,` affects the behavior we are seeing here."

"How so?" Nathan asked.

"By default," I said, "when the pop-up menu is displayed to the user, they can then only select an item from it by using the left mouse button. By default, the right mouse button is used to display the pop-up menu, and the left mouse button is used to select a menu item. Likewise, the pop-up menu only disappears when the user left-clicks the mouse outside of the pop-up menu structure."

"That's right," Nathan agreed, "and that's what I'm looking to change."

"We can do that," I said, "by passing the `PopupMenu` method the optional flag argument, `vbPopupMenuRightButton`. This tells Visual Basic to allow the user to make a selection of a menu item in the pop-up menu using *either* the left or right mouse button. As a result, if the user clicks the left or right mouse button outside of the pop-up menu structure, Visual Basic closes that pop-up menu, and displays a new one."

"That's exactly the behavior I want," Nathan said. "I think I better have a look at some of those other flag settings to see what else they can do for me. Thanks, Professor Smiley."

"Glad I could be of help, Nathan," I said, "and now it's time for caller number five."

Question 55: Can I change the font of every control on my form?

"This is Rick, and I'm calling from Teaneck, New Jersey," the caller said. "I was wondering - is there any way to change the font of every control on a form so that they are all the same *without* having to change them all individually? I'm writing a program for my parents who are getting on in years, and I want to display the `Captions` of all of the label controls on the form in a large font. For lack of a better way, I've been placing all of my label controls on the form, and then manually changing the font size of each of them individually. That can really be time consuming, and I keep thinking that there must be a better way."

"Hi, Rick," I said. "Welcome to the show. Yes, there is a better way – maybe even *two* ways. First, did you know that the default font of every control you place on a form is determined by the font properties of the form itself?"

"No I didn't," Rick answered. "Are you saying that if I change the font of the form from its default type and size to – say – Arial 24, every label control I add will have that same font type and size?"

"That's right," I said. "Why don't we try it?"

I started a new Visual Basic project. Prior to placing any controls on the form, I brought up the Properties window for the form…

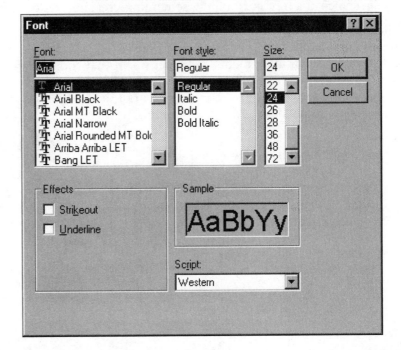

…and changed the font type from its default of 'MS Sans Serif' to 'Arial', and changed its default size from 8 to 24:

"Most programmers," I said, "think that changing the font properties of the form only affects text that you write to the form using the `Print` method – but it *also* affects the font of any control placed on the form thereafter. Watch this – I'll now place a label, a text box and a command button on the form."

I did just that, and the form now looked like this:

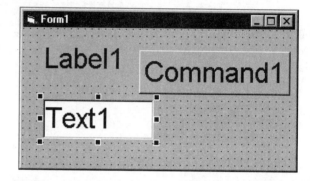

"I see what you mean," I heard Rick say. "You're right. Did I hear you correctly when you said that changing the font properties of the form only affects *new* controls that you place on the form – not controls that are already on the form?"

"That's right," I said. "If we were to change the font properties of the form at this point, the font properties of the controls already on the form wouldn't change."

"So the choice of a font is definitely something you should do up-front," Rick said.

"That's true," I said, "but there is something you *can* do after the fact. Suppose you do already have controls on your form and, for some reason, you want to change the font type and size of some or all of them. I've already said that changing the font properties of the form won't affect controls already on the form. But there is something you can do. Suppose, for instance, that we'd like to change the font of the label and text box controls on our form from Arial-24 to Courier-8. Take a look at this."

I then selected *both* the label control and the text box control by pressing and holding the *Ctrl* key on my keyboard and clicking first on the label control, and then on the text box control. This is the screenshot that the viewing audience saw at home, with the two selected controls showing their grab handles:

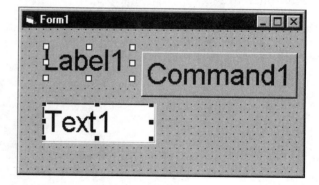

234

"Notice," I said, "that both the label control and the text box control are now selected."

"How did you do that again?" Rick asked.

"All I did was hold down the *Ctrl* key on my keyboard while selecting the label and text box on the form," I said. "That's very much like multi-selecting files in Windows Explorer, except that here we're multi-selecting controls. Now let's bring up the Properties window:"

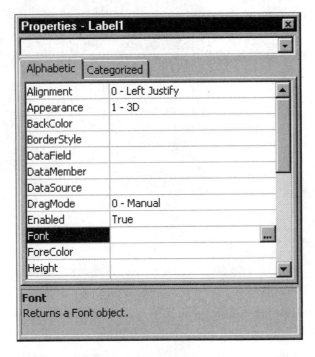

"Do you notice anything funny about the Properties window, Rick?" I asked.

"Yes," he said quickly. "I don't see a name for the control listed in the Object list box at the top of the window. What is this – a hybrid Properties window?"

"That's a great description of it, Rick," I said. "Since we selected two controls – the label and the text box controls – at the same time, when we display the Properties window, we are really seeing the properties that are common to both controls. This is a great feature, because it allows us to change the properties of *every* selected control in a single Properties window."

"So," Rick said, "if we change the font property in this window, the selected font properties will be applied to both the label control and the text box control?"

Rick was catching on quickly.

"That's exactly what that means," I said. "Let's make a selection now."

I clicked on the **Font** property, and the font dialog box appeared. I changed the font to 'Courier' and the size to '10'...

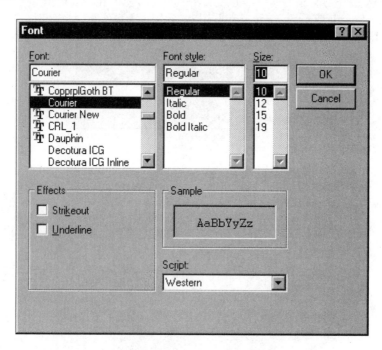

...and clicked on the OK button. When I did, the font type and size of the two selected controls – the label and text box – were immediately changed:

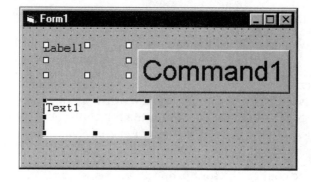

"Wow, that's great," Rick said. "Can this technique be used to change the properties of any set of controls that have been multi-selected?"

"Yes," I answered, "but remember, you'll only see properties in the Properties window that are common to all of the selected controls. If you include a control in the multi-selection that has properties that are not common to all of the selected controls, you won't see the unique properties in the 'hybrid' Properties window. Also note that the font properties are reset if you start a new project."

"I understand," Rick said. "Thanks very much. This will be a great time saver for me."

"Glad I could help, Rick," I said. "Thanks for calling, and now let's move onto caller number...six."

Question 56: Is it possible to build a Visual Basic program for the Mac?

"Hi, my name is Martin, and I'm from Atlanta, Georgia," he said. "I wasn't sure if your producer would accept this phone call, but my family and friends tell me I can be pretty persistent, and I think I just wore her out. My question is this: is it possible to write a Visual Basic program that can run on a Macintosh?"

"Welcome to the show, Martin," I said. "I can understand my producer's reluctance – after all, this is a show about Visual Basic running on the PC. However, I do have an answer for you. I've had a number of students who were Mac users, and who wanted to run the programs they had written in class on a Macintosh. What they did was to import their Visual Basic programs into a product called 'Real Basic', which apparently has some kind of 'Visual Basic-like' environment. From what they told me, Real Basic reads Visual Basic project and form files. You can find out more about it by checking out this website:"

http://www.realsoftware.com.

"Do you happen to know how seamless the transition is?" Martin asked. "Does Real Basic just read the files, or is there some kind of conversion involved?"

"From what my students told me," I said, "I understand that the transition is pretty seamless, but like all PC to Mac conversions, there are bound to be some things that need tweaking. You should check out their website for more information."

"Thanks very much," Martin said.

"Thank you for calling," I said. "And now it's time for our final commercial break of the day. We'll be back in a short while."

I'd scarcely had time to relax for a moment than it was time for caller number seven.

Question 57: Is there a way to hide the Mouse Pointer in a Visual Basic Program?

(see also questions 68 & 75)

"Hi, my name is Maureen, and I'm from Scottsdale, Arizona, but originally from Dublin, Ireland," she said. "I've written a Visual Basic program that displays a very pretty splash screen for about ten seconds upon start up. While that splash screen is displayed, I'd like to hide the mouse pointer from the user. I've experimented with the `MousePointer` and `MouseIcon` properties of the form, trying to adjust them to hide the mouse pointer – but there doesn't seem to be a way to adjust these properties to specify 'no mouse pointer icon'. Is this something that just can't be done in Visual Basic?"

"That's an excellent question," I said. "I think you're right about the a splash screen, Maureen – you probably don't want the mouse pointer displayed. I'd *like* to tell you that you were on the right track, but I can't. The `MousePointer` property of the form allows you to specify one of sixteen different values for a mouse icon – one of which includes selecting a custom mouse icon that is then specified in the `MouseIcon` property. However, there is no way to specify 'no mouse pointer at all' using these properties."

"So it can't be done?" Maureen asked. "There's absolutely no way no hide the mouse pointer?"

I thought for a moment, then said, "I don't know if you saw the show a few weeks ago, but I was asked a question about placing an icon on a menu bar."

"I remember that well," Maureen said. "As I recall, you mentioned something about using the Windows API."

"You have a good memory!" I said. "The Windows API gives the programmer access to Windows functionality that Visual Basic itself does not provide."

"Like hiding the mouse pointer," she said.

"Exactly," I replied. "In fact, using the Windows API to hide the mouse pointer is really pretty easy – and would probably be a great way to introduce everyone to the Windows API."

"That would be great," she said. "What do we need to do to use the Windows API?"

I started a new Visual Basic project with a single command button.

The Windows API," I said, "is a term that collectively describes a series of functions and procedures that exist outside of the Visual Basic environment. These functions and procedures are contained in any one of a number of **Dynamic Link Libraries**, or **DLLs**, found somewhere on your PC's hard disk drive. Using the API is really just a matter of naming the procedure or function that we want to use, and specifying the name of the DLL that contains it."

"That doesn't sound all that bad," Maureen said.

"In this case, it's not," I said. "Probably the hardest thing is knowing which function or procedure to call. Once we know that, the first thing we need to do is to use the Visual Basic `Declare` statement to declare the function `ShowCursor`. The `Declare` statement must be coded in the General Declarations section of a code module (either a form module or a standard module). To keep things simple here, let's declare this function in the General Declarations section of the form."

I then typed the following code in the General Declarations section of my form:

```
Option Explicit

Private Declare Function ShowCursor Lib "user32" (ByVal bShow As Long) As
Long
```

"Yuck!" said Maureen, "maybe I spoke too soon when I said this didn't sound too bad to me. Can you explain that horrible-looking syntax for the `Declare` statement?"

"Sure thing," I said. "First, the words `'Private Declare Function'`, announce to Visual Basic our intention to use a function contained in a Windows DLL. What function? `ShowCursor`. `Lib` stands for **Library**, and `user32` is the name of the Windows DLL that contains the function `ShowCursor`."

"The rest of the line," Maureen said, "I think I can guess. It looks like `ShowCursor` is a function that requires a single argument called `bShow`, whose data type is `Long`. And since `ShowCursor` is a function, it returns a value – and it looks like the return value is `Long` also."

"Excellent analysis," I said. "For my viewers at home, all of this will make more sense to you when we call the function. Let's look at that code now."

I typed the following code in the command button's `Click` event procedure:

```
Private Sub Command1_Click()

Dim lngCounter As Long

Call ShowCursor(False)

For lngCounter = 1 To 20000000
Next lngCounter

Call ShowCursor(True)

End Sub
```

I ran the program and clicked on the command button. When I clicked on the command button, my mouse pointer disappeared and reappeared in about three seconds.

> **If you're trying this yourself, you might want to try it with a smaller loop first, as the length of time it takes to execute depends on your processor. You might have to test it a few times to get the best loop size.**

"You did it," I heard Maureen say. "You made the mouse pointer disappear."

"That wasn't too bad," I said. "Notice in the code that we actually call the `ShowCursor` function twice. Once with a `False` argument, which makes the mouse pointer disappear. Then, after a loop of 20 million iterations has executed, we call it again, this time with a `True` argument, to make the mouse pointer reappear again."

"So that accounts for the three second delay," Maureen said. "The `For...Next` loop. If you don't mind me saying so, this Windows API business doesn't seem all that difficult to me. Why don't we hear more about it?"

"I think there are three reasons," I said. "First, most everything you need to do in a Windows program can be done using Visual Basic – so there really isn't a need to go outside of VB. Secondly, documentation to use the Windows API functions and procedures isn't supplied with Visual Basic. I should mention that there is a tool supplied with Visual Basic called the API Text Viewer that lists Declaration statements for the more common API functions and procedures. But no documentation is provided to tell you what these API functions and procedures do, or - more importantly - how to work with them. To get that documentation, you either need to purchase a Software Developer's Kit from Microsoft, or purchase a book like Daniel Appleman's *Visual Basic Guide to the Windows API*."

"The third reason," I continued, "is that not all functions and procedures are as easy to work with as this one was – others can be much harder. An incorrect call to a Windows function or procedure could lock up your Windows session – so you really do need to be careful, particularly when you're developing and testing your programs. The rule of thumb when working with the Windows API is to make sure you save all of your work beforehand, including anything you may be doing outside of Visual Basic at the time."

"I have two other questions," Maureen said. "First, if the argument data type is a `Long`, why did you pass values of `True` and `False`? And second, what's the return value of this function, and why did you choose to ignore it?"

"Those are both intelligent questions, Maureen," I said. "You're right – `ShowCursor` is built to look for a `Long` data type as its single argument. Using the documentation I found in Daniel Appleman's book, I found that the function was *really* only expecting two values: 0 or -1. In Visual Basic, the `Boolean` value of `False` equates to 0, and the `Boolean` value of True equates to -1. So, by passing `ShowCursor` either a `True` or `False` value, we were passing it exactly what it was expecting."

"OK," she said, "that makes sense – but we *could* have passed it either 0 or -1 just the same? Why didn't we do that? Let me guess, you did this to make the program more readable?"

"That's correct," I said. "You know how I feel about code readability. Now to your second question – the return value of the `ShowCursor` function. The answer to that is a little more difficult to answer, and will begin to give you a flavor for the complexity of working with the API – here goes."

"Windows maintains a system variable which it uses to determine whether or not the mouse pointer should be visible. If this variable is greater than or equal to 0, the mouse pointer is visible. If it's any number *less* than 0, the mouse pointer is *invisible*. Now, whenever you call the `ShowCursor` function with a `False` argument, Windows subtracts 1 from this counter. Whenever you call the `ShowCursor` function with a `True` argument, Windows *adds* 1 to this counter. The return value of the `ShowCursor` function is the value of this system variable. If it's 0 or greater, then the mouse pointer should be visible. If it's less than 0, the mouse pointer should be invisible. In this little program, there wasn't any gain in dealing with the return value – so I just discarded it."

"That means," Maureen said, "that when we called the `ShowCursor` function with a `False` argument, the value of this system variable was set to -1, which meant that the mouse pointer was invisible. When we called the `ShowCursor` function with a `True` argument, the value of this system variable was set to 0 – which means that the mouse pointer was visible again."

"Right on the mark," I said. "It's confusing because of the two separate variables we have. One is the argument passed to the ShowCursor function, where –1 indicates that we want the cursor to be visible, and 0 that we don't. Then we have the *system variable*, where a value of –1 equates to the pointer being *invisible*, and 0 that it's visible. Do you see?"

"Yes, I can see how that could be confusing," Maureen said, "I'm beginning to feel that this can be a bit more complicated than it appears at first."

"Just remember," I said, "with a set of good documentation on the Windows API, you'd be amazed at some of the things you can do with it from within a Visual Basic program."

"Thanks for your help," Maureen said. "You've solved my problem, at least. It's quite difficult, this API business, isn't it?"

"It can be. You really have to know exactly how each API call works, otherwise it can have strange and unforeseen effects on your program. But with a little work, (and nobody ever said there was no work in programming) you can unleash a fair bit of power. Thanks for your call, Maureen," I said. "And now on to our next caller."

Question 58: Is there an easy way to re-center a form when it's been resized?

(see also question 2)

"Hi, my name is Louis, and I'm from New Orleans," said a gravelly voice from the other end of the phone. "I was wondering, is there an easy way to re-center a form when the user re-sizes it?"

"Hi, Louis," I said, "I'm frequently asked how to center a form when it's first loaded. *You're* asking how to center the form *after* the user re-sizes it, is that right?

"That's right," he said.

"What version of Visual Basic are you using?" I asked.

"I'm using Visual Basic version 3," he answered. "Why?"

"In Version 5 and above," I said, "Microsoft introduced a new property of the form that can automatically center your form for you when it's *first loaded*. This property *doesn't* center the form if the user resizes it, but I'd be remiss if I didn't discuss it here. It's called the StartUpPostion property, and you won't find it in Visual Basic 3 or 4; and remember, it won't help you if the user resizes the form. Let me show you and the rest of the viewing audience who may be running version 5 or 6 of Visual Basic how this works at startup, and then I'll give you a solution to the resize issue. Is that OK?"

"That's fine with me," Louis answered.

I started a new Visual Basic project and brought up the Properties window for the form:

"Centering the form when it's first loaded," I said, "was such a popular 'wish list' item that Microsoft added the **StartUpPosition** property to the list of form properties starting in Version 5. If we set the **StartUpPostion** to **2-Center Screen**, then the form will be perfectly centered within the **Screen** object whenever our program starts up."

I ran the program and, as predicted, the form was perfectly centered upon startup. However, when I resized the form, it wasn't automatically re-centered.

"That's something we'll have to take care of ourselves," I said, "by putting some code into the form's **Resize** event procedure. By the way, for those of you who don't have Visual Basic 5 or 6, and therefore don't have access to the **StartUpPosition** property, this code will also center the form when your program first starts up, since the form's **Resize** event is executed as part of the start up process. Here's the code:"

```
Private Sub Form_Resize()

Form1.Top = (Screen.Height - Form1.Height) \ 2
Form1.Left = (Screen.Width - Form1.Width) \ 2

End Sub
```

"To test this, I'd better set the value of the `StartUpPosition` property back to its default of `0-Manual`, and run it," I said, and did so. When the form appeared, it was perfectly centered within the screen. I resized the form several times, and each time the form was perfectly centered.

"That works very nicely," Louis said, slowly and evenly. "Can you explain how you did that?"

"The `Top` and `Left` properties of the form," I said, "control the location of the form within the screen. When the form is first shown, and each time it's re-sized, the `Resize` event of the form occurs. All we did here was to recalculate new `Top` and `Left` coordinates for the form each time the `Resize` event took place, using the form's `Height` and `Width` in a little formula I created. Actually, this formula is one that I demonstrated way back in our second show, when I was asked how to center a command button on a form whenever the form was re-sized. Here, we use the same type of calculation – calculating the `Left` property of the form to be equal to the width of the screen, minus the width of the form, divided by 2. The same formula can be applied to calculate the `Top` property of the form, this time using the height of the form and the height of the screen."

"When does the `Resize` event get triggered again?" Louis asked.

"The `Resize` event," I replied, "is triggered whenever the form is first 'shown' upon program startup, and whenever it is resized by the user."

"Thanks for your help," Louis said. "You've answered my question."

"Before you hang up, Louis," I said quickly, "let me show you another variation on this code that you might see somewhere else in the future."

I displayed this code to Louis and the viewers at home:

```
Private Sub Form_Resize()

Me.Top = (Screen.Height - Me.Height) \ 2
Me.Left = (Screen.Width - Me.Width) \ 2

End Sub
```

"`Me`?" he said, puzzled. "What's `Me`?"

"I wanted to show you this," I said, "because experienced programmers frequently replace the name of the form with the keyword '`Me`'. It's one of those Visual Basic shortcuts you see from time to time that you should be familiar with."

"Professor Smiley," Louis said. "I just ran this code on my PC at home, and when I minimized the form, the program bombed."

"Let's check that here," I said. I minimized the form myself. Louis was right. The program did bomb. Oh, the perils of live television! The following screen shot was displayed to one and all:

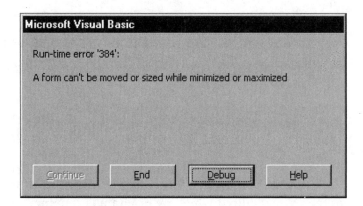

"You're right, Louis," I said, "thanks for pointing that out. I forgot that when you minimize or maximize your form, the **Resize** event is triggered *after* the form has been minimized or maximized – and in Visual Basic, you are not permitted to change the size of a form or move it while the form is either minimized or maximized."

"Now what can we do?" Louis said. "Does this mean that our formula won't work?"

"Not a problem, Louis," I answered. "All we need to do is add an '**If**' test in the **Resize** event procedure to determine if the form is either minimized or maximized *before* we attempt to resize it. This code should do it…"

```
Private Sub Form_Resize()

If Me.WindowState = vbMinimized Or Me.WindowState = vbMaximized Then Exit
Sub


Me.Top = (Screen.Height - Me.Height) \ 2
Me.Left = (Screen.Width - Me.Width) \ 2

End Sub
```

"By checking the form's **WindowState** property," I said, "we can determine if the form is minimized or maximized. If it *is*, we just bypass the rest of the code by exiting the event procedure."

I ran the program, and the form was perfectly centered at startup. Then I minimized the form. No problem. Then I maximized the form. Again, no problem.

"Louis," I said, "I'm glad you thought to minimize the form. Thanks for catching that error."

"Thanks, Professor Smiley," he said. "This is exactly what I needed."

It was time for our ninth caller.

Question 59: Is there a way to determine the number of elements in an array?

(See also questions 49 & 60)

"Hi, my name is Edgar, and I'm from Chicago," he said. "My question is a little theoretical. Is it possible to determine programmatically the number of elements in an array? In a program I'm writing, I'm using file processing to read data from a disk file into a dynamic array; so you see, I'm never quite sure how many elements are going to be loaded in my array, because I can't be certain of what's in the disk file before I've read it. I'd like to be able to determine the size of the array required while my program is running."

"Yes, Edgar," I said, "you can determine that information at run time. Visual Basic has two functions that make finding the number of elements in an array very easy – the LBound and UBound functions. Let me demonstrate this by first declaring an array."

I started a Visual Basic project and placed a single command button on the form. Then I typed up the following code into the command button's Click event procedure:

```
Private Sub Command1_Click()

Dim intArray(20) As Integer

End Sub
```

"With this code," I said, "we're declaring a static array of Integers called intArray. Can you tell me how many elements are in this array, Edgar?"

"20?" Edgar said, obviously not sure of his answer. "When you declare a static array like this, isn't the number within the parentheses the total number of elements in the array?"

"Not quite," I said. "Many beginners - and even experienced Visual Basic programmers - believe that the number within the parentheses is the total number of elements in the array. But this number is actually something called the **Upper Bound** of the array, which is really the upper limit of the array. In my *Learn to Program with Visual Basic* book, I liken the upper bound of an array to the top floor of a high-rise hotel or skyscraper."

"I guess," Edgar said, "the question that begs to be answered is, what about the bottom floor?"

"Right on cue," I said, smiling. "The bottom floor is known as the **Lower Bound** of the array, and is - typically - not explicitly specified. If not specified in the array declaration, Visual Basic assumes that it's equal to the Option Base value – which by default is 0."

"Where is Option Base specified, and can it be anything else?" Edgar asked.

"There are only two possible values for Option Base," I said, "0 and 1. Like the phrase Option Explicit, Option Base (if specified) must appear in the General Declarations section of the form. If Visual Basic doesn't find an Option Base statement there, then the Option Base value is assumed to be 0."

"That helps," Edgar said. "So with the declaration we have now, with the number 20 in parentheses, that means that there are actually 21 elements in this array – since the array elements are numbered starting with 0, and working their way up consecutively to 20."

"That's spot on," I said. "In fact, Edgar, we could have declared our array in the following way – leaving absolutely nothing to the imagination:"

```
Private Sub Command1_Click()

Dim intArray(0 To 20) As Integer

End Sub
```

"I've never seen an array declaration like that," Edgar said. "You've explicitly declared both the lower and upper bound of the array?"

"Right," I said. "It's also possible to declare an array with a lower bound *other* than 0 or 1 – provided you do it in the array declaration, like this:"

```
Private Sub Command1_Click()

Dim intArray(4 To 20) As Integer

End Sub
```

"I didn't know you could do that, either," said Edgar. "I must confess that all of the examples I've seen only seem to specify the *upper* bound of the array. Now getting back to my question; I presume that the LBound and UBound functions you mentioned earlier are used to determine the lower bound and upper bound values of an array – just like we did here by examining the declaration?"

"Right again, Edgar," I said. "Now, since array elements must be consecutive, and knowing both the upper bound and lower bound of an array, we can easily calculate the total number of elements in an array. All we need to do is take the upper bound of the array, subtract the lower bound from it, and add 1. Like this…"

I modified the code in the `Click` event procedure of the command button to look like this:

```
Private Sub Command1_Click()

Dim intArray(4 To 20) As Integer

MsgBox UBound(intArray) - LBound(intArray) + 1

End Sub
```

I ran the program, clicked on the command button, and the following screen shot was displayed:

"Seventeen, that's correct," Edgar said. "But what about dynamic arrays? That's the type of array I'm dealing with."

"Determining the number of elements in a dynamic array," I said, "is really no different, Edgar. With a dynamic array, you don't know at the time you declare the array how many elements it will hold. That's why we declare the dynamic array like this…"

```
Dim intArray() As Integer
```

"…with an empty set of parentheses to tell Visual Basic that we don't know the number of elements in the array at this point. Then, later on – when we *do* know – we use the `ReDim` statement to tell Visual Basic how many elements are now in the array. Like this…"

```
Dim intArray() As Integer

ReDim intArray(20)
```

"Of course," I said, "the exact number of elements in your array will depend on what your program is doing. In your case, you're reading records from a disk file – so the code that you write to read the data from a disk file (most likely within the body of a loop) should also include a `ReDim` statement somewhere within the body of the loop as well. And in order to preserve any data that you've already read into the array's elements, the `Redim` statement should be a `ReDim Preserve` statement. Like this..."

```
ReDim Preserve intArray(20)
```

"As I mentioned a moment ago, Edgar," I continued, "determining the number of elements within the dynamic array is no different than determining the number of elements within a static array. You can use the same code..."

I modified the `Click` event procedure of the command button to look like this:

```
Private Sub Command1_Click()

Dim intArray() As Integer
Redim intArray(4)

MsgBox UBound(intArray) - LBound(intArray) + 1

End Sub
```

I ran the program, clicked on the command button, and the following screen shot was displayed.

"You're right," Edgar said. "It *is* no different. Thank you so much – that will come in quite handy."

"Thank you for your phone call, Edgar," I said. "And now, let's take our final caller of the day."

Question 60: Is there an easy way to erase every member of an array?

(see also questions 49 & 59)

"Hi, my name is Amelia, and I'm from Atchison, Kansas," she said. "While we're on the subject of arrays, is there an easy way to erase the value in *every* element of an array?"

"Hi there, Amelia," I said. "It's a little known fact, but all of the elements of a static array can be erased using the Visual Basic **Erase** statement. Like this..."

I opened up a clean project and placed a single command button on the form. In the command button's **Click** event procedure, I keyed in the following code:

```
Private Sub Command1_Click()

Dim intArray(1 To 10) As Integer
Dim intCounter As Integer

For intCounter = 1 To 10
    intArray(intCounter) = intCounter * 2
Next intCounter

For intCounter = 1 To 10
    Form1.Print intArray(intCounter)
Next intCounter

End Sub
```

Then I ran the program and clicked on the command button:

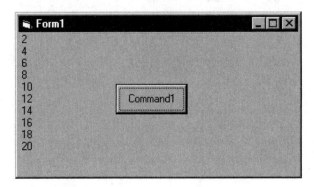

"All we've done here," I said, "is to initialize a 10-element static Integer array:"

```
Dim intArray(1 To 10) As Integer
```

"Notice," I continued, "that in the declaration of the array we specified both a lower *and* an upper bound for the array. Then, using a `For...Next` loop, we assigned values to the ten elements of the array – in this case, a value equal to the element number of the array multiplied by two:"

```
For intCounter = 1 To 10
    intArray(intCounter) = intCounter * 2
Next intCounter
```

"And that final `For...Next` loop," Amelia interjected, "just moves through all of the elements of the array and prints their values on the form."

"Quite so," I confirmed. "Now that we have written code to load and initialize the values of an array, let's see how easy it is to erase those same values."

I modified the code in the `Click` event procedure to look like this:

```
Private Sub Command1_Click()

Dim intArray(1 To 10) As Integer
Dim intCounter As Integer

For intCounter = 1 To 10
    intArray(intCounter) = intCounter * 2
Next intCounter

For intCounter = 1 To 10
    Form1.Print intArray(intCounter)
Next intCounter

Erase intArray

Form1.CurrentY = 0

For intCounter = 1 To 10
    Form1.CurrentX = Form1.CurrentX + 500
    Form1.Print intArray(intCounter)
Next intCounter

End Sub
```

I re-ran the program and clicked on the command button once more, with this result:

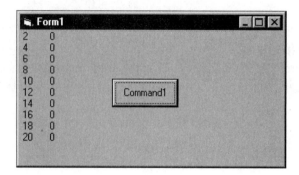

"The first 'column' of numbers is the array with its values," I said. "The second column of numbers is the array *after* we use the Erase statement to delete all of its values. Notice that the Erase statement requires only a single argument – the name of the array:"

```
Erase intArray
```

"I see," Amelia said, "that even though we erased the array, it still has values of zero – why's that?"

"That's because we originally declared the array as an Integer array," I answered. "If we had initially declared the array as a String type, then we would have an array of empty strings after executing the Erase statement."

"I see what's going on here with the Erase statement," Amelia said, "but I must say, I've never seen this column-type display on a form before. How did you manage to do that?"

"I did that by using the CurrentX and CurrentY properties of the form," I explained. "To make this demonstration even more powerful, I wanted to display the values of the populated array and the erased array side by side. So, prior to printing the values of the array after executing the Erase statement, I set the CurrentY value of the form equal to 0. CurrentX and CurrentY are X and Y coordinates of the form, which designate the next printing position for the Print method. If CurrentY is 0, we are telling Visual Basic to print the next character it is asked to print at the *top* of the form:"

```
Form1.CurrentY = 0
```

"Likewise," I continued, "so that I wouldn't print the values of the erased array on top of the previous values, I adjusted the CurrentX property of the form to effectively create a second column of values 500 twips to the right of the first 'column'. I executed this statement just before each execution of the Print method of the form:"

```
Form1.CurrentX = Form1.CurrentX + 500
```

"That's cool," Amelia said. "I haven't seen that technique before. I think I can also use that in my programs. You certainly do learn something here every week. Must fly - bye!""

"Thanks for calling, Amelia," I said. "Well, it looks like we are just about out of time for today's show. I hope everyone enjoyed it, and I hope to see you all again next week. Many thanks to all of my callers. And if you called today but couldn't get through, I'm sorry about that, but we'll be right here next week, at the same time."

As I left the set, I asked Linda how she thought today's show had gone.

"Fine - a little lighter than last week's, I thought. I don't think we've ever had a hiccupping Visual Basic teacher before," she replied, "It's good to bring something new to the show every week!"

"Thanks a lot," I said. "See you next week, I guess."

"I'll get some fresh sea bass in, just in case," she called after me, but I didn't look back. I just chuckled to myself as I got into my car for the trip home.

Week 7

Thursday afternoon found me in Tim's office. I had barely sat down in the chair across from Tim's desk when he asked me if I had made up my mind about the long-term contract. I smiled and told him I had already made up my mind to accept the offer. Tim shook my hand, then asked why I'd been reluctant to commit myself earlier.

"I really didn't think," I told him, "that viewers would call in week after week with good Visual Basic questions. But they have – and I guess if that changes, we'll find out pretty quickly."

"As they say," Tim said, "that's show business. Still, the show has been great for everyone so far; you, me, the audience, and the advertisers. Our ratings in the last few weeks have been excellent. That popularity brings me to the second item I need to discuss with you."

"What's that?" I asked casually, feigning ignorance of what was coming next.

"Well," he continued, "we've worked out a deal to provide a satellite feed of the show to some international networks, starting next Saturday."

I tried to maintain my calm pose, but I was still thrilled.

"An international market," I said, "that's fantastic. So, starting with show number eight we'll be reaching Europe?"

"Not only Europe," Tim said. "It's everywhere. Europe, Asia, South America, Australia, Japan. We've still got to work out some technical details – but a week from Saturday, you could be answering Visual Basic questions from anywhere in the world."

"That's unbelievable," I said. "In eight weeks, we've gone from a local cable television show in northeast Philadelphia to a world-wide audience."

"It's still too early to pat ourselves on the back," Tim said. "But I agree with you, this is phenomenal. Now, back to business. One of the remaining technical issues is the time difference. We need to change the time of the show from 1 pm to 10 am on Saturday mornings. That would give us an air time of 3 pm in London and 4 pm in Paris. Our research indicates that wouldn't severely impact our current viewership."

"That would be fine with me," I said. "As long as we don't offend our established audience. I'm a morning person anyway."

"Great, John," Tim said. "Let's do it!"

Learn to Program with Visual Basic Examples

When I arrived at the studio on Saturday for our seventh show, trusty Linda was already there setting up.

"Congratulations," she said, "I hear we've been extended. That's great news – now I know what I'll be doing with my Saturday mornings for the next few years."

"Congratulations to you too," I said, "you've done a great job."

"And," Linda continued, "I also heard the news that it's 'official' that we're going international. Isn't that great? I think I better ask for a raise. *Our* show is the only international one at the station."

Linda and I talked animatedly while the studio's technical preparations went on around us. I seemed to float through my standard routine until, eventually, Linda's voice cued me in.

"You're on the air."

"Before we introduce our first caller," I began, "I have a couple of announcements to make. First, this show has been extended indefinitely. That means we'll be here each and every week. Secondly, starting next week, we'll be welcoming an international audience, which means that our broadcast will start at 10 am, Eastern Standard Time. I hope you can continue to join me at our new time. Now let's go to the phone lines. Caller number one, you're on the air."

Question 61: Why does the Separator Bar in the General Declarations section act so weird?

"My name is Jim. I'm from Greenville, Mississippi," the caller announced sonorously. "I've been following along with your *Learn to Program with Visual Basic* book, and I've got a question that I bet other beginners have too."

"Hi, Jim," I said, "Go ahead."

"Sure. Here I go. Whenever I try to declare a variable in the General Declarations section of a form," he said, "my cursor moves out of the General Declarations section – where the words 'Option Explicit' appear – and into the next section below, as soon as I start typing. My question is this: how can I get my code typed into the General Declaration section of the form?"

"Well, Jim," I said, "you're not alone – many beginners *do* have this same problem. But the problem is really one of *perception* than anything else, and it really only happens if your code window is open in Full Module view. Is that how you are viewing your code window?"

"Let me double-check on that..." I heard him say. "Yes, you're right, I am viewing my code window in Full Module view. Why would that make a difference?"

"Let me try to duplicate what is happening to you for the rest of the viewing audience," I said, "and then I can show you how to cure it."

I opened a new Visual Basic project and double-clicked on the form to open up the Visual Basic code window:

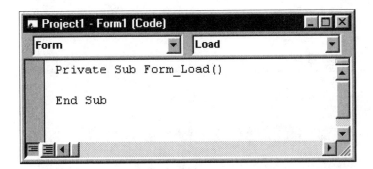

"I think I've mentioned in previous shows," I said, "that the Visual Basic Code window is displayed in Procedure view by default. In Procedure view, you see the code in only *one event procedure at one time*. The alternative, Full Module view, allows you to see *all* of the code in your form at one time – with optional separator bars between the procedures. In a way, Jim, you might be better off with Procedure view, as this view is sometimes less confusing to beginners, at least in the early stages of their Visual Basic careers. Let me explain why. If I'm viewing the code window in Procedure view and I want to declare a variable in the General Declarations section of the form – as you've been trying to do – I need to select (General) from the Object list box at the top of the code window."

"The Object list box?" Jim asked. "That's the list box on the left, yes?"

"That's correct," I said, as I clicked my mouse pointer in the code window's left-hand list box:

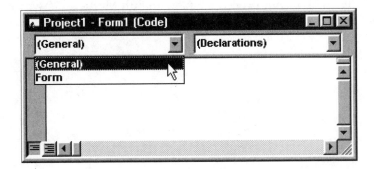

"Once I select **(General)** in the Object list box," I said, "the General Declarations section of the form is displayed in the code window..."

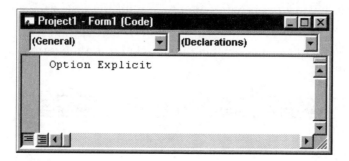

"...and I can declare the variable with no problem. Like this..."

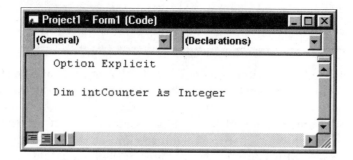

"Now, Jim," I said, "let me show everyone what happens if you're viewing the code window in Full Module view when you attempt to add that variable to the General Declarations section."

I created another Visual Basic project and once again double-clicked on the form to open up the code window.

"As I said earlier," I continued, "Visual Basic displays the code window in Procedure view by default. We can easily switch from Procedure view to Full Module view by clicking on the Full Module view button; that's the second button from the left at the bottom of the code window:"

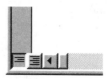

I then clicked on the button with the following result:

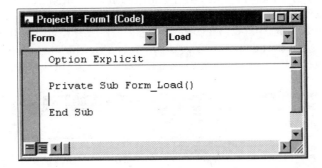

"This is the Full Module view of the code window," I said. "Notice that the mouse pointer is sitting in the `Load` event procedure of the form, and that the words `Option Explicit` appear at the top of the code window. That's the General Declarations section of the form, and it's separated from the `Form_Load` event procedure by a separator bar."

"This is where my problem lies," Jim said. "Try declaring a variable in the General Declarations section of the form, right after the words `Option Explicit`."

"I'll do that in a moment, Jim," I said. "But before I do, I just want to point out that the line we see after the words `Option Explicit` – the Procedure Separator – doesn't really exist as far as the code is concerned. It's just a guide that Visual Basic inserts in the code window to show us where one event procedure ends and another begins. The problem with the procedure separator is that it becomes 'confused' – for want of a better word – whenever you enter code into the General Declarations section. Watch what happens when I position my mouse pointer after the words `Option Explicit` and press the *Enter* key:"

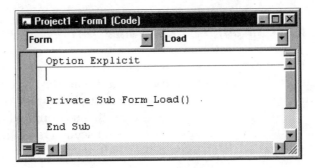

"That's exactly what happened to me," Jim said. "As soon as I started typing into the General Declarations section, Visual Basic moved my mouse pointer down below the separator bar."

"It sure looks that way, doesn't it Jim?" I asked. "Do you remember what I said a second ago – that this problem is more one of perception than reality? Remember, that procedure separator *doesn't really exist*. As soon as you hit the *Enter* key, Visual Basic *appears* to move the mouse pointer out of the General Declarations section. But if you just keep typing and hit the *Enter* key, you'll see that as soon as you finish typing the variable declaration, Visual Basic will move the procedure separator bar back underneath the variable. Like this..."

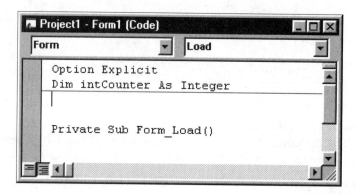

"That's *so* strange," Jim said. "Was that all it was then? I'm really embarrassed – I should have just gone ahead and continued typing – but as soon as I saw the procedure separator bar move, I guess I just panicked..."

"There's no need to be embarrassed," I said. "We've all done the same thing. I'm glad I could help."

"So am I," Jim replied. "Thanks again."

"My pleasure," I said. "And now, let's take call number two."

Question 62: Why do I get an 'Ambiguous Name' error?

"Hi, my name is John," the caller said, "and I'm an expatriate Liverpool lad living in New York City. I bought your book about three weeks ago and read through it with no problem at all, and then wrote my very own Visual Basic program to keep track of my record collection. Everything was going along really cool until this morning when I tried to run my program – now I'm getting an error message I haven't seen before, and it doesn't appear in my Visual Basic documentation. Won't you please help me?"

"Welcome to the show, John," I said. "I'll try – what does the error message say?"

"Something about an 'ambiguous name' being detected," John said. "If you hang on a minute, I can get you the exact wording."

"That's OK, John," I said, "I think I know what the problem is, and it's not difficult to fix. It will actually be more difficult to determine *why* this happened than to fix the problem."

"What's the problem then?" John asked.

"This error message," I answered, "indicates that you've somehow created two event procedures with identical names in your form. I'm not sure how you did this, but I *do* know that I see this kind of error message frequently with beginners, and I've never quite figured out exactly how they do it. Let me try to duplicate this problem for the home audience."

Creating a new project, I placed two command buttons on the form.

"Now let's add some code to the `Click` event procedures of each command button," I said, starting to type:

"Now watch what happens," I said, "if I change the name of the `Command2_Click` event procedure to `Command1_Click`:"

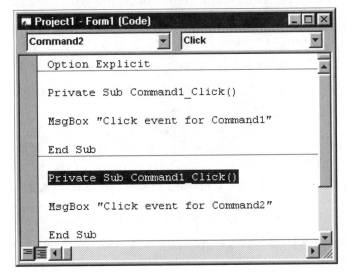

"Why would we want to change the name of an event procedure?" John asked.

"We wouldn't, John," I answered quickly. "But that's what *has* happened here. Somehow or other, you managed to name two event procedures identically. How, I'm not sure. Let's see what happens when we run this program."

I ran the program, which generated John's error message:

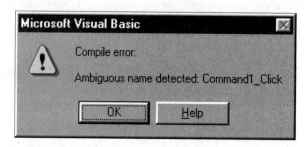

"That's it," John interjected. "That's the error message I'm getting when I try to run my program. So you're right – somehow, I managed to create two event procedures with identical names. I wonder how I could have done that?"

"I can't be certain why this happened, but I have a theory," I replied. "Beginners tend to take liberties with event procedure headers, much like we did in this little demo I did here. Is it possible that perhaps you thought you could rename a control by changing the name of the control's event procedure header?"

"Maybe," John said. "I wish I knew for sure. But just to let you and the rest of the audience know, I just found the villains of the piece; I've got two `Text1_Click` event procedures. I suppose if I delete one or the other, everything will be fine."

"Just a second, John," I interrupted. "First, make sure you're not deleting any useful code. Are any of the event procedures empty of code?"

I waited a moment while John clicked away faintly with his mouse.

"Er - yes," he responded, "one of the event procedures contains the code I want to use, but the other one's empty."

"OK," I said, "select the empty event procedure with your mouse, and then press the *Backspace* or *Delete* key. That will erase the duplicate event procedure, and should take care of your problem."

"Thanks for your help," John said. "I just did that myself, and the program is now running fine. It's time to update my record collection now. As one of my colleagues once said, programming is a long and winding road."

"Good luck with your program, John," I said, "now let's take call number three."

Question 63: I can't click and drag a control from the Toolbox to my form – I just see an icon with a circle around it. Why?

(see also question 47)

"Hi, I'm Dean, from Steubenville, Ohio," the next caller said. "I've only been programming in Visual Basic a few days. I know this is a very basic question to be asking, and I'm sure I'm doing something wrong..."

"Take it easy, Dean," I said, "that's why I'm here – to help beginners with the problems that beginners have. Heck, even experienced programmers learn new things every day!"

"Thanks," Dean said. "I've been trying to place a command button on a form, but I just can't seem to do it. Whenever I try, Visual Basic displays an icon with a circle around it."

I must confess I was puzzled. This was a new one on me. Immediately I thought of an installation problem, or a Windows Registry malfunction of some kind.

"Offhand, Dean," I said, "I'm not sure what may be happening there. Would you try to help me duplicate the problem? Let me start a new Visual Basic project..."

I did just that.

"OK now, Dean," I said, "can you tell me exactly what technique you're using to place the command button on your form? Are you double-clicking the control in the Toolbox, like this...?"

I double-clicked the command button in the Toolbox, and a command button appeared in the middle of my form.

"No, I'm not double-clicking on the command button in the Toolbox," Dean said. "To tell you the truth, I didn't even know you could do that. That's the first time I've seen that illustrated."

"OK," I continued, "are you selecting the command button in the Toolbox by clicking on it with your mouse and then drawing the control on the form, like this...?"

I deleted the first command button, single-clicked the command button control in the Toolbox, clicked on the form, and drew a command button on the form using the cross-hairs that appeared where the mouse pointer was located:

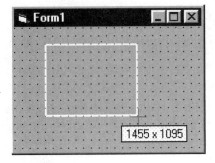

"Unfortunately, I'm not *exactly* using your second technique either. Now I think I know what my problem may be. I've been trying to click *and* drag the command button directly from the Toolbox to my form."

I smiled. "That sounds like a reasonable idea, doesn't it? To be honest with you, Dean," I said smiling, "I've never tried *that* technique myself. Why don't we try that now and see what happens?"

My interest aroused, I deleted the existing command button. Then, using Dean's technique, I clicked on the command button in the Toolbox and tried to drag the command button onto the form. Here's the result of this operation:

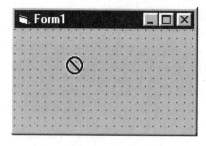

"Well, Dean," I said, "looks like we've both learned something today. Although your technique seems perfectly reasonable, that icon is Visual Basic's way of telling us that this is one technique that you just can't use."

"I told you I was probably doing something stupid," Dean said.

"On the contrary, Dean," I said. "There's nothing stupid about this at all – there's certainly nothing obviously wrong with this technique – in fact, I would bet there are other software packages which allow you to perform operations very similar to this with tools in their Toolbox. And let me tell you one more thing – if you, a beginner, have been trying to use this technique, you can bet that there are hundreds of other beginner programmers trying to do the same thing. You've done them all a great service by calling in with your question – and a service to me also. I pride myself on knowing every possible mistake a beginner can make in Visual Basic – you've just added another one to my inventory. Now whenever anyone mentions this 'forbidden' icon, I'll know right away what's going on."

"Hang on," Dean said, "I just thought of something – what happens if you let go of the mouse button *now*?"

I retried dragging the control from the Toolbox, but this time released the mouse button when the 'no drop' circle was over the form. Hey presto, the crosshairs appeared and I was able to draw the command button on the form.

"Thanks," Dean said. "I feel better now. By the way, I just double-clicked the command button onto the form – that worked great. I'm happy now, and ready to begin programming in earnest."

"Glad I could help, Dean," I said, glancing at the clock on the studio wall. "It looks like it's time to take our first commercial break of the day. We'll be back!"

After a short break, we were ready for caller number four.

Question 64: Is there a way to change the default location for saving files in Visual Basic?

(see also question 23)

"Hi, my name is Bruce, and I am in San Francisco," the caller said. "This isn't a major problem, but I'm curious about it just the same. By default, whenever I save a project for the first time, I'm always prompted to save it in the same directory where Visual Basic is installed. Is there any way I can change things so that the default save location is a directory called **Practice** that I've created on my hard disk drive?"

"Yes you can, Bruce," I said. "First, let me show the home viewers exactly what you mean."

I started a new Visual Basic project and clicked on the **Save** icon on the Visual Basic Toolbar, with this result:

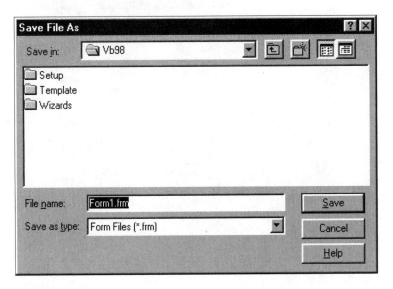

"This is what Bruce is talking about," I said. "By default, when we try to save a project, Visual Basic will save both our forms and the project itself in the same directory that Visual Basic is installed in."

"But there's a way to change that default?" Bruce asked rhetorically.

"Yes," I said. "Personally, I override this default behavior by creating a Desktop Shortcut for the Visual Basic program itself, and specify the directory of my choice in the shortcut's Start in text box. Then, when I save either a form or a project, Visual Basic uses the directory that I've typed in as the default 'save to' directory."

"Do I have to create a desktop shortcut to do this?" Bruce asked.

"No, you don't *have* to do it that way," I said. "Instead, you can adjust the Start in property for Visual Basic in your Visual Basic program group by clicking on your Start button, and use the Taskbar and Startup menu options to navigate to the Start in property. But let's stick with our original technique; let me show everyone the desktop shortcut method now to illustrate what I'm talking about."

I exited Visual Basic, before right-clicking on the desktop and creating a new desktop shortcut for Visual Basic via the New I Shortcut menus:

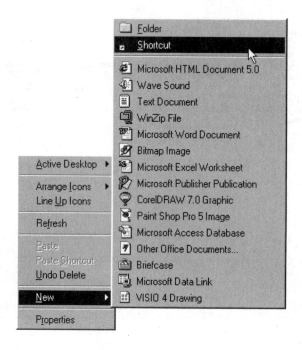

Next, I navigated (via the Browse button) to the location of the Visual Basic executable in the Visual Studio directory on my PC. This path was automatically entered in the Command line argument of the shortcut:

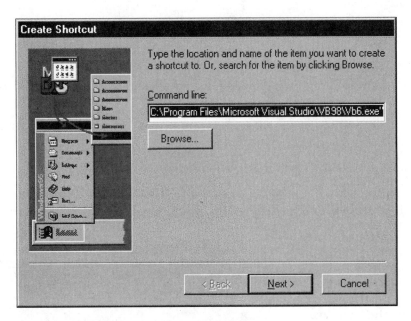

Clicking on the Next button, I then specified a name for the shortcut:

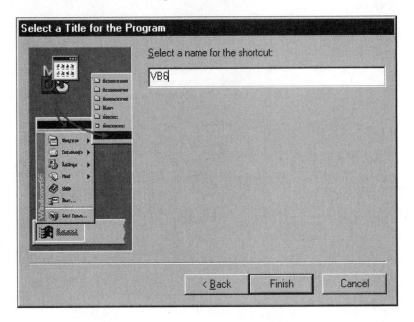

Learn to Program with Visual Basic Examples

Finally, I clicked on the Finish button, and my desktop shortcut was created:

VB6

"Now we have a desktop shortcut which, when we double-click it, will start up Visual Basic," I said.

"But we haven't done anything to have it point to another directory as its default, have we?" Bruce asked.

"No, not yet, Bruce," I replied. "To do that, we need to adjust the Start in property of the desktop shortcut."

To follow this process through successfully, you'll have to create a directory called `C:\Vbfiles\Practice`, **or substitute a directory path of your choice.**

I right-clicked on the desktop shortcut icon for Visual Basic to bring up the Properties window for the shortcut, and changed the Start in property of the shortcut to point to `C:\Vbfiles\Practice`:

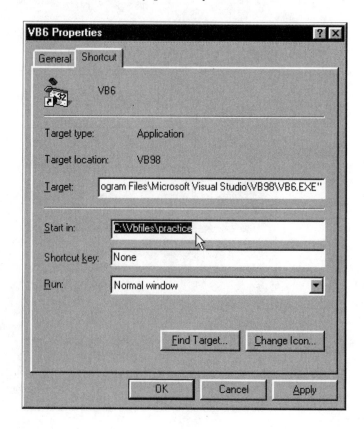

...and clicked on the OK button.

"I should stress," I said, "that `C:\Vbfiles\Practice` is the name of the `Practice` directory that I use here in the studio – you may not have a directory of this name on your PC. Now if we start up Visual Basic again and click on the Save icon on the Toolbar, we should automatically see the new default directory. Let's see..."

I started Visual Basic using the desktop shortcut, started a new project, and clicked on the Save button on the Toolbar. This brought up the Save File As dialog box again:

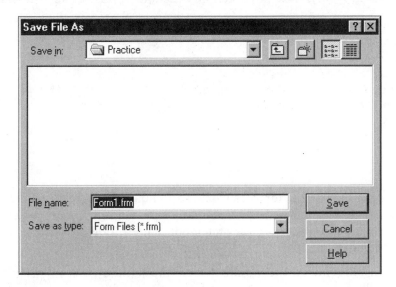

"Do you see the difference now, Bruce?" I asked. "The default directory is now `C:\Vbfiles\Practice`. Is this what you were looking to be able to change?"

"Yes, that's exactly it," Bruce answered. "Thanks for your help."

"To change it back," I added, "You just amend the Save in property to point to the directory where Visual Basic is installed. And now, let's take our next caller."

Question 65: How can I detect the difference between numbers pressed on the standard keyboard and on the numeric keypad?

"Hi, my name is Glenn," caller number five said, "and I'm in Clarinda, Iowa. Can VB detect whether a number typed by the user is being typed from the standard portion of the keyboard or from the numeric keypad? I want to use the numbers from each section of the keyboard to trigger different actions in a program that I'm working on."

"That's a pretty intriguing question," I said. "It *is* possible to detect the difference between the two pretty easily by using the `KeyDown` or `KeyUp` event procedures of the text box control. Take a look at this code and I'll show you what I mean."

I created a new Visual Basic project and added a text box control to the form. I cleared the `Text` property of the text box, and keyed the following code into the text box's the `KeyDown` event procedure:

```
Private Sub Text1_KeyDown(KeyCode As Integer, Shift As Integer)

Select Case KeyCode

    Case vbKey0 To vbKey9
        MsgBox "Keyboard Number"
    Case vbKeyNumpad0 To vbKeyNumpad9
        MsgBox "Numeric keypad"

End Select

End Sub
```

"Very well," I began. "Since the numbers from the standard keyboard and the numeric keypad are represented by different `KeyCode` values passed to the `KeyDown` event procedure, we can use a `Select...Case` statement to identify which group of keys the keyboard input came from."

I ran the program, and entered the number 5 from the standard portion of the keyboard into the text box, and this message box was displayed:

Next, I cleared the number in the text box and entered the number 5 into the text box using the Numeric keypad. This time, the alternative message box appeared:

"That's works great," Glenn said. "I presume that `vbKey0` through `vbKey9` are the Visual Basic intrinsic constants for the keyboard numbers – and that `vbKeyNumpad0` through `vbKeyNumpad9` represent the numeric keypad?"

"That's exactly right, Glenn," I said.

"Thanks, Professor Smiley," Glenn said, "this is just what I need."

"I'm glad I was able to help, Glenn," I said. "Now can you answer a question for me?"

"Sure," he said, "what is it?"

"What kind of program are you writing where you need to be able to detect the difference between the two sets of numbers?" I asked.

Suddenly the phone went dead. Linda signaled to me that we had lost him.

"Looks like we lost Glenn," I said. "Maybe he'll get back to us later. Let's move on to our next caller."

Question 66: Why are there names with colons in the argument list of a MsgBox?

"Good day," the caller began, "I'm Agnes from Skopje, Macedonia..."

'Huh?' I thought, *'an international call?'*

"...but I'm in your country visiting Washington DC," she finished.

"Welcome to the show, and to our country," I said. "How can I help you?"

"One of the Visual Basic programmers at my company has left their job," she said, "and I've been looking at some code they wrote. Specifically, the code in the `Click` event of a command button. I'm a bit baffled by their code, because this programmer did not follow any advice about making their code readable for those that came after them. Anyway, I've come upon something I've never seen before, and I was wondering if you could help me interpret it. If I e-mail you the code right now, would that be OK?"

"Yes, that would be fine, Agnes," I said, "Go right ahead."

In a matter of seconds, I had the code in front of me, via e-mail. *'How computers have shrunk the world and compressed time,'* I thought.

"I see why you're confused, Agnes," I said. "Let me write a modified version of this code and display it to the viewers at home."

I started a gleaming new project and placed a single command button on the form before writing the following code in the command button's `Click` event procedure:

```
Private Sub Command1_Click()

MsgBox Prompt:="I love Visual Basic", Title:="Optional Arguments"

End Sub
```

When I ran the program and clicked on the command button, the following message box popped into view:

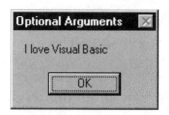

"Is this code similar to the code that's puzzling you, Agnes?" I asked.

"Yes, it's similar," she said. "What's going on here with the colon and the equal sign in the `MsgBox` line of code? I'm afraid that syntax has me confused."

"The colon and equal sign (`:=`) tells Visual Basic that we're passing **Named Arguments** to the `MsgBox` function," I said. "Named arguments are great, in that they provide built-in documentation for your program – the *actual* name of the argument appears *explicitly* in the argument list, just before the colon and the equal sign:"

```
MsgBox Prompt:= "I love Visual Basic", Title:="Optional Arguments"
```

"One benefit of named arguments is how easy they make passing optional arguments to a procedure or a function. With named arguments, it's not necessary to provide a place holder comma in the argument string; we saw in a previous show that when you're passing optional arguments in an argument string, you can use a comma to indicate that you're *not* passing a value for a particular argument. These multiple commas can be difficult to interpret when reading other people's code, especially if you're not sure what the *possible* arguments are. With named arguments, you can see the arguments there in the code in black and white, and so your code is self-documenting."

"Yes," Agnes agreed, "I've seen myself that passing optional arguments to a procedure or function can be a real pain."

"So," I continued, "with *named* arguments, all you need to do is pass the individually named arguments that you actually want to use – and no placeholder commas. Because of the explicit argument names that we're passing along with their values, Visual Basic knows *exactly* which arguments we are supplying and which ones are missing."

"I have a question," Agnes said. "How do you know *what* to name the argument?"

"Good question," I said. "You need to check the definition of the function or procedure in on-line help. Any arguments, and their names, are listed there. Let's check the definition of the `MsgBox` function to see."

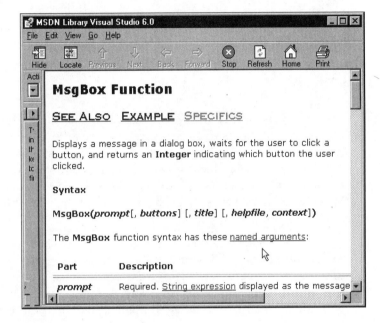

I selected the word `MsgBox` in the code window and pressed the *F1* function key to trigger the display of context sensitive help:

"This is the Help definition for the `MsgBox` function," I said. "Notice that this definition indicates that the `MsgBox` function has **named arguments**."

"I see that," she said, "so those are the names that we can use when passing named arguments – `Prompt`, `Buttons`, `Title`, `Helpfile`, and `Context`?"

"Exactly," I said. "And just to repeat, all you need to do to pass a named argument is to use this syntax:"

```
argumentname := value
```

"I think I can handle that," she said. "I can definitely see the value of named arguments in my program. I just wish our programmer had explained this to me. Let me ask you this; do all Visual Basic procedures and functions support named arguments?"

"Most of them do," I said. "If you don't see a phrase in the Help file referring to named arguments, then the procedure or function does *not* support named arguments."

"I just thought of something," Agnes said. "What about procedures or functions that I've written myself? Can I use named arguments in those also?"

"You sure can," I said. "And you don't need to do anything special to implement them. The names that you define the arguments when you *create* your procedure or function are the names you pass to that procedure or function via any argument list you write in your code."

"I think I may just do that," she said. "Thanks for clearing this up for me."

"My pleasure, Agnes," I said. "And now I think it's time we took our final break of the day."

After the break, we resumed with caller number seven.

Question 67: Is there a form property that allows 'tabbing' via the Enter key?

"Hello, this is Grace from New York City," she said. "Here's my question: if you press the *Enter* key in a Microsoft Access form, you're automatically 'tabbed' to the next entry box on your form. Is there a way to do this in Visual Basic? I've figured out that when you hit the *Enter* key on a Visual Basic form, the cursor just stays where it is. It seems that the only way to move from one entry box to another is to use the *Tab* key, or to click the mouse. I was looking for some property of the form to do the trick, but I couldn't find anything. Can you help?"

"Hi, Grace," I said. "Let me welcome you to the show. This is a classic question, especially for people coming to Visual Basic from a product like Microsoft Access. Just so everyone understands exactly what you're asking, let's use a hypothetical situation. You have a form that contains several text boxes. After the user makes an entry in one of the textboxes, you want them to be able to move to the next text box in the correct `Tab Order` when they press the *Enter* key. Is that right?"

"That's correct," Grace said. "Is there a form property that can do that for me?"

"No, Grace," I said, "I'm afraid there isn't a form property. But I can think of a way to achieve this behavior using Visual Basic code. Would that be OK for you?"

"Whatever works," she answered.

"OK," I said, "let's take a shot. Let's first look at the default behavior of the form and the text boxes."

I opened up a new Visual Basic project and put three text boxes on the form. Using the Properties window, I cleared the text properties of each text box.

"If I run this program now," I said, "and make an entry of some kind into the first text box, I can only move to the *second* text box if I press the *Tab* key or click in the second text box with the mouse."

I ran the program, typed the letter 'I' into the first text box, and pressed the *Enter* key.

"Notice," I said, "that pressing the *Enter* key has absolutely no effect on our program. The focus remains on the first text box. If I press the *Tab* key however, I can move the focus to the second text box."

I pressed the *Tab* key and typed 'love' into the second text box. I pressed the *Tab* key again and focus moved to the third text box, where I typed 'Visual Basic'. My form now looked like this:

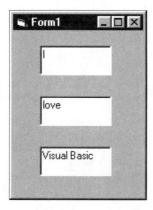

"What you just saw," I said, "is the default behavior of the text box controls and the form. The only way to move the focus from a text box to another control on the form is to press the *Tab* key, or to click the mouse on the other control."

"Let me just say," Grace said, "that this behavior is extremely awkward for the users of my Visual Basic program. Since many of them are familiar with the Access version of my program, they habitually press the *Enter* key expecting the focus to move to the next field on the form."

"I understand, Grace," I said. "But don't despair – we can build this behavior into your program – it's just going to take more effort than setting a property. In fact, in order to make coding this as easy as possible, I'm going to suggest that you use a control array of text boxes on your form. Are you familiar with control arrays, Grace?"

"Yes, I am," she replied emphatically, "they're groups of controls that have the same *name*, but a unique `Index` property that identifies individual instances of the control."

"Wow, that was *good*," I said. "That's a large part of it. In addition, and very importantly, all of the member controls in a control array share the same event procedures. You'll see in a minute that we'll be placing code in the `KeyPress` event procedure of the text box. Because we'll use a control array of text boxes, we only need to place this code in the single shared `KeyPress` event procedure of the text box control array – not in a whole bunch of individual text boxes."

"And suppose we choose *not* to create a control array?" Grace asked.

"Then," I said, "we would have to copy and paste the code into the `KeyPress` event procedure of *every* text box control on the form."

"It sounds like a control array will be a lot easier to maintain," Grace said, "after all, the code only appears *once*."

"Exactly," I replied. "Let's get rolling on this code. First, we have three individual text box controls on the form. We can convert these into a control array."

"I thought you needed to create a control array when you first placed the controls on the form?" Grace asked. "I didn't know you could do it after the fact."

"You can create a control array at *any* time," I said, "As you pointed out, a control array is just a collection of identical controls, all sharing the same name, but each having a unique `Index` property. Creating a control array up front – by placing a single text box on the form and then copying and pasting it onto the form – is probably a little easier on the programmer because Visual Basic will take care of assigning the unique `Index` properties for you. But we can also create the control array after we've created a number of individual controls. All we need to do is change the `Name` property of each one of the text boxes so that they are all identical, and then assign unique `Index` values to each. Let me show you."

I stopped the program and, using the Properties window, changed the **Name** property of each text box to **txtDemo**. I then assigned **Index** properties of **0**, **1** and **2** respectively to each of the three text boxes:

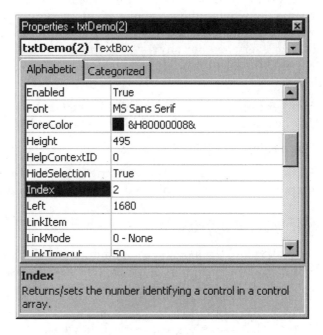

"Now," I continued, "let's enter some code into the control array's shared **KeyPress** event procedure. This code will check to see if the user has pressed the *Enter* key; and if they have, it will generate a *Tab* character in the text box, just as if the user had pressed it themselves. Here's the code:"

```
Private Sub txtDemo_KeyPress(Index As Integer, KeyAscii As Integer)

If KeyAscii = Asc(vbCrLf) Then SendKeys "{TAB}"

End Sub
```

"I'm familiar with the **KeyPress** event of the text box," Grace said, "but I'm not clear about this code. What is the **Index** argument doing inside the brackets in the event procedure header?"

"Remember, Grace," I said, "this event procedure is associated with a control array, and the code in it is executed whenever *any* of the three text boxes have text entered into them. Therefore, the designers of Visual Basic thought it would be a good idea to let us know exactly *which* of the textboxes actually triggered the **KeyPress** event."

"And that's done through the use of the **Index** argument?" Grace queried.

"Yes," I confirmed. "So, if the control the user typed into had an **Index** property of 1, the argument passed to the **KeyPress** event procedure would be 1. In our example, the **Index** property doesn't actually affect the behavior of our code, since we want to execute the *same* code for every text box anyway. But our code *could* be dependent upon which control triggered the event procedure, in which case we would want to check the **Index** property first."

"Another thing," Grace continued, "the **KeyAscii** argument. Just to be sure – is that the ASCII value of the key that the user just pressed?"

"That's right," I said.

"So, the Visual Basic intrinsic constant **vbCrLf** represents the *Enter* key, and..." Grace faltered, presumably nonplussed by the **SendKeys** portion of the **If** statement:

```
If KeyAscii = Asc(vbCrLf) Then SendKeys "{TAB}"
```

"Let me explain the **SendKeys** statement," I said. "**SendKeys** is used to send *keystrokes* to the Active Window in your application, just as if the user had *typed* them on the keyboard."

"Really? Now let me get this straight," she said, "if the user presses the *Enter* key, we translate that input by using the **SendKeys** statement to simulate the user having hit the *Tab* key? That's sounds great to me. Can we see this in action?"

"Sure thing," I said, as I ran the program. I began by typing the letter 'I' into the first text box. I then pressed the *Enter* key – and the focus moved immediately to the second text box.

"Beautiful," I heard Grace say, "that's pretty elegant."

I then typed 'love' into the second text box, and pressed the *Enter* key; focus then moved to the third text box.

"Outstanding," Grace said. "That did it. Thanks very much – this is *exactly* what I needed. Believe me, my users will be very happy."

"I love happy users," I said. "Thanks for calling, Grace, and good luck with your programming. Who's our next caller, please?"

Question 68: Can I have a different mouse icon?

(see also questions 57 & 75)

"Hi, my name is Eleanor, and I'm from New York City," the voice on the other end of the line said. "My husband Frank telephoned you several weeks ago with a question about the common dialog control, and he just got around to telling me about your show the other day. That man can really keep a secret, believe me. I had no idea that a show like yours was on the air. What a great idea!"

"Thank you, Eleanor," I said, "How can I help you?"

"I'm writing a Visual Basic program," she said, "and during the course of the program, I want to disable several of the controls on the form. My program's users are primarily senior citizens whose eyesight isn't quite what it used to be, and I want to change the mouse icon when the user moves the mouse pointer over a disabled control. I know that disabled controls look 'disabled' to most people, but to members of my age group, disabled controls don't always stand out – hence the need for a change of the mouse pointer to indicate their status. Is there a way to do this?"

"Yes there is, Eleanor," I said, "but I must warn you, this isn't going to be easy. Are you up to it?"

"If it will do the job," she answered, "I'm all for it."

I started a new Visual Basic project and added two check boxes to the form.

"Let's disable one of the checkboxes," I said, "and leave the other one enabled."

Using the Properties window, I set the **Enabled** property of the first check box, **Check1**, to **False**:

I left the second check box Check2 enabled and ran the program. When I moved my mouse pointer over the disabled check box, Check1, we saw the following effect:

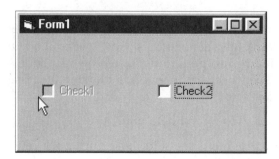

"Notice," I said, "the default nature of the mouse icon when the mouse pointer moves over a disabled control – it doesn't change. Now correct me if I'm wrong, Eleanor, but you would like the mouse pointer to change shape here to signal to the user of your program that the control is disabled – is that right?"

"That's it," she agreed. "And you say that's difficult?"

"Difficult may not be the correct word," I said, "how about 'tedious'? You'll need to follow along with me carefully. Let me explain what I propose to do in a nutshell. Basically, we're going to change the MousePointer property of the form from its default value of 0 to a value of 12, which equates to the vbNoDrop value. But we only want to do this when the mouse pointer is moved over the disabled check box. That's the tricky part."

Eleanor interjected at this point; "Why not use the MouseMove event of the disabled Check1 check box? That's what I was experimenting with."

"Well, therein lies the problem," I said. "The MouseMove event of a disabled control is *never* triggered. For that reason, we can't put code in that event procedure to change the mouse pointer – it would never get executed."

"So that's why my attempts failed," Eleanor said.

"Unfortunately for us," I continued, "the MouseMove event of a disabled control isn't recognized by Windows. But we *can* use the MouseMove event of the form, although it will be a challenge to determine when the mouse pointer is 'over' the disabled control."

"I would think so," Eleanor said. "Does the MouseMove event procedure of the form give us enough information to determine that?"

"Yes, it does," I replied, "although it will require some translation. The MouseMove event procedure of the form is passed the X and Y coordinates of the mouse pointer on the form. Using those coordinates, and knowing where on the form the disabled checkbox is located, we can determine if the mouse pointer is over the disabled check box."

"This I want to see," Eleanor said.

"I'll show you," I said. "Let's start by declaring four module-level variables that we will use to represent the dimensions of our disabled check box."

"Why module-level variables?" Eleanor asked.

"We want to declare these variables as module level in the form's General Declarations section," I said, "because we'll be referring to them in two event procedures; both the Load event *and* the MouseMove event procedure of the form. When a variable needs to be accessed from more than one procedure on a form, it must either be declared as a form- or module-level variable on the form, or possibly as a global variable in the General Declarations section of a standard module. For our demonstration, we'll declare these variables in the General Declarations section of the form. That way, *both* event procedures will be able to 'see' them."

I wrote the following code in the General Declarations section of the form:

```
Option Explicit

Private m_intLeft As Integer
Private m_intRight As Integer
Private m_intTop As Integer
Private m_intBottom As Integer
```

"Now," I continued, "we need to create some code in the form's Load event procedure to calculate the disabled check box's dimensions, and to assign those values to our four module level variables. Here's *that* code:"

```
Private Sub Form_Load()

m_intLeft = Check1.Left
m_intRight = Check1.Left + Check1.Width - 1
m_intTop = Check1.Top
m_intBottom = Check1.Top + Check1.Height - 1

End Sub
```

"These variables' values will represent the location of the check box on the form," I explained. "When the form loads, we use this code to calculate the dimensions of the disabled check box (Check1). The assignment of m_intLeft and m_intTop are relatively easy – those are just the built-in Left and Top properties of the disabled check box. m_intRight and m_intBottom are a little more difficult. To calculate the 'bottom' coordinate of the check box, we need to take the Top property of the check box, add its Height, and subtract 1 (because the coordinate system is zero-based). To calculate the right-hand side coordinate of the check box, we need to take the Left property of the check box, add its Width, and subtract 1."

"Now, what exactly do those numbers give us?" Eleanor asked.

"This is the key thing," I said. "They give us values that we can use to compare with the X and Y coordinates passed to us in the MouseMove event procedure of the form. Remember, these X and Y coordinates tell us the position of the mouse pointer at the instant that the MouseMove event is triggered. In other words, we can use these coordinates to determine if the mouse pointer is within the boundaries of the check box. Here's the code we'll use to do this:"

```
Private Sub Form_MouseMove(Button As Integer, Shift As Integer,
    ↳ X As Single, Y As Single)

   If (X > m_intLeft And X < m_intRight) And
     ↳ (Y > m_intTop And Y < m_intBottom) Then

      Form1.MousePointer = vbNoDrop

   Else

      Form1.MousePointer = vbDefault

   End If

End Sub
```

"Picture this, Eleanor," I said. "When the mouse is moved, it passes an X and Y coordinate to the MouseMove event procedure of the form. At that point, this code compares the X coordinate of the mouse pointer to the range of values from the left side of the disabled check box to the right side of the disabled check box:"

```
If (X > m_intLeft And X < m_intRight) And
```

"The code also compares the Y coordinate of the mouse pointer to the top and bottom coordinate range of the disabled check box:"

```
(Y > m_intTop And Y < m_intBottom) Then
```

"If both X and Y coordinates are inside these ranges, we know that the mouse pointer is within the disabled check box, and at that point, we use this code..."

```
Form1.MousePointer = vbNoDrop
```

"...to change the mouse pointer to one the user will clearly recognize as being 'over' a disabled control. And if the X and Y coordinates are not within the dimensions of the disabled control, we then use this code to change the MousePointer property back to its default value..."

```
Form1.MousePointer = vbDefault
```

"Can we see this in action?" Eleanor asked.

"Sure thing," I said, and ran the program. As I moved the mouse pointer over the form, there was no obvious difference. However, when I moved the mouse pointer over the disabled check box, the following screen shot was displayed:

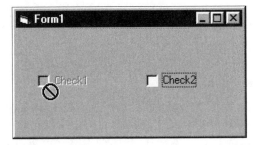

"That's the icon you were talking about," I heard Eleanor say. "The vbNoDrop pointer. Yes, that will do quite nicely."

I moved the mouse pointer away from the disabled checkbox, and sure enough, the mouse pointer changed back to its default look.

"That's excellent, Professor Smiley," she said. "Thanks so much."

"You're quite welcome, Eleanor," I said, "and say 'hello' to your husband for me. And now on to caller number nine."

Question 69: Why won't my executable file run on another PC?

"Hi, my name is Bess, and I'm from Independence, Missouri," she said. "My husband Harry is on an extended business trip to Washington, DC, so I've been taking a Visual Basic course at our local community college here in Independence. I wrote a program last week that I was very proud of, and I wanted to send it to Harry. I generated an executable of the program, just like we do in the classroom at college, and sent it off to Harry. But when he tried to run it on his PC in his office, it wouldn't function...something about a 'missing DLL'. Can you tell me what's going on?"

"This is a familiar problem, Bess," I said. "The Visual Basic executable you sent to your husband Harry *cannot* run on its own – it needs some Visual Basic DLLs to go along with it. As you may know, Bess, DLLs (Dynamic Link Libraries) are used to store functions which your operating system and programs can use. In many cases, Visual Basic uses functions in these basic 'libraries' without any intervention from you, which is why it's easy to forget they are there. Since they are linked *dynamically* at run time, rather than compiled into your program, when your program tries to find them – and can't – you get the machine equivalent of a *huh*?"

"But," she said, "why did the executable run in the classroom? I wrote the program at home but could still run it at college – is that because the college machines have the Visual Basic DLLs installed?"

"That's right, Bess," I said. "If a PC contains Visual Basic, then the DLLs your executable needs to run are already installed on that PC. The problem is that Harry needs them to see your executable in action – and they're not on his PC."

"How can I get him those DLLs?" she replied. "If you give me a list of them, I can copy them onto a diskette and mail them to him."

"I'm afraid it's not that simple, Bess," I said, "I *could* give you a list of the DLLs that you need to give him. But there are a few other files he needs in addition, and it would be easy to miss one. Furthermore, Harry needs to install these files in specific directories on his PC and, in some cases, he needs to register them in his Windows Registry."

"That sounds pretty difficult," Bess said. "Maybe I should just wait until he's back home."

"That's probably not necessary," I said. "I'm not sure of which version and edition of Visual Basic you are running at home or in the classroom, but most versions have an Application Setup Wizard which will lead you through the process of copying the necessary support files – DLLs among them – onto a diskette. This wizard will generate a professional looking setup program so that all Harry needs to do is click on the `setup.exe` file on the diskette using Windows Explorer and your program, plus all the DLLs it needs, will be installed on his PC, ready to run."

"That's great," Bess said, "but it sounds too easy. Can you show me how to run the Wizard?"

"I sure can," I said. "First, let me create a simple little program – a form with a command button – to use in our demonstration. Then I'll generate an executable file that can run independently of whether VB is installed on the machine it's run on, and finally use the Setup Wizard to create a set of setup diskettes."

I started yet another new Visual Basic project and placed a single command button on the form.

"The first thing we need to do," I said, "is to save this project, then compile the program so that we have something to distribute."

"Compile?" queried Bess.

"Yes," I said, "that essentially means that the code we've written is compacted into a format we can run."

I saved the project as **Bess** in my **C:\Vbfiles\Practice** directory, and then selected Make Project1.exe from the Visual Basic Menu Bar:

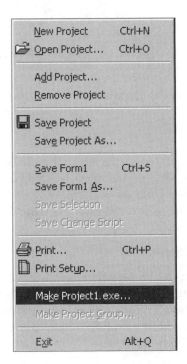

"Rather than accept the default name of `Project1.exe`," I said, "let's generate the executable as `Bess` and save it in the `\Vbfiles\Practice` directory:"

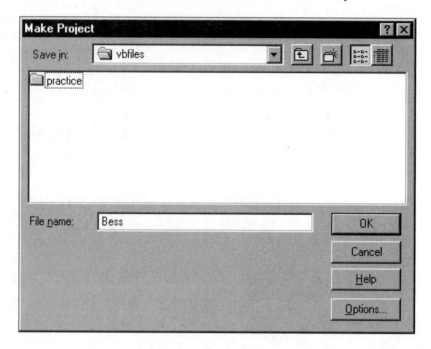

"At this point," I said, "we now have an executable file called `Bess.exe`. This is as far as you got, I guess, Bess?"

"That's right," she confirmed.

"OK," I said, "Now, we could easily run this program using the Start I Run button, since all of the Visual Basic support DLLs are already installed on this PC. But this executable *will not* run on any PC that does not have Visual Basic installed. I should mention that in rare instances, the Visual Basic DLLs *might* be present on a PC which has not had Visual Basic installed, but that is a little haphazard."

"Do we run the Wizard now?" Bess asked.

"Yes," I replied, "now it's time to run the Wizard. Perhaps the hardest part of that process will be finding it. In Visual Basic 6, the Wizard can be found either in the Visual Basic 6 group on this PC, in the Visual Studio 6.0 Tools folder. Alternatively, it can be run from within Visual Basic itself, under the Add-In menu. In Visual Basic 5, the wizard will only be found in the Visual Basic program group itself."

I opened up the Visual Basic program group on my studio PC and selected Microsoft Visual Studio 6.0 Tools from the menu...

...before selecting the Package and Deployment Wizard...

"Didn't you say that the Wizard was called the Application Setup Wizard?" Bess asked.

"My apologies, Bess," I said, "that's the name of the Wizard in the Visual Basic 5 world. The name of the Wizard changed in Visual Basic 6, mainly because Microsoft added an additional step to the distribution process, where we need to create something else first – a **Package**."

"So both processes do essentially the same thing?" Bess asked, "but the Visual Basic 6 version is doing something more. Does that complicate things?"

"A bit," I said. "People using Visual Basic 5 don't need to worry about first creating a package, that's all. They go straight to the deployment part of the Wizard. It's a few more steps away in Visual Basic 6. In VB 5, the detail of the process differs, but the principles are similar. When in doubt, follow the Wizard's instructions and accept its defaults."

I waited for a moment to see if Bess had any questions, and then selected the Wizard in the tools submenu.

"Our first step, then," I continued, "is to select a project – in this instance, `Bess.vbp` in our `Practice` directory. We can do that now by using the Browse button in the Wizard to find and select it..."

I did that.

"Once our project is selected,"
I said, "we then need to click
on the Package icon..."

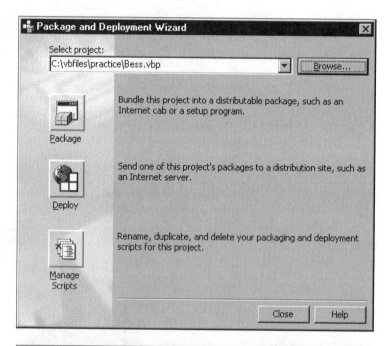

I clicked on the icon and, after
a few seconds, the following
screen shot appeared:

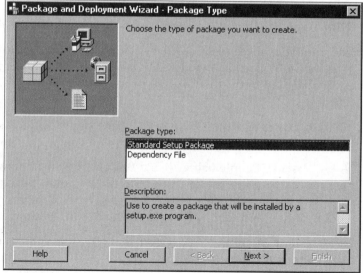

"Just let the Wizard lead you through this, Bess," I said. "For the most part, we'll accept the Wizard's defaults, and click the Next button."

"What is this screen asking us to do?" Bess asked.

"The Wizard is asking us to specify the **Package** type," I said. "We want to create a **Standard Setup Package**, which will then allow us to create a `setup.exe` program. A **Dependency File** would just list the files necessary to run our executable on another PC – like the list of DLLs you originally asked me for."

I then selected **Standard Setup Package** and clicked on the **Next** button:

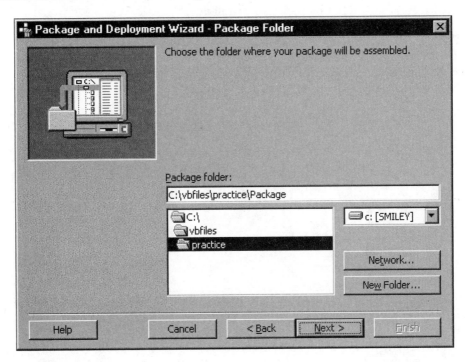

"This screen is prompting us to select a location for our Package directory or folder," I said. "The Package is just a group of temporary files that hold the data that we use to create the distributable program, and the Wizard wants to know where we want to store them. By default, the Wizard will create a Package directory 'underneath' the directory where the executable is located. As is the case most times with Wizards, the default is usually fine – so we'll just click on the **Next** button here."

Learn to Program with Visual Basic Examples

I did this, with the following result:

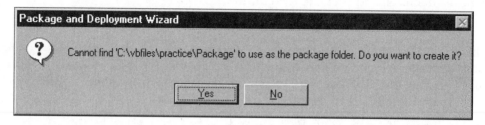

"Uh oh..." I heard Bess say. "That looks like a problem..."

"It's OK," I said. "The Wizard is just telling us that a Package Directory does not yet exist in our **Practice** directory, and wants to know if it's OK to create one. If we click the Yes button here, the Wizard will create the directory or folder for us."

I clicked on the Yes button, and this screen was displayed:

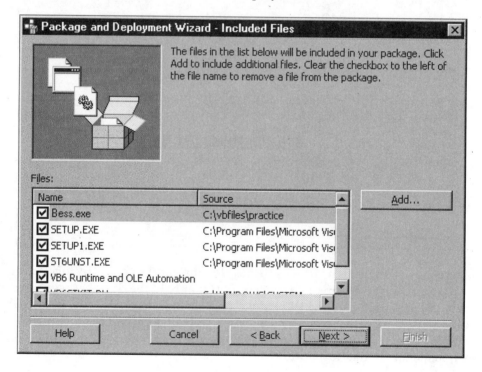

"I'm just guessing," Bess said, "but are these the files that Harry needs to run my executable on his PC?"

"Some of them are," I said. "Our executable and those DLLs I mentioned are included in this list of files – if you scroll down far enough, that is. Other files are those that the Setup program requires. I should mention that if we click on the Add button here, the Wizard will provide us with an opportunity to add any other files to our Package that our program might need at run time."

"Such as?" Bess asked.

"Such as," I said, "graphic files that we want to load into the form or picture box using the **LoadPicture** method; or disk files that the program reads at startup; or maybe a database that we intend to write records to during the program's execution, etc. We have no files to add at this time, so all we need to do here is click on the Next button."

I did that, and the following screen shot was displayed:

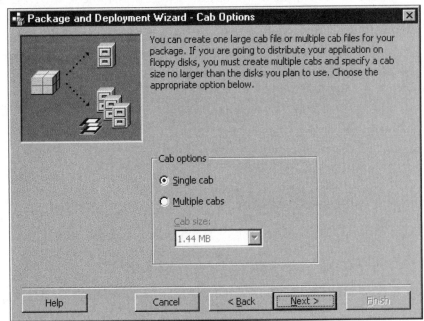

I gave Bess and the viewing audience a chance to read this screen.

"This is a bit odd," Bess said. "What do we do now? What's a Cab?"

"I agree," I said, "the first time I saw this screen, I spent about five minutes reading it and re-reading it. But I can summarize this pretty easily. *Cab* stands for 'cabinet', and it forms the basis of the distribution package in Visual Basic. There are many options for creating and distributing Cabinet files – for example, as a single file over a network, as a writable CD-ROM device, over the Internet, and – as in our case – via floppy diskettes. Since we will be distributing our package via floppy diskettes, we need to specify the Multiple cabs option here."

"Why multiple cabs?" Bess asked.

"Well," I replied, "that's because the Wizard knows that even the *smallest* Visual Basic executable requires at least two floppy diskettes for the distribution files."

"Is that right?" Bess inquired. "Those DLLs must be pretty large!"

"The Visual Basic runtime DLL," I said, "which is just one of the DLLs that we need to put onto your husband's PC, is over a megabyte and a half in size – which means it takes more than one floppy just to store that file. So let's select Multiple cabs here..."

I also accepted the default Cab size of 1.44 MB – the capacity of a standard floppy diskette drive:

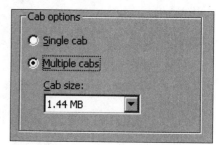

I then clicked on the Next button, and the next screen appeared:

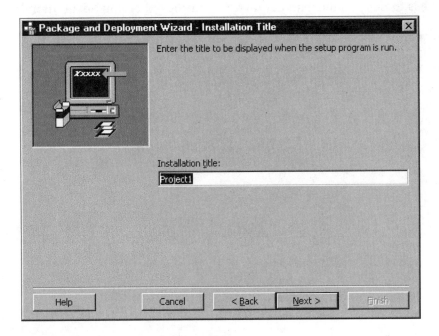

"What's this asking us to do?" Bess said. "I thought we had already changed the name of our executable from `Project1.exe` to `Bess.exe`?"

"Oh," I said, "I forgot to change the name of our project in Visual Basic," I said. "That's where this default for the installation title is coming from."

"What's the installation title?" Bess asked.

"As I mentioned earlier," I replied, "the Wizard will generate a professional quality setup program for us. Part of that is a very spiffy looking splash screen when it fires up – and that's what we're being asked about here – the title for that splash screen. How about if we get fancy, Bess, and customize the title to read From Bess to Harry for now."

"That's great," she said, "I know he'll love that."

I entered From Bess to Harry as the installation title and clicked on the Next button:

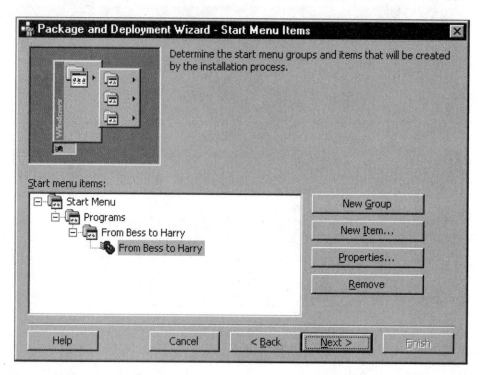

"What's that?" Bess asked.

"This is a neat little feature of the Wizard," I said, "It allows us to specify *exactly* where the program will be installed on Harry's Start menu. By default, our program will be installed in the Program group of the user's Start menu – but we could change that if we wanted. My advice is to go with the defaults here, Bess. That means that the Wizard will create a Program Group called From Bess To Harry on Harry's PC."

I accepted the default by clicking on the Next button:

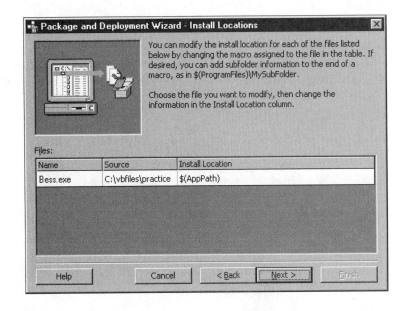

"Whereas the previous screen allowed us to specify where the *icon* representing our executable would be placed in the user's Start menu," I said, "this screen allows us to specify the actual location of the *executable*. As you can see, the default location is the same directory as on my studio PC. This means that the Setup program will create a directory of the same name on the recipient's PC. Again, unless you have a good reason to change this location, you should probably accept the default. Let's do that now by clicking on the Next button:"

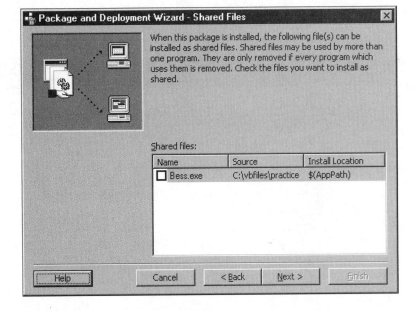

"More confusion," I heard Bess say. "What's a shared file?"

"Try not to worry, Bess," I replied. "If you continue to accept the defaults in the Wizard, everything will work out fine. The defaults are really set for a 'stand-alone' executable like the one you want to give Harry. This window is asking us if we want to designate our executable as a shared file – something we would do only if more than one application needed to use it. In our case, our executable is definitely stand alone, so we just need to click on the Next button here."

I did so and the following screen was displayed:

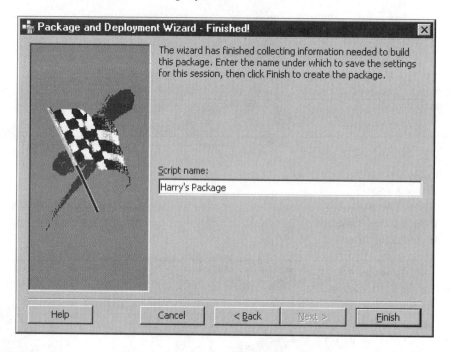

"Ordinarily," I said, "I like to accept defaults in the Wizard – but when it comes to a script name, I like to customize them. Let's change the name of the script to Harry's Package, and click on the Finish button."

"Script? What's that?"

"It's the saved set of instructions that'll let you perform your packaging or deployment again, using the same set of instructions," I said.

When I clicked on Finish, the following screen appeared:

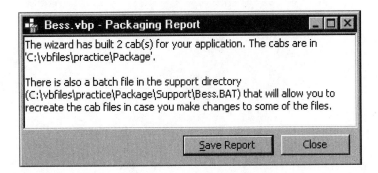

"This is a Packaging Report," I said. "It provides us with a little information about our package – the number of cabs in it, and its location. At this point, you can either save the report, or just close the window."

"Great, we're finished," I heard Bess say. "I guess that wasn't too bad after all. But I must have missed something somewhere. I don't remember you inserting any diskettes."

"You're right, Bess," I said. "I didn't insert any diskettes. The first time I ran this myself, I figured I was done at this point, and asked myself the same question. I didn't realize that now that I had the *Package*, I then needed to *deploy* it – in our case, to floppy diskettes."

"So this is really a two-phase operation," Bess said.

"That's right, Bess," I said. "First we create the package, then we deploy it."

I closed the Packaging Report window, and we were taken back to the initial screen of the Package and Deployment Wizard:

"It won't be much longer now, Bess," I said. "From this main screen of the Wizard, we now need to select Deploy. Here goes:"

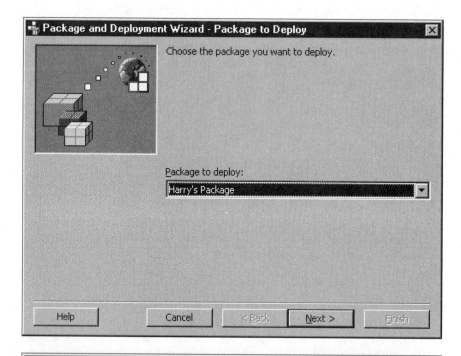

"This screen is just asking us to select a package for deployment," I said. "A few minutes earlier, we named our package 'Harry's Package' – that makes it easier to pick out of a list here. Once the Package is selected, we just need to select the Next button:"

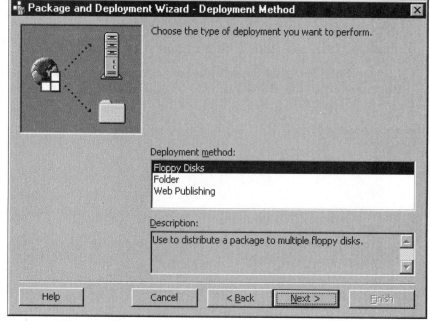

"The Wizard wants to know about our Deployment method," I said. "In our case, we need to select Floppy Disks and then click on the Next button."

"Didn't we tell the Wizard that we wanted floppy disks a while back?" Bess asked. "In the Package Creation portion of the wizard?"

"When we specified multiple cabs," I said, "we needed to tell the Wizard the size of our distribution media, which was 1.44 MB. Despite that, this is – strictly speaking – the first time we've told the Wizard that we want to place our `Setup.exe` on floppies:"

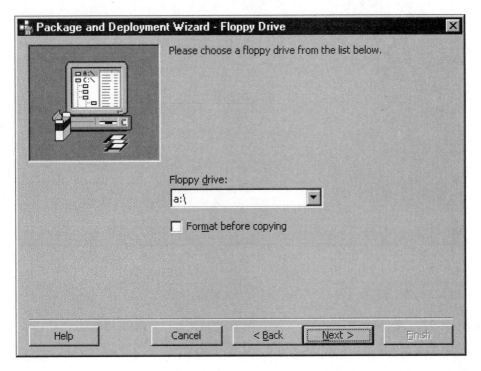

"This one's easy," Bess said. "We just need to specify the drive letter for our floppy drive."

"That's right," I agreed. "Do you see that there's an option here to format the diskette before the Wizard begins copying? It's a good idea to check that 'on' – the Wizard requires 'empty' formatted diskettes anyway. If you format before copying, you'll verify the data integrity of the diskette and ensure that it's empty prior to copying the setup files to it."

I checked 'on' the option to Format before copying and clicked on the Next button:

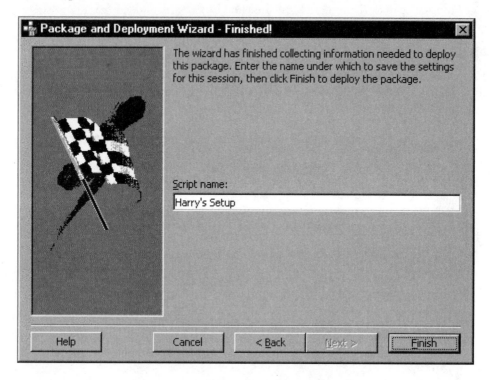

"The Wizard wants *another* name?" Bess asked. "I though we already named this script."

"That was the *Package* Script," I said. "Now the Wizard wants a name so that it can save the settings for this Deployment's Script. We need to take care not to name the Script the same name as the Package Script. Let's call this 'Harry's Setup'."

I did so, and clicked on the Finish button.

"Now we're getting close, Bess." I said.

We were then prompted to insert the first diskette into our floppy diskette drive, and after a minute or so a prompt for the second diskette appeared. After a few seconds of copying files to the second diskette, the following screen shot appeared:

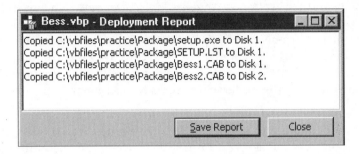

"*Another* report?" I heard Bess say.

"Yes, another report, " I replied, "but this is the final one – the Wizard process is complete. This report is giving us a list of the files that it has copied to our diskettes."

"Does this mean I can just send those files off to Harry now?" she asked. "Where are the DLLs you mentioned? And what about our executable?"

"Our setup program," I said, "like many others in use today, has compressed the files that it placed on the diskettes. These compressed files contain everything that Harry needs to install and run your program on his PC: the code you wrote, the DLLs, the Setup program – in fact, the whole darned shooting match. The .cab files you see are the compressed files, and they will be uncompressed when Harry runs the setup.exe program that you see listed in the report."

"So all I need to do is send Harry the diskettes that the Wizard produced?" she asked.

"That's right," I said, "just tell Harry to insert the first diskette into his diskette drive, open up Windows Explorer, and double-click on the setup.exe file – he'll be prompted for the rest. I guarantee you he'll be wildly impressed with your setup program, and in no time at all, he'll be running the program you wrote for him."

"I want to thank you for taking the time to show me how to do this," Bess said. "I'm sure there are others in the viewing audience who had the same problem."

"You're quite welcome, Bess," I said, "and thanks for calling. By the way, I mentioned earlier that versions of Visual Basic prior to Version 6 have a different version of the wizard than the one I demonstrated today. It's called the Application Setup Wizard. It's similar in many ways to the one we used here today – but there are some obvious differences – the main one being that the Visual Basic 5 Wizard doesn't first create a package on your hard drive – it starts immediately with the creation of the setup.exe to your floppy diskette. And now on to our final caller of the day."

Question 70: The underscore in a variable name in the General Declarations section disappears – why?

"Hi, my name is Flo, and I'm from Los Angeles," the caller said. "I've been trying to declare a variable in the General Declarations section of my form. A friend of mine who read your book suggested naming variables that appear in the General Declarations section of a form with the letter m, followed by the underscore, to signify that they're module-level variables. My problem is this – when I use an underscore in the variable name in the General Declarations section, the underscore seems to disappear."

"Hi, Flo," I said, "welcome to the show. What you are seeing here is an optical illusion of sorts in Visual Basic. You wouldn't believe how many times I'm asked this same question – so this is a familiar one. Let me ask you a question – when you encountered this problem, were you viewing your code window in Full Module view or Procedure view?"

"I think it was Full Module view," she said, "is that where you can see all of the code in your *entire program* at one time?"

"Well then," I said, "that explains it – that's the reason for the optical illusion. Let me show you."

I started a new Visual Basic project and double clicked on the form.

"Let me specify Full Module view," I said, "I do that by clicking on the second button from the left at the bottom of the code window."

I did that...

"Now let me declare a variable that begins with 'm_'," I said.

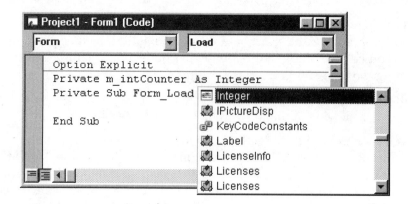

"Everything's fine up to this point," I said, "the underscore is still intact. Notice that the Procedure separator bar is still above the variable declaration. Now watch what happens as soon as I hit the *Enter* key:"

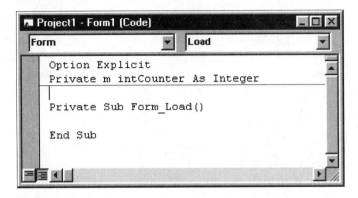

"You see," Flo interjected, "the underscore has disappeared."

"I see." I said, "It *appears* as though the underscore has disappeared. But let me assure you, this is an optical illusion, caused by the Procedure separator bar. Here, watch what happens if I add another variable declaration beneath the first one and hit *Enter* – you'll see that the underscore is still really there:"

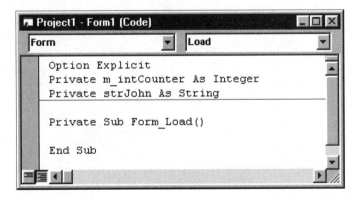

"Gee," she said, "it *is* there after all. I can't believe that I could get hung up on something as stupid as that."

"Now, Flo," I said, "don't be so hard on yourself. It did *appear* to be missing. I get this question many times a semester. I'm sure other members of the viewing audience had the same question."

"Thanks for your help, Professor Smiley," Flo said. "Now maybe I can get back on track."

"Thanks for your call, Flo," I said.

I looked at the clock – just about 2:30 pm. As ever, my timing was impeccable.

"It looks like we are just about out of time for today's show," I said. "I hope you all enjoyed it. For those of you who may have missed my announcement at the top of the show, next week we'll be broadcasting at a new time – 10 am Eastern Standard Time. As always, many thanks to all of my callers. And if you called today, but couldn't get through, remember, we'll be here next week, *new* time, same channel."

Once we were off-air, the normally infallible Linda apologized to me.

"What's that for?" I asked.

"You remember that caller, Glenn, who got cut off? I spoke to him later and he told me that it was a games program he was working on, but I didn't get the chance to tell you straight away, and it kinda slipped my mind. Sorry."

"Ah, I see," I said. "Don't worry about it. What do you say we go refresh our brain cells with some coffee and a couple of donuts?"

"Oh, all right then – you talked me into it."

Week 8

As I drove to the studio the following Saturday, I noticed that there was less traffic around; the new start time of 10am certainly made for a much more relaxing journey. While I waited at a red light, I reflected on what Tim had told me earlier in the week – for the first few international shows, callers from outside the US would be given priority in an effort to boost the show's popularity overseas. I still felt a scintilla of discomfort about the compromises that I had to make to the station executives, but it wasn't like I was selling my soul, was it?

"Good morning," said Linda as I made my way through the door. "We've actually been a little sneaky with the phone lines today – to make sure we got international callers, we opened the lines a few minutes ago. We should have a fully international show today."

"What about my loyal US audience?" I asked, as I began to set up my equipment. "It's a little rude to exclude them, isn't it?"

"I guess you could say something about it being our first show, and us wanting overseas viewers to feel like they were part of it, so for this show we snuck them in early. I'll still put the phone line on the screen in case we're not fully queued up by the time we start."

It felt pretty strange to know that I'd be presenting my show live to countries across the globe. Wow. Hopefully we wouldn't have too many language barrier difficulties; I was wondering if I should maybe talk slower when Linda's voice in my earpiece startled me. I stood up and brushed myself down, ready for the world to see me. Linda cued me in, and I began.

"Hi, everyone," I said, "welcome to Professor Smiley's Visual Basic Programming Workshop. Each week at this same time, I'll be answering your questions about Visual Basic. I'd like to thank everyone for tuning in at this new time, and I'd also like to welcome our expanded audience of international viewers. Don't forget, in order for us to have a show at all, we need you, the viewers, to phone in with your Visual Basic questions. Here's our toll-free number, so just call right in."

Linda signaled me that we ready for our first caller.

"Caller number one? You're on the air," I said.

Question 71: All other things being equal, is it better to set a property or execute a method?

"Good morning, my name is Emily, and I'm from Thornton in Yorkshire, England," said a quiet, faltering voice. "I'm not sure if you've been asked this question before. It troubles me."

"Hi, Emily," I said, "Welcome to the show. Go ahead. What is it?"

"I've only been programming in Visual Basic for a short while," she said, "but it seems to me that there are instances in Visual Basic where the same result can be achieved by setting the value of an object's property or by executing an object's method."

"I understand what you mean perfectly, Emily," I said, "can you give us an example?"

"Certainly," she said. "For instance, you can make a form invisible by setting its `Visible` property to `False`. You can also make a form invisible by executing its `Hide` method. My question is this: is there a 'best' way to do this, or is this duality just an accident? My sister Charlotte, who is also a beginner in Visual Basic, was reading through the postings on a Visual Basic newsgroup, and she said that someone there had posted a message saying that, given the choice, you should always execute a method of an object, instead of setting the property. What's your opinion?"

"That's really an excellent question, Emily," I said, "and I'm glad you brought this up, as this is a question that I am asked regularly in the classroom. I should tell you that as your programming prowess increases you'll find yourself creating objects of your own, and you'll be faced with deciding what the properties and methods of your own objects will be."

"So I could create a property *and* a method, where setting the property to a certain value would have the same effect as using the method?" she asked.

"Exactly," I said. "And that's probably the explanation for the duality that you've observed. Virtually every control in Visual Basic has a `Visible` property – the form also happens to have the `Hide` method. Someone at Microsoft undoubtedly believed strongly that the form should have a `Hide` method, even though setting the `Visible` property to `False` accomplishes the same thing."

"But which technique is *better*?" Emily persisted. "Is it better to set the form's `Visible` property to `False` or to execute the `Hide` method?"

"I'd love to give you a hard and fast rule," I said. "Unfortunately, I'm not intimately familiar with 'behind the scenes' the code for each technique. The bottom line is, use the one that processes fastest and uses the least amount of resources in terms of RAM. I can tell you this; I've heard the same rumor that your sister has, although for the life of me, I can't find it in my Visual Basic documentation anywhere. I guess I'm just reluctant to cast my vote unequivocally in one direction or another; and without a clear mandate from Microsoft, I quite honestly can't say 'set the property instead of executing the method' or vice versa. However, that doesn't mean you can't do a little experimentation of your own."

"What do you mean?" Emily asked.

"Well, for instance," I said. "Take the check box control. A few months ago, in response to a similar question in my university Visual Basic class, we performed a little experiment. We placed a check box control on the form with two command buttons. Now, theoretically there are two ways to move a check box control on the form. We can change its `Top` and `Left` properties. We can also execute the `Move` method of the check box. In our classroom experiment, we wrote code in one command button to move the check box to the upper left hand corner of the form and *back* to the lower right hand corner of the form 500 times; we did this by varying the check box's `Left` and `Top` properties. We put code to do the same thing in the other command button, but this time by executing the `Move` method of the check box."

"I'm curious," Emily said. "Which one ran faster?"

"The `Move` method," I said, "was just about twice as fast – but those results were deceptive. After thinking about the results of our experiment for a few minutes, we realized that using the property technique involved two Visual Basic statements – setting the `Left` property and then setting the `Top` property. Executing the `Move` method involved only *one* statement."

"So it wasn't really a fair experiment?" Emily asked.

"That's right," I replied. "Then one of the students suggested doing the test by setting only the `Left` property of the check box 500 times. This would mean only one Visual Basic statement for the property technique – just like we were using only one Visual Basic statement for the `Move` method technique. Here's the code..."

I started a new project and placed a single check box and two command buttons on the form.

"Let's put this code in the `Click` event procedure of the first command button," I said, "to test the processing speed of the property technique:"

```
Private Sub Command1_Click()

Dim datStartTime As Date
Dim datStopTime As Date
Dim strDuration As String
Dim sngCounter As Single

datStartTime = Now

For sngCounter = 1 To 80000
   Check1.Left = lngCounter
Next sngCounter

datStopTime = Now

strDuration = DateDiff("s", datStartTime, datStopTime)

MsgBox strDuration

End Sub
```

I ran the program and clicked on the command button, and six seconds later a message box was displayed on the form with the number '6' in it.

"Six seconds," Emily said. "That's pretty fast to move that check box 80,000 times."

"I agree," I said, "that is pretty fast. The actual number may be different on your PC at home. Do you see what's going on in this code, Emily?"

"I think so," she said. "It looks like you've declared two **Date** type variables to help you calculate the duration between the start and the stop of the code in the **Click** event procedure. Then you set the value of the variable **datStartTime** equal to the system date and time prior to moving the check box. After that, you executed a loop in which you repeatedly set the **Left** property of the check box equal to the value of the loop control variable, which moves it along as the loop variable increases. Finally, when the loop finished, you set the value of the variable **datStopTime** to equal the current system date and time, and then calculated the duration using the **DateDiff** function with the value in those two variables."

"That's an excellent analysis, Emily," I said.

"Thank you – you're very kind. I do have a question, though," she continued. "Why doesn't the program crash when the check box runs off the edge of the form?"

"The edge of the form doesn't really exist," I said. "By that, I mean there's nothing to let Windows know where the edge of the form (or even the edge of the screen) is. That the check box has run off what appears to be the right edge of the form means nothing to Visual Basic. The `Left` property is defined in Visual Basic as a `Single` data type – so as long as we don't attempt to assign a value to the `Left` property that exceeds the valid value range for the `Single` data type, the program won't bomb."

"I guess I hadn't really thought about that. Can we code up the `Move` method now?" she asked.

"Sure thing," I said, "here's the code."

I stopped the program and rapidly typed the following code into the `Click` event procedure of the second command button:

```
Private Sub Command2_Click()

Dim datStartTime As Date
Dim datStopTime As Date
Dim strDuration As String
Dim sngCounter As Single

datStartTime = Now

For sngCounter = 1 To 80000
    Check1.Move sngCounter
Next sngCounter

datStopTime = Now

strDuration = DateDiff("s", datStartTime, datStopTime)

MsgBox strDuration

End Sub
```

"This code is virtually identical to the code in the first command button," I said, "except that in this case, we're using the `Move` method of the check box to move the check box across the form. Let's see what happens when we run it. Which technique will be faster – setting the property, or executing the method?"

When I ran the program again and clicked on the command button, a message box was generated after six seconds, containing the number '6'.

"They're identical?" Emily said. "Both the property technique and the `Move` technique took the same amount of time?"

"For the purposes of live TV, I had to choose a loop small enough to be executed in a reasonable length of time. For more accurate tests, you should increase the length of the loop," I said. "Now I should tell you that when I've run this test on other PCs, the property technique seemed to win by a millisecond or so. But still, both techniques are pretty close."

"Can we run this test one more time?" Emily asked.

I did exactly that – ran the program, and clicked on each command button three times. Each time, the results were identical – 6 seconds for the property, 6 seconds for the method.

"I want to caution you not to draw any deep conclusions from this little experiment," I said. "I think the key point of our tests here today is that using either technique generates the same kind of basic Windows instructions to perform the task we want to accomplish. This may not *always* be the case."

"You mean there may be instances," Emily said, "where using one technique over the other has a clear advantage?"

"Exactly right," I said. "The bottom line is that if processing speed is crucial to the program you write, you may want to do a test like this to prove to yourself which technique really produces the fastest results."

"Thank you so much for your help, Professor Smiley," Emily said.

"My pleasure, Emily," I said. "Thanks for calling, and be sure to tell your sister Charlotte that I said hello. And now it's time for our second caller."

Question 72: Is there a way to extract icons from other programs for use in my own Visual Basic program?

"Hello," the voice on the phone line said tentatively, "my name is Louis, and I'm from the town of Dole in France. Thanks so much for taking my call. I've been looking for a way to place a custom icon on my form. An e-mail friend of mine told me that when he was programming in Visual Basic 3, there was some kind of utility program or tool that came with it that allowed him to extract an icon from an existing program. Do you know if this utility program is available in Visual Basic 5?"

"Welcome to the show, Louis," I said. "I know what your friend is talking about. Before I talk about that program, are you aware that there are a number of icons supplied with Visual Basic when you install it on your PC?"

"Yes, I am," he said, "but I haven't found quite the right one. I've also tried looking on the Internet with no luck. However, there is an icon in another program that I think would be perfect."

"Are you aware that extracting that icon could be a copyright infringement, Louis?" I asked.

"Yes, I am," he said. "I sent an e-mail to the program's author, and he sent me a response telling me that if I could find a way to use the icon, to go ahead. Unfortunately, I haven't been able to figure out a way to get to it. That's why I was very excited when my friend said that he thought Visual Basic had an icon extractor program. Are you familiar with what he is talking about?"

"Yes indeed," I said. "I used it once or twice when I was programming in Visual Basic 3. It was actually a program installed in the Visual Basic 3 Samples subdirectory, and I think it was meant to be more of a demonstration program than anything. But it was a marvelous tool. It allowed you to specify an `.exe` or `.dll` file, and it would display all of the icons contained in the file, and give you an option to save the icon to your hard drive."

"Does Microsoft still supply this program as a sample program?" Louis asked.

"It didn't come with my copy of Visual Basic 6," I said. "To be honest, Louis, I think it's probably something they would shy away from now – especially since Visual Basic comes shipped with so many icons of its own."

"I wonder," he mused, "if I found an old copy of that sample program for Visual Basic 3, would it run in the Visual Basic 5 environment?"

"I'm afraid I don't know, Louis," I said. "Somehow, I would really doubt it."

"Someone in a newsgroup told me that there's something posted on the Microsoft web site about using the Windows API to extract icons," Louis said.

"That's right," I said, "if you check the Microsoft Knowledgebase (`http://www.support.microsoft.com`) on their web site, they *do* have some techniques documented that enable you to use the Windows API to extract icons – but using the Windows API can be pretty complex for a beginner, particularly the API calls necessary to extract icons. But all's not lost – I know of an easier way."

"What's that?" Louis asked excitedly.

"One of my associates needed to create a custom icon, just like you," I said, "and while surfing the Internet, he came across an icon editor he's really pleased with. One of its features is the ability to extract icons from `.exe` and `.dll` files."

"Where can I get it?" he asked.

"The name of the program is *AX Icons from Axialis* (`http://axialis.com`)," I said, "and he found it and downloaded it from Shareware.com at `http://www.shareware.com`."

"That's great," Louis said, "and you said that not only can I create my own icons, but I can also extract them from other files?"

"That's right," I said. "My associate has done some great work with it. But don't forget – and this program will warn you – that extracting icons from an `.exe` or `.dll` file written by someone else may be a copyright infringement, and you should never do so *without their permission*."

"I understand," Louis said. "Thanks for your help, Professor Smiley – this is a life saver."

'You're welcome, Louis, " I said, "and thanks for calling. And now it's time for our third caller."

Question 73: Can you explain what the dollar sign means in a function name?

"Hi, my name is Marie, and I'm calling from Warsaw, Poland," said the caller. "I was recently looking through the Visual Basic Help index when I noticed that, in addition to the `Left` function (which I'm familiar with) there is also a `Left$` function. Seeing it in the index made me curious, but when I selected `Left$` in the index, Visual Basic just took me to the definition for the `Left` function. I then spent the next half hour searching for information about the `Left$` function, but without any success. Can you explain the difference between `Left` and `Left$`?"

"That's a very perceptive question, Marie," I said, "and it's one that pops up inevitably in all of my Visual Basic classes. And by the way, this pair of functions is not the only one with a dollar sign twin, so to speak. There are others – such as `Right`, `Mid`, `UCase` and `LCase`, which also have dollar sign equivalents."

"Why aren't these functions documented? Marie asked.

"I can't speak for Microsoft," I said, "but these functions have existed since Visual Basic 1. But you have to go back pretty far in the Visual Basic documentation – probably Visual Basic 3 – to see the definition for them. Later versions of the documentation seem to have dropped the definitions altogether."

"Are the functions identical?" she asked.

"Yes, in general, the dollar sign and their non-dollar sign equivalents function identically," I said. "For instance, the two functions you cited, `Left` and `Left$`, both return the `Left` portion of a string."

"Then what's the difference?" Marie asked.

"The difference is how they react to a string that contains a `Null` value," I said. "In short, dollar sign functions bomb when asked to perform an operation on a string containing a `Null` value."

"Oh," Marie said, sounding surprised. "Can a string contain a `Null` value? I didn't think that was possible."

"Yes, a string can contain a `Null` value," I said. "And if you pass a string containing a `Null` value to the `Left$` function, it will bomb."

"Maybe that's why Microsoft doesn't mention the `Left$` function in their documentation," Marie suggested. "Although I think they should drop the function altogether."

"In order to provide backward compatibility for older programs," I said, "Microsoft is very reluctant to pull existing functionality out of Visual Basic. But the fact that you don't see `Left$` defined may be a clue that Microsoft would *prefer* you not to use it."

"You said that `Left$` will bomb if the string that is passed to it contains a `Null` value," Marie said. "What happens with the `Left` function?"

"The `Left` function," I said, "if it's passed a string with a `Null` value in it, returns a `Null`. That's the general rule in programming – an operation performed on a `Null` returns a `Null`."

"How does a `Null` value get into a string in the first place?" Marie asked.

"Good question. There are two ways," I said, "and the first is the most likely possibility. Most databases – such as Microsoft Access and Oracle – have a special value called `Null`, which is contained in the field of any record that has not yet had a value placed in it. So, if you read data from a database within your Visual Basic program, it's conceivable that the field value could contain a `Null` value."

"So if we are using string manipulation functions on data read from a database," she said, "we should use the non-dollar sign function equivalent – that is, `Left`, *not* `Left$`?"

"That's correct," I said.

"You said there are two ways," Marie said. "What's the second way that a `Null` value could be contained in a string?"

"The second way is if your code *explicitly* assigns the `Null` value to a variant variable," I replied. "And that would take a conscious effort on your part."

"That's not likely to happen," Marie said. "At least, I wouldn't do it."

"I should also mention," I said, "that in addition to the dollar sign functions bombing if asked to work with a string containing a `Null` value, the dollar sign functions also differ from their non-dollar sign equivalents in one other important way – the data type of their return value."

"Wait. Do you mean that because these are functions that we're talking about, and because a function by definition returns a value, that the data types of the return values are different?" she asked.

"That's correct," I said. "The return values of the dollar sign equivalents of these functions are `Strings`, while the return values of the non-dollar sign equivalents are `Variants`. And if you think about it, that makes sense; only a `Variant` variable data type can contain a `Null` value – so in order for the non-dollar sign functions to be able to pass a `Null` value back to the calling program, they require a `Variant` data type."

"This is beginning to make some sense to me now," Marie said. "I guess if you want to be on the safe side, just use `Left` instead of `Left$`."

"That's the safe approach," I said.

"Thanks for your help, Professor Smiley," Marie said. "You've cleared up this mystery for me."

"I'm glad I could help, Marie," I said. "Thanks for calling."

I saw Linda signaling that it was time for our first commercial break of the day, and so I announced one. A few minutes later, we were ready to pick up with our fourth caller of the day.

Question 74: I'm trying to use the Shell command to process a file with a long file name in Word

(see also questions 17, 24 & 33)

"Hi, my name is Grace, and I'm calling from Philadelphia," she said. "I have a question about the `Shell` function in Visual Basic. Your producer explained to me that you discussed the `Shell` function a few weeks ago, and how it can be used to execute other programs. I've been successful using it, except in certain instances."

"Welcome to the show, Grace," I said. "What problem are you having with the `Shell` function?"

"I've written a program," she continued, "and I want to let the user of my program select a document and open it in Microsoft Word. My first thought was to use the `Shell` function with Word, and to specify a document for Word to open when it started up. Unfortunately, when the user selects a document that has a space in its name, the `Shell` function is not working. In fact, it's becoming royally messed up. I know – I should say I *believe* – this can be done, since I've opened up Word with this same document by typing the command string directly into the Run box in Windows. I have no problem with the `Shell` function if the document name does not contain spaces. I guess there's just a trick to getting this to work. Can you help me?"

"Yes, Grace," I said, "I can help you. Before I show you the trick of getting this to work, let me first give our viewers at home a sense of the frustration you're experiencing."

I started Microsoft Word, created a new document, typed in my favorite phrase - 'I Love Visual Basic' - and saved the document as `I Love Visual Basic.doc` in the root directory (`c:\`) of my hard drive. I then closed Microsoft Word.

"There," I said, "we now have a Word document on my hard drive named with a long file name containing spaces. That will give us something to experiment with."

I then started a new Visual Basic project, and placed a command button on the form.

"Let's write some code to shell Word, and to open up our document," I said.

I placed the following code in the `Click` event procedure of the command button:

```
Private Sub Command1_Click()

Dim dblRetval As Double

dblRetval = Shell("c:\office95\winword\WINWORD.EXE
    ↳c:\I Love Visual Basic.doc", vbNormalFocus)

End Sub
```

"In case anyone missed the show where I talked about the `Shell` function," I said, "the `Shell` function allows us to asynchronously run another program from within Visual Basic."

"Can you clarify that word **asynchronously** for me?" Grace asked.

"Oh, I'm sorry," I said. "Asynchronously just means that Visual Basic starts up the program, and as far as Visual Basic is concerned, that's the end of it. Visual Basic has no control over it after that, and your code continues to execute normally."

"So asynchronously means," Grace said, "that we can't use the `Shell` function to start a program, and then have Visual Basic wait for it to finish."

"That's exactly what that means," I said.

I waited a moment to see if Grace had any other questions.

"We can run just about any program from within Visual Basic," I continued. "A few weeks ago we ran the Windows calculator. In this code, we're doing something a little extra, in that we are using the `Shell` function to start Word, *and* pass the program a file name argument ('`I Love Visual Basic.doc`'). Now, we hope, Word will start up, and when it does, it'll automatically open the document we pass as a file name argument."

When I ran the program and clicked on the command button, the following message box appeared:

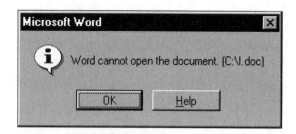

"This," I said, "is an obvious problem. Word is telling us that it can't find a file called '`I.doc`'. Of course, I told Word that the file name was '`I love Visual Basic.doc`'. So, something we did has confused Word."

"That's exactly the type of error message I'm getting," Grace said. "It seems as soon as the `Shell` function sees the space in the file name argument, it gets perplexed. And it doesn't stop there. Hit the OK button."

I clicked on the OK button, and this screenshot appeared:

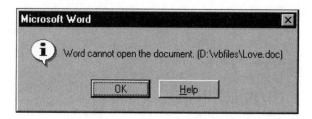

Followed by this one...

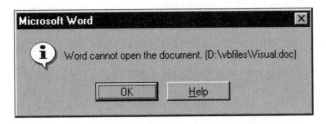

...and finally *this* one...

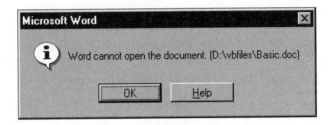

"You're right, Grace," I said. "Word is *highly* perplexed. Instead of interpreting our statement as a request to open up a single file with a long file name containing spaces, it thinks we're trying to open up four different word files named 'I.doc', 'Love.doc', 'Visual.doc' and 'Basic.doc'."

"That's beginning to sound like characters from Snow White," Grace said. "Is there anything we can do to make this work?"

"At this point," I said, "some programmers would be inclined to include the file name argument within apostrophes – like this..."

I then modified the code in the Click event procedure of the command button to look like this...

```
Private Sub Command1_Click()

Dim dblRetval As Double

dblRetval = Shell("c:\office95\winword\WINWORD.EXE
    'c:\I Love Visual Basic.doc'", vbNormalFocus)

End Sub
```

...and ran the program.

"Notice that I have now included the file name argument within apostrophes," I said. "Let's see if that makes a difference."

I ran the program, clicked on the command button, with the following result:

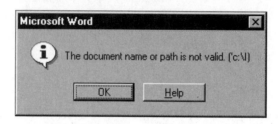

"Uh oh," I heard Grace say. "That didn't work either."

I clicked on the **OK** button and, just as before, three consecutive error messages were displayed, similar to the first batch.

"Visual Basic seems even more rattled than the first time!" I said. "But don't worry – there is a way to make this work. Instead of using apostrophes, use a *pair* of quotation marks around the file name argument and everything will be fine. Look at this code..."

```
Private Sub Command1_Click()

Dim dblRetval

dblRetval = Shell("c:\office95\winword\WINWORD.EXE
    ⬂""c:\I Love Visual Basic.doc""", vbNormalFocus)

End Sub
```

"A *pair* of quotation marks?" Grace said in surprise. "You mean that works for this as well?"

"It may look a bit peculiar," I said, "but it works like a charm. And *that's* what counts."

I ran the program and clicked on the command button. This time, Word started up and opened my document:

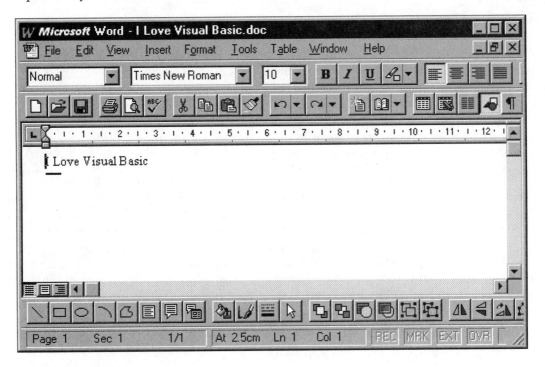

"There it is," I said.

"That's beautiful," Grace said, "and this is just what I needed. I even saw that show of yours earlier where you used the same trick to display quotation marks in a string, and I *still* didn't think to use a pair of quotation marks around the file name argument. I can't thank you enough."

"I'm glad I could help, Grace," I said. "By the way, if you're ever in the vicinity of our studio, stop by and visit."

"I may just do that," she said. "Thanks again."

"And now let's go to our next caller," I said.

Question 75: Is it possible to block Ctrl+Alt+Delete and Alt+Tab in a Visual Basic program?

(see also questions 57 & 68)

"Hi, my name is Jim, and I'm from Dublin," said a smooth Irish voice. "I was working on the 'China Shop' project in your *Learn To Program with Visual Basic* book, and it occurred to me that it might not be a good idea if the user could either press the *Ctrl+Alt+Delete* combination to bring up the Task Manager, or the *Alt+Tab* key combination to switch to another application. Is there a way to disable these keystroke combinations? I've been experimenting with the `KeyDown`, `KeyUp` and `KeyPress` events of the form – but without any luck so far. Or is this something that just can't be done in Visual Basic?"

"Hi, Jim," I said, "welcome to the show, and thanks for calling. I'm very tempted to just say 'no way' to this one. Microsoft has designed the *Ctrl+Alt+Delete* and *Alt+Tab* combinations to give the user the ability to switch out of a badly behaving program, or to end it altogether. In just about every case I can think of, disabling this facility is a bad idea. However, you just named the prime example where it's a good one; a kiosk program used in a public place, where you want to prevent (or eliminate as much as possible) mischievous attempts to shut down your program. You cited the China Shop program in my book – we prevent the program itself from being shut down by unauthorized users, but you're right in that we didn't prevent the user from getting to the Task Manager and shutting down the program that way, or even from exiting Windows altogether."

"You're implying there *is* a way to do this," Jim said.

"In a way, Jim," I said. "There is no way to disable these keystroke combinations within Visual Basic itself – but you *can* do it by using the Windows API. I think that in prior shows I've mentioned the Windows API once or twice. I don't necessarily encourage beginners to code Windows API calls in their programs, but on the other hand, there's no need to shy away from the Windows API if the need arises. And if disabling these keystroke combinations is what needs to be done, the only way to disable them is via the Windows API. But I must warn you – once you disable the *Ctrl+Alt+Delete* and *Alt+Tab* key combinations, you must explicitly enable them again. Just ending your Visual Basic program won't enable them. So if you forget to enable them and then end your Visual Basic program, the keystrokes are disabled until you either write some code to enable them again, or re-boot your PC."

"I understand," Jim said, "Believe me, I won't take this step lightly. Now, how do we code this?"

I started a new Visual Basic project, and placed two command buttons on the form.

"Ordinarily," I said, "in a quick demo like this, I would accept both the default name and captions for these command buttons. But I don't want to get mixed up, so let's name them `cmdDisable` and `cmdEnable` respectively, and change their captions to `Disable` and `Enable`."

I brought up the Properties window and changed the `Name` and `Caption` properties for both command buttons.

"A few weeks back," I continued, "I spoke about using the Windows API to hide the mouse pointer. Calling a function or a procedure in the Windows API first requires that we place a `Declare` statement in the General Declarations section of the form, like this..."

```
Private Declare Function SystemParametersInfo Lib
    ↳"user32" Alias "SystemParametersInfoA"
    ↳(ByVal uAction As Long, ByVal uParam As Long,
    ↳lpvParam As Any, ByVal fuWinIni As Long) As Long

Private Const SPI_SCREENSAVERRUNNING = 97
```

"What I'm doing here," I said, "is declaring a function called `SystemParametersInfo`, which is a function contained in the `user32.DLL` which can be found in the \Windows\System directory on my PC. This function allows us to change a number of Windows System parameters, one of which we'll see is the parameter that allows the keystroke combinations we are trying to disable. I should tell you here that the documentation I found on this function by using the API Text viewer (which I mentioned a few weeks ago when I first introduced the Windows API) is virtually useless in determining how to call this function. There is some information about this function in Daniel Appleman's *Guide to the Win 32 API* book – but even that excellent guide doesn't tell us what we need to do to disable these keystrokes."

"How did you figure out how to use this function, then?" Jim asked.

"From Microsoft," I said. "Microsoft has a Knowledgebase article which explains how to do this. I just copied and pasted the code directly out of there, and it worked great. If you want to check the article for yourself, here's the link. I'm not sure if the article is still there, but it was there not too long ago..."

http://support.microsoft.com/support/

"...then go to Search Support and enter these keywords as your search criteria:"

SystemParametersInfo SPI_SCREENSAVERRUNNING

I then placed the following code in the `click` event procedure of `cmdDisable`:

```
Private Sub cmdDisable_Click()

Dim intRetval As Integer

intRetval = SystemParametersInfo(SPI_SCREENSAVERRUNNING, True, False, 0)

End Sub
```

"This code," I said, "will disable the user's ability to bring up the Task List, or to switch to another application. It achieves this by calling the function `SystemParametersInfo`, which we declared in the General Declarations section of our form; we also pass it the four arguments necessary to disable *Ctrl+Alt+Del* and *Alt+Tab*. Hold onto your hats..."

"The `SystemParametersInfo` function lets us modify System variables. It takes four arguments: the first argument, `uAction`, is supplied by the constant value `SPI_SCREENSAVERRUNNING` that we declared in the General Declarations section, and tells Windows which System variable we wish to change. The second argument, `uParam`, is passed as `True`, and this tells Windows to change the System variable's value to `True`. This has the effect of telling Windows that a screen saver is running – the implication being that nothing, including *Ctrl+Alt+Del* or *Alt+Tab*, should interrupt it. The third argument, `lpvParam`, is passed a value of `False`. Nobody knows what this does...well, I'm sure somebody does, but I've never found out. Finally, the fourth argument, `fuWinIni`, is passed as 0, and this tells Windows *not* to update the Registry with this change."

"This is a more complicated than most of the other API calls I've made," Jim said. "I'm almost afraid to try this."

"The Windows API," I said, "is like a frontier. If you have good documentation, like a good scout, you'll be OK. But you may want to avoid calls to the API that are not well documented. In this case, we really have nothing to fear, since we found the instructions for using this function on the Microsoft site – plus I've already tested this code. Now let's take a look at the code necessary to re-enable those keystrokes."

I then entered the following code in the `Click` event procedure of `cmdEnable`:

```
Private Sub cmdEnable_Click()

Dim intRetval As Integer

intRetval = SystemParametersInfo(SPI_SCREENSAVERRUNNING, False, False, 0)

End Sub
```

"This is nearly identical to the code in the other command button," I said, "except that this time we are passing a `False` value as the second argument to the function. That tells Windows to re-enable the keystrokes by changing the value of the Windows System variable, `SPI_SCREENSAVERRUNNING`, to `False`."

"You mentioned earlier," Jim said, "that we'll get ourselves into trouble if we end our program without re-enabling these keystrokes. Should we also put this code in the `Unload` event of the form?"

"Great observation," I said. "Microsoft's article suggests that instead of repeating the code in the `Click` event of `cmdEnable`, we just execute the code *directly* using this syntax…"

I keyed the following code into the `Unload` event procedure of the form:

```
Private Sub Form_Unload(Cancel As Integer)

cmdEnable_Click

End Sub
```

"I didn't know you could do that," Jim said. "That line of code will execute the code in the `Click` event procedure of `cmdEnable`?"

"That's right," I said. "Of course, if you were putting this functionality in a real application, you wouldn't have the `Enable`/`Disable` buttons at all, and the code would go directly in the `Unload` event. OK, why don't we run the program now and see how it works? If you are following along with me at home, you should save any other work that you may be doing on your PC. Whenever you test any program involving the Windows API, it's always a good idea to save any work you're doing. If you miscode the call to the API, there's a very good chance you can lock up your PC, with the only escape route being a re-boot."

I ran the program, and to be sure that I could bring up the Windows Task List, I pressed the *Ctrl+Alt+Del* combination – and the Windows Task List appeared. I then pressed the *Alt+Tab* combination, to check that I could switch from my Visual Basic application to another running program.

"That's the normal behavior," I said. "Now let's click on the `Disable` button, and see if we're able to disable those keystrokes."

I clicked on the `Disable` button, with no obvious reaction.

"If the code worked," I said, "then if I press the *Ctrl+Alt+Del* combination, nothing will happen."

I pressed the *Ctrl+Alt+Del* combination, and no Task List appeared.

"No Windows Task List," I heard Jim say. "Good job."

I then pressed the *Alt+Tab* combination. Again, that keystroke was disabled.

"We can't switch out of this application either. Right now, we have totally disabled those keystroke combinations. Now let's see if we can enable them again," I said, as I clicked on the `Enable` command button.

Again, as was the case when I clicked on the `Enable` command button, there was no obvious reaction. I pressed the *Ctrl+Alt+Del* combination, and this time the Windows Task List appeared. I then pressed the *Alt+Tab* combination, and was able to switch to another Windows application.

> **To test this, you'll have to have another application running already – try bringing up the Calculator or something like that.**

"Looks like we're back to normal," Jim said. "This is great. I'll really be able to use this. Thanks for your help."

"My pleasure, Jim," I said, "and thanks for calling. Just remember to be careful using the API. And now, let's take caller number six."

Question 76: Can you pass parameters from one form to another?

"Good day, my name is Jacques, and I'm from St. André-de-Cubzac," said a French-accented voice. "This is probably a very basic question, but I was wondering if it is possible to pass values from one form to another."

"Hi, Jacques," I said. "Welcome to the show. I'm a bit stumped by your question. What do you mean by values? Can you give me an example?"

"Yes, I can give you an example," he said. "I've written a program that prompts the user for their name when it starts up. I then take their name and append it to the end of a friendly greeting in the form's Caption. But my program has several forms, and I haven't been able to figure out a way to carry that value to the next form's caption. Am I making sense? I was hoping that when I loaded the second form, I could just pass it a value – almost like an argument to a procedure or a function, I guess. I tried passing the value along with the Load statement of the second form, but that didn't work at all."

"No, I'm afraid you can't pass a value to a form via the Load statement," I said. "But there are a number of different things you *can* do that will work here. But first, let me show the audience viewers exactly what it is you are trying to accomplish."

I created a fresh Visual Basic project and placed a single command button on the form. Then I typed the following code into the form's Load event procedure:

```
Private Sub Form_Load()

Dim strRetval As String

strRetval = InputBox("What is your name?")

Form1.Caption = "Good day, " & strRetval

End Sub
```

"I would think this is something similar to what you want to do, Jacques," I said. "When this program is run, this code will prompt the user for their name and then display the message 'Good day', along with the user's name in the form's caption."

"Yes," Jacques said, "that's exactly what I want to do."

"Now, we need a way to load up a second form," I said. "We'll use the command button for that. This code will do the trick..."

This is the code I keyed into the command button's Click event procedure:

```
Private Sub Command1_Click()

Form2.Show

End Sub
```

"I notice," Jacques said, "that you're not using the `Load` statement to load `Form2`. In my code, I used `Load Form2`, then I set the `Visible` property of the form to `True`. Can you use just the `Show` method by itself?"

"Yes," I said, "using the `Show` method alone is fine. As it turns out, when you set a property for an unloaded form, that action causes Visual Basic to automatically *load* the form. I had discussed this in our very first broadcast, but since our early shows were not broadcast to Europe, you missed it."

I then added another form to the project by selecting Project | Add Form from the Visual Basic menu bar.

"Now let's run the program," I said.

Immediately, the program prompted for my name.

"I'll enter my name, 'John', into the input box," I said:

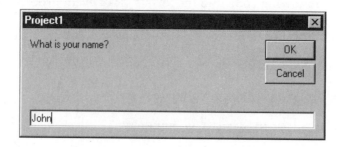

I entered my name into the input box and then clicked on the OK button. Our friendly greeting was displayed:

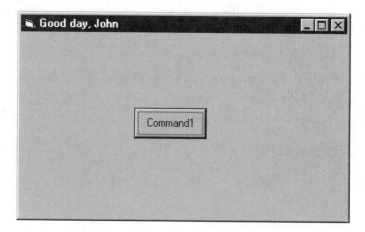

"Notice how the `Caption` of the form is now customized," I said, "to include my name. This is a nice touch, and I can see why you would want that 'friendliness' to carry over to `Form2`. Unfortunately, look at what happens when we click on the command button to load `Form2`."

I clicked on the command button, and we saw this:

"Notice that the caption of this form is the rather drab 'Form2'," I said. "That's just the default caption – and that's our problem. Jacques would like the information that the user provided to the program via the input box on `Form1` to be available on `Form2` also. This is actually pretty easy to do, and there are three techniques we can use. Let's look at the first technique now."

I stopped the program, brought up the `Load` event procedure of `Form2`, and placed the following code in it:

```
Private Sub Form_Load()

Form2.Caption = Form1.Caption

End Sub
```

"All I'm doing here is setting the `Caption` of the second form equal to the `Caption` of the first form," I said. "Let's run the program and see this in action."

I ran the program once again entered my name in the input box, and then clicked on the command button to load up `Form2`. When I did, `Form2` was displayed, and Jacques and the home viewers saw this screen:

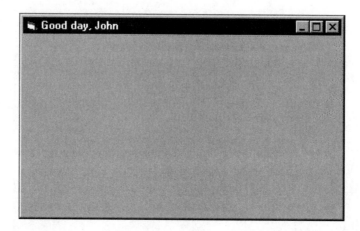

"That worked," Jacques said excitedly. "I had no idea you could reference the property of a form from another form. Can you also reference properties of controls from other forms?"

"Yes, you can," I said. "You can refer to properties of controls on other forms. As we saw here in this code, you need to preface the control reference with the form name. For instance, you could refer to the command button's `Caption` property on `Form1` from `Form2` using this syntax:"

```
Form1.Command1.Caption
```

"That's good to know," Jacques said. "What are the other two techniques?"

"This technique is fine," I said. "But you may need to refer to something other than a form or control property from another form. For instance, you may need to refer to a variable instead. In that case, you can use a form-level variable to accomplish the same thing. Let's modify the code in the `Load` event of the form slightly; what we'll do is move the declaration of the variable for the `InputBox`'s return value out of the `Load` event procedure and put it in the General Declarations section of the form."

I then added this line to the General Declarations section of `Form1`:

```
Option Explicit

Public m_strRetval As String
```

"**m_strRetval**," I said, "is just a module-level variation of the variable we had previous declared in the **Load** event procedure. Notice that I added the **m_** prefix to denote that the variable is a module-level (or form-level) variable. These terms are interchangeable if you're working in a form's code module. You wouldn't call a variable 'form-level' if you were in a standard code module, though."

"I remember that notation from your book," Jacques said. "That makes it easier to identify where it was declared – is that correct?"

"That's right, Jacques," I said.

"Why did you declare the variable as **Public**?" Jacques asked. "Why didn't you use the **Dim** statement?"

"Another good question," I said. "The use of **Dim** in these situations is frowned upon by Microsoft, probably for reasons of clarity. They prefer **Private** or **Public** as the declaration statement in the General Declarations section of a form or standard module. I chose **Public** here so that **Form2** could see the variable. If we had declared it as **Private**, **Form2** wouldn't be able to see it."

"I see," Jacques said.

"Now we need to modify the code in the **Load** event procedure slightly:"

```
Private Sub Form_Load()

m_strRetval = InputBox("What is your name?")

Form1.Caption = "Good day, " & m_strRetval

End Sub
```

"Since we are now declaring the **InputBox** return value variable as a module-level variable," I said, "we *remove* it from this event procedure. Notice that we also needed to change the assignment of the **InputBox** return value to the form-level variable."

"Will we also need to change the code in the **Load** event procedure of **Form2**?" Jacques asked.

"Yes, we will, since we've changed the name of our variable," I said. "Here it is:"

```
Private Sub Form_Load()

Form2.Caption = "Good day, " & Form1.m_strRetVal

End Sub
```

I opened up the code window for Form2, and started to change the assignment statement of Form2's Caption to the module-level variable m_strRetVal (defined in the General Declarations section of Form1). As soon as I typed 'form1.m', this screen shot appeared:

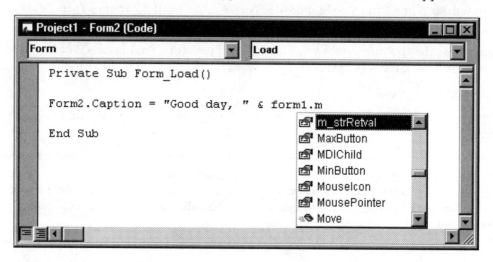

"That's really neat," I heard Jacques say. "Form2 knows all about the properties and variables on Form1!"

"Yes, that comes in quite handy," I said, "but remember – Form2 only knows about the variables if they are declared in the General Declarations section of the form – and *only* if they are declared as Public variables. If m_strRetVal had been declared as Private, then it never would have appeared in this drop-down list box."

I completed my editing of the code in the Load event procedure of Form2 and, as before, ran the program and entered my name at the input box prompt. When I clicked on the command button, the second form was displayed once again, with the customized prompt.

"Two down and one to go," I said. "There's one other technique I want to show you, very similar to the last technique where we used a form-level variable, and that's to use what's known as a Global variable in a standard module."

"What's a standard module?" Jacques asked.

"Microsoft defines a standard module," I said, "as a container for procedures and variable declarations that will be accessed by other modules within your application. Variables, procedures and functions declared as Public in a standard module have what is known as **global** scope – meaning they can be seen from anywhere within our program. Like this…"

I stopped the program and selected Project | Add Module from the Visual Basic menu bar:

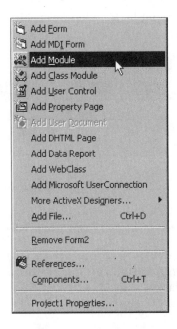

I then selected New…

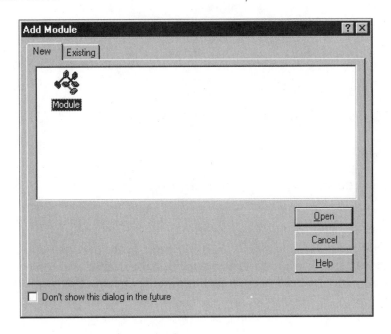

...and the code window for `Module1` appeared.

"Now we'll take the module-level variable, `m_strRetVal`, out of the General Declarations section of `Form1`," I said, "rename it slightly, and place it in the General Declarations section of our standard module. Like so..."

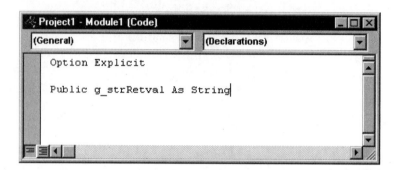

"Notice," I said, "that I've changed the name of our variable from `m_strRetVal` to `g_strRetVal`, to emphasise the fact that this variable is now a *global* variable – that is, a variable declared as `Public` in a standard module. At this point, all we need to do is change the assignment statement in the `Load` event of `Form1` to this..."

```
Private Sub Form_Load()

g_strRetval = InputBox("What is your name?")

Form1.Caption = "Good day, " & g_strRetval

End Sub
```

"...and then change the code in the `Load` event of `Form2` to this..."

```
Private Sub Form_Load()

Form2.Caption = "Good day, " & g_strRetval

End Sub
```

"The important thing to notice about the code in the `Load` event procedure of `Form2`," I said, "is that because the variable `g_strRetval` is now a global variable, we don't need to prefix its name with a form name – since it's now declared in the General Declarations section of a standard module."

"I also noticed," Jacques said, "that when you entered the name of the variable `g_strRetval` in the `Load` event procedure of `Form2`, you typed it in all lower case letters – Visual Basic then changed it to mixed case. I know you mentioned that as a tip in your book, and I thought you might want to point that out to the other viewers at home."

"Thanks, Jacques," I said, "that's a good point. You should always declare variables and control names in mixed case – a mixture of upper and lower case. That way, if you type the name of the variable or the control in lower case and you notice that Visual Basic hasn't automatically changed the name to mixed case, something is wrong. Usually, you either named the variable or control differently from what you typed, or you did what we all do from time to time – made a typo. Let's run this code now and see what happens."

As I had done before, I ran the program, entered my name at the input box prompt, and then clicked on the command button to load `Form2`. When I did, the second form was displayed, once again with the customized caption.

"Thanks, Professor Smiley," Jacques said. "This opens up a whole new horizon for me."

"Thanks for calling, Jacques," I said. "I see that it's time for our final commercial break of the day. We'll be back in just a few minutes, and then we'll take some more questions. See you then."

After a commercial break, it was time for caller number seven.

Question 77: How do I turn the NumLock key on in my Visual Basic code?

"Hi, my name is Leo, and I'm calling from Anchiano, Italy," he said. "I was wondering, is there a way in Visual Basic to automatically turn the *NumLock* key on? I teach art, but I also dabble in scientific calculations, and I've written a program that requires quite a bit of numeric entry. I want to ensure that when my users start typing numbers on the numeric keypad that they are actually typing in numbers, and not using the arrow keys."

"Hi, Leo," I said, "and welcome to the show. It's funny you should ask about this. A few weeks ago, a client of mine requested that I build this functionality into a program I was writing for her. Never having done this before, I tried everything I could think of, but nothing worked. There was nothing I could do, short of using a complicated call to a Windows API function call that would do the trick – and even that API function call, from the reports I had seen from other developers, seemed very inconsistent."

"Does that mean this is hopeless?" Leo asked.

"No, not at all, Leo," I said. "I keep an e-mail folder of a VB newsletter I get each day. As it turned out, someone on the mailing list asked the same question, and someone else responded by saying that there's a control called the *Microhelp Key State* control, which can be found on the Visual Basic 5 and 6 installation CD-ROM."

"So that control isn't installed as part of the standard installation?" Leo asked.

"That's right," I agreed. "You'll need to look for it on one of the installation CD-ROMs, and I'll show you how in moment. Its file name is '`KEYSTA32.OCX`', and once you install it and include it in your Visual Basic project, you can use it to obtain (and alter) the state of your user's *NumLock*, *CapsLock*, *ScrollLock*, and *Insert* keys."

"That sounds exactly like what I need," Leo said. "Can we try to do that today?"

"Sure thing," I said.

I placed the third CD-ROM of my Visual Studio installation CD into my studio's PC.

"After some exploring," I said, "I discovered the file I needed was on the third CD-ROM of my Visual Studio 97 set. Now we need to find a directory called 'VB'. Once we find it, then we need to look in the \Tools\Controls subdirectory. By the way, the CD-ROM and this path may be slightly different for you viewers at home, and also for you, Leo."

In no time at all I found the directory. In the directory, along with about forty other controls, was the file '`KEYSTAT32.OCX`'.

"That's the file," I said. "For those of you unfamiliar with the file extension '`.OCX`', that indicates an ActiveX control – in other words, a control that we can add to our toolbox. Now we just need to copy this file to our \Windows\System directory using Windows Explorer."

Under Windows NT, the equivalent directory is the \WINNT\SYSTEM32 directory.

I copied the file to the \Windows\System directory of my hard drive, and then started a new VB project.

"Now that the file is in our \Windows\System directory," I said, "we need to add the control to our toolbox by selecting Projects | Components from the Visual Basic menu bar."

I found the control in the list box and selected it:

Then I clicked on the OK button. At this point, the KeyState control appeared in my toolbox:

"Now that the KeyState control is now in our Toolbox," I said, "we can place it on our form."

I did, and the following screen shot was displayed:

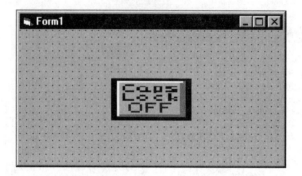

"Notice that by default," I said, "the KeyState control displays the status of the PC's *CapsLock* key. We can easily change the key that the control is linked to by changing its `Style` property to `1 - NumLock`."

I made that change:

"I'm glad that this will do the job," Leo interjected, "but this control is pretty intrusive. I was hoping that the user wouldn't notice what I was doing."

"No problem, Leo," I said. "We can change the `Visible` property to `False`, and the user will never know what you're doing."

I then changed the `Visible` property of the `KeyState` control to `False`...

"That's better," I said. "We don't want the KeyState control visible to the user at run-time. All we want to do is automatically turn *NumLock* on. And we can do that very easily by placing this single line of code in the `Load` event procedure of the form:"

```
Private Sub Form_Load()

MhState1.Value = True

End Sub
```

"This code," I said, "sets the `Value` property of the `MicroHelp` KeyState control to `True`. With a `Style` property of *NumLock*, that means that the *NumLock* key will be turned 'on' when our program starts up. Let's test that now – but before I do, let me first make sure that *NumLock* is currently off."

I checked. It *was* 'off'.

I ran the program and, as advertised, when it started up, my *NumLock* light lit up – and stayed lit.

"That's great, Professor Smiley," Leo said. "By the way, I have good news – I just found this control on my Visual Basic CD-ROM. I just wish there was a way to keep the user from turning the *NumLock* 'off'."

"There is, Leo," I replied. "The KeyState control has a `Changed` event – which means you can place that same single line of code in the `Changed` event procedure. Whenever the user presses the *NumLock* key, that event procedure will be triggered, and you can just set it back."

"That's beautiful," he said, "a real masterpiece, as we say in the art world. I thank you very much."

"Leo, glad I could help, and thanks for calling," I said, "and now on to our next caller."

Question 78: I want to be able to prevent the user from exiting my application, but still be able to display the Max and Min buttons on my form. If I disable the ControlBox, I lose the Min and Max buttons. Help!

"Hi, my name is Vasco, and I'm from Sines, Portugal," said the voice, on a very crackly phone line. "I've written a Visual Basic application, and I want the user of my program to be able to close the single form in my application *only* by choosing the Exit menu item from my menu bar."

"Hi, Vasco," I said, "welcome to the show, and thanks for calling. Creating a menu item that allows the user to exit your application should be no problem."

"I'm having no problem with that," he said. "Here's my question. I don't want the user to be able to close the form any other way – that is, I don't want them to be able to click on the Control Menu Box, or be able to click on the Close button in the upper right hand corner of the form."

"Again," I said, "that should be no problem. All you need to do is set the `ControlBox` property to `False`."

"Now that's my problem," Vasco said. "If I do that, the Maximize and Minimize buttons disappear. But I want the user to be able to maximize and minimize the form!"

"Now that *is* a good question," I said, "and it's one I hear a lot. The short answer is no, there is no way to display both the Maximize and Minimize buttons, and *not* the Close button (the 'X') – or the Control Menu icon in the upper left hand corner of the form."

"So I'm stuck, then," Vasco said, "If I want the user to be able to maximize or minimize my form, I have to take the chance that they will close the form, and therefore shut down my program, whenever they want."

"All is not lost," I said. "Are you familiar with the `QueryUnload` event of the form?"

"No, I'm not," he said. "When does the `QueryUnload` event take place? Is that the same as the `Unload` event of the form? If not, how are they different?"

"The two events are different," I said. "Of the two, the `QueryUnload` event occurs first, just prior to the `Unload` event of the form, which occurs right before the form is unloaded. We can place code in the `QueryUnload` event to cancel the unloading of the form."

"Why not place that code in the `Unload` event?" Vasco asked.

"The `QueryUnload` event," I explained, "provides us with a little more information than the `Unload` event – in particular, what caused the form to be unloaded in the first place. Because of that, we can make a better determination about whether to cancel the unload of the form. Take a look at this code…"

I created a new Visual Basic project and placed the following code in the `QueryUnload` event procedure of the form:

```
Private Sub Form_QueryUnload(Cancel As Integer, UnloadMode As Integer)

MsgBox "Vasco asks that you close the program via the menu"
Cancel = True

End Sub
```

"This event procedure," I said, "will take place whenever the form is about to close. Notice that I display a message box to alert the user, then I set the `Cancel` argument to `True` – which tells Visual Basic to cancel the unloading of this form."

"Why `True`, when it's declared as an `Integer`?" asked Vasco.

"Well, it's more readable that way, and it has the same result behind the scenes," I said.

I ran the program and double-clicked on the Control Menu icon in the upper left hand corner of the form, with this result:

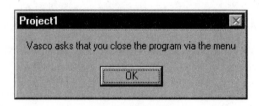

When I clicked on the OK button of the message box, the form remained opened.

"The code we keyed in the `QueryUnload` event procedure," I said, "has defeated the user's attempt to close the form. By setting `Cancel` = `True`, we told Visual Basic *not* to close the form."

"That's a beautiful thing," I heard Vasco say.

I then clicked on the Close button in the upper right hand corner of the form – again, the message box was displayed, and the form remained open.

"We have just one little problem," I said. "Vasco, you said you want the user to be able to shut down your program via a menu item. What code do you have in the `Click` event procedure of that menu item?"

"Well," he said, "I do a little bit of housekeeping – closing files, and writing some values to the Windows Registry, but the last statement I have is '`Unload Me`.' Is that OK?"

"Ordinarily, that would be fine," I said. "But let's see what happens if we execute that code now."

I created a quick File | Exit menu structure using the Visual Basic menu control. In a menu item named '`mnuExit`', I wrote the following code:

```
Private Sub mnuExit_Click()

Unload Me

End Sub
```

I ran the program, clicked on the File I Exit menu item, and the following message box appeared:

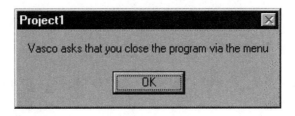

"Uh oh," Vasco said. "What happened? Does this mean that there's no way to close the form?"

"We do have a *slight* problem," I said. "The 'Unload Me' statement we have in the Click event of the menu item is triggering the same QueryUnload event procedure that the user triggers when they click on the Control Menu box or click on the Close button."

"What can we do now?" Vasco asked.

"Do you remember, Vasco," I said, "that the QueryUnload event procedure gives us information about why the form is closing? If you take a look at the procedure header for the QueryUnload event procedure, you'll see that in addition to the Cancel argument, there is also another argument called UnloadMode. UnloadMode is the argument, passed to the QueryUnload event, that tells us why the form is being unloaded. Using this argument, we can determine if the QueryUnload event was triggered by the user, or more importantly, triggered by our own code."

"That's great," Vasco said excitedly. "So if the QueryUnload event was triggered by code, we can allow the form to close normally?"

"You catch on quickly, Vasco," I said. "That's right. I invite my viewers to check out Visual Basic Help for more details on the UnloadMode argument, but I can tell you that if the UnloadMode argument is equal to 1 - the intrinsic constant vbFormCode - we know that the QueryUnload event was triggered by Visual Basic code. If the value of the argument is 0 – the intrinsic constant vbFormControlMenu – we know that the QueryUnload event was triggered because the *user* tried to close the form. Here's the code..."

```
Private Sub Form_QueryUnload(Cancel As Integer, UnloadMode As Integer)

If UnloadMode = vbFormCode Then
   MsgBox "Thank you for using my program"
   Exit Sub
Else
```

```
    MsgBox "Vasco asks that you close the program via the menu"
    Cancel = True
End If

End Sub
```

"In this code," I said, "we check to see if the `UnloadMode` is equal to `vbFormCode` – meaning that the form is being unloaded due to Visual Basic code being executed. If this is `True`, then we display a message box thanking the user for using our program, and bypass the rest of the code via the `Exit Sub` statement. This results in the `Unload` event taking place next as it normally would, and the form is then unloaded. However, if the value of `UnloadMode` is *not* equal to `vbFormCode`, we display a message box asking the user to properly exit the program, and set the `Cancel` argument to `True`. Again, this results in the form not being unloaded, and our program continues to run."

I ran the program and, as before, clicking on the Control Menu box or the Close button generated a message box warning the user to exit the program properly, and the form remained loaded. However, when I clicked on the Exit menu item, a message was displayed...

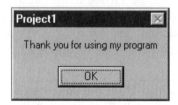

...the form closed normally, and the program ended.

"That's great," Vasco said. "That's exactly what I need. Thanks so much for your help. This will save me many headaches, believe me."

"You're quite welcome, Vasco," I said, "and thanks for calling. Now let's move on to our next caller."

Question 79: Where can I get a list of those VB intrinsic constants I've heard about?

"Hi, my name is Agatha, and I'm calling from Torquay, England," she said. "You just referred to another one of those Visual Basic intrinsic constants. Is there a comprehensive list of these constants anywhere?"

"Hi, Agatha," I said, "welcome to the show. That's another terrific question. I'm not aware of any comprehensive list of these Visual Basic intrinsic constants. In fact, if you go out to the Microsoft web site, and search for the phrase 'Intrinsic Constant', Microsoft will tell you that intrinsic constants are listed in the **Object Library**."

"Isn't there anything in Help that lists them?" Agatha asked.

"You can find individual intrinsic constants listed in the Visual Basic documentation, along with the statement, function or procedure that uses them. Unfortunately, trying to find intrinsic constants in Visual Basic Help can be frustrating. For instance, if we pull up Visual Basic Help and type the words `'UnloadMode'` in the Index search box, you won't find a match. If, on the other hand, we look up `'QueryUnload'` in the Index search box, you'll find a list of argument values, along with their Visual Basic intrinsic constant names."

"That's not a great deal of help, is it?" Agatha said. "That's like trying to look up a word in the dictionary when you don't know how to spell it."

"You're right," I agreed, "which is why Microsoft's suggestion to use the Visual Basic Object Library is probably best."

"I've heard of the Object Browser," Agatha said. "Is that the same as the Object Library? And where can I find it?"

"The Object Browser," I said, "is used to display the contents of the Object Library – which lists the hierarchies of controls and objects in Visual Basic, including all the controls you've set up in your project. While objects are a bit beyond the scope of our show, I can certainly show you how to use the Object Browser."

"Is the Object Library like Visual Basic Help?" she asked.

"I wouldn't go that far, Agatha," I replied. "The Object Library is a bit sketchier than that – however, the Visual Basic intrinsic constants are all listed in the Object Browser, *if* you know how to find them. But I must warn you – they're *listed* there, but not explained."

"I think I'd be content to just know what their names are," Agatha said. "Can you show me how to find them?"

"Sure thing," I said. "To view the Object Library using the Object Browser, we can either press the *F2* function key, or select View | Object Browser from the menu bar."

I started a new Visual Basic program, and pressed the *F2* function key. This brought up the Object Browser:

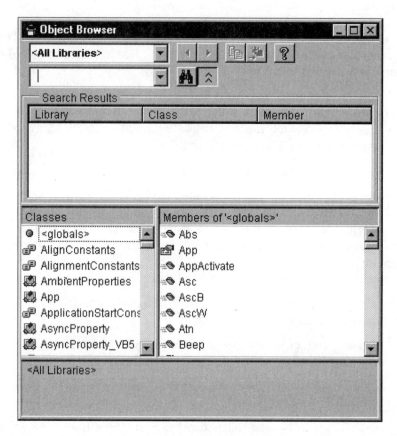

"The Object Browser is a pretty busy window," I said, "and contains a lot of information. If we want information on a Visual Basic intrinsic constant we already know exists, we can do that pretty easily – how about the one we just used in our previous question, **vbFormCode**?"

I entered vbFormCode into the search box of the Object Browser, clicked on the binoculars icon, and the following screen shot was displayed:

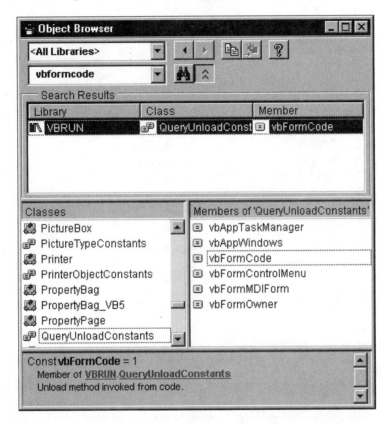

"There, that was fast," I said. "Take a look at the Classes window pane in the Object Browser. Notice how 'QueryUnloadConstants' is selected. That indicates that **vbFormCode** is one of the group of QueryUnloadConstants. If you look at the Members pane to the right of the Classes pane, you'll see that '**vbFormCode**' is selected. You'll also see the other five members of the QueryUnloadConstants class. Finally, notice that in the bottom window of the Object Browser, the value for the constant **vbFormCode** is defined, along with a *brief* explanation of what it means – and I do mean brief. At this point, you might want to experiment just a bit by typing the word 'Constant' or 'Constants' into the Search box. Let's do that now…"

I typed the word 'constants' into the search box of the Object Browser and clicked on the binoculars. The results of the search were displayed:

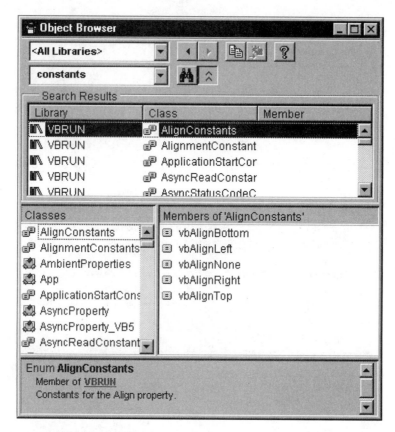

"That's more like it," Agatha said. "At least now I know where I can find these. It's not ideal – I wish these were all listed in one place – but this *is* valuable information. As long as I know where I can find a list of these, I feel better. You saved me some detective work. Thanks for your help."

"I'm glad I could help, Agatha," I said. "And thanks for calling. Now it's time to take our last phone call of the day."

Question 80: In a Select Case statement where two of the Case statements can be true, why don't both sets of code execute?

"Hi, my name is Hans," our final caller of the day said, "and I'm from Odense, Denmark. I have a little problem. I coded a `Select Case` statement, and it doesn't seem to be working."

"Hi, Hans," I answered, "tell me a little bit more – what kind of condition were you evaluating in the `Select Case` statement? And what you do you mean when you say it isn't working?"

"I was testing a number that the user entered in a text box," he said, "to see if the number fell within three possible ranges."

"What ranges?" I asked.

"Well," he continued, "If the number is between 1 and 50, I want to display a message box and execute a subprocedure I've written. If the number is between 30 and 60, I want to display a *different* message box and execute a different subprocedure. Finally, if the number is between 51 and 100, I want to display still another message box and execute a third subprocedure."

I thought for a moment, and then asked Hans to repeat this scenario. When he was finished, I said:

"Are you aware that there are numbers within the first range that overlap with the numbers in the second range? And numbers that fall within the second range, that also fall within the third range?"

"Yes, I am," said Hans. "Is that a problem in Visual Basic? I have no trouble coding that same `Case` structure logic in C."

"Visual Basic `Select...Case` structure is different than the `switch...case` structure in C," I said. "In Visual Basic, once a `Case` statement in the `Select...Case` structure evaluates to `True`, all of the other `Case` statements are then bypassed."

"I didn't know that," Hans said, "that's the exact opposite of C's behavior. In C, each `case` statement is evaluated in turn, regardless of whether the previous `case` statement evaluates to `True`. In fact, in C, you need to explicitly exit the `case` structure if that's the sort of behavior you're trying to achieve."

"Before we get too far into this, Hans," I said, "I think it would be a good idea if I showed the viewers at home exactly what we're talking about here."

I started a new project and placed a text box and a command button on the form. Using the Properties window, I cleared the `Text` property of the text box, and keyed the following code into the command button's `Click` event:

```
Private Sub Command1_Click()

Select Case Val(Text1.Text)
    Case 1 To 50
        MsgBox "1 to 50"
    Case 30 To 60
        MsgBox "30 to 60"
    Case 51 To 100
        MsgBox "51 to 100"
End Select

End Sub
```

"This pretty much simulates what you are trying to do, doesn't it, Hans?" I asked.

"Yes," he said. "I have just one question – why are you using the `Val` statement here?"

"The `Text` property of the text box is of the `string` data type. The `Val` function takes a string, and returns the numeric equivalent of it," I said. "Beware of using strings in comparison operations with numeric literals. The results may not be quite what you expect. For instance, here's an example I give my students in class all the time."

I displayed this `Select Case` structure on my electronic whiteboard:

```
Select Case Text1.Text

Case 1 To 10

MsgBox "1 to 10"

Case Is > 11

MsgBox "Greater than 11"

End Select
```

"Would it surprise you to learn that if the user enters the number 2 into the text box," I said, "a message box would be displayed saying 'Greater than 11'"?

"Yes, that would surprise me," Hans said, "why is that?"

"Many programmers make the mistake," I said, "of believing that Visual Basic sees that the *string* '2' is a valid number and converts it to the *number* 2 before performing the comparison with the range '1 to 10'. However, I have found this particular type of comparison to be a problem. It appears that the comparison is actually being done at the string level, which is done left to right, character versus character. Here, the condition '1 To 10' is interpreted as any text string alphabetically between '1' and '10'. Anything that starts with '1' comes before everything that starts with '2'. So '2' isn't considered to be between '1' and '10'."

"Hmm...," muttered Hans. "So the first `Case` statement is false, and we pass to the next one. But here, we're using the '>' operator. Surely VB should know that this is a numerical comparison?"

"Visual Basic knows that the two terms you're comparing aren't of the same data type. It knows, therefore, that it has to change *one* of them. But you can't necessarily count on it changing it to the same one you expect. The bottom line is this: If you intend to do a numeric comparison, it never hurts to use the `Val` function on the `Text` property of the text box. And it can save you some grief in the end."

"Wow," Hans said, "that's shocking. And if we use the `Val` function on the text box, then we ensure that all comparisons are done numerically?"

"That's right," I said. "That's why we use the `Val` function."

"Thanks for that tip," he said.

"Let's run the original program now," I said, "and see what happens when we enter the number 15 into the text box."

I ran the program, entered 15 into the text box, and clicked on the command button. This is what we saw:

"No surprise here," I said. "Since 15 is a number between 1 and 50, this message box gets displayed. Now, suppose that I enter the number 33, which is between 1 and 50, and *also* between 30 and 60. In some other languages, most notably C, we would see two message boxes displayed – one indicating that the number is between 1 and 50, and the second indicating that the number is between 30 and 60. But in Visual Basic, once one of the case conditions evaluates to `True`, testing for the rest of the `Case` conditions comes to an immediate stop. Look at this..."

I entered 33 into the text box, clicked on the command button, and the following message box was displayed:

"That's the message box for the first `Case` condition that evaluates to `True`," I said. "Now let's see if we get another message box."

I clicked on the OK button and nothing else was displayed.

"No other case conditions were evaluated," I said.

"You're absolutely right," Hans said. "I was expecting that a second message box would be displayed reading '30 to 60'. Coming from the 'C' world, this is a bit shocking."

"It will take some getting used to," I agreed.

"So how can I get this behavior in my program?" he asked. "Will I need to use a series of `If...Then` statements?"

"That's right," I said, "but that shouldn't be too big a deal. Let's take a shot at that here:"

```
Private Sub Command1_Click()

If Val(Text1.Text) >= 1 And Val(Text1.Text) <= 50 Then
    MsgBox "1 to 50"
End If

If Val(Text1.Text) >= 30 And Val(Text1.Text) <= 60 Then
    MsgBox "30 to 60"
End If
```

```
If Val(Text1.Text) >= 51 And Val(Text1.Text) <= 100 Then
    MsgBox "51 to 100"
End If

End Sub
```

"Now let's run the program..."

I ran the program, entered 33 into the text box, and clicked on the command button. This time, we got...

"Just like before," I said, "since the number 33 is between 1 and 50, this message box is displayed. As you'll recall, with the **Select Case** structure, that was as far as our code went with this. But since we've converted our **Select Case** statement into a series of **If...Then** statements, if we now click on the OK button ..."

I did, and the following screen shot was displayed:

"...we'll get a second message box."

"I can live with that," Hans said, "I'll just need to keep those differences in mind if I find myself switching back and forth between the two languages – thanks for your help, Professor Smiley."

"Glad I could help, Hans, and thanks for calling," I said, as I glanced at the clock on the wall.

"It looks like we're all out of time for today. I want to thank everyone who called in today with those great questions. If you didn't get through, please try again next time. Remember, we'll be here next week – same place, same new time, same channel. See you then."

As I removed my earpiece, I sat down and wiped my brow. "That was definitely more difficult than earlier weeks," I said to Linda.

"Yeah, the questions seemed harder, and a bit more theoretical," she agreed. "I have a question, actually, about the very last item – I'm no programmer, but you do pick stuff up when you produce a show – I was trying to figure this out and I couldn't. You had a message box, and you clicked on its OK button. Then, even though you hadn't put any code in that button, another message box popped up. How does that message box know what to do next?"

"What? Oh, I see. The thing about a message box is that it just pops up when you call it, and its OK button really just tells it that the message has been read and it can go away. You don't have to put code behind a normal message box – your program runs the very next line of code after the one that called it up," I explained.

"So the message box popped up, you dismissed it, and your program ran the next part of its code, which was to bring up the next message box? I think I get it. This programming thing isn't as hard as everyone makes it out to be," said Linda.

"You're right, and it's exactly that which makes me want to encourage all the beginners out there who think it's just too hard for them," I said. "This show really took it out of me. I think I'll go home and relax a little. See you next week!"

Week 9

The week leading up to our ninth show was fairly uneventful. On Monday morning, Tim had called to tell me that our first week of international broadcasting had gone extremely well, as evidenced by the fact that the bulk of our callers had been international callers. Our domestic viewing numbers continued to be impressive.

"Good morning," said Linda when I arrived in the studio early on Saturday morning. "I must tell you, the international viewers are extremely anxious to get through. I already have ten callers waiting on the line. I suspect we may be getting some complaints from our United States callers – this will be the second week they've been shut out – but the phones were already ringing like crazy when I arrived at the studio an hour ago."

"It's great to be popular," I said. "Let's hope it keeps up."

Running all of my equipment and software through a quick test, everything performed perfectly. It wasn't long before Linda gave me a wave and said:

"Ten seconds."

I cleared my throat and faced the camera. Right on cue, I came in with my introduction.

"Good morning, everyone," I said, "welcome to Professor Smiley's Visual Basic Programming Workshop. Let's go straight to the phone lines. Caller number one, you're on the air."

Question 81: I specified a picture for a command button, so why doesn't my picture show up?

(see also questions 17, 24 & 33)

"Hello, my name is Victoria, and I live in London, Great Britain," said the caller. "I have a graphics file that I want to load into the `Picture` property of a command button, and no matter what I do, the graphic just won't show up. Can you tell me what you think the problem is here?"

"Hi, Victoria," I said, "and welcome to our show. This is a complaint I hear from time to time in my classes – and I think I have a good idea of what the problem may be. Just so everyone fully understands your question, let me try to duplicate your problem here in the studio."

Learn to Program with Visual Basic Examples

I opened a new Visual Basic project (this was pure instinct to me now) and placed a command button on the form. Bringing up the Properties window for the command button, I cleared the `Caption` property of the button, and then located and specified a graphics file for the `Picture` property of the command button:

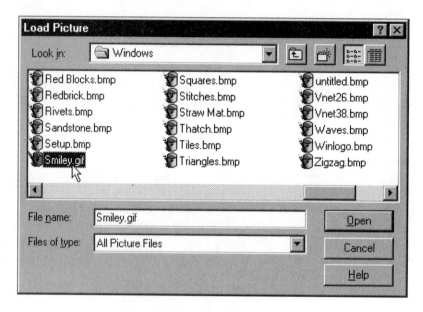

"Let's try the `Smiley.gif` file," I said, "I think it's pretty appropriate."

I selected `Smiley.gif` and clicked on the **Open** button:

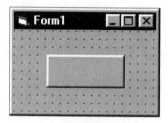

"Shouldn't that command button have a picture displayed in it now?" Victoria asked. "We don't have to wait until the program is run to see it, do we?"

"No, Victoria," I said, "you're right – we *should* see a picture displayed in the command button right now. However, there's one more thing we need to do first."

"I thought I might have forgotten something," I heard Victoria say. "Well, what is it?"

"Well," I said, "you *did* forget something – but that's very easy to do. The additional thing you need to do is open up the Properties window for the command button and change the `Style` property of the command button from its default value of `0-Standard` to `1-Graphical`. I'll do that now..."

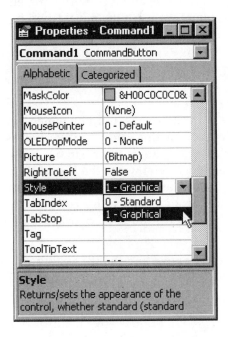

"... and the missing picture in the command button will appear:"

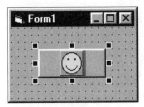

"Normally at this point," I said, "we would resize the command button to make it look a bit neater. Like this..."

"I find this difficult to believe," Victoria said, obviously chastened. "That's all there was to it. You wouldn't believe how much time I spent trying to get that picture to appear. Thank you so much for your help, Professor Smiley."

"My pleasure, Victoria," I said, "And don't be annoyed with yourself; sometimes these frustrating problems are the ones where we learn the most. Good luck with your programming. And now it's time for our second caller."

Question 82: What does the 1 in EOF(1) mean?

(see also question 89)

"*Buon giorno*, my name is Dante. I'm from Firenze, in Italy, which you may know as Florence," the voice on the other end of the line said fluently. "I work for a publishing house, and we're using a Visual Basic program to maintain our books inventory in a file on the hard disk drive of my PC. The person who wrote the Visual Basic program (my cousin Michael) has been in the hospital for the last month after falling from a scaffold while painting a ceiling. I've been looking through some of his code, and there's a statement in his program that I just don't understand. It's in the section where he reads records from the disk file. Can you help me?"

"Hi, Dante," I replied, "welcome to the show, and thanks for calling. I'll be glad to try to help you. Can you tell me what the statement is that's confusing you?"

"Sure," Dante said, "the line reads `Do While Not`, followed by the word `EOF`, followed by the number 1 in parentheses."

"OK," I said, "let me put that on my electronic whiteboard to make it clear:"

Do While Not EOF(1)

"That's right," confirmed Dante. "I checked Visual Basic Help, and I've figured that `EOF` stands for End Of File, but I'm befuddled as to what the number 1 stands for."

"You're right, Dante," I said. "`EOF` *does* stand for End Of File. `EOF` is a function that is used to tell us if we have reached the End Of File of an opened file, and the number 1 here represents the file opened with File Argument Number 1."

There was silence, and it became evident that Dante probably didn't know what a File Number Argument was.

"Perhaps I should clarify this," I suggested. "Let me do a little demonstration to give everyone a better feel for disk file processing – that is, how we write data to disk files, and how we retrieve it."

I created a new project and placed a single command button on its form.

"I'm going to write some code to read data from a file on my hard disk," I said. "First, I need to create the file itself. Here's how."

I started Notepad and created a three-line file consisting of one of my favorite phrases – you may recognize it:

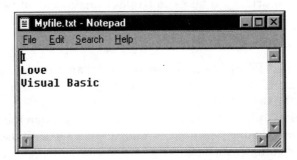

I saved the file as MYFILE.TXT in the root (C:\) directory of my hard drive, and closed Notepad. Next, I typed the following code into the Click event procedure of the command button:

```
Private Sub Command1_Click()

Dim strData As String

Open "C:\MYFILE.TXT" For Input As #1

Do While Not EOF(1)
    Line Input #1, strData
    Form1.Print strData
Loop

Close #1

End Sub
```

"This line of code," I said, "will look for the MYFILE.TXT file I just created and open it up in **Input mode**, which allows us to read the text in the file:"

```
Open "C:\MYFILE.TXT" For Input As #1
```

"There's that number 1 again," commented Dante. "Is that the same number 1 that appears in the EOF function?"

"That's right," I said. "It's the File Number argument again. When we open a file using a particular File Number argument, from that point forward, that's how the program refers to the opened file. Using the File Number argument eliminates the need to refer to the file by its actual name again."

"So it's like a shortcut?" Dante asked.

"*Perfetto*," I said. "Just like a shortcut – it takes us straight there without having to explicitly reference the full file name every time."

"Is the File Number argument always 1?" Dante asked.

"That's a fine question, Dante," I said. "You can open more than one file at the same time in your Visual Basic program, and the convention is that the first file you open is opened with File Number Argument 1, the second with number 2, and so on. But a File Number argument can range from 1 to 512, so if you wanted to you could open the first file in your program with File Argument number 333 – but it really makes sense to use number 1 for your first file, number 2 for your second, etc."

"I see that," he said. "What about the rest of the code? Can you explain that to me, please?"

"Sure thing," I said. "Once we've opened the file for input, we use the `Line Input` statement to read a line of text from the open file into our program. The syntax for the `Line Input` statement requires that we read single lines of text, one at a time, into a variable – in this case, that variable is `strData`, which we declared earlier:"

```
Line Input #1, strData
```

"And you're using the `Line Input` statement within a `Do...Loop` construct ," Dante said, "because the code needs to be able to read three lines of text?"

"*Bravo*," I said. "More specifically, the program needs to be able to read a *variable* number of lines of text. This file could contain anywhere from zero lines to a million. Since we don't know how many lines of text will be in the file we open, we use a `Do...Loop` with a conditional expression of `Not EOF(1)`, to tell Visual Basic to continue reading the file until the End Of File has been reached:"

```
Do While Not EOF(1)
    Line Input #1, strData
    Form1.Print strData
Loop
```

"So," I continued, "when the end of the file is reached and there are no more lines to read, the loop terminates because its `Do While` condition is no longer true. The icing on the cake is that we also display the line of text we've read on the form, using the form's `Print` method."

"OK," Dante said, "now I realize that the number 1 in the `EOF` function refers to the File Number argument. By the way, is EOF the last line of text in the file?"

"No," I replied, "EOF is actually an invisible file marker *after* the last line of text in the file. Do you understand what's going on with the rest of the code?"

"I think so," Dante said, "At the end of the code you close `MYFILE.TXT` using the `Close` statement – again, using the File Number argument of 1."

"Excellent, Dante," I said, "you're a quick student. Your cousin Michael better get back up on his feet soon, or he's going to have a little VB competition to contend with. Let's run this code now and see what happens when we click on the command button:"

"There," I said, "that did the job. This file reading technique can be used to pull in data from files; you can then use that data in your programs – assigning it to variables, properties and so on – just as if you had coded the data into the program itself."

"I want to thank you, Professor Smiley," Dante said. "You've really cleared this up for me."

"Glad I could help," I said. "*Ciao*! Now, who's next on the line?"

Question 83: The IsMissing function isn't working – why?

"Hi, my name is Elizabeth, and I'm from Greenwich, in the United Kingdom," proclaimed caller number three. "I've been doing a little experimentation lately by writing my own subprocedures in Visual Basic. I've been very pleased with the progress I've made so far – at least I was until today, when I decided to become perhaps a little too sophisticated, and wrote a procedure with two arguments, one of which is optional."

"The procedure worked fine, but then I got even more elaborate by using the `IsMissing` function to determine whether the calling procedure had passed the optional argument. Everything seemed to be working – the program didn't fail, anyway – but then I discovered that when the calling procedure *doesn't* pass the optional argument, `IsMissing` still thinks that it *has*. Although the program isn't failing, I was depending upon the `IsMissing` function to allow me to fine-tune my code in the event of the optional argument not being passed. I realize that there are other ways to determine if the optional argument has been supplied – but it just irritates me that something doesn't work as advertised. Could it be that this is a Visual Basic bug?"

"I think I know what the problem might be here, Elizabeth," I said. "By the way, I really appreciate you asking this question. This will give me a chance to show our home viewers how to create a procedure of their own that executes code, and gets passed an argument that lets you qualify the procedure in some way. Let me take a minute here to code up an example for everyone. Let's start out with a simple procedure – that is, one that has no arguments."

In time-honored fashion, I started a clean Visual Basic project and placed the trusty single command button on the form.

"There are a number of ways to go about creating your own procedures or functions," I said. "Probably the easiest way is to open up your code window, go to the General Declarations section of the form, and start coding, like this…"

I typed the following code into the General Declarations section:

```
Private Sub MyProcedure()

Form1.Print "I love Visual Basic"

End Sub
```

In the code window, this code appeared as follows:

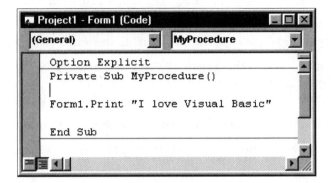

"This is a pretty simple procedure," I said. "When it's called, all it will do is print I love Visual Basic on the form. Notice that the first line of the procedure, the Procedure Header, contains the name of the subprocedure:"

```
Private Sub MyProcedure()
```

"We can name the procedure virtually anything we want, and since our procedure has no arguments, we include an empty set of parentheses at the end of the procedure to indicate that to Visual Basic."

I ran the program, clicked on the command button – and nothing happened.

"Oops," I said, "I forgot to *call* the subprocedure."

"I was about to say that, actually," Elizabeth said.

"Nothing like live television to humble one," I said. "You're quite right, Elizabeth. We've written the procedure, now we need to 'call' it. In other words, the code to print the words on the screen is just sitting there in the General Declarations section of the form; nothing's yet been done to make the code actually *run*. Like this..."

I bashfully typed this code into the code window:

```
Private Sub Command1_Click()

Call MyProcedure

End Sub
```

"There, that's better," I said. "Now when the `Click` event is triggered, the code in the `Click` event procedure will call our custom-written `MyProcedure` procedure. Let's do that now and see if it works."

"Before you do," Elizabeth said, "may I ask a question? Is the word `Call` essential?"

"That's a pertinent question, Elizabeth," I replied. "No – *technically*, the `Call` part is not required to run the subprocedure. I always use it when I want to execute a procedure or function of my own, but we *could* execute `MyProcedure` without using the word `Call`."

"I see," Elizabeth said. "Using `Call` does make the line of code stand out a bit."

I ran the program and clicked on the command button. This time, we generated the following result:

"As we expected," I said, "our procedure was executed, and the phrase I love Visual Basic was printed on the form. Now let's modify the subprocedure so that it accepts a single, mandatory `Integer` argument."

"What kind of argument?" Elizabeth asked. "What will we do with that?"

"How about an argument," I replied, "that determines the number of times that we print I love Visual Basic on the form?"

"Sounds good to me," Elizabeth said.

Thus encouraged, I modified the procedure declaration like so:

```
Private Sub MyProcedure(intTimes As Integer)

Dim intCounter As Integer

For intCounter = 1 To intTimes
    Form1.Print "I love Visual Basic"
Next

End Sub
```

"As we mentioned when I first declared the procedure," I said, "any arguments are specified in the parentheses following the procedure name. Our first iteration of this procedure was simple – no arguments, and therefore a pair of empty parentheses. This time around, we've complicated things a bit by having the subprocedure accept one mandatory argument – we *have* to pass a value for the integer variable intTimes to this procedure when we run it."

"And that argument is specified in the parentheses, is that right?" Elizabeth asked. "How does Visual Basic know that it's a *mandatory* argument?"

"Well, Elizabeth, the argument is certainly specified within the parentheses. Visual Basic knows that the argument is *required* because the keyword Optional does *not* precede the argument name. So, this code..."

```
Private Sub MyProcedure(intTimes As Integer)
```

"... tells Visual Basic that the subprocedure requires one argument, intTimes, whose data type is type Integer."

"I notice," Elizabeth said, "that the argument intTimes isn't declared anywhere within the body of the procedure itself, like a variable would be."

"That's right," I said. "Arguments are really declared within the procedure header itself – so there's no need to further declare them within the body of the procedure. By the way, did you notice how we used the argument intTimes as the end parameter of our For...Next loop?"

```
For intCounter = 1 To intTimes
```

"Yes I did," Elizabeth said. "That certainly highlights how powerful an argument passed to a procedure can be. I would imagine that the code to call this subprocedure needs to change a bit, now that the subprocedure requires an argument – isn't that right?"

"You're right on the mark, Elizabeth," I said. "Let's take a look at that code now."

I modified the code in the Click event procedure to look like this:

```
Private Sub Command1_Click()

Call MyProcedure(3)

End Sub
```

I started to explain this code: "We now need to pass the subprocedure an integer value. We can do this in a number of ways; the easiest way is to pass a numeric literal within parentheses – so that's what we've done here. This value will then be used to determine the number of times that the loop in the subprocedure is executed."

I ran the program, with this result:

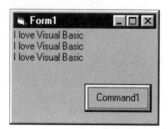

"What happens if you call the procedure and forget to pass the required argument?" Elizabeth asked.

"We'll soon find out," I replied, "let's try it."

I quickly removed the argument-passing code from the call statement in the `Click` event procedure:

```
Private Sub Command1_Click()

Call MyProcedure

End Sub
```

When I reran the program and clicked on the command button...

"As you can see," I said, "Visual Basic is well aware that the procedure requires an argument. The error message isn't the greatest in the world; it should really say 'a required argument has not been provided' – but it does the trick. By the way, let me show you some code that confuses the heck out of my students at the university:"

I amended the code in the `Click` event again, so that it now looked like this:

```
Private Sub Command1_Click()

Dim intValue as Integer

intValue = 3

Call MyProcedure(intValue)

End Sub
```

When I ran the program and clicked on the command button with this code in place, we saw the same result as in the previous run:

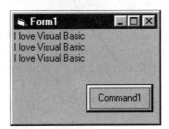

"Something in your tone tells me I should be baffled, but I'm *not*," Elizabeth said lightheartedly. "I understand that instead of passing the procedure a numeric literal as an argument, you're substituting the name of the variable `intValue`. I guess my only question is, shouldn't the variable be named `intTimes`? That's what the variable name is in the procedure. Don't they have to be the same?"

"That's what many of my students believe," I said. "But arguments in Visual Basic are passed *positionally*. If you choose to pass an argument using a variable instead of a numeric or string literal, the name of the variable *doesn't* need to match the argument name as declared in the header. Visual Basic will know what the argument is by its position in the argument list in the call statement. So long as the value-providing variable is the right position, it doesn't matter what it's called."

"OK," Elizabeth said, "now what about specifying an `Optional` parameter?"

"All right," I said, "let's get a little more elegant here – let's modify the procedure so that the name of the person who loves Visual Basic is displayed on the form. But let's make it an *optional* argument, like this:"

```
Private Sub MyProcedure(intTimes As Integer, Optional strName As String)

Dim intCounter As Integer

For intCounter = 1 To intTimes
    Form1.Print strName & " loves Visual Basic"
Next

End Sub
```

"Notice," I said, "that we now have *two* arguments included in the procedure header – intTimes, which we had already, and a new argument called strName, which we've declared as a string data type. Notice also that strName has been declared as an optional argument through the use of the Optional keyword. Also, we've modified the line of code that prints I love Visual Basic to include the value of the argument strName:"

```
Form1.Print strName & " loves Visual Basic"
```

"As I recall," Elizabeth said, "*optional* arguments need to be specified after all *required* arguments have been named in the header – is that right?"

"You're correct, Elizabeth." I said. "Any optional arguments that you declare *must* appear at the end of the declaration list – you can't, for instance, declare an optional argument, and follow it with a mandatory argument. You may have more than one optional argument, though – but remember, once you declare an optional argument, any subsequent arguments you declare must *also* be optional."

I paused to let that sink in before continuing: "Let's take a look at the code to call the procedure now."

I modified the code in the Click event procedure again, so that it now looked like this:

```
Private Sub Command1_Click()

Call MyProcedure(3, "John Smiley")

End Sub
```

"I've gone back to passing a numeric literal," I said. "And even though the second argument to the subprocedure is optional, I've passed it anyway. Let's run this code:"

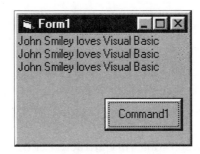

"That worked beautifully," I said. "We're now passing two arguments to our procedure – the number of times to print the I love Visual Basic statement, and an optional argument to specify the name of the person who loves Visual Basic. Now remember, the second argument was *optional*. Whenever you have declared a procedure with an optional argument, you need to be able to handle *not* receiving it."

"Exactly!" Elizabeth said, "which is why I was so frustrated when IsMissing failed to work for me. Remember, I'm trying to use IsMissing to detect if an argument has been passed to my program."

"The answer to your problem is imminent," I assured her. "But first, let's modify our Call statement so that we do *not* pass the optional strName argument."

Once more, I modified the code in the command button's well-worn Click event procedure so as *not* to pass the optional argument:

```
Private Sub Command1_Click()

Call MyProcedure(3)

End Sub
```

This time we got the following result when we ran the program:

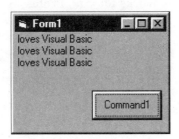

"See what happens," I said, "when we don't pass the optional argument for `strName`? Our code just blindly goes through the process of printing the value of the declared argument `strName`."

"Which I can see," Elizabeth said, "contains an empty string."

"That's right," I said. "The argument was declared as a string in the procedure header, so as far as Visual Basic is concerned, it contains an empty string – which it dutifully prints with this line of code:"

```
Form1.Print strName & " loves Visual Basic"
```

"I see that," she said. "That doesn't look very attractive. I think it would be reasonable to check to see whether the optional argument has been passed to the procedure and, if not, revert back to the old standard I love Visual Basic."

"That sounds good to me," I agreed, "and we can do that through the use of the `IsMissing` function. Look at this code..."

I modified the procedure's code one more time, so that it looked like this:

```
Private Sub MyProcedure(intTimes As Integer, Optional strName As String)

Dim intCounter As Integer

If IsMissing(strName) Then
  For intCounter = 1 To intTimes
    Form1.Print "I love Visual Basic"
  Next
Else
  For intCounter = 1 To intTimes
    Form1.Print strName & " loves Visual Basic"
  Next
End If

End Sub
```

"I'll be very surprised if this code works for you, Professor Smiley," Elizabeth said. "This code is very similar to mine."

"Actually, Elizabeth," I said, "you're right. There's a subtle error in this code, which ensnares a lot of programmers – beginner and intermediate alike. But let's pretend for the moment that all is well. What we want to do here is use the `IsMissing` function (which checks for the presence of arguments) with the `strName` argument. The `IsMissing` function will return a value of `True` if the optional argument *has not* been passed to the procedure, and a value of `False` if the optional argument *has* been passed."

I waited a moment before pressing on.

"If the return value of `IsMissing` is `False`, we know that our optional argument `strName` *has* been passed, and we use the passed name to custom print (Jane Doe) loves Visual Basic. However, if the `IsMissing` function returns a value of `True`, we know that the optional argument `strName` has *not* been passed and, per your suggestion, we just print the standard phrase I love Visual Basic."

"Of course, this is exactly where I had my trouble," Elizabeth said. "I'm anxious to see what happens when you run this and don't pass the subprocedure the optional argument. You're keeping me in suspense."

To ease that tension, I ran the program and clicked on the command button:

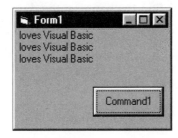

"As I suspected." Elizabeth said, "Now I don't feel so bad – it's happening to you as well. Is this a bug in Visual Basic?"

"As I mentioned earlier, this is a pretty common *error* people make in Visual Basic," I said. "In fact, I've even seen it in some textbooks."

"Where's the error?" Elizabeth asked.

"The problem isn't with the code in the *procedure*," I said. "The problem is with the procedure *declaration*, particularly our optional argument declaration."

"We declared the optional argument after the required argument?" Elizabeth queried.

"No, that was fine," I said. "However, in order for the `IsMissing` function to tell us whether an optional argument has been passed to a procedure, the argument *type* must be declared as a **Variant** – but if you check our procedure header, you'll see that we defined our optional argument as a *string* data type."

"That made perfect sense at the time," Elizabeth said. "After all, a person's name *should* be a string."

"Yes, it did make perfect sense," I agreed. "However, if you check Visual Basic Help, you'll see that `IsMissing` only works with `Variant` optional arguments – and we certainly proved that here. If you use the `IsMissing` function on anything but a `Variant` data type, it always returns `False` – meaning that it always tells you the optional argument has been passed to the procedure. Let's change our procedure header by changing the data type of the optional argument to a `Variant`, and see if that cures the problem."

I changed the header declaration to look like this:

```
Private Sub MyProcedure(intTimes As Integer, Optional varName As Variant)
```

"To adhere to Hungarian notation," I said, "we should change the name of the argument from `strName` to `varName` in addition to changing the data type. We'll also need to change the rest of the procedure slightly to incorporate the change in the argument name:"

```
Dim intCounter As Integer

If IsMissing(varName) Then
   For intCounter = 1 To intTimes
     Form1.Print "I love Visual Basic"
   Next
Else
   For intCounter = 1 To intTimes
     Form1.Print varName & " loves Visual Basic"
   Next
End If
```

This time, we got this result:

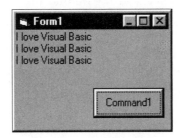

"That worked!" Elizabeth said excitedly. "Imagine that – just by changing the optional argument *type* to `Variant`, the `IsMissing` function worked. That seems so obscure."

"Another one of those famous tricks of the trade!" I laughed. "Thanks for calling, Elizabeth," looking up to see that it was time for the commercial break.

"Now for a word from our sponsors," I said. "We'll be back in a matter of minutes. See you then."

After the break, it was time for caller number four.

Question 84: Problems with the Timer control in Step Mode – why?

(see also question 86)

"Hi, my name is Werner, and I'm calling from Cologne, Germany," the caller said. "I've read your book and I've taken to heart your suggestions about running programs in Debug mode, or Step mode, as you call it. I must tell you, running a program in Step mode, even a program that isn't giving you any problems, is a wonderful way to see what's going on behind the scenes. I've learned so much about my programs this way, I can't recommend it enough. However, I'm having one tiny little problem running my program in Step mode."

"Let's try, Werner," I said. " What's the nature of your problem?"

"Well," he continued, "I have a Timer control on the form, and when I run my program in Step mode it seems like the Timer control just takes over. Every time I try to step through my code, the code in the Timer event procedure of the Timer control is displayed. As soon as I step through that code, it appears again, and I can't see the code in any of my event procedures run. Is there any way around this?"

As soon as Werner mentioned the Timer control and Step mode, I had an inkling of what he was getting at.

"Step Mode or Debug Mode – whatever you choose to call it," I said, "is a wonderfully effective way to see how your code is executing behind the scenes – but if you have a Timer control on your form, it becomes an exercise in massive frustration. Let me show everyone the execution of a program in Step mode, where you can watch each line of code being executed one at a time."

I opened a new project and placed a single command button on the form. I then entered the following code in the `Click` event procedure of the command button:

```
Private Sub Command1_Click()

Dim intCounter As Integer

For intCounter = 1 To 10
    Form1.Print intCounter
Next intCounter

End Sub
```

"Nothing too testing here," I said. "All this code does is print the numbers from 1 to 10 on the form when the command button is clicked. Now let's run this program in Step mode by pressing *F8*, and see what happens."

I pressed the *F8* function key and clicked on the command button:

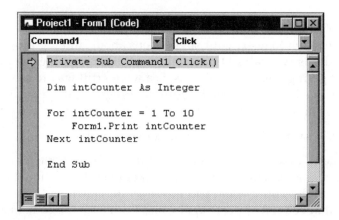

"For those of you who haven't seen it," I said, "this is **Debug** or **Step** mode. In Step mode, the Visual Basic code window opens up as your program is running and Visual Basic displays, in yellow, the line of code that is *about* to be executed."

"That's right," Werner said. "It took me quite a while to get used to that fact – that the line of code in yellow wasn't the one that had just *been* executed."

I pointed out to Werner that it's possible to have the form and the code window displayed side by side in the IDE – and therefore to see how the code being executed in the code window is affecting the form and the controls on it. I continued to press the *F8* function key; doing this executes the code a line at a time. We watched the yellow line in the code window advance through the code, and watching the numbers appear on the form:

Finally, the **For...Next** loop finished execution, and the event procedure ended.

"Now," I said, "let's see the effect of placing an enabled timer control on the form."

I stopped the program and added a timer control to the form. Using the properties window, I set the timer control's **Interval** property to 1000 – which tells Visual Basic to trigger the **Timer** event procedure every 1000 milliseconds (which is equivalent to one second):

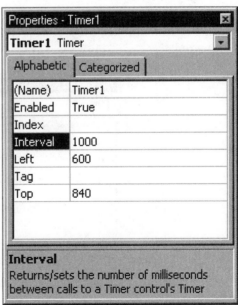

"If we put some code into the `Timer` event procedure of the timer control," I said, "I think we can show everyone just how annoying the `Timer` event can be when running in Step mode. Here's the code:"

```
Private Sub Timer1_Timer()

Dim intCounter As Integer

For intCounter = 1 To 10
    Debug.Print intCounter
Next intCounter

End Sub
```

"This code," I said, "will display the numbers from 1 to 10 in the Immediate window whenever the `Timer` event procedure is triggered – which is every second. The line..."

```
Debug.Print intCounter
```

"...uses the `Print` method of the `Debug` object to print the loop counter's value in the Immediate window. Let's see what effect this code has when we run this program in Step mode."

I pressed the *F8* function key but before I clicked on the command button, the following screen appeared:

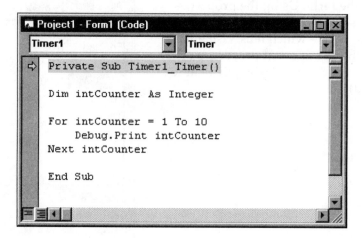

"That's the code in the Timer event procedure being executed," I said, "and that's the behavior Werner is complaining about. In Step mode, any code in the **Timer** event procedure interferes with Visual Basic's ability to step through the code in your program. As you can see, even before I had a chance to click on the command button, the timer control's **Timer** event was triggered and its code window displayed. Let me press *F8* to step through the lines of code one by one in the **Timer** event procedure until we reach the *end* of the procedure..."

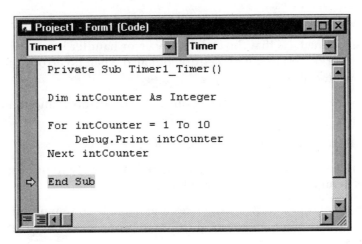

As soon as I reached the last line of the **Timer** event subprocedure, it fired up again.

"As you can see," I said, "the **Timer** event is triggered again one second after its first run ends, and the code in the **Timer** event procedure is displayed *all over again*. In Step mode, with an enabled Timer control on the form whose **Interval** property is set to trigger frequently, and with code in the **Timer** event procedure, there's just no way to see any other code execute."

"So I'm out of luck?" Werner asked. "I can't use Step mode?"

"Well," I said, "I have a very simple solution for you. Why not just disable the timer control by setting its **Enabled** property to **False** in the Properties window prior to running your program in Step mode? I know this isn't the most ideal of solutions, but it *will* work."

"Thanks for your help, Professor Smiley," Werner said.

"Glad I could help, Werner," I said. "And now let's take our next question. Who's calling, please?"

Question 85: My error handler code is being executed regardless of whether an error occurs. Why?

"Hi, my name is Fyodor, and I'm calling from Moscow," a deep, gravelly voice said. "I've been programming in Visual Basic for a little while, and I decided to incorporate error handling in my program. That seemed like a good idea – but the results have left me a bit frustrated."

"Hello, Fyodor," I said, "What's the source of your frustration?"

"My problem," he explained, "is that the code in my error handler is not only being executed when an error occurs in the procedure, but also when no error occurs at all. Do you have any idea what could be happening?"

"Let's see, Fyodor," I replied, "can you check your code for me now, and tell me if you have any **Exit Sub** statements coded in your procedure?"

"No, I don't see an **Exit Sub** statement," he said, "should I?"

"You should have at least one," I said. "The error here is very easy to put right – but before we fix it, I'd like to demonstrate what the problem is to everyone."

I started a new project and placed two text boxes and a single command button on the form. Using the Properties window, I cleared the **Text** properties of both text boxes.

"Let's write a program," I suggested, "that will generate an error – this will let me demonstrate how to set up an error handler. We'll take a number entered into the first text box, and divide it by a number entered into the second textbox – and then display the answer in a message box."

"That's very similar to what's going on in my program," Fyodor said. "A friend of mine told me that whenever you write code that's performing division, you should have an error handler coded into the procedure because of the possibility of division by zero."

"Your friend gave you good advice," I agreed. "Division by zero will generate an error and crash your program. Let me show you."

I quickly keyed the following code into the **Click** event procedure of the command button in my latest project:

```
Private Sub Command1_Click()

Dim dblResult As Double
```

```
dblResult = Val(Text1.Text) / Val(Text2.Text)

MsgBox "The answer is " & dblResult

End Sub
```

"Before I run the program," I said, "let me explain what's going on here. First, we declare a variable to hold the result of the division operation of text box 1 and text box 2 – `dblResult`:"

```
Dim dblResult As Double
```

"The next line of code performs the division operation..."

```
dblResult = Val(Text1.Text) / Val(Text2.Text)
```

"...and assigns the result to our variable. Finally, we display the result in a message box:"

```
MsgBox "The answer is " & dblResult
```

"Of course," I added, "if this program were a commercial program, we would include code to ensure that the user actually enters valid numbers into both text boxes. Watch what happens now if I enter the number 4 into the first text box, and then enter 2 into the second..."

"May I ask a question before you run the program?" Fyodor interjected. " I understand that the `Val` function returns a numeric value from a string. But why are you using it on the `Text` properties of both text boxes – is that really necessary? It's my understanding that Visual Basic will *automatically* convert the `Text` property of the text box to a number prior to performing the division operation."

"You raise a good point there, Fyodor," I said. "Every property in Visual Basic has a defined data type, and the `Text` property of the text box control is defined as a `string` data type."

"How can you determine the data type for a property?" Fyodor asked.

"You can check Visual Basic Help," I said, "or use the Visual Basic Object Browser. Either one will give you the data type for a property. Now, getting back to your point about the `Val` function; in Visual Basic, arithmetic operations (such as the division operation we're using here) must be performed using operands with *numeric* data types. And you were right – Visual Basic will automatically convert the string in the `Text` property of the text box to a number before performing the division."

"So why did you use the `Val` function?" he said, puzzled.

"Out of habit – a good habit, I think." I responded. "Most of the other programming languages I've used would not be kind enough to perform this data conversion for me. In fact, in Visual Basic, data conversion like this is subject to a pretty complex set of rules. Here, Visual Basic is very explicit as to what it will do – convert the strings to numbers. But there are other operations where this explicitness *can't* be guaranteed. I guess the bottom line is that it never hurts to explicitly perform the data conversion yourself – and that way, you can always be confident about the outcome."

"I see what you mean," Fyodor said. "In your show last week we saw the problems that can come when you used the `Text` property of a text box in a `Select Case` range statement."

"Yes," I said, "I had forgotten about that. Let me run the program, and make those entries in the text box now..."

I entered the number 4 in the first text box and 2 in the second:

When I clicked on the command button, we saw this message box:

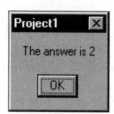

"Nothing surprising there." I said. "4, divided by 2, is 2. Now let's see what happens to the program if I divide 4 by 0..."

In the next run of the program, I entered 0 into the second text box...

...and clicked on the command button. The following screen shot was displayed:

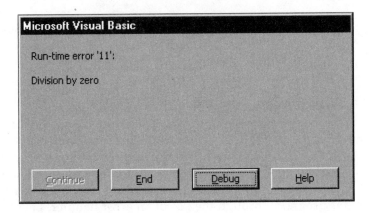

"I'm sure just about everyone has seen this window," I said. "This is the Visual Basic error dialog box, and it is displayed in the Visual Basic IDE whenever an error is generated. In this case, division by zero generates a run-time error of '11'. Just about all we can do here is click on the End button and end the program. Errors like this are what we refer to as *unhandled* errors in Visual Basic. Our program just bombs, and if you are writing a professional Visual Basic program – that is, accepting money for your work, something many of you aspire to do – an unhandled error can be very embarrassing, and makes you and your program look stupid. Fortunately, Visual Basic provides us with a more graceful way to handle errors."

"You mentioned that this is the error dialog box that is displayed in the IDE," Fyodor said. "Is the same dialog box displayed if your program runs as an executable?"

"No," I said. "In that case, a dialog box is displayed, with just a single button – an OK button. Let me show you."

I took a moment to generate an executable of the program, named it **Fyodor.exe**, and then used Windows explorer to run it. As I had done when I ran the program within the Visual Basic IDE, I entered 4 into the first textbox, 0 in the second, and then clicked on the command button:

"As you can see," I said, "the user of your program receives a dialog box informing them of the error. All they can do next is click on the OK button."

"And then what happens?" asked Fyodor.

"The program ungracefully comes to a grinding halt," I said, "which is why unhandled errors in your program are so bad. Any data files opened in your program are automatically closed, with the potential loss of data. The same thing happens to any database files you may have been working with. Plus, all the user remembers about your program is how it blew up in their face in a totally unforgiving way. It's not a good memory for them to have – especially if you would like to do more work for them in the future. Fortunately – as I mentioned earlier – Visual Basic gives us the ability to handle errors more gracefully in our program, through the use of an error handler. Let's code one up now."

I modified the code in the **Click** event procedure to look like this:

```
Private Sub Command1_Click()

Dim dblResult As Double

On Error GoTo Fyodor:

dblResult = Val(Text1.Text) / Val(Text2.Text)

MsgBox "The answer is " & dblResult
```

```
Fyodor:

If Err.Number = 11 Then
    MsgBox "You can't divide by zero..."
    Text2.Text = ""
    Text2.SetFocus
Else
    MsgBox "Error code " & Err.Number & " was generated"
End If
```

```
End Sub
```

"Before I start receiving phone calls and emails from the viewers at home," I said, "I want you to know that I have *intentionally* coded into this procedure what I believe is Fyodor's mistake. Let's leave that as is for a moment while I explain Visual Basic error handlers for those of you who are unfamiliar with them. By the way, I have a chapter devoted to error handling in my book, so you may want to check my book for wider coverage of this issue. But let me give you an overview here. This line of code..."

```
On Error GoTo Fyodor:
```

"...tells Visual Basic that we want to enable an error handler named **Fyodor**."

"I'm flattered that you named the error handler after me," Fyodor said. "May I presume you did that to illustrate to the viewers at home the fact that you can name an error handler in VB just about anything you want?"

"That's right," I said. "By the way – notice the use of the GoTo statement. In Visual Basic, the use of the GoTo statement is discouraged – but ironically, GoTo is the *only* way to enable an error handler. The word following GoTo (Fyodor in this case) is a **line label**, which is a line of code somewhere else in the event procedure bearing that same name and ending with a colon. If you look further down in the event procedure, right after the MsgBox line, you can see the line label itself:"

```
Fyodor:
```

"Everything that follows this line label," I said, "is the code for the error handler, and will automatically be executed if a Visual Basic error occurs while this event procedure is running. The code in the error handler is intended to let your program deal with the error that's been generated and, most importantly, it bypasses the intrinsic treatment of errors – which is to display the Error dialog box and end the program. If you take a look at the code following the line label..."

```
If Err.Number = 11 Then
    MsgBox "You can't divide by zero..."
    Text2.Text = ""
    Text2.SetFocus
```

"... you'll see that we have an `If...Then...Else` statement coded to check for the Error number that we know equates to division by zero."

"The `Number` clause in this code..." Fyodor said, "...that's a *property* isn't it?"

"That's right," I said. "`Number` is a property of the `Err` object. The `Err` object is a Visual Basic system object whose properties are populated – have values entered into them – whenever a Visual Basic error occurs. By checking for a `Number` property of 11, we can determine if division by zero was attempted and, if it was, we display a much friendlier message to the user, clear the second text box, and then set focus to it."

"Why the `Else` statement?" Fyodor asked.

"That's to cover the possibility that some other error *besides* division by zero may occur in the event procedure and trigger the code in the error handler. If that's the case, then – as a minimum – we should display the error to the user in a helpful message box:"

```
Else
    MsgBox "Error code " & Err.Number & " was generated"
End If
```

"The bottom line," I continued, "is that by coding an error handler in this event procedure, we can intercept Visual Basic's nasty default error dialog box, display a user friendly version of our own, stop the program from collapsing gracelessly. The user is notified of their mistake, given a way to fix it, and the program continues to run. Let's see this code in operation."

As I had done before, I entered 4 into the first text box, 0 into the second text box, and clicked on the command button. The following screen shot was displayed:

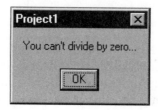

"The invalid division operation generates this user-friendly message," I said. "The user reads it, processes the information, and then clicks on the OK button."

I clicked on the OK button – the second text box was cleared, and focus was set to it.

"Isn't that much better?" I asked. "Now, Fyodor, you said that your error handler seemed to be executing regardless of whether your code encountered an error or not. Let's check that here by dividing 4 by 2. Nothing in that division operation should generate an error, so when I click on the command button we should see a message box with the answer 2 displayed in it."

I entered the usual formula of 4 into the first text box, 2 into the second, and then clicked on the familiar command button:

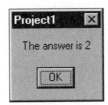

"That's fine," I said. "The answer is 2. Now let's click on the command button."

I did, and we saw the following screen:

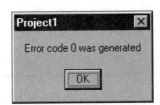

"Well, there's obviously something wrong here," I said. "Nothing we did should have generated an error."

"That's exactly what's happening in my code," Fyodor said, emphatically. "The error handler is being executed *even when no error is generated*. By the way, what exactly is Error code 0?"

"Error code 0," I said, "believe it or not, is really no error at all – it's an `Err` object whose properties have not been set, because no error has occurred."

"So why is this happening?" Fyodor asked.

"It's all because of one tiny error you made," I replied. "If we run this program in Step mode," I said, "by starting the program using the *F8* function key, we'll see that after we enter non-zero values into both text boxes and click on the command button, the division operation is performed normally, followed by the display of the message box."

To confirm this, I followed the steps I'd just described, and the next line of code following the display of the message box was...

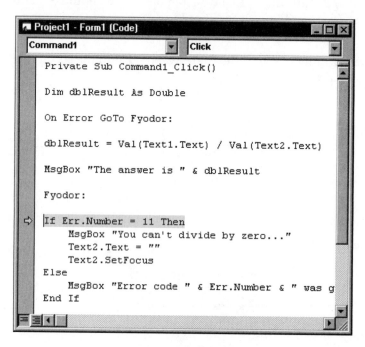

"The first line of the error handler!" I heard Fyodor exclaim. "What happened?"

"Well," I said, "that *was* the next line of code to be executed after the display of the message box."

"I guess," he said, "that somehow I thought that the code in the error handler was special in some way – and would only be executed if an error occurred in the event procedure."

"There's really nothing special about the code in an error handler," I said.

"How do we stop it from executing then, if no error occurs in the procedure?" Fyodor asked.

"We just need to put a barrier between the error handler and the rest of the procedure above it," I said. "We do this by inserting an **Exit Sub** statement *above* the error handler label. Like this..."

I altered the click event procedure of the command button to look like this:

```
Private Sub Command1_Click()

Dim dblResult As Double

On Error GoTo Fyodor:

dblResult = Val(Text1.Text) / Val(Text2.Text)

MsgBox "The answer is " & dblResult

Exit Sub

Fyodor:

If Err.Number = 11 Then
    MsgBox "You can't divide by zero..."
    Text2.Text = ""
    Text2.SetFocus
    Exit Sub
Else
    MsgBox "Error code " & Err.Number & " was generated"
    Exit Sub
End If

End Sub
```

"Yes, I see it now," he said. "That's the 'barrier' you were referring to."

"That's right. Now let's see if this corrects our problem," I said, as I ran the program, and entered the usual digits before clicking on the command button.

As before, a message box was displayed telling us that the answer was 2. However, when I clicked on the OK button of the message box, we weren't presented with the redundant Error Code 0 message box.

"That Exit Sub statement has fixed it," Fyodor said. "I should have thought of that myself. In fact, I just checked Visual Basic Help for On Error – and Microsoft's example has Exit Sub coded just like this – right before the error handler line label."

"It's easy to forget to insert it," I said. "But when you do, it makes sure that the error handler only runs if the conditions that you specify in your GoTo make the code jump to the error handler. Otherwise, the error handler never runs because the End Sub exits the procedure."

"Thanks for your help," Fyodor said. "I just made this change to my program – and it's working fine now."

"My pleasure," I said. "Now, let's move on to our next caller."

Question 86: I set a Watch Expression, but my program never displays the Watch window. What's happening here?

(See also question 84)

"Hi, my name is Florence, I'm from Firenze, Italy," she said. "I also have a question about a Debugging tool – but in my case, not Step mode, but on setting a Watch Expression."

"Ah," I said puckishly, "Florence from Florence! What's your question?"

"In a nutshell," she said, "I'm setting a Watch Expression, and nothing is happening; I was hoping you could tell me how to repair this situation."

"I'll try, Florence," I said. "For those of you at home who are not familiar with Watch Expressions, here's a little background. We can set a Watch Expression in Visual Basic on either a variable or an expression, and have Visual Basic automatically display a Watch window whenever the variable or expression changes, or when the variable or expression reaches some predetermined value. Florence, what type of Watch Expression are you setting?"

"I don't know exactly what you call it," she said, "It's that first one in the **Add Watch** window."

"That explains your statement that 'nothing is happening'," I said. " I call that Watch type the 'Vanilla Watch type'. The problem with it is that if your program never pauses, the Watch window that you're expecting never appears."

"Is that right?" she gasped, surprised. "I was hoping that I would see a dynamically changing Watch window."

"You and many others, Florence," I said. "That would be a nice feature, but unfortunately it's not available in Visual Basic. Before we get too much further into this discussion," I said, "let's illustrate what we're talking about."

I generated a new project and placed a single command button on the form. I typed the following code in command button's `Click` event procedure:

```
Private Sub Command1_Click()

Dim intCounter As Integer
```

390

```
For intCounter = 1 To 20
   Form1.Print intCounter
Next intCounter

End Sub
```

"This code," I said, "is nearly identical to the code I used to answer Werner's question just a few minutes ago. The 'vanilla' Watch type that Florence described only displays a Watch window when the program is paused. Let me show you."

I opened up the code window for the command button's click event procedure, selected the word intCounter in the variable declaration statement, and right-clicked my mouse to display a Visual Basic pop-up menu:

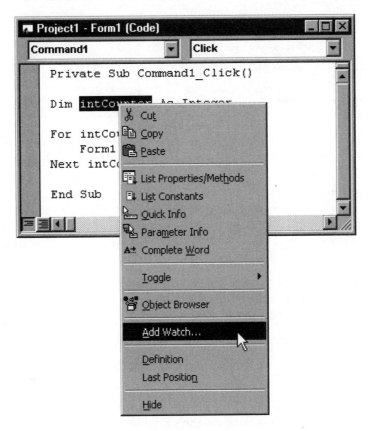

"The quickest way to set a Watch Expression," I said, "is to bring up the code window, select the variable or expression for which you wish to set a Watch, and right-click your mouse. This will bring up a pop-up menu, and at that point you can select **Add Watch**."

I followed my own suggestion, with this result:

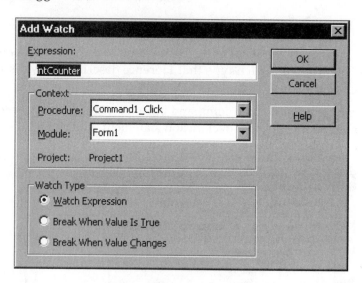

"This is the **Add Watch** window," I said. "Notice that there are three sections to it: **Expression**, **Context**, and **Watch Type**. By pre-selecting the variable in the code window, the **Expression** is already filled in for us. The **Context** section is also filled in, based on where you selected the variable or expression in the code window. The last section, **Watch Type**, is – pretty logically – where you specify the *type* of Watch you want to set. As I mentioned a minute or so ago, the first type, **Watch Expression**, is what I call the vanilla Watch type. If you select this Watch type, you'll *never* see a Watch window appear unless the program is paused."

"That's the Watch type I picked," Florence said. "If the Watch window never appears until the program is paused, that doesn't seem like a very worthwhile choice. As I said before, I really wanted to be able to see the values of my variable change as the program ran..."

"Almost like a `Debug.Print` statement in the Immediate window? " I interjected.

"Exactly," she said. "But as you said, that's not going to happen with this, or any other Watch type."

"Unfortunately, that's right," I said. "Let me continue this illustration for our home viewers by continuing to set the Watch Expression on the variable `intCounter`."

I left the Watch Type set at Watch Expression, and clicked on the OK button. The following screenshot was displayed:

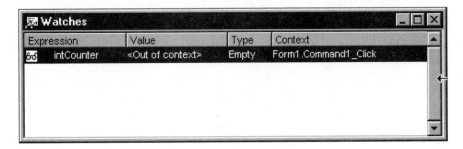

"This is the Watch window that Florence hoped would be visible while her program ran," I said. "Unfortunately, as soon as we run the program, this window disappears..."

I ran the program and, as promised, the numbers from 1 to 20 printed on the form, but no Watch window ever appeared:

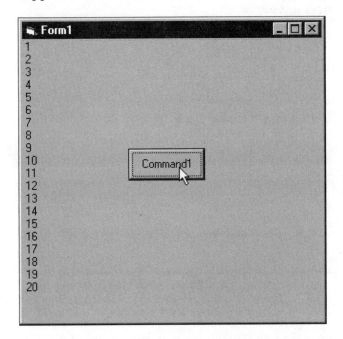

"I really thought I was doing something wrong," Florence said.

"It isn't you, Florence," I said. "With the vanilla Watch Type, if we want to see the Watch window, we'll need to *pause* our program. I'd like to do that now, but the loop we coded here is too fast to allow us to get our pause in. Let me change the End parameter to 20000, and then put a `DoEvents` statement in the body of the loop. Then we should be able to pause the program, and see the Watch window."

"`DoEvents`?" I heard Florence ask.

"`DoEvents` allows us to pause a program that is running a long loop," I said. "If we don't put `DoEvents` within the body of the loop, our program won't stop until the code in the event procedure wraps up."

I changed the `Click` event procedure of the command button to look like this:

```
Private Sub Command1_Click()

Dim intCounter As Integer

For intCounter = 1 To 20000
   Form1.Print intCounter
   DoEvents
Next intCounter

End Sub
```

...and then ran the program. I waited a second or two, and then paused the program by clicking on the Break button on the Visual Basic toolbar. This is what we saw next:

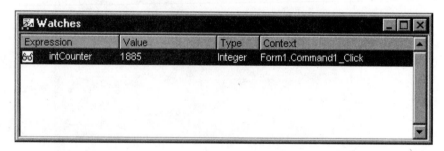

"So that's how that works," Florence said. "Again, I don't think this is very practical, do you?"

"Not really," I said, "the other two Watch type expressions are of much more use to me: Break When Value is True, and Break When Value Changes."

"Can you explain those once again for me?" she asked.

"I'd be glad to, Florence," I answered. "Let's start with **Break When Value Changes**. Whenever the variable or expression that we selected changes, Break When Value Changes tells Visual Basic to pause the program and display the Watch Expression window. Let me show you how this Watch type works by editing the Watch Expression we already have in place. To do that I need to stop the program, and edit the Watch by selecting Debug| Edit Watch from the Visual Basic menu bar:"

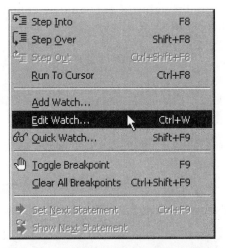

"Doing so brings up the Edit Watch window," I continued, "which is identical to the Add Watch window we looked at earlier. Let's change the Watch Type from the vanilla Watch Expression to Break When Value Changes:"

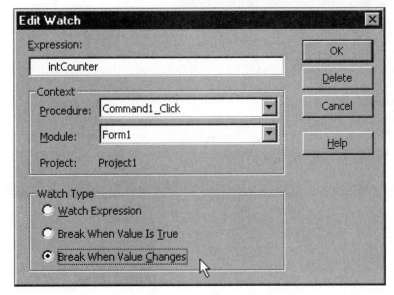

"...and then rerun the program. Now the program will pause as soon as the value of our expression (the variable `intCounter`) changes."

I reran the program and clicked on the command button. As soon as I did, the loop started executing, the value of intCounter changed, and the program automatically paused. The Watches window was then displayed:

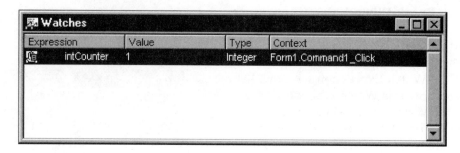

"That's more like it," Florence said. "When might you use this type of Watch type?"

"This type of Watch," I said, "can be very effective if, for some reason, you suspect that a variable you have declared is *never* changing, and you want Visual Basic to alert you immediately if the value of the variable *ever* changes during the running of your program."

"I can see that being valuable," Florence said.

"In most cases, though," I said, "I think the most valuable Watch Type is Break When Value Is True, which tells Visual Basic to pause the program and display the Watch Expression window when the value of a variable or an expression reaches a specified value. For instance, suppose we want to pause our program when the value of intCounter is equal to 123. Once again, let's edit the Watch Expression, this time selecting Break When Value Is True, and specifying an expression that tells Visual Basic when to pause the program..."

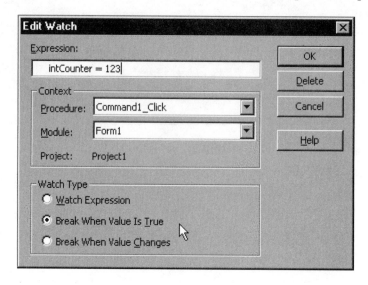

"I think I understand," Florence said. "We can't just place 123 in the Expression text box on its own – we need to specify that we want Visual Basic to pause the program when the value of intCounter is equal to 123?"

"Exactly right, Florence." I said. "Let's see this in action."

I then ran the program and clicked on the command button. Almost immediately the program paused and the Watches window appeared:

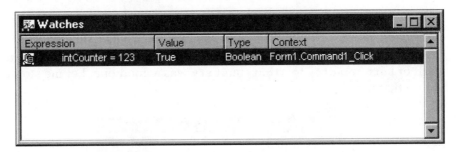

"I'm happy with that," Florence said. "Watches aren't *quite* what I expected or wanted, but I've got a much better idea about how to use the Watch window now. Thanks for your help, Professor Smiley."

"You're welcome, Florence," I said. "I see from the clock here in the studio that it's time for our final commercial break of the day. We'll be back in five."

Question 87: Right Justification alignment doesn't work in a text box – why?

(see also questions 21, 22, 39 & 98)

"Hi, my name is Audrey," she said, "and I'm calling from Brussels. I need some help in using the Alignment property of a text box control. I've been trying to right justify numbers in the text box, but even though I've set the Alignment property to Right Justify, the numbers in the text box are still aligned on the *left* side. I must be missing something somewhere, I guess."

"Good day, Audrey," I said, "I think I know what's wrong. Let me demonstrate this for everyone at home," I said.

I closed the Watch window from the previous questions and started a new project before placing a text box on the form. I cleared the text box's Text property and ran the program.

"The text in a text box control defaults to `Left Alignment`," I said. "That is, if I type I love Visual Basic into a text box, the default will display it like this:"

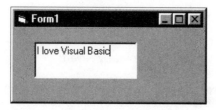

"Audrey," I continued, "your idea about changing the `Alignment` property of the text box from its default of `Left Justify` to `Right Justify` was a good one. Let me stop the program, and do that now..."

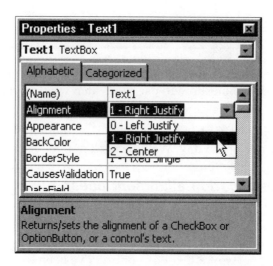

The next time I ran the program and typed I love Visual Basic into the textbox, we saw the following result:

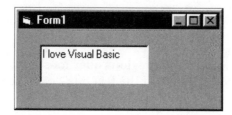

"As you can see," I said, "there is no change in the alignment of the text in the textbox – it's still left justified. Audrey was tripped up by not knowing that you also have to change the `MultiLine` property to `True` – and in case anyone at home is wondering, *this* little quirk of Visual Basic *is* mentioned deep in the recesses of the Visual Basic Help file – and I mean deep. It isn't until we change the `MultiLine` property of the text box from its default `False` value to `True`..."

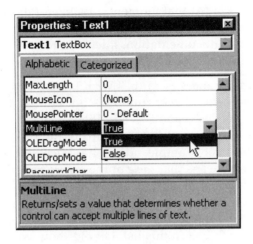

"...that the `Alignment` property finally takes effect. Let's see the difference."

I ran the program again, and when I typed those four little words into the text box this time...

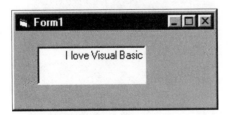

"Now I see the difference," Audrey said. "Thanks for your help. I'll remember – change both the `Alignment` property *and* the `MultiLine` property."

"Glad I could help, Audrey," I said. "And now, here's caller number eight – go ahead, caller."

Question 88: Is there a way to print out every error code?

(see also question 85)

"Thank you. My name is... Frances," she said hesitantly, "and I was born in Sandringham, England. I was reading some postings on a Visual Basic bulletin board when I noticed a posting referring to Error Code 424. At that moment, I realized I didn't have a comprehensive list of Visual Basic Error codes, and furthermore, I didn't know *where* to find such a list in the Visual Basic documentation. I decided to call to ask *you* if there is any one place where all of the Error codes are listed? "

"Well, I hear you loud and clear, Frances," I said. "I wish *I* had a comprehensive list of every Visual Basic error that you would ever run into – but I don't. There *is* a list of what I call 'intrinsic Visual Basic Error codes' – and that's in Visual Basic Help. The problem is that Visual Basic is very flexible in allowing you to use controls and objects that are *not* part of the Visual Basic intrinsic toolbox (for example, additional Microsoft controls, and controls from third-party suppliers). This means that *some* of the errors generated in your program might *not* be generated from within Visual Basic, but from within the additional control or object you're using – and to maintain a comprehensive list of those Error Codes is just impossible. But I *can* help you find the Visual Basic Intrinsic Error Codes – and the one you mentioned earlier is definitely included in this list. Let me show you."

I selected Help from the Visual Basic menu bar, and selected the Index menu:

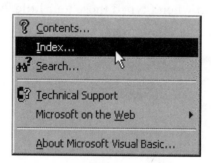

When the Visual Basic Help window appeared, I typed the word 'trappable' into the Search box. This selected the phrase 'trappable errors' in the list box...

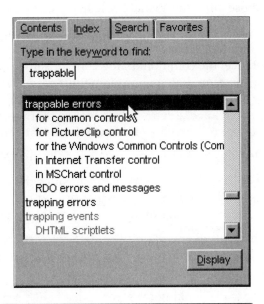

...and then pressed the *Enter* key, displaying a list of Visual Basic Trappable Errors:

Trappable Errors

SEE ALSO   SPECIFICS

Trappable errors can occur while an application is running. Some trappable errors can also occur during development or compile time. You can test and respond to trappable errors using the **On Error** statement and the **Err** object. Unused error numbers in the range 1 – 1000 are reserved for future use by Visual Basic.

Code	Message
3	Return without GoSub
5	Invalid procedure call
6	Overflow
7	Out of memory
9	Subscript out of range
10	This array is fixed or temporarily locked
11	Division by zero

"Are those all of the Visual Basic Error Codes, then?" Frances asked.

"No," I said. "These are the *intrinsic* Visual Basic Error codes. Errors that are generated as the result of your program's interaction with controls not part of the Visual Basic toolbox – for instance, the common dialog control – aren't listed here. For example, suppose you place a common dialog control on your form, set the `CancelError` property to `True`, and use the `ShowColor` method to display the Color dialog box. If the user presses the Cancel button, the `CancelError` setting means that we generate an error – error number 32755. If we go down our displayed list, we'll see that code is not listed here."

I scrolled down the list and, true enough, the 32755 error code was not listed.

"There are many controls available besides the controls supplied in the basic toolbox," Frances said. "I would imagine that they are all capable of generating their own unique errors. Are you saying there is no list of those error codes anywhere?"

"Certainly not in one place," I said. "Some are listed by the individual control in Visual Basic Help. For instance, if you look up the `CancelError` property, Visual Basic Help mentions what Error Code 32755 means."

"So," she said, "looking for error codes is like searching for a needle in a haystack?"

"Maybe not quite *that* bad," I said. "Of course, if you have enabled an error handler, then if and when an error occurs, you can display the `Number` and `Description` properties for the `Err` object and find out the description of the error code that way."

"A friend of mine told me," Frances continued, "that you can use the `Raise` method of the `Err` object to fool Visual Basic into thinking that an error has occurred. If I did that, and raised an error, could I print the number and description for the error in the Immediate window?"

"That's not a bad idea, Frances," I said. "Unfortunately, there's a problem with that technique; you can only use it to raise errors that are part of the Visual Basic intrinsic error codes! For instance, if we use the `Raise` method to raise the 32755 error we've just discussed, Visual Basic displays a dialog box with the error code – but only includes a generic description essentially says that it doesn't really know what the error message is. Watch, and I'll use the Immediate window to raise Error 32755..."

I brought up the Immediate window, and typed in the following statement:

```
Err.Raise 32755
```

When I hit the *Enter* key, we saw the following screen was displayed:

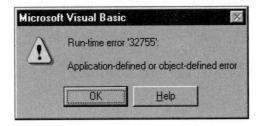

"The purpose of the `Err` object's `Raise` method is to convince Visual Basic that an error has been generated," I said. "Unfortunately, Visual Basic doesn't have a description for this error – other than to say that it's Application-defined or object-defined. The description for this error code is buried deep in the recesses of the common dialog control. And we will only see the actual description when this error occurs as a result of the user interacting with the common dialog control itself."

To emphasize my point, I created a new program and added a common dialog control to the form, along with a command button. I changed the common dialog control's `CancelError` property to `True` and keyed the following code into the command button's `Click` event:

```
Private Sub Command1_Click()

CommonDialog1.ShowColor

End Sub
```

I ran the program and clicked on the command button; when the Color dialog box was displayed and I clicked on the Cancel button, the following result was generated:

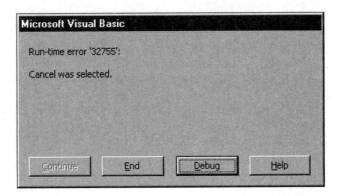

"This is the *real* error message, Frances," I said. "Do you notice the difference between this error and the error we craftily raised a minute ago? The explicit Cancel was selected error description is emanating from the common dialog control itself – and it's this description that Visual Basic *didn't* have for us when we used the **Raise** method of the **Err** object."

"I understand now," Frances said, "having a list of all the error codes would be great – but at least I know where to find the list of trappable intrinsic Error codes in Visual Basic Help. Thank you."

"No problem," I said. "Now then, who is next up?"

Question 89: Can I tell that the # (pound sign) in the Close statement is optional by reading Visual Basic Help?

(see also question 82)

"Good morning. My name is Carl, and I'm from Basel , Switzerland. I've read your book with interest, and I believe I have a pretty simple question. From what I've observed so far in Visual Basic, there are quite a few instances where procedures and functions have optional arguments. Specifically, I was thinking of the **Close** statement, where there is an optional file number argument; also, you said in your book that this statement could also be coded with or without a pound sign. My question is, how would I know that the pound sign (#) is optional by looking in Visual Basic Help?"

"Hi, Carl," I said, "Hope you liked my book. I can give you a quick answer to this one – whenever you see an argument for a statement, function, or procedure listed in Visual Basic Help, if the argument has square brackets – [ ] – around it, this indicates that the argument is optional."

"So *that's* what they mean," Carl said. "I had seen them before, but never put two and two together."

"It's not obvious, by any means," I said. "Let take the example you cited, the **Close** statement in Visual Basic Help…"

It took me just a moment or two to open Visual Basic Help and to locate the `Close` statement:

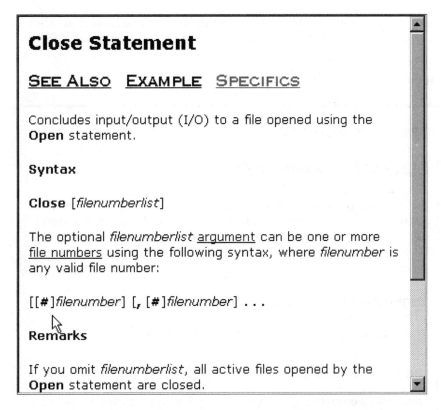

> # Close Statement
>
> <u>SEE ALSO</u> <u>EXAMPLE</u> SPECIFICS
>
> Concludes input/output (I/O) to a file opened using the **Open** statement.
>
> **Syntax**
>
> **Close** [*filenumberlist*]
>
> The optional *filenumberlist* <u>argument</u> can be one or more <u>file numbers</u> using the following syntax, where *filenumber* is any valid file number:
>
> [[*#*]*filenumber*] [**,** [*#*]*filenumber*] . . .
>
> **Remarks**
>
> If you omit *filenumberlist*, all active files opened by the **Open** statement are closed.

"Notice, Carl," I said, "that both the `filenumberlist` argument and the pound sign are enclosed in brackets. The brackets tell us that the argument is optional. Notice too that the comma is *also* enclosed in brackets, meaning that you could close more than one file in a single `Close` statement by passing more `filenumber` arguments separated by commas. Like this…"

```
Close #1, #2
```

"What about those three dots?" Carl queried. "I think you called them 'ellipses' in your book."

"Good question," I replied. "When you see ellipses in Visual Basic Help it means that the arguments can be repeated indefinitely, for a large number of different files. So we could code a `Close` statement like this:"

```
Close #1, #2, #3, #4, #5
```

"Just to make sure that everyone understands," I said, "let's take a look at another Visual Basic statement – one that we've talked about quite a bit in our broadcasts – the MsgBox function."

I located the MsgBox function in Visual Basic help:

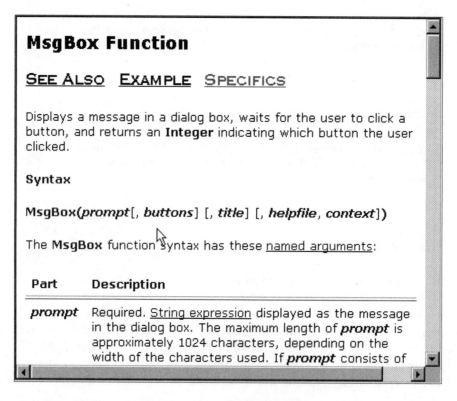

"This function is pretty challenging syntax to read," I said. "The MsgBox function accepts five arguments, but only one – the prompt – is mandatory. We can see this, because it's the only one *not* enclosed in brackets. The last four arguments: buttons, title, helpfile, and context – are optional; as you can see, all are enclosed by brackets."

"Yes I see that," Carl said, "but can you tell me why both the helpfile and context arguments are contained within the *same* pair of brackets?"

"That's because if you specify the `helpfile` argument you must also specify the `context` argument. These two arguments are dependent upon one another – VB needs to know the context so that it can supply the right help file."

"I understand," Carl said. "So there is some method to the madness of these cryptic characters in Help. I'll need to read these more carefully in the future. Thank you."

"Thanks for calling, Carl," I said, "and now it's time for our final caller of the day."

Question 90: Problem with the option button's Value property

"Hello there, my name is Roddy, and I'm calling from London – near the zoo, in fact," he said. "I'm having a problem with the option button control, and it's got me climbing up the wall."

"Oh dear," I said, soothingly, "What is it that's driving you bananas, Roddy?"

"I have a program where I display two option buttons in a frame control," he said, "and I'm evaluating the `Value` property of each option button to see which choice the user has made. Unfortunately, my code just doesn't seem to be working, and I have no clue about what's wrong."

"I think I can guess what your problem might be, Roddy," I said. "But first, as usual, let me try to duplicate what is happening to your program. I'll create a program that has a frame containing two option buttons, plus a command button. Like this..."

I started a new Visual Basic project, and placed a frame on the form, followed by two option button controls within the frame control and, finally, a command button.

"Let's use these two option buttons to ask the user what their favorite programming language is," I said.

I then changed the frame's `Caption` property to What Is Your Favorite Programming Language?, the names of the option button controls to `optVB` and `optC` respectively, and their captions to Visual Basic and C++.

"For good measure," I said, "let's also set the `Value` property of the Visual Basic option button to `True` to establish it as the default – after all, what else would it be?"

My form now looked like this:

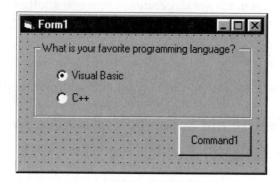

"What I'd like to do," I continued, "is to display a message box saying That's my favorite too! if the user selects the Visual Basic option button, and one that says What can I do to change your mind? if the user selects the C++ button. Roddy, not to put you on the spot, but can I ask you how you would code that?"

"Hmm," mused Roddy momentarily, "I would check the **Value** property of the option buttons with an **If...Then...Else** statement," Roddy said. "If the **Value** property of **optVB** is equal to 1, then we know that the user has selected Visual Basic as their favorite language. Otherwise, they've selected C++ as their favorite language."

"I thought that might be your problem, Roddy," I said. "You should really be checking for a **Value** property equal to **True** or **False**, *not* 0 or 1."

"But isn't the **Value** property of an option button an **Integer** data type?" Roddy asked.

"No," I replied, "The *check box* **Value** property is an **Integer**. The *option button* **Value** property is a *Boolean* data type. Checking for a **Value** property equal to an **Integer** can lead to incorrect results – as you've been experiencing at home. Let me demonstrate."

I keyed the following code into the command button's **Click** event procedure:

```
Private Sub Command1_Click()

If optVB.Value = 1 Then
   MsgBox "VB? That's my favorite too!"
Else
   MsgBox "C++? What can I do to change your mind?"
End If

End Sub
```

"Now watch what happens," I said, "if I run the program and click on the Visual Basic option button."

I ran the program and selected Visual Basic as my favorite programming language (actually, it already was selected, because I had set its `Value` property to `True`), then clicked on the command button, with the following result:

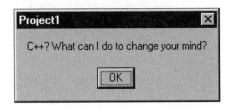

"Oops," I heard Roddy say. "That's not right – and it's similar to what's been happening in my program. You selected Visual Basic, but the program thinks that you selected the C++ button. And this is the result of comparing the `Value` property to 1 instead of `True` or `False`?"

"Exactly," I said. "You wouldn't believe how often I see this in my university classes. I suspect students code it like this because the `value` property of a check box is an `integer` data type with possible values of 0, 1 and 2, and students presume that the `value` property of an option button works in the same way. But remember, for properties defined as a `Boolean` data type, you really need to compare them to `True` or `False`."

"I think you're right," Roddy said. "I guess I just didn't think about it before coding it."

"It's easy enough to fix, though," I said. "All we need to do is change the comparison of the `Value` property from `1` to `True`..."

```
Private Sub Command1_Click()

If optVB.Value = True Then
    MsgBox "VB? That's my favorite too!"
Else
    MsgBox "C++? What can I do to change your mind?"
End If

End Sub
```

"...and run the program."

Learn to Program with Visual Basic Examples

I ran the program, selected Visual Basic as my favorite programming language (what else?), and clicked on the command button:

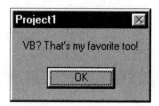

"That's better," I heard Roddy say.

"And just to make sure our code is really working," I said, "let's select the C++ option and click on the command button..."

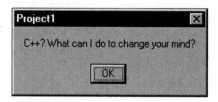

"That's one mistake I won't be repeating, I can assure you," Roddy said. "Thanks."

"I'm glad I could help," I said. "By the way, Roddy, I don't want to overplay the teacher role here, but the statement you just made is very profound. In my experience, I find we learn much more from making the mistakes than we would if we just lucked into the correct code the first time. It's best to get these little problems out of the way early in your Visual Basic career. And better to make them at home rather than during the first week at your new programming job. Thanks for calling!"

"Well, we're all out of time for today's show," I said. "I want to thank everyone for tuning in, especially those of you who called in with questions. Remember, we'll be here next week – same time, same channel. See you then."

"Phew," said Linda, "that was a tough set of questions this week, John."

I nodded in agreement. "Yes, I feel pretty drained – somehow, the theoretical questions take it out of me more."

That said, I was really feeling like I was getting the hang of this. The fact that we'd gone international was quite insane, but that wasn't what made me enjoy it. It was the interaction with so many different people, being able to help with their problems, that I liked about the show. I wondered if I'd be able to give as much time as I'd like to both this project and my normal teaching. As exciting as this was, I'd never want to let my students down. But as long as I could continue to help everybody a little, I was OK with that.

I made my way home, on what had turned out to be quite a warm spring day. I'd still got the rest of the afternoon ahead of me and today, I decided, I'd relax and spend time with my kids. People say I work too hard, but they don't realize that the work I do is so enjoyable to me that it doesn't *feel* like work all the time. That's the best kind of job.

Examples

Week 10

During the week leading up to our tenth show, I realized that I would have felt a little down if they hadn't extended the series. This coming Saturday's show would have been the last one, and I would have seriously missed the regular routine. I'd come to thoroughly enjoy the show; meeting new people (albeit by telephone) and helping them with their VB questions. I could see myself doing this for a while.

During Tim's customary Monday morning call, he maintained that the show was going well, but something about his tone of voice made me think that something was up. He didn't let on what it was, though, so I assumed it must be something unrelated to my show.

On Friday afternoon he called me again and asked me if I would have some time early next week to see him.

"Is anything wrong?" I asked.

He assured me that nothing was wrong; if it had been, he said, he wouldn't wait until next week to tell me. That reassured me a bit, and we agreed to meet on Monday afternoon at his office – and he insisted on leaving it at that.

On edge, I arrived at the studio good fifteen minutes earlier than usual on Saturday morning.

"Good morning," said Linda. "Up with the lark this morning, huh?" Her voice was bright, but she looked a little strained, I thought.

"I wanted to have a chance to speak with you," I said. "Is anything wrong? You seem a bit down."

"No, I'm not feeling real great," she said. "I've had a head cold all week, and the medicine I've been taking is making me feel sluggish. But I'm sure I'll get through this show OK. How are you?"

"I'm fine," I said, "although I did get a puzzling phone call from Tim yesterday. He wants to see me on Monday. Do you have any idea why? You usually have the scoop before anyone else."

"No, I haven't heard anything," she said. "If anything is brewing, he's done a great job of keeping it a secret. You know, there's not much you can do about it. Whatever it is, you'll find out about it on Monday – until then, just have a great show!"

Linda was right. As I ran through my pre-show checklist, I made a decision to savor this, our tenth show of the series, as if it were to be our last.

"We have quite a mix of callers today," Linda said. "Some more of the U.S. callers have managed to get through, including an extremely interesting guy from Tennessee."

I relaxed for a few minutes before the start of the show, passing the time by thinking about how elated I'd been when the station had actually agreed to screen the show. We'd come a long way in a very short space of time.

I looked up in time to see Linda give me a wave, and a hand signal for 30 seconds. I readied myself and waited for her to cue me in.

"Good morning, everyone," I said, "welcome to Professor Smiley's Visual Basic Programming Workshop. Each week at this same time, I'll be answering your questions about Visual Basic. Of course, in order for us to have a show, we need members of our viewing audience to phone in with Visual Basic questions. That's *you guys*."

Linda signaled me that we had our first caller of the day.

"Let's go to the phone lines. Caller number one, you're on the air," I said.

Question 91: How can I replace characters in a string variable?

"Hi, my name is Jeanne, and I'm calling from Domremy-la-Pucelle, France," said a young, yet confident, voice. "I've written a Visual Basic program where I read from a data file on my hard disk drive and then write that information to a Microsoft Access database. My problem is this: one of the fields in the data file is a date field, but it's not properly formatted for Access – it contains dashes between the month, day and year. I've been looking for an easy way to replace the dashes with a slash. I say 'easy way', because I discovered that I could probably do this by using the `Mid` statement (I found that out from your book, actually!) But my attempts with that technique so far have been a little frustrating. There must be an easier way – is there?"

"Hi, Jeanne," I said, "and welcome to our show. The answer is 'yes', there is an easier way, provided you're using Visual Basic 5 and up. If you're using Visual Basic 4 and below, then the `Mid` statement is the only way to go. But in Visual Basic 5 and 6, you can use the `Replace` function."

"That's a new one on me," she said. "How does it work?"

"Before I show you the `Replace` function," I said, "I better recap how to do this using the `Mid` statement, particularly for those viewers using earlier versions of Visual Basic. Anyway, it's always good to see alternative ways of solving a problem."

I started a new Visual Basic project and added a command button to the form. I then wrote the following code in the command button's `click` event procedure:

```
Private Sub Command1_Click()

Dim strOld As String
Dim intWheresTheDash As Integer

strOld = "06-18-83"

Do While True
    intWherestheDash = InStr(strOld, "-")
    If intWherestheDash = 0 Then Exit Do
    Mid(strOld, intWherestheDash, 1) = "/"
Loop

MsgBox strOld

End Sub
```

"This code," I said, "starts out by declaring two variables that we'll use to find the dashes in a string, and replaces them with slashes. The first, `strOld`, is a variable where we'll store the string we want to work with – in this case '`06-18-83`'. The second, `intWheresTheDash`, is an `Integer` variable that we'll use to store the location of the dash in the string. This statement..."

```
strOld = "06-18-83"
```

"...is just an assignment of the string we wish to search through. At this point, we set up a `Do...Loop` structure in which we'll search through the string, looking for dashes, and replace each one we find with a slash."

"What's that `Do While True` syntax?" Jeanne asked. "I don't believe I've ever seen that before."

"`Do While True`," I said, "is just a little programming trick that sets up an endless loop structure. `True` is a Visual Basic keyword that is *always* true, and never changes. As a result, setting up a `Do...Loop` like this results in a loop that has no end built into it – we have to provide a method that tells VB when we want to break out of the loop. We use this kind of loop because we want to keep replacing until we run out of characters to replace, and we don't know beforehand how long the string is or how many of the characters there are that we want to replace. Let's take a look at the first statement in the body of the loop:"

```
intWherestheDash = InStr(strOld, "-")
```

"This line of code uses the `InStr` function to determine where the dash character is found within `strOld`. For those of you not familiar with the `InStr` function, it returns a value equal to the location of the *second* argument (in this case the dash) within the first argument, `strOld`. If the return value is 0, then we know that there are no dashes in the string – either because there never *were* any, or because the code we wrote to replace them has completed its work."

"I guess that's why the next line of code is so important," Jeanne said:

```
If intWherestheDash = 0 Then Exit Do
```

"You exit the loop whenever the return value of `InStr` is 0 – meaning there are no longer any dashes," she added.

"You hit the nail on the head there, Jeanne," I said. "When `InStr` returns 0, we exit the loop through the use of the `Exit Do` statement. Let's take a look at the next line of code now:"

```
Mid(strOld, intWherestheDash, 1) = "/"
```

"This is the code," I said, "that does the actual replacement, using the `Mid` *statement* (not to be confused with the `Mid` *function*). The `Mid` *function* returns a string from another string, but the `Mid` *statement* is used to change a character or characters within a string at a specified location. The `Mid` statement accepts three arguments – *stringvar*, *start*, and *length*. The first argument, *stringvar*, specifies the string in which the change is to be made. The second argument, *start*, specifies the starting location of the change, and the final argument, *length*, specifies how many characters to be change. We follow that up with an equals sign, followed by the character that will be the replacement character in the string – in this case, the slash."

I waited a moment to see if Jeanne had any questions.

"This process is repeated within the body of the loop," I said, "until no more instances of the dash character are found – at which time we exit the loop and display the fruits of our labor in a message box."

"I see what's going on," Jeanne said. "Maybe this isn't so bad after all – I thought it would be much more difficult."

"I think you'll find the `Replace` function a lot easier to work with, Jeanne," I said. "But let's run this code and see how it works."

I ran the program, clicked on the command button, and the following screenshot was displayed:

"That worked beautifully," I heard Jeanne say. "And you say the `Replace` function is easier to use."

"I think so," I said. "But remember, it's only available in Visual Basic 5 or 6. The `Replace` function takes the code we wrote ourselves just a minute ago, and encapsulates it in a single function. The `Replace` function, simply speaking, is used to replace a character or characters within a string. We can use it to search for a dash and replace it with a slash character. Let's add another command button to the form, and place this code in the `Click` event procedure:"

```
Private Sub Command2_Click()

Dim strOld As String
Dim strNew As String

strOld = "06-18-83"
strNew = Replace(strOld, "-", "/")

MsgBox strNew

End Sub
```

"As before," I said, "we declare some variables for use in the procedure. `strOld` is used to store the string containing the dashes. Unlike the `Mid` statement, the `Replace` function doesn't alter the original string – its return value is the *altered* string, so we've declared a string variable, `strNew`, to store the return value. This line of code is the wonder:"

```
strNew = Replace(strOld, "-", "/")
```

"The `Replace` function," I said, "requires three arguments: *expression, find* and *replacewith*. There are some optional arguments you may want to check out on your own in Visual Basic Help, but these three provide us with all that we need to do what we need here. *Expression* is just the name of our string variable containing the string we want to search through, *find* is the argument specifying the character to find in the expression, and *replacewith* is the character to replace the found character with."

"This is simpler," Jeanne said. "No loop to code, no checking on your own to see if there are any more characters to replace, like the line in the first set of code that exited the loop…"

"That's right," I said, "if the version of Visual Basic you are using supports this function, this is the way to go."

I then ran the program, and we saw that the same result was achieved:

"This worked beautifully too," Jeanne said. "But with a lot less code. Thank you so much for your help."

"My pleasure, Jeanne," I said, "and thanks for calling. And now, who's next, please?"

Question 92: I tried to load up a Visual Basic project someone else gave me, and my common dialog control has been replaced with a picture box

"Hello, my name is Henry, and I'm from Greenwich, England," caller number two said. "I'm having the strangest problem. My wife, Anne, who's away in the country visiting some friends, sent me a Visual Basic program she's currently working on. I started Visual Basic, selected the project from the diskette drive, and as it was loading up, I received some kind of Visual Basic warning message. I clicked on the OK button, and the form finally appeared. I didn't notice anything at first, but when I clicked on a command button - which in turn triggered the ShowColor method of the common dialog control– an error message appeared. It turns out that the common dialog control is missing – and that it has been turned into a picture box control. When I called my wife about it, she got a little mad, and said I ruined her project, but I'm sure I didn't do anything wrong. It's the strangest thing – have you ever heard of anything like this?"

"Thanks for calling, Henry," I said. "The answer to your question is yes, I have seen this phenomenon before – many times in fact. What you described – where a control referenced in and saved in a project on one PC, can't be loaded by Visual Basic on another PC – is pretty common – especially with controls that are not one of the intrinsic controls found in the toolbox."

"By *intrinsic* controls," Henry said, "you mean the ones always found in the toolbox when Visual Basic first starts up – such as the command button, option button, and check box?"

"That's right, Henry," I said. "Controls that you add to the toolbox via the Project | Components tab of the Visual Basic menu bar (the common dialog control is a good example) sometimes confuse Visual Basic when it tries to load them up on a different machine. And when Visual Basic becomes confused and finds itself unable to load the control, it displays a warning message and replaces the control with a picture box – something Visual Basic doesn't actually bother to tell you."

"I see," Henry said. "That seems to be exactly what happened to me. But let me ask you this question. Why would Visual Basic be confused? Isn't the common dialog control the same on my PC as it is on my wife's?"

"Not necessarily," I answered. "The common dialog control, unlike the intrinsic Visual Basic controls, is stored on the PC as a separate file, called an ActiveX control, with an .ocx file extension. All ActiveX controls, when they're installed on the PC, also make an entry in the Windows Registry to 'register' the fact with Windows that they are there. This entry, called a CLSID – pronounced 'class I.D.' – contains, among other things, the version number of the ActiveX control, important licensing information, and also its location on the PC. Each ActiveX control loaded on a PC has a different CLSID, although the same control loaded on different PCs should have the same CLSID in the Windows Registry – provided they are the same version."

I waited a moment.

"When your wife saved the Visual Basic project on her PC," I continued, "the CLSIDs of any ActiveX controls included in her project were written to the project file."

"And that should mean," Henry added, "that my PC should be able to load up the common dialog control just by looking at the CLSID in the project file?"

"Theoretically, yes," I answered. "If you have Visual Basic loaded on your machine – and you obviously do – then your Windows Registry will also contain an entry for the common dialog control – with a unique CLSID."

"Then why the confusion on Visual Basic's part?" Henry interjected. "Why couldn't it load up the common dialog control?"

"Because the CLSID on your PC for the common dialog control," I said, "didn't match the CLSID in the project file."

"I thought the common dialog control on her PC and the common dialog on mine would be identical," Henry said.

"The CLSID," I said, "will be identical only if the *versions* of the common dialog controls are identical. In your case, they must be different."

"What would make them different?" Henry asked. "Aren't *all* the common dialog controls identical?"

"No," I said. "Since the introduction of the common dialog control, there have been many versions. Different versions of Visual Basic may come with different versions of the common dialog. Even downloading a Service Pack from Microsoft could place a newer version of the common dialog control on your PCs."

"So this is what is causing Visual Basic's confusion, then," Henry said. "Is there anything we can do about it?"

"Fortunately, Henry, there's an easy fix," I said, "but before I show you that, I'd like to reproduce this problem for our viewers at home. I can create a simple program containing a common dialog control and a command button which, when clicked, shows the Color dialog box."

I started a new project, and added a command button and a common dialog control on the form (I first needed to select Project-Components from the Visual Basic menu bar, and add it to my toolbox):

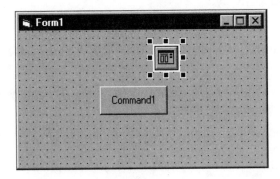

I quickly typed this code into my command button's `Click` event procedure:

```
Private Sub Command1_Click()

CommonDialog1.ShowColor

End Sub
```

"Quite simply," I said, "when we click on the command button, we'll display the Color dialog box."

I ran the program and clicked on the command button, and – hey presto – the Color dialog box was displayed:

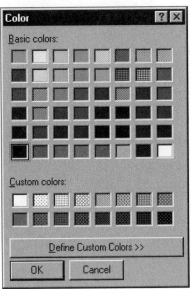

421

"OK, Henry," I said, "now let's experiment a bit. I know of a way I can alter the CLSID in the project file slightly so that it *doesn't* match any CLSID found in my Windows Registry. We'll save this project and form in our \vbfiles\Practice directory on my hard drive as Henry.vbp and Henry.frm respectively."

I then saved both the project and the form in my practice directory and exited Visual Basic.

"So altering the CLSID will simulate the problem I'm having with my wife's project?" Henry asked.

"That's right," I said. "By the way, do not attempt this at home! Altering your project file is something you should never do on your own."

At this point, I killed the video feed from my PC to my home viewers – all they could see was my face. I didn't want them to be able to see how I altered the project file – it's not something you should really do.

After I had altered the CLSID for the common dialog control in the project file, I started Visual Basic, selected Project I Open from the Visual Basic Projects window, and told Visual Basic to open up the project I had just saved – Henry.vbp. This generated the following error message:

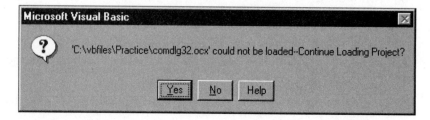

"*That's* the error message I received," Henry said. "At that point, I just clicked on the Yes button."

I did so myself, with this result:

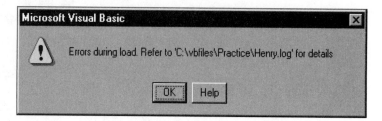

"Did you hit the OK button at this point, Henry? " I asked.

"Yes I did," he said. "But I entirely forgot to view the log file."

"It wouldn't have helped much, really," I said. "Let me show you."

I then used Notepad to view the log file...

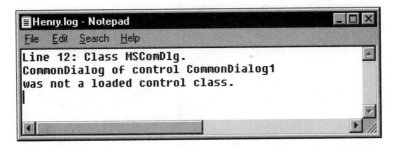

"You're right," Henry said, "that isn't of much help."

I then clicked on the OK button, and the following screen shot was displayed:

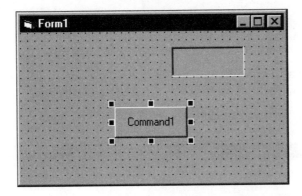

"I don't know whether you and the viewers at home noticed, " I said, "but when the form was loaded we lost our common dialog control – which had been in the upper right hand corner of the form. In its place we now have a picture box control – although interestingly enough, Visual Basic has retained the common dialog control's name for the picture box control. We can see that by looking at the Properties window:"

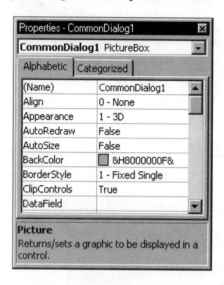

"But that's not all," I said. "Now that our project no longer has a common dialog control, if we run the program and click on the command button, look at what happens..."

When I did this, we were presented with a compile error:

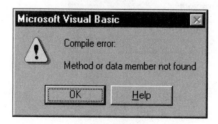

"That's similar to the problem I'm now having with my wife's program," said Henry. "With the common dialog control gone, the `ShowColor` method crashes. Is there anything we can do about this?"

"Up until a few weeks ago," I said, "my solution to this problem had always been to delete the picture box control and manually add the common dialog control to the form."

"I would imagine," Henry said, "that this technique isn't bad if you have just one control in the project that has been loaded as a picture box. But suppose you have *many* controls that have been converted to picture boxes?"

"You raise a good point, Henry," I agreed. "And there's another thing – there are other types of controls susceptible to this problem besides the common dialog control. Some of those controls would be a real pain if you had to replace them on the form, adjust their properties, and even re-write code in their event procedures. It sure would be nice if you could just flip a switch and have Visual Basic fix this for you. As I mentioned, up until a few weeks ago I didn't think this was possible. But an associate of mine showed me a technique which takes care of this problem quickly and painlessly."

"I can't wait to hear this," Henry said. "What is it? "

"In short," I said, "we need to remove our form from the project, and then add it back. Doing that will cause Visual Basic to add the common dialog control back to the form."

"Sounds great," Henry said. "But how do we do that?"

"First," I said, "we need to select Project | Remove Henry.frm from the Visual Basic menu bar. That will remove the form from the project:"

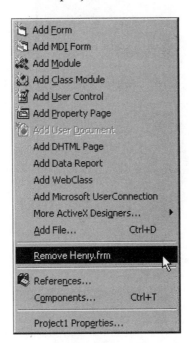

"That actually sounds pretty drastic, " I heard Henry say.

"Removing the form from the project doesn't erase the form from your hard drive," I said. "It's not permanent – removing the form from the project just removes the *entry* for the form from the project file – and as an added benefit, Visual Basic also removes the CLSIDs for any ActiveX controls on the form. Then, when we add the form back to the project, Visual Basic recreates the entry in the project file for the ActiveX controls using the CLSIDs from your PC."

"That means that the common dialog control will show up on the form?" Henry asked.

"That's right," I said. "Watch this."

I then selected Project | Add Form from the Visual Basic menu bar...

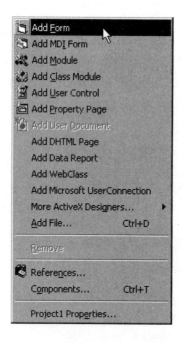

"When this window appears," I said, "we need to find the form we just removed by selecting the Existing tab..."

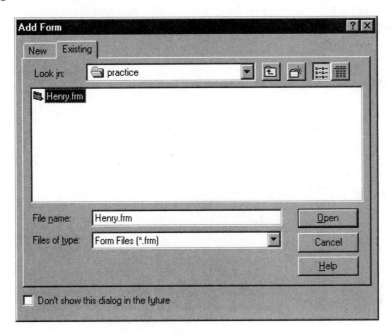

"...and clicking on the Open button."

I did that, and the form was then re-added to the project. The common dialog control was back:

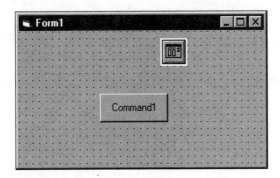

"There it is!" Henry exclaimed. "That's great. So, just by removing the form, and then adding it back, we cured the problem."

"That's right," I said, "this will work fine, provided the control that couldn't be loaded the first time around is registered on your PC. But be careful – it's possible that the version of the control that has just been placed on your form may not be the same version as the code in your project was written for, and so some of its functionality might be missing. By the way, there's one more thing we need to do before we can run this program. In fact, if we run it now, you'll see what I mean..."

I ran the program, and immediately a more frightening-looking error message was displayed:

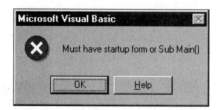

"What happened?" Henry asked.

"We removed the one and only form in our project," I said, "and it was the startup object for the project. Every project needs to have either a form, or a procedure called **Main** in a standard module, designated as the startup object. That's the thing that VB looks at first, and starts up in."

"Is this a big problem?" Henry asked.

"Not at all," I said. "If we just click on the OK button, Visual Basic will present us with the **Projects Properties** window where we can specify **Form1** as the startup object..."

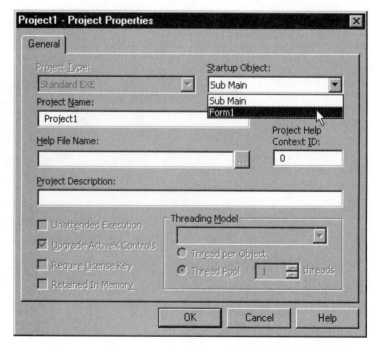

"... and then click on the OK button."

When I had done that, I was prompted to save both the project and form. I reran the program and clicked on the OK button. This time around, the Color dialog box was displayed.

"Thanks, Professor Smiley," Henry said. "I just used your technique, and it worked flawlessly in placing the common dialog control back on the form. I'm running my wife's program, and I must say, I'm very impressed with it. Thanks for your help."

"One more thing, Henry, before you go," I said. "If you save the project and send it back to her, she may very well have the same problem as you had with hers. Make sure you warn her about it, and tell her not to lose her head."

"Oh," Henry said, "I didn't think about that. Thanks again for your help."

"I'm glad I could help," I said. "And now let's take another question."

Question 93: How can I turn off case-sensitivity?

"Hello – my name is Charles, and I'm from London," caller number three said. "I've been reading your *Learn to Program with Visual Basic* book, and I have a question about the use of the function UCase."

"Welcome to the show, Charles," I said, "and thanks for calling. What's your question?"

"I'm an engineer by trade, but I'm helping a local school by writing a Visual Basic program that asks the children questions – about twenty-five questions in all," he said. "The children are young enough that they don't yet have much of a sense for upper and lower case. I'm comparing their answers to a set of correct ones, and because the children have been typing in answers in a mixture of upper and lower case, I had been pulling my hair out trying to anticipate all of the combinations. Fortunately, I picked up a copy of your book, and saw that you discuss taking responses, uppercasing them, and then comparing the values to the answers in all uppercase. I did that, and that's working fine. My question is this: is there some kind of global option I can turn on that tells Visual Basic that I don't care about case sensitivity at all? That would save me some coding."

"Yes, Charles," I said, "there is a way to do that. However, before I show you how to do that, let me show the viewers at home what we're talking about here..."

I opened up a new project and placed a text box and a command button on the form. Using the Properties window, I cleared the **Text** property of the text box, and then typed in the following code in the **Click** event procedure of the command button:

```
Private Sub Command1_Click()

If Text1.Text = "Visual Basic" Then
    MsgBox "I love it too"
Else
    MsgBox "Sorry to hear that"
End If

End Sub
```

"This code is probably similar to the code you are using in your program," I said. "The user makes an entry in a text box, and then we compare what they have entered to the correct answer. In this case, we take the contents of the text box, and compare it to the phrase 'Visual Basic'. If the user enters that phrase *precisely* in the text box – matching upper and lower case also – we display a message box saying 'I love it too'."

I ran the program, entered 'Visual Basic' into the text box...

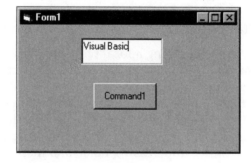

...and then clicked on the command button. The following message box was displayed:

"The program behaved the way we expected," I said. "Of course, what are the chances the user will enter 'Visual Basic' into the text box just the way we are expecting it? You probably know that there are 1,024 different ways to type the phrase 'Visual Basic'. Suppose the user picks one of the other choices – like this..."

Once again, I ran the program, this time entering Visual Basic into the text box in this format:

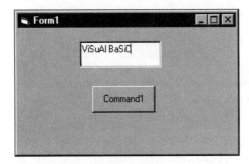

When I clicked on the command button, we were presented with this message box:

"That's my basic dilemma," Charles said. "The children type the 'correct' answer into the text box in many different ways."

"One way to handle this, Charles," I said, "*is* to use the **UCase** function that you mentioned a minute ago, and which I'll just demonstrate to everyone at home. If we compare the uppercase value of the user's text box entry with the upper case **string** literal of the correct answer, we can handle all 1,024 possibilities. Like this:"

```
Private Sub Command1_Click()

If UCase(Text1.Text) = "VISUAL BASIC" Then
    MsgBox "I love it too"
Else
    MsgBox "Sorry to hear that"
End If


End Sub
```

"The new line of code is taking the string in the text box, turning it to all uppercase, then comparing it to an all-uppercase version of our answer, 'VISUAL BASIC'," I said. I re-ran the program, once again entered a mixed case combination of 'Visual Basic' into the text box, and clicked on the command button. This time, the correct message box was displayed:

"That works," Charles said. "And that's basically what I've coded – my problem is that I have twenty-five questions I'm asking – with twenty-five correct answers. This increases the code I need to write."

"There's another method, Charles," I said, "in which you can place code in the **KeyPress** event procedure of the text box and convert whatever text the user enters into the uppercase equivalent. We can do that by using a nifty little trick here. The lowercase alphabetic characters fall within the ASCII code range of 97 through 122. If you then subtract 32 from the lowercase ASCII value, guess what – you have the uppercase equivalent."

"So in effect..." Charles said, "whatever the user enters, you make it uppercase automatically. That's ingenious."

"Exactly," I said. "So you no longer need to handle the comparison in your code – everything in the text box will be uppercase by the time you evaluate it. Here's the code for the **KeyPress** event procedure of the text box."

I entered this code into the **KeyPress** event procedure of the text box:

```
Private Sub Text1_KeyPress(KeyAscii As Integer)

If KeyAscii >= 97 And KeyAscii <= 122 Then
   KeyAscii = KeyAscii - 32
End If


End Sub
```

"Each keystroke that the user makes into the text box," I said, "has a corresponding ASCII code equivalent which is passed to this event procedure. All we need to do is use an **If...Then** statement to determine if the character the user just pressed is a lower case letter. If it is, we subtract 32 from it, and *that's* the ASCII character that then appears in the text box."

"Wouldn't you need a loop to do this for each character?" Charles asked.

"No, no – the **KeyPress** event is triggered separately for every single press of a key, remember – the checking routine will be triggered again each time a new character is entered," I said.

"Oh, yes, of course – I wasn't thinking straight," he said.

"This code is impressive," I said, "but you'll see in a minute, Charles, that the easiest way to accomplish a case-insensitive text comparison is to do what you thought was possible in the first place – and that's to turn on a global option. Before I do that, however, let's change the code in the **Click** event procedure of the command button to look like this…"

```
Private Sub Command1_Click()

If Text1.Text = "VISUAL BASIC" Then
    MsgBox "I love it too"
Else
    MsgBox "Sorry to hear that"
End If

End Sub
```

"That simplifies things quite a bit," I said, "since all of the code in the text box will now be uppercase."

I then entered 'visual basic' in mixed case into the text box – or, I should say, I *tried* to enter it. As I had promised Charles, as soon as I entered a lower case letter, the code in the **KeyPress** event procedure of the text box immediately converted it into uppercase:

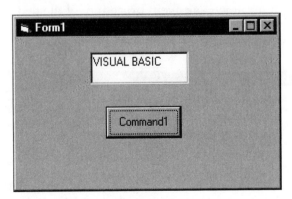

"That's great," I heard Charles say.

I clicked on the command button, and we saw this message box:

"The technique of automatically upper casing the characters that the user enters into a text box," I said, "although dazzling from a programming point of view, sometimes makes the user feel uncomfortable. Your users will undoubtedly do a 'double take' when they see everything they type appearing in the text box in uppercase. For that reason, this technique is not always my first choice."

"What about that global option?" Charles asked.

"Yes, let's look at that now," I said. "If case sensitivity is not crucial in your program, all you need to do is place the statement `Option Compare Text` in the General Declarations section of your form or standard module. If that statement is found there, all the code text comparisons are performed on a case insensitive basis."

"I knew there had to be an easy way," Charles said happily. "If we need to explicitly code `Option Compare Text`, what is the default?"

"The default is `Option Compare Binary`," I said, "It basically means that when string comparisons are made, capital letters are treated as different from lowercase ones. Being the default, it obviously doesn't need to be coded anywhere. Let's add `Option Compare Text` to the General Declarations section of the form now."

I first removed the code from the `KeyPress` event procedure of the text box – we didn't need it any more – and then added the `Option Compare Text` line to the General Declarations section of the form:

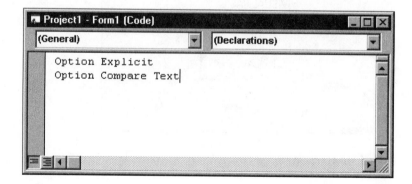

I then ran the program, and entered 'visual basic' into the text box– entirely in lower case...

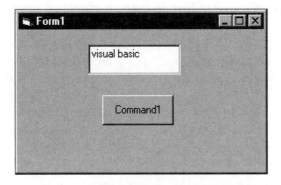

...and clicked on the command button. The following message box was displayed:

"Because of **Option Compare Text**," I said, "'Visual Basic' in upper case letters is considered to be the same as 'Visual Basic' in lowercase letters. Do you think this will help you, Charles?"

"Yes, I think that's great," Charles said. "Professor Smiley, thanks for your help."

"I'm glad I could help, Charles," I said, as I glanced at the studio clock. "And now it looks like it's time to cut to a break. We'll be right back – don't touch that remote! Hah – I always wanted to say that. We'll see you in a sec."

During the break, I went to get a can of soda from the machine in the hall, but the machine ate my change. Well, I thought, you can't have everything. I have my own TV show, for goodness' sake.

When we resumed, Linda put our next caller on the line.

Question 94: I'm trying to keep track of the number of times that a command button has been clicked – but it keeps getting zeroed out. Why?

"Hi, my name is Ada," said a frenetic female voice, "and I'm also from London. What's *really* freaky is that the last bloke was my boyfriend, Charles. How weird is *that*? At any rate, I've always been fascinated with numbers, and I wanted to write some code that would show me the number of times that the user of my program had pressed a command button. I whacked some code into the `Click` event of a button to count the number of times that someone clicked it, and then it was supposed to display it on the command button's caption, but far from being a complete wow, like I thought it would be, it's gone wrong. It's stuck on 1, you know what I mean? What's up with it?"

"Hi Ada, welcome to the show, and wow, slow down a little!" I said.

"Sorry, mate, I'm just well-freaked out by my boyfriend calling just before I did. He's supposed to be *here*."

"Well, anyway, I think I know what the problem may be. Please e-mail me your code, and I'll take a look at it."

"Yeah, OK," she said. "It should be there in a minute or two."

Actually, through the magic of telecommunications, Ada's e-mail was there in *seconds*. I displayed Ada's code for the home viewers:

```
Private Sub Command1_Click()

Dim intCounter As Integer

intCounter = intCounter + 1

If intCounter = 1 Then
  Command1.Caption = "This button has been clicked " & intCounter & " time"
Else
  Command1.Caption = "This button has been clicked " & intCounter & " times"
End If

End Sub
```

"I like this code, Ada," I said. "Each time the user clicks on the command button, you add 1 to your counter variable – that's fine. And it's very clever of you to use an `If...Then...Else` statement to vary the caption you display..."

"That's all very well, but it's not working," Ada said.

"Let's code this up," I said, "and see what is happening with your program."

I started a new Visual Basic project and placed a single command button on the form. I copied and pasted Ada's code from her e-mail into the `Click` event procedure of the command button, and then ran the program. After clicking on the command button once, we saw the caption reading correctly:

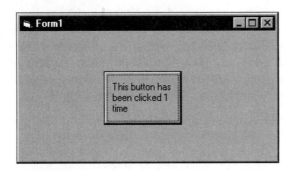

"Yeah, see, that's what it's supposed to do, but after that, it goes wrong," Ada said. "Hit it again; I bet nothing happens."

I clicked on the command button again, and indeed, the button's caption still read 'This button has been clicked 1 time.'

"I won't keep you in suspense any longer, Ada," I said. "I know what the problem is. In your code, the variable you use to count the number of times that the command button has been clicked is declared locally using a `Dim` statement..."

```
Dim intCounter As Integer
```

"Yeah, and?" Ada said, seeming a little irritated.

"In short, Ada," I said, "a variable declared in an event procedure using the `Dim` statement is born, initialized, and dies each time the event procedure is run."

"Oh," she said, a little humbler this time.

"What happens," I continued, "is that each time the event procedure is triggered, the code to declare the variable is executed. You then increment the value of the variable by 1, display it, but then the end of the procedure is encountered – and the variable dies, along with its value. Then the process is repeated all over again when the user clicks on the command button again."

"Whoops. I reckon I must have thought the variable and its value would hang around for the duration of the program," Ada said.

"Many beginners believe that," I said. "But variables declared within procedures using the Dim statement 'die' when the End Sub statement of the procedure is executed."

"Can you help me fix it?" she asked. "Or is what I'm trying to do...I mean, is it impossible, or something?"

"Not at all," I said, "in fact, there are two ways to do it. You can change the declaration statement of the local variable from Dim to Static, or you can declare the variable in the General Declarations Section of a form or standard module. Let's look at the Static variable technique first. Unlike a variable declared using the Dim statement, a Static variable declared using the Static keyword lives for the duration of the program. Let's modify our code to use a Static variable..."

I changed the Click event procedure of the command button to look like this...

```
Private Sub Command1_Click()

Static intCounter As Integer

intCounter = intCounter + 1

If intCounter = 1 Then
    Command1.Caption = "This button has been clicked " & intCounter & " time"
Else
    Command1.Caption = "This button has been clicked " & intCounter & " times"
End If

End Sub
```

"Now," I said, "let's see what difference this can make to our program."

I then ran the program, and clicked on the command button:

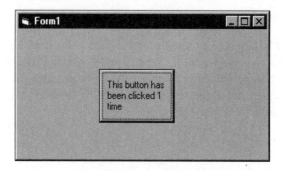

"So far, that's the same as before," I said. "Let's click on the command button again…"

I did, with this effect:

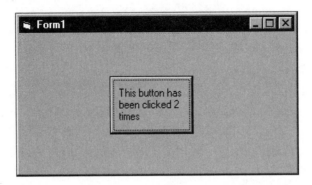

"That's an improvement," I said. "The counter has incremented past 1."

I continued to click on the command button, and the caption continued to increment.

"Wicked, man," Ada said. "That's excellent. I thought I'd totally mucked it up."

"Well, you weren't too far off," I said. "Now let me show you that second method I mentioned. This time, instead of using a `static` variable to declare our counter variable as we did here, let's declare the counter variable either in the General Declarations section of the form or standard module. You may have seen me discuss form-level or global variables in an earlier show. A variable declared in the General Declarations section of a form is known as a *form-level* variable, and can be seen anywhere within the form. A variable declared in the General Declarations section of a standard module is known as a *global* variable, and the variable can be seen anywhere within your application."

I opened up the code window, and keyed the following code into the General Declarations section of the form:

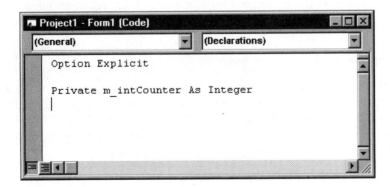

"Because we are declaring this variable in the General Declarations section of the *form*," I said, "this is a form-level, or module-level variable. By convention, variables declared in the General Declarations Section of the form should begin with the prefix 'm_'. Variables declared here have form-level scope – that means they can be seen by code anywhere within the form and, most importantly, since they are declared in the General Declarations section of the form, they exist for as long as the form does."

"Wow, do they really?" Ada asked.

"Yes, they do. Now," I said, "we just need to change the code in the click event procedure of the command button to refer to this form level variable instead of the static variable we declared earlier..."

I modified the code in the click event procedure of the command button to look like this:

```
Private Sub Command1_Click()

m_intCounter = m_intCounter + 1


If m_intCounter = 1 Then
   Command1.Caption = "This button has been clicked " & m_intCounter & "
time"
Else
   Command1.Caption = "This button has been clicked " & m_intCounter & "
times"
End If

End Sub
```

"We need to remove the declaration of the static variable," I said, "and change the code to refer to m_intCounter instead of intCounter."

I ran the program, and clicked on the command button once – then again and again. The program worked properly, incrementing the caption of the command button each time the button was clicked.

"So which one's the best then? static, form-level, or global variable?"

"Microsoft's rule of thumb," I said, "is to declare the variable as close as possible to where you need it. In this instance, since the counter variable is only used by the code in the click event procedure of the command button, it makes sense to declare the variable there as a static variable. By the way, declaring a variable in the General Declarations section of a standard module requires that we add a standard module to our project."

"What's the point of a standard module anyway?" Ada asked.

"Well, quite simply," I explained, "there are some times when you want certain code to live in a central location for use in more than one form or program. Let's say you wrote a whole bunch of functions or procedures that performed string manipulation. You could create a standard module to hold all these, then wherever you were in code, you could just call these functions, and you wouldn't have to write the same code twice. It also makes it easier to incorporate code you've used in one project into another project you write, as you can just import the standard module."

"Massive," Ada said. "Hang on a second, Charles has just arrived."

"Hi, Charles," I said, and heard a muffled 'hi'.

[The moments that followed were all a little unclear, but on watching a tape of the show, I could just make out what they were saying in between the dialogue between Ada and myself:]

Ada: "Where have you been, you maniac? You were supposed to be here an hour ago."

Charles: "I just had this one question I had to ask Mr. Smiley. How's my little fairy-lady?"

Ada: "If you ever call me that again I'll slap ya."

"Uh, Ada, we're going to have to move on. Thanks to you both for calling."

"Thanks for your help, Professor Smiley."

"I'm glad I could help," I said, trying not to laugh. "And now on to our next caller."

Question 95: I'm trying to set the focus on a text box in the Form_Load event procedure – but the program bombs

(see also questions 21, 22, 39, 87 & 98)

"Hi, my name is Helen," caller number five said. "And I'm from Tuscumbia, Alabama. I'm writing a Visual Basic program for the visually impaired, and I'm having a little problem with it."

"Let's see what we can do, Helen," I said, "What's your problem?"

"I have several text box controls on my form that can receive focus," she said. "When my program starts up, I want to set the focus to a particular text box – although it won't always be the same one. I use the Windows Registry to store the user's preference for which one needs the focus. Anyway, I tried to use the `SetFocus` method of the text box control, but when I do, my program bombs. Can you help me?"

"I think I know what the problem may be, Helen," I said. "Where are you coding the `SetFocus` method?"

"I'm coding it in the Load event procedure of the form," she said. "Is that a problem?"

"It can be," I said. "If you attempt to set focus to a control on the form and the form has not yet become visible, that means that the *control* isn't visible yet either. That can generate a VB error, since only a visible control can receive the focus. Let me see if I can duplicate your problem here."

I started a new Visual Basic project, and placed two text box controls on the form. I brought up the Properties window for the text boxes, and cleared the `Text` properties of each. I then wrote the following code into the Load event procedure of the form:

```
Private Sub Form_Load()

Text2.SetFocus

End Sub
```

"Nothing fancy here," I said. "Let's try to set focus to the second text box when the form loads."

I then ran the program and the following screen was displayed immediately:

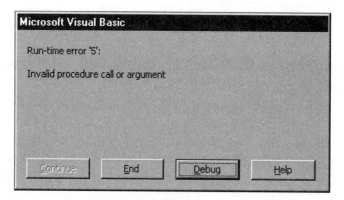

"That's the error message I'm receiving," Helen said. "I really had no idea what was wrong with this. I couldn't see anything wrong with my code – but you're saying that my problem is that I'm trying to set focus to a control that isn't visible?"

"That's right," I said. "When Visual Basic runs your program, the `Activate` event of the form designated as the startup form is triggered first, followed by the `Load` event procedure for that form. When the `Load` event procedure begins, the form, and all of the controls on it exist, but they don't yet have a visual interface. This means you can refer to their properties in code in the form's `Load` event, but you can't execute any code that requires the form or control to be visible. Setting the focus to a control on the form violates that rule – since the control must be visible in order to receive the focus. As a result, this error message is generated."

"I guess the question that begs to be asked," Helen said, "is *when does the form become visible?*"

"Good question," I said. "The form and all of the controls on it become visible after all of the code in the form's `Load` event procedure has been executed."

"So there's no way I can set focus to one of my text box controls using the Load event procedure?" Helen asked.

"Yes, there is a way," I replied, "because there's a way to force the form to become visible prior to the `Load` event procedure ending. The way to do that is to code the `Show` method of the form in the `Load` event procedure. And if you code this prior to executing the `SetFocus` method of the text box, the program won't bomb. Look at this…"

I modified the code in the `Load` event procedure of the form as follows:

```
Private Sub Form_Load()

Form1.Show
Text2.SetFocus

End Sub
```

"As you can see," I said, "all we're doing here is using the form's `Show` method to make the form, and all of the controls on it visible, prior to setting focus to the second text box."

I then ran the program, and focus immediately moved to the second text box:

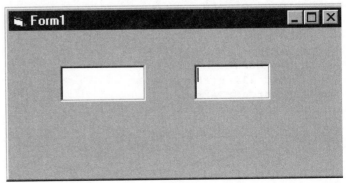

"That's great," Helen said. "This solves my problem. Thanks very much for your help."

"Helen," I said, "I realize this doesn't apply in your situation since you want to set focus to a different control each time your program starts up, but I wanted to remind everyone that we could also set focus to the second text box just by setting its `TabIndex` property to 0. The control with the lowest `TabIndex` property automatically receives the focus when your program starts up."

"Thanks again, Professor Smiley," she said.

"I'm glad I was able to help," I said. "And now it's time for caller number...six."

Question 96: Is there a way to determine if a file exists?

(see also question 82)

"Hi, my name is Jesse," caller number six said. "Like your previous caller, I'm also from Alabama – Danville to be exact. I read your book, and was fascinated by the chapter where you show how to read data from a disk file into your Visual Basic program. One thing I'd like to be able to do is to determine ahead of time if the file I want to open exists on my hard drive. If the file doesn't exist, I want to display a message to the user. Does VB have a way to determine if a file exists?"

"Hi there, Jesse," I said. "Yes, there is a way to determine if a file exists. First, let's write a little program that opens and reads a file. Then I'll show you how you can check to see that the file exists before you try to open it. Last week, by the way, I was asked a question about file processing, so I just happen to have a file already prepared on my hard drive to open and read. It contains three lines of text."

I created a brand new project, and added my trusty single command button to the form before placing the following code in the `Click` event procedure of the command button:

```
Private Sub Command1_Click()

Dim strData As String

Open "C:\MYFILE.TXT" For Input As #1

Do While Not EOF(1)
    Line Input #1, strData
    Form1.Print strData
Loop
```

```
Close #1

End Sub
```

"This code," I said, "is probably identical to the code I used last week. It will look for the file `'MYFILE.TXT'` on the root directory of my hard drive, open it for input, read each line or record in the file, and then use the `Print` method of the form to display each line on the form."

I then ran the program and clicked on the command button:

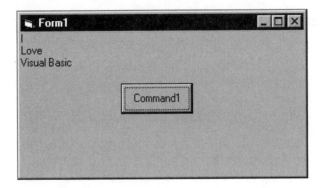

"That was pretty straightforward," I said. "Now let me show you and the home viewers what happens if the file can't be found."

I used Windows Explorer to rename the file `'MYFILE.TXT'` to `'MYFILE.OLD'`.

"I've renamed the file `MYFILE.TXT` to `MYFILE.OLD`," I said, "which means if I now click on the command button, the code in the `Click` event procedure will try to locate and open that file and..."

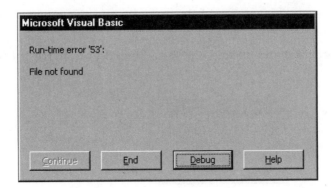

"...a nasty error is generated telling us that the file cannot be found," I said. "By the way, since you mentioned my book, Jesse, you probably noticed that I discussed this particular error and how to deal with it via error handling."

"Yes, I noticed that," Jesse said, "but I'd prefer to check first to see if the file exists."

"I can understand that," I said. "As you suspected, there is a way to check for the existence of a file, and that's to use the Dir function. The Dir function requires just one single argument, the full path of the file you are looking for. If the file is found, Dir returns a value equal to the full path name – if the file does *not* exist, it returns a zero length string. Here, take a look at this code."

I changed the code in the Click event procedure of the command button to look like this:

```
Private Sub Command1_Click()

Dim strData As String

If Dir("C:\MYFILE.TXT") = "" Then
    MsgBox "Oops...the input file is missing"
    Exit Sub
End If

Open "C:\MYFILE.TXT" For Input As #1

Do While Not EOF(1)
    Line Input #1, strData
    Form1.Print strData
Loop

Close #1

End Sub
```

"Let's see the difference between this version of the program and the one in which the 'File not found' error was generated," I suggested.

This time when I ran the program and clicked on the command button, we got the following message box:

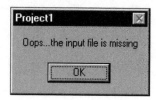

"That's great," Jesse said. "This time the program didn't bomb, and a much more user-friendly error message was generated."

"You're right, this is better than that nasty error message," I said. "The key to this code is the `Dir` function. Let's take a look at that line of code:"

```
If Dir("C:\MYFILE.TXT") = "" Then
```

"As I mentioned a moment ago," I said, "the `Dir` function is used to determine if a file exists. You supply the function with a single argument consisting of the full path name of the file you are looking for. If that path name does't exist, a zero-length string is returned. By the way, there is an optional argument that can be supplied – for instance, if you need to look for hidden files."

"A zero-length string," Jesse said, "can be determined by using an `If` statement to compare the return value with an empty set of quotation marks? Is that correct?"

"That's right," I said, "a zero-length string, sometimes called an **empty** string, is represented by two quotation marks with nothing in between. Remember, *nothing at all* between them – not even a space."

I waited a moment.

"Let's rename the file **MYFILE.OLD** back to **MYFILE.TXT**," I said, "and make sure the code works when the file is found."

I then used Windows Explorer to rename **MYFILE.OLD** to **MYFILE.TXT** and reran the program. When I clicked on the command button, the following screen shot was displayed:

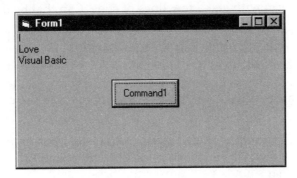

"Works like a charm," Jesse said. "That's great – this is exactly what I need. Thank you."

"I'm glad I could help," I said. "I see that it's now time to take our final commercial break of the day. We'll be back after these messages."

Linda approached me and told me she had a potential 'situation' on her hands.

"It's our tenth caller," she said. "He called from a car phone, and he's been circling the studio in a pink Cadillac for the last hour. I don't know whether you noticed, but he's also knocked on the door a couple of times. Apparently, he's on his way from Atlantic City back to his home town of Memphis, and he'd like to present his question live and in person – he claims to be an entertainer, and told me he'd love to sing a song on the show."

"Have you called security?" I asked.

"Yes I did," she said, "and they verified his identity and checked with the casino lounge he said he played and sang for last night. He is who he says he is – I guess they just have suspicious minds – and he sounds kind of familiar...but I can't quite place the voice. Stay tuned for more. This could get interesting."

"Don't tell me if it's someone famous or something, I really don't want to know," I said. "Don't ask me why, but I have a funny feeling about this."

But anyway, it was time to introduce the next caller.

Question 97: Is there a way to set the same property on all of the controls of my form at once?

"Hi," said our seventh caller. "My name is Sessue, and I'm calling from Honshu, Japan. I was browsing through the VB Help files the other night, and I found something called the `Controls` Collection. From what I read, it appears that I should be able to use the `Controls` Collection to update a property – such as the `FontSize` property or the `BackColor` property – for every control on a form with just a few lines of code. Can that be done?"

"Hi Sessue," I said, "welcome to the show. Yes, you have found a very powerful feature of Visual Basic. A Collection in Visual Basic is very much like an array, containing items or *elements*. The `Controls` Collection is one of several System collections that Visual Basic maintains on its own. Each time you place a control on the form – either at design time or run time via the `Load` statement – Visual Basic creates an entry in the `Controls` Collection for it."

"So you mean that if I have three command buttons and a text box on my form, I can treat them as a group using the `Controls` Collection, which will contain them all without my having to do anything? That sounds very powerful," Sessue said.

"It can be extremely useful," I said. "I must warn you though, to fully tap into the features of the controls collection, we need to use a loop structure called 'For Each', and that syntax requires that we declare something in our code called an **Object Variable**, which is then used to reference each item in the collection. That syntax can be a bit strange at first. Let me show you."

I opened a new project and put a list box, two text box controls, a label, a check box, an option button and a command button on the form. "I want to have quite a few controls on the form," I said, "to fully demonstrate the power of the Controls Collection."

In the Click event procedure of the command button, I wrote this code:

```
Private Sub Command1_Click()

Dim MyControl As Control

For Each MyControl In Form1.Controls
    List1.AddItem MyControl.Name
Next MyControl

End Sub
```

"This code is straight out of Visual Basic Help," I said. "It will read each item in the Controls Collection, and add an entry for it in a list box."

"So every control on the form will appear in the list box when we click on the command button?" Sessue asked.

"That's right," I said.

"Here you see the declaration of the **Object Variable**..." I said.

```
Dim MyControl As Control
```

"...specifically, a variable called MyControl of type 'Control'. An object variable is used to refer to an object, or as is the case in this code, to a control. It is possible, in Visual Basic, to create many types of object variables. For instance, we can declare a variable as a text box type or a label type as well."

"You were right," Sessue said. "This syntax is a little strange."

"An object variable," I said, "is really not much different than the types of variables you may be used to. For instance, an `Integer` variable really points to a location in memory that contains a value – a number that we want to store. An object variable points to a location in memory, but instead of a value being stored there, we'll store the name of an object, such as a control. From that, you can access its properties, methods, and so on. I'm oversimplifying here – object-oriented programming is a fairly deep subject, and I can't get into a lot of detail in the time allowed. But does that help?"

"That's a little better," he said. "The `For Each` syntax is new to me also. You mentioned that it's a loop structure. Is it used specifically for collections?"

"`For Each`," I said, "is like a normal `For...Next` loop, used to repeat a group of statements, but instead of going around a specified number of times, you go through each element in an array or a collection, one after the other. You basically are saying 'for each item, no matter what it is, in this `Whatever` collection, I want you to...' whatever."

"What does `MyControl.Name` refer to within the `For Each` loop?" Sessue asked:

```
For Each MyControl In Form1.Controls
    List1.AddItem MyControl.Name
Next MyControl
```

"`MyControl`," I said, "is the name of our object variable, and the `For Each` loop uses it to point to a particular control in the `Controls` Collection. Notice how we can use standard object notation to append the `Name` property of the control to the object variable `MyControl`..."

"Object notation?"

"Also known as *dot notation*," I said. "What I mean is that we can say `MyControl.Name` instead of, say, `Command1.Name`, and whichever control is being worked on at the time will know that the object variable is referring to it."

I sensed some confusion.

"Often in programming," I said, "a picture is worth a thousand words. Let's run the program and see what happens."

I ran the program and clicked on the command button, and the form ended up displaying like this:

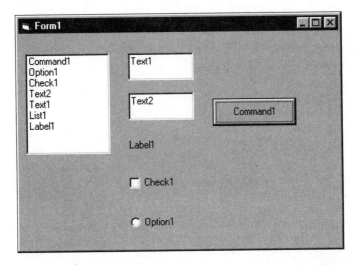

"Notice," I said, "that the list box contains a entry for each control on our form. You'll notice that they don't appear in the order they were placed on the form, but the order *is* related to the **TabIndex** property."

"That technique seems useful," Sessue said. "I would think that if you can add each control to the list box using its **Name** property, it isn't much of a jump to do something else – like change their font size or style."

"That's right," I said. "Let me add a second command button to the form which, when clicked, will allow us to change the **Font** name of every control on the form to 'Comic Sans MS', the Font Bold attribute to bold, and the **Font** Size to 11."

"Now that will be impressive," Sessue said, "and that's exactly the kind of thing that I want to be able to do."

I added a second command button to the form, and typed this code into its **Click** event procedure:

```
Private Sub Command2_Click()

Dim MyControl As Control

For Each MyControl In Form1.Controls
    MyControl.Font = "Comic Sans MS"
    MyControl.Font.Bold = True
    MyControl.FontSize = 11
```

```
Next MyControl

End Sub
```

"This code is very similar to the code in the `Click` event procedure of `Command1`," I said. "Once again, we declare an object variable..."

```
Dim MyControl As Control
```

"...which will be used within the `For...Each` loop to point to each control in the `Controls` Collection. Within the `For Each` loop..."

```
For Each MyControl In Form1.Controls
    MyControl.Font = "Comic San MS"
    MyControl.Font.Bold = True
    MyControl.FontSize = 11
Next MyControl
```

"...we have a little more code this time, but the principle is the same. We can use the object variable, plus a dot (.) plus a property name, to refer to the individual properties of the controls in the `Controls` collection. In this case, we are modifying three properties: `Font`, `Font.Bold`, and `FontSize`."

I waited a moment to see if Sessue had any questions.

"Let's run the program," I said. "Once again, I'll click on the first command button, to load up the items in the list box. Then I'll click on the second command button. We should see the font style and size of every control on the form change."

I ran the program, clicking first on `Command1` and then on `Command2`. Here's what we saw:

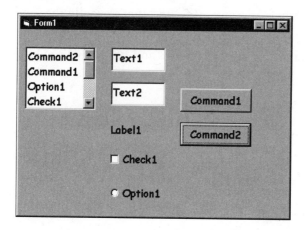

"That's great," Sessue said. "The font style and size has been changed for *every* control on the form. This will really come in very handy."

"There's something I need to warn you about," I said. "What happens if you refer to a control property within the **For Each** loop structure that the control being pointed to by the object variable **MyControl** does not support?"

"Can you say that again?" Sessue said. "Doesn't support?"

"For instance," I said, "within the body of the **For Each** loop, we really assumed that *every* control on the form had a **FontSize** property. Suppose one of the controls didn't?"

"Oh, I see what you're saying now." Sessue said. "Suppose there had been a Timer control on the form. That doesn't contain a **FontSize** property, does it?"

"Exactly," I agreed, "no, it doesn't. Or suppose we decide to change the **ForeColor** property for each control on the form. Does every control have a **ForeColor** property?"

"I'm not sure," Sessue said.

"We can find out very quickly," I said, "by modifying our code to change the **ForeColor** property of each control in the **Controls** Collection as well. Let's modify the code in the **Click** event procedure of **Command2** to assign the Visual Basic intrinsic constant **vbRed** to the object variable's **MyControl.ForeColor** property and see what happens."

I stopped the program, and modified the code in the **Click** event procedure of **Command2** to look like this:

```
Private Sub Command2_Click()

Dim MyControl As Control

For Each MyControl In Form1.Controls
    MyControl.Font = "Comic San MS"
    MyControl.Font.Bold = True
    MyControl.FontSize = 11
    MyControl.ForeColor = vbRed
Next MyControl

End Sub
```

Once again I ran the program, clicked on the first command button to load the list box, and then clicked on the second command button. This time...

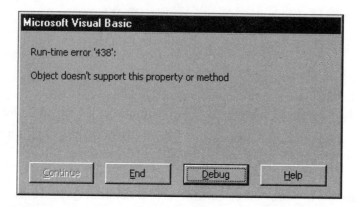

"The program bombed," Sessue said. "I guess that means that one of the controls doesn't have a **ForeColor** property?"

"That's right," I said. "This error code indicates that we tried to assign a value to a property of a control that doesn't exist."

"But how do we determine which one?" Sessue said. "Is there a way to determine which control the **For Each** loop was working with at the time the program bombed?"

"Excellent point," I said. "Yes, there is. First, if we click on the Debug button, Visual Basic will verify exactly which line of code was the one that generated the error..."

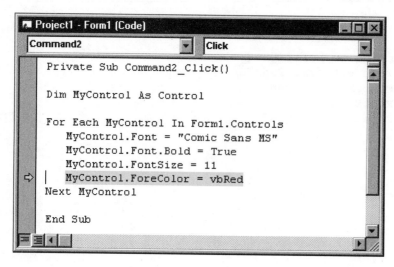

"No surprise there," I said, "we knew that – it's the line of code where we attempted to set the `ForeColor` property of the control our object variable pointed to equal to red."

"But this doesn't tell us the control name," he said.

"No it doesn't," I said. "We need to determine that ourselves. But that's easy enough. Since our program is now in Break mode anyway, all we need to do is bring up the Immediate window, and type this line in…"

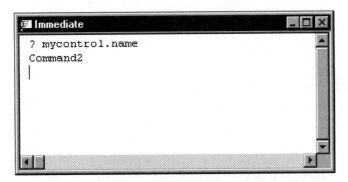

"I see," Sessue said. "The object variable is still pointing to the control in the `Controls` Collection that it was working on when the program bombed."

"You're catching on fast," I said. "Using the `Name` property of the object variable in the Immediate window, we can then determine the control in the `Controls` Collection that doesn't have a `ForeColor` property – in this case, `Command2`."

"But what about this error?" Sessue said anxiously. "I'm really looking forward to working with the `Controls` Collection – but if my program is going to bomb every time I refer to a control property that doesn't exist, this isn't going to be very useful to me."

"Don't worry," I said, "you'll still be able to use the `Controls` Collection – but you will need to handle the potential errors it can generate. There are two ways of dealing with this. One way is to use the `TypeOf` keyword, which could be used to determine if the Object variable in our `For Each` loop is pointing to a command button. For instance, you could code the `Click` event procedure like this."

I changed the `Click` event procedure of `Command2` to look like this:

```
Private Sub Command2_Click()

Dim MyControl As Control
```

```
For Each MyControl In Form1.Controls
   MyControl.Font = "Comic Sans MS"
   MyControl.Font.Bold = True
   MyControl.FontSize = 11
   If TypeOf MyControl Is CommandButton Then
      ' Nothing to do
   Else
      MyControl.ForeColor = vbRed
   End If
Next MyControl

End Sub
```

"Here we use the `TypeOf` keyword to determine if the object variable is pointing to a `CommandButton`," I said. "If it is, we just bypass setting the `ForeColor` property."

I ran the program, and clicked on the first command button, then the second. On this occasion this evoked the following response:

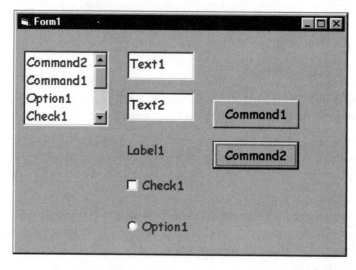

"For those of you at home with black and white television sets," I said, "all of our text is now red."

"Except for the command buttons," Sessue exclaimed, "which don't support the `ForeColor` property. This is great."

"Yes," I said, "the `TypeOf` keyword bailed us out of this one, but in order to use it here in our code we really needed to know exactly which control, and which property, would cause us a problem. But we may not always know this. You might have a form with close to one hundred controls on it, many of them third party controls not supplied with Visual Basic. How do you know which ones have a particular property and which ones don't? Oh sure, you can dig through the documentation, but that takes time, something you may not have. Rather than code a series of `If...Then` statements with a variety of `TypeOf` keywords, why not just use error handling?"

"Error handling?" Sessue asked.

"That's right," I said. "Remember earlier when we tried to assign a value to the `ForeColor` property of the command button? Because the command button does not have a `ForeColor` property, Visual Basic generated an error code of `438`. It's a simple matter to write an error handler, and check for that error code. Then, regardless of which control generates the error, we can tell VB to continue processing with the next control in the `Controls` collection by using the `Resume Next` statement of the error handler. That'll make it essentially ignore the error and continue with the statement after the one that caused the error. Here, let me show you..."

I modified the code in the `Click` event procedure of `Command2` to look like this:

```
Private Sub Command2_Click()

Dim MyControl As control

On Error GoTo Sessue

For Each MyControl In Form1.Controls
    MyControl.Font = "Comic San MS"
    MyControl.Font.Bold = True
    MyControl.FontSize = 11
    MyControl.ForeColor = vbRed
Next MyControl

Exit Sub
```

```
Sessue:

Select Case Err.Number
   Case 438
      Resume Next
   Case Else
      MsgBox "Error Number " & Err.Number & " generated"
End Select

End Sub
```

"In honor of you, Sessue," I said, "we'll name the error handler after you. Did you see our show last week? One of the questions dealt with error handlers."

"I sure did," he answered. "I haven't missed a show since you started broadcasting here in Japan a few weeks ago."

"You're familiar with error handlers, then," I said. "As soon as we try to assign a value to a property that a control does not have, error 438 is generated. Within the error handler..."

```
Sessue:

Select Case Err.Number
   Case 438
      Resume Next
```

"...we check for error number 438. If the error handler is triggered by that code, the `Resume Next` statement tells VB to continue processing at the next line of code. That's called 'trapping' an error – just because technically something's an error doesn't mean your program has to fall over. Let's see how this code works."

I ran the program and clicked on the first command button. As before, the list box was populated. When I clicked on the second command button the text on the controls, with the exception of the command buttons, became red.

"I want to thank you, Professor Smiley," Sessue said. "This works great. The `Controls` Collection will come in very handy for me, believe me."

"Glad I could help, I said. "Thanks for calling, Sessue."

"Before we take the next caller, I'd like to say something about the use of objects in VB programming. We haven't time to go into as much detail as I'd like here. It's a big subject, and there's more to it than we've had a chance to see. I'm glad it came up here, to give you a taster for what it's like. I've been thinking for a while now that it's something that I'd like to make less scary for the beginner, and I'm planning to write a book about it. Look out for it in the stores in the fall of 1999! And now, it's time for caller number eight."

Question 98: I want to select the contents of the text box automatically when it gets focus

(see also questions 21, 22, 39, 87 & 95)

"Hi, my name is Michael A. Buonarotti III, and I'm calling from Caprese, Italy," our next caller introduced himself. "I'm actually from New York, but I'm over here visiting old family. I thought I was going to miss your show, but then, wow, you went international, man! Anyway, I've been trying to build a special effect into my Visual Basic program that I've seen in other Windows programs, and I'm hoping you can help me."

"Welcome to the show, Michael," I said. "What special effect is that?"

"You've probably seen Windows programs," he said, "where the entire contents of a text box are selected when it receives focus?"

"Yes, I have," I answered. "We can do that pretty easily in Visual Basic. First, let me show the viewing audience exactly what you mean."

I started a new Visual Basic project and placed two text boxes on the form.

"By default," I said, "this program already has some behavior built in. For instance, the first text box I placed on the form, `Text1`, will receive the focus when the program starts up, since it has the lowest `TabIndex` property." I ran the program and, as promised, the first text box I placed on the form received the focus:

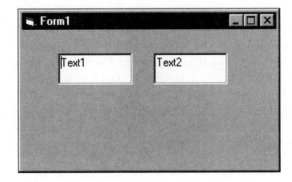

"...if we now press the *Tab* key, focus will move to the second text box, pressing it again will move us back to the first, and so forth..."

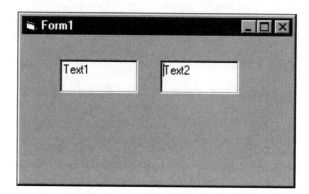

"Notice," I said, "that when the focus moves to the first text box, Visual Basic places the insertion point right before the letter 'T' in **Text1**. If we press the *Tab* key, focus will move to the second text box, and once again the insertion point appears before the letter 'T'."

"Exactly," Michael said. "I'd like all of the text in the text box to be selected when the text box receives focus."

"We can do that pretty easily by using two properties of the text box control," I said. "**SelStart** and **SelLength**, which we can demonstrate in the **GotFocus** event of our second text box. Look at this code:"

```
Private Sub Text2_GotFocus()

Text2.SelStart = 0
Text2.SelLength = Len(Text2.Text)

End Sub
```

"These two properties," I said, "can be used to select text in the text box. By putting this code in the **GotFocus** event procedure of the second text box, it's triggered whenever the focus is moved to the second text box. **SelStart** specifies the starting point of the selected text, and **SelLength** specifies the length. By setting **SelStart** to 0, we tell Visual Basic that the selected text starts immediately before the first character of text in the text box. We then use the **Len** function to determine the length of the text in the text box, and set the **SelLength** property equal to that. The result is that when the second text box receives the focus, the text within it will be selected. Let's run the program now, and see the differences in the behavior of the two text boxes."

I ran the program, and as before, the first text box received the focus at startup. However, when I tabbed to the second text box, not only did it receive the focus, but its entire contents were selected as well:

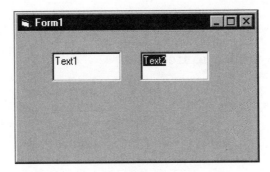

"Is this the effect you were looking for, Michael?" I asked.

"That's it," he replied. "Thanks – this will work out quite nicely."

"Glad I could help, Michael, and goodbye." I said. "And hello, caller number nine."

Just then, I noticed a bit of confusion at the back of the studio. I saw Linda head towards the studio access door and disappear out of view. I couldn't spend time watching her, though. One of the other crew gave me the go-ahead, and I went to the next caller.

Question 99: Can I detect the Cancel button being pressed in an input box?

"Good day. My name is Bill, and I'm from Stratford, in England," he said. "I've been writing a program that accepts a response from the user via a Visual Basic input box. My problem is this: I haven't figured out a way to determine if the user has pressed the Cancel button in the input box window, and it's been wreaking havoc with my program. Can you help me?"

"Hi, Bill," I said, "thanks for calling. Yes, there is a way to determine if the user has pressed the Cancel key in your input box. All you need to do is check the return value of the input box for a zero length. Let me show you."

I started a clean project and located a single command button on the form before writing the following code in the click event procedure of the command button:

```
Private Sub Command1_Click()

Dim strRetval As String

strRetval = InputBox("What is your favorite programming language?")

If UCase(strRetval) = "VISUAL BASIC" Then
   MsgBox "I love it too"
Else
   MsgBox "Sorry to hear that"
End If

End Sub
```

"This code," I said, "displays an input box, asks the user to indicate their favorite programming language, and then evaluates their answer – by comparing the uppercase value of the return value of the input box to 'VISUAL BASIC'. If the user enters 'Visual Basic' into the text box, then we display a message box congratulating them on their good taste."

I ran the program, clicked on the command button, and entered Visual Basic into the input box:

When I clicked on the *OK* button, the following message box appeared:

"That works well," I said. "Now suppose the user enters something other than 'Visual Basic'..."

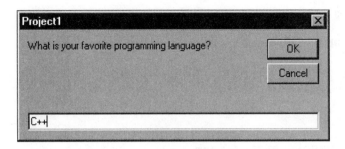

"...the program will then display an 'I'm Sorry' message:"

"Now Bill's problem is that the user may not enter anything at all into the input box," I said, "and immediately click on the Cancel button, in which case the 'I'm sorry' message box is also displayed, as we'll see."

I clicked on the command button, and immediately clicked on the Cancel button. As expected, the 'I'm sorry' message box was displayed.

"The important thing to note here," I continued, "is that if the user presses the Cancel button, VB doesn't differentiate between the empty string this returns and any other language name that the user might have typed. It thinks that the empty string *is* the user's entry. This is exactly what you want to be able to detect, isn't it Bill?"

"That's right," he said. "If the user presses the Cancel button, I want to display a message box telling them they need to make an entry."

"Fortunately," I said, "that's easy to do. All we need to do is insert an `If...Then` statement into the `Click` event procedure, and we'll be able to detect if the user clicked on the Cancel button. Watch this."

I then made the following changes to the `Click` event procedure of the command button:

```
Private Sub Command1_Click()

Dim strRetval As String

strRetval = InputBox("What is your favorite programming language")

If strRetval = "" Then
    MsgBox "You forgot to make an entry"
    Exit Sub
End If

If UCase(strRetval) = "VISUAL BASIC" Then
    MsgBox "I love it too"
Else
    MsgBox "Sorry to hear that"
End If

End Sub
```

"What we've done here," I said, "is add code to check for a zero-length string. Remember, the user's response from the InputBox function is returned to our program via a return value. If the user clicks the Cancel button, the return value contains a zero-length string. Knowing that, we can then display a message box telling them that they have forgotten to make an entry in the input box. At that point, we just bypass the rest of the code with an Exit Sub statement."

I then ran the program and clicked on the command button, and when the input box was displayed, immediately clicked on the Cancel button:

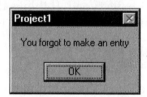

"That's perfect," Bill said. "That's exactly what I needed to know how to do. Thanks for your help."

"My pleasure, Bill," I said. "And now it's time for our final caller of the day."

464

Question 100: I was calculating the average of three numbers, and my result is wrong

"Hi, my name is Elvis," our last caller said, except that his voice wasn't coming from the speakerphone in the studio; he was standing right in front of me!

"Where do you come from? Let me guess," I said, "you're from Memphis!"

"How'd you guess?" he said very seriously, looking very much like the famous celebrity. "I'm a professional entertainer, and I'm on the road quite a bit, you know what I mean? Still, I have plenty of time to, uh, dabble in programming, and Visual Basic is my favorite programming language. I have a question about a program I've been writing to keep track of my record sales."

"Go ahead, ask me," I said.

"It's basically just a form with three text boxes. In each text box, I enter the number of records I've sold for each of my last three albums. My intention is that the program will take the three values, and average them – but the results I'm getting are totally wrong. Can you help me, sir?"

"I'm sure I can, Elvis," I said, as I continued to gaze at the person who appeared to be the real thing. "Can I offer you a seat?"

"No thanks," he said, "I'm used to being on my feet – concerts, recording studios and all. I'll just stand."

"Let me try to duplicate your problem here in the studio," I said.

"No need for that," Elvis said, "I brought my program disk with me."

With that, he handed me the diskette, and I inserted it into the diskette drive of my PC. In no time, we had Elvis's project loaded into Visual Basic. As he had said, it contained three text boxes and a single command button. He had cleared the `Text` properties of each text box, and in the `Click` event procedure of the command button he had placed the following code:

```
Private Sub Command1_Click()

Dim intResult As Long

intResult = Val(Text1.Text) + Val(Text2.Text) + Val(Text3.Text) / 3

MsgBox "The average of your last three recordings is " & intResult

End Sub
```

"I like most of what I see here, Elvis," I said. "Your code is easy to read, and you use Hungarian Notation. I like the fact that you used the `Val` function on the `Text` properties of the text box..."

"Uh, thank you very much. I picked up that tip from your show," he said proudly.

"However, I do see a problem," I said, "and that would get your average calculation all shook up and befuddled. Let's run the program so our home viewers can see."

I ran the program and the input form appeared.

"What are those sales figures, Elvis?" I asked.

"That's 300,000, and 600,000 and, uh, 900,000," he said. "Sales figures are going up. Who says my popularity is waning?"

I entered the sales figures for Elvis's last three recordings into the text boxes (without the commas, though, as VB is easily confused by things like that):

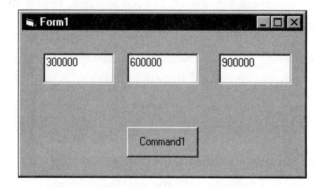

"That should average out to 600,000," Elvis said, as I clicked on the command button, with this result:

"See what I mean?" Elvis said. "That result is wrong. The average should be 600,000 and *not* 1,200,000. Can you tell me why?"

"You forgot about the 'Order of Operations', sometimes called the 'Order of Precedence'," I said. "That's causing the problem with your average calculation."

"Order of Operations?" he asked. "Sounds familiar."

I displayed this line of code on my electronic whiteboard:

intResult = Val(Text1.Text) + Val(Text2.Text) + Val(Text3.Text) / 3

"I know what you intended to do, Elvis," I said. "But the problem is, Visual Basic *didn't*. Visual Basic evaluated this line of code and recognized that it contained three separate arithmetic operations. Reading from left to right, there's an addition, another addition, and then finally a division. Visual Basic – and other programming languages – use a set of rules, called the Order of Operations, to decide which of those mathematical operations to perform first. The rules state that, from left to right in an expression, it will perform exponentiation, then multiplication and division, and then finally addition and subtraction."

"Are you saying that Visual Basic performed the division operation first, sir?" Elvis asked.

"That's right," I agreed. "That means that Visual Basic divided the third text box – 900,000 – by 3, yielding a result of 300,000. At that point, Visual Basic performed the addition operations, adding 300,000 to 600,000 giving 900,000 and finally adding that number – 900,000 – to the result of 900,000 divided by 3. That's where the 1,200,000 came from."

"You know," Elvis said, "this all sounds familiar to me. Forgive me, but I've been on the road a lot lately, and I think I've probably forgotten some of what I've learned about Visual Basic. Now and then, there's a fool such as I who forgets things. So, how can we fix this?"

"That's easy," I said, "We want Visual Basic to perform the addition operations, and *then* divide the total by 3. We can tell Visual Basic to do that my placing parentheses around the addition operations, like this…"

I made the following change in the `Click` event procedure of the command button:

```
Private Sub Command1_Click()

Dim intResult As Long

intResult = (Val(Text1.Text) + Val(Text2.Text) + Val(Text3.Text)) / 3

MsgBox "The average of your last three recordings is " & intResult

End Sub
```

"Well, it's now or never," I said, as I ran the program again. "Putting the parentheses around the operations makes VB perform the addition first, and then the division. When the form appeared, I entered the three values again – 300,000; 600,000; and 900,000 – into the three text boxes and clicked on the command button. This time, we got this result from the calculation:

"That's great," Elvis said. "I feel so bad about making such an easy mistake."

"Don't be cruel to yourself," I reassured him. "Learning VB doesn't happen overnight; it's a matter of time."

"I guess I'll be able to trust this program now. I want to thank you for your help. I'd like to say 'hi' to my best friend's little sister, if I may – she's a hard headed woman, but I'd like her to know she's always on my mind."

"Sure thing, and next time you see her, just tell her John said hello," I said.

With that, it was time to wrap up the show. With no idea of what Tim wanted to see me about, I assumed the show would be continuing, and told our audience that. Once the cameras clicked off and the studio lights went down, I turned to my final questioner.

"I'm sorry, Elvis, that there wasn't time for you to sing on the show," I said. "But I know Linda here is one of your biggest fans, so would you care to sing something for the crew? It would just about make our day," I said.

"I'm yours," he replied. A few minutes later, we had the studio (which was to be unused until later that afternoon) set up for Elvis to play a few numbers. We had a great time, especially Linda, when Elvis dedicated *'Are You Lonesome Tonight?'* to her...

In the quiet that descended on the studio after all the excitement, I said goodbye to Linda, Elvis, and the crew, and – at least for that day – we went our separate ways.

As I walked across the parking lot, noting the slightly dilapidated pink Cadillac that was coated with dust from the highway, the spring sunlight was warm on my face. I felt that familiar end-of-term feeling, a mixture of relief, freedom and possibility. Whatever the future – and especially my next meeting with Tim – might bring, I was so glad that I had been given the opportunity to do this show. I'd had a great time, and realized a dream.

Examples

In Other News...

"Following the success of his second book, John Smiley, acclaimed author and self-confessed programmer, denied today that he was close to signing a contract to write monthly web-based articles relating to Visual Basic programming for beginners."

"The publishing house 'Active Path' has reportedly been in negotiations with Mr. Smiley, and last week expressed 'encouraging' results regarding the talks. We've been able to obtain details of the proposal, which would launch a series of articles written specifically for the novice VB programmer. The content would be posted on Active Path's website and provided free to the public, as what should become an extremely valuable resource."

"However, at the close of the talks yesterday, John Smiley was reported to have rejected the current plans in what an AP spokeswoman said 'felt like a delaying tactic'. She went on to say that Active Path wouldn't rest until Mr. Smiley signed with them. 'John Smiley is a brilliant, brilliant teacher. We want to know that our readers are getting the best information, presented in the most understandable way it can be. To me, that has 'John Smiley' written all over it.'"

"The news of the failed talks has hit the beginning VB community hard. When told the disappointing news, novice programmers became outraged at the result. Earlier today, in the author's home town of Philadelphia, police clashed with protesters in what started as a friendly demonstration. 'We just wanted to show John just how many of us he'd be letting down – we never meant to cause any trouble,' said one fan, who is not being named for legal reasons."

"I'm sorry – this just in. Within the last hour, John Smiley called an emergency meeting of the AP council, and agreed terms for the articles proposal, reportedly in response to the demonstrations. 'My concern was about readership figures. My goal is to reach as many people as I can, yet still provide them with high-quality teaching,' he said. 'The negotiations dragged on because of my concern that nobody wanted that kind of teaching. Well, it looks like I was wrong. You'll get your articles. If you'll excuse me, I have a deadline to meet! Look on www.activepath.com in a few days' time. I just wish we could have reached that decision without the protests, and I'm sorry.'"

Index

Index

Index

Index

Index

W

Z

Examples

Forthcoming Titles from Active Path

We will continue to expand our output to teach you the programming skills that you need.

Our next publications are:

Learn to Program with HTML by Chris Ullman

Learn to Program with Visual Basic Databases by John Smiley

Learn to Program with Visual Basic Objects by John Smiley

Learn to Program with Visual Basic on the Web by John Smiley

Examples

Be an Author

Ever heard yourself thinking "I know enough about this to write a book!"?

If you answered **yes**, good! Now read on.

If you answered **no**, then maybe it's about time you did think it, so read on too!

Here at Active Path we can help you turn your teaching and programming experience into an education resource for instructors and students alike with our proven **Learn To Program** book format.

Let us teach you how to recreate your learning environment in the pages of a book and become a universal teacher!

Active Path is dedicated to the creation of learning materials that enable the novice to develop real world programming skills and a solid knowledge base for future learning.

Active Path is about providing structured learning, NOT a shallow overview.

If you have experience of teaching Java, Access, VBA (all areas), C++, Visual Basic, or any form of web development, and you subscribe to our teaching ethic, we want to hear from you NOW!

Contact Us

Contact Sarah Inston at Active Path on *authors@activepath.com*. She can tell you more about the company, about how you can share your programming and teaching knowledge on an international scale, and about our acclaimed instruction book format Learn To Program.

We're also interested in hearing from you if you'd like to contribute to the other learning materials that we create, including support materials for academics, and workbooks for online training courses. Tell us about your expertise and aspirations.

You can also visit our web site at `http://www.activepath.com`

Examples

NOTES

NOTES

NOTES

NOTES

NOTES

NOTES

activepath

If you enjoyed the book, and

you're interested in other titles

by Active Path, why not drop in

to our web site at:

www.activepath.com

Support • Sample Code • New Titles • News

active path

Active Path writes books for you. Any suggestions,
or ideas about how you want information given in
your ideal book will be studied by our team.
Your comments are always valued at Active Path.

Free phone in USA 800-873-9769
Fax (312) 397 8990

UK Tel. (0121) 687 4100 Fax (0121) 687 4101

——————— *Computer Book Publishers* ———————

NB. If you post the bounce back card below in the UK, please send it to:
Active Path Ltd., Arden House, 1102 Warwick Road,
Acocks Green, Birmingham. B27 6BH. UK.

NO POSTAGE
NECESSARY
IF MAILED
IN THE
UNITED STATES

BUSINESS REPLY MAIL
FIRST CLASS MAIL   PERMIT#64   CHICAGO, IL

POSTAGE WILL BE PAID BY ADDRESSEE

WROX PRESS
1512 NORTH FREMONT
SUITE 103
CHICAGO IL 60622-2567